The American Social Experience Series

GENERAL EDITOR: JAMES KIRBY MARTIN

EDITORS: PAULA S. FASS, STEVEN H. MINTZ,
CARL PRINCE, JAMES W. REED & PETER N. STEARNS

Lewis M. Terman

LEWIS M. TERMAN

Pioneer in Psychological Testing

___

HENRY L. MINTON

NEW YORK UNIVERSITY PRESS
NEW YORK AND LONDON
1988

LIBRARY OF CONGRESS
Library of Congress Cataloging-in-Publication Data
Minton, Henry L.
Lewis M. Terman : pioneer in psychological testing / Henry L.
Minton.
p. cm. — (The American social experience series : 11)
Bibliography: p.
Includes index.
ISBN 0-8147-5442-2 (alk. paper)
1. Terman, Lewis Madison, 1877–1956.   2. Psychologists—United
States—Biography.   3. Stanford-Binet Test—History.
4. Intelligence levels—United States—History—20th century.
5. Psychological tests—United States—History.   I. Title.
II. Series.
BF109.T39M56   1988
153.9'3'0924—dc19   88-12274
[B]   CIP

New York University Press books are Smyth-sewn
and printed on permanent and durable acid-free paper.

Book design by Ken Venezio

To my parents,
and in memory of
Gary McDonald

Contents

Illustrations

Preface

Psychological tests, since their inception during the first two decades of the twentieth century, have been sources of great controversy. In America they played an influential role, especially in education. Testing became a generally accepted practice in the schools by the 1920s. In many instances, a child's test score could determine how much and what kind of education he or she received. By the 1960s the civil rights movement had sensitized parents, teachers, school officials, and social scientists to the race, class, and sex bias that was often an inherent part of the tests. Consequently, testing came under considerable attack and subsequently there has been a movement to develop tests and interpret results, taking into account the impact of cultural differences and social discrimination.

The challenge to traditional testing practices has also aroused interest in reappraising the contributions by those psychologists who first developed the tests. Questions have been raised about the motives of the test constructors; for example, did they harbor race, class, or sex prejudice, and was such prejudice used to legitimate the inequities of capitalist society?[1] Lewis M. Terman was one of the leading members of this group of pioneering test advocates, and he has been, therefore, the subject of much criticism. This biography seeks to provide a balanced view of this influential and controversial psychologist.

My interest in Terman first began when I started my graduate program in clinical psychology at Pennsylvania State University. However, it was little more than a passing curiosity about the man who was the senior author of the first clinical tool that I had been exposed to—the 1937 Stanford-Binet, Form L. (I have since learned that the L stood for Terman's first name, Lewis.) This interest, however, was quickly lost by the myriad of events that I experienced in my subsequent graduate training. It would not be until midcareer when a change in professional direction would lead me once again to a consideration of Terman. After being engaged in traditional empirical research in the area of personality and individual differences, I became interested in the history of psychology. Though I had had a longstanding attraction to history, I had no training in the historical method. My first exposure to historiography was a workshop given by Michael M. Sokal at the 1980 meeting of the American Psychological Association. This whetted my appetite for historical research, and the following year I presented a paper dealing with the history of social psychology at the meeting of the Cheiron Society. This interdisciplinary group, concerned with the history of social science, has been a rich source of intellectual stimulation and support ever since I attended my first meeting. I owe particular gratitude to Cheiron members Lorenz J. Finison and Jill G. Morawski, because of their encouragement in my first research effort in the history of intelligence testing, and Michael M. Sokal for his interest and support throughout this project.

During 1983–84 I was granted sabbatical leave from the University of Windsor, supported with a Leave Fellowship and Research Stipend from the Social Sciences and Humanities Research Council of Canada. This enabled me to spend several months at the Stanford University Archives where the Lewis M. Terman papers are located. Roxanne Nilan, curator of the Stanford University Archives, and her staff were most helpful and accommodating during my stay. Many other librarians and archivists were of aid in my research. I am particularly grateful to Stuart W. Campbell, university archivist, Clark University Archives; Maxine B. Clapp, former archivist, University of Minnesota Archives; James H. Hutson, chief, Manuscript Division, The Library of Congress; Elisabeth R. O'Lessker, archives associate, Indiana University Archives; John A. Popplestone, director, and Marion White McPherson, associate director, Archives of the History of American Psychology, the University of Akron; and Patricia B. Stark, principal reference archivist, Yale University Library.

I would like to thank several individuals who were kind enough to share, their personal impressions of Terman with me. These include

Nancy Bayley, Lee J. Cronbach, Ernest R. Hilgard, Robert R. Sears, and Ruth Tinsley Storey, each of whom agreed to an interview. This material was provided through correspondence by Roger G. Barker, Jean Carson Challman, Dale B. Harris, C. Mansel Keene, the late E. Lowell Kelly, Neal E. Miller, and Anne Roe. In addition, interviews with Marie Skodak Crissey, Orlo L. Crissey, and the late Ronald Lippitt provided recollections of the 1940 debate on intelligence between Terman and George D. Stoddard.

I am most grateful to the Terman family for their support in carrying out this project. Fred W. Terman, Terry Terman, and Doris Tucker granted me interviews about their grandfather. Doris Tucker also gave me the opportunity to make use of family photographs and diaries.

Special thanks go to James Reed whose editorial comments and suggestions were instrumental in the completion of this work. Finally, I want to express my appreciation to the following individuals at the University of Windsor for their secretarial services: Betty Mercer, Claire Rabideau, Marilyn Vasily, and Veronica Edwards and her staff at the Word Processing Centre.

Permission to quote from the Frederick E. Terman and Lewis M. Terman papers has been granted by the Stanford University Archives, Stanford University Libraries. Doris Tucker, for the Terman family, has provided permission to quote from the personal documents of Lewis Terman that are contained in other collections. For quotations from the personal papers of other individuals, the following permissions have been obtained: Barbara S. Burks (Stanford University Archives), Florence L. Goodenough (Howard L. Goodenough, executor of estate of Florence L. Goodenough), G. Stanley Hall (Clark University Archives), and Ray L. Wilbur (Ray L. Wilbur, Jr., executor of estate of Ray L. Wilbur).

Permission to quote from Lewis M. Terman's published work has been granted from the following:

Lewis M. Terman, "Trails to Psychology," in C. A. Murchison, ed., *A History of Psychology in Autobiography*, vol. 2. Copyright © 1932 by Clark University. Used by permission of Clark University Press, Worcester, Massachusetts.

Lewis M. Terman, *The Measurement of Intelligence*. Copyright © 1916 by Houghton Mifflin. Used by permission of Doris Tucker, for the Terman family.

Lewis M. Terman and Catharine Cox Miles, *Sex and Personality: Studies in Masculinity and Femininity*. Copyright © 1936 by McGraw-Hill. Used by permission of Doris Tucker, for the Terman family.

Permission to include material from my own previously published work has been received from the following:

Henry L. Minton, "Femininity in Men and Masculinity in Women: American Psychiatry and Psychology Portray Homosexuality in the 1930s," *Journal of Homosexuality*, vol. 13, no. 1. Copyright © 1986 by Haworth Press. Used by permission of Haworth Press, New York, New York.

Henry L. Minton, "Lewis M. Terman and Mental Testing: In Search of the Democratic Ideal," in Michael M. Sokal, ed., *Psychological Testing and American Society, 1890–1930*. Copyright © 1987 by Rutgers, The State University. Used by permission of Rutgers University Press, New Brunswick, New Jersey.

Henry L. Minton, "Charting Life History: Lewis M. Terman's Study of the Gifted," in J. G. Morawski, ed., *Exploring Inner Space: The Rise of Experimentation in American Psychology*. Copyright © in press by Yale University. Used by permission of Yale University Press, New Haven, Connecticut.

CHAPTER I

Hoosier Roots
(1877–1892)

In planning a discussion of the factors that may have influenced a career
. . . it would be a mistake to ignore the indications of childhood experiences
and preoccupations.[1]

On the ground floor of Stanford University's Jordan Hall, the building
that houses the psychology department, is an office that contains about
a dozen old-fashioned wooden filing cabinets. Another notable feature
of the room is a bust of a fatherly looking man with a faint, benign
smile. The cabinets contain files on a sample of some fifteen hundred
individuals who were identified as intellectually gifted children six and
a half decades ago. The bust depicts the psychologist who launched
this study in 1921, Lewis M. Terman, and is the work of Betty Ford
Acquina, one of the subjects in the study who, as an adult, became an
accomplished sculptor. This room is not part of an archive, library, or
museum. It is the central office for an ongoing research project, the
field study that Terman began in 1921. The surviving subjects of this
study are now mostly in their seventies.

Terman's longitudinal study of gifted children was the centerpiece
of his career as a psychologist. His pathways or "trails to psychology"
(the title of his autobiography) were spurred by an early interest in
children of exceptional ability. In order to study such children, he
searched for ways in which he could assess individual differences and
subsequently select those at the upper end of the distribution of ability

or intelligence. Toward this end, he produced the first widely used individual measure of intelligence in America—the Stanford-Binet Scale, published in 1916.[2] The total score earned on this scale was expressed as an Intelligence Quotient or "IQ," that is the ratio of mental age (average test performance for a given age) to chronological age (multiplied by 100). While Terman did not originate the IQ, he was the first to make use of it in a published test. As other intelligence tests followed, it became the standard mode of expressing a total score, and teachers, parents, and children grew increasingly familiar with it. Terman can thus be credited with introducing the IQ to the American vocabulary.

Terman was a pioneer in the study of individual differences and the development of psychological tests (measuring nonintellectual as well as intellectual qualities). He was among the first generation of American psychologists who received all of their graduate training in America. He was a product of the changing patterns of American society in the late nineteenth and early twentieth centuries—the shift from a rural agrarian culture to an urban industrial way of life. His work as a psychologist contributed in many significant ways to America's emergence as a corporate-industrial power. An expanding and more diversified labor force required techniques for sorting individuals according to their vocational potential. Terman's skills as an assessor of individual differences fitted in well with the needs of the changing American scene. He was also alert to new roles and sources of influence that he and other psychologists could provide. He was thus not only a product of his times but also a shaper of his social context.

In 1928 Terman was one of fifty eminent psychologists selected to contribute to a new series of edited books, entitled *A History of Psychology in Autobiography*.[3] Terman wrote his chapter-length autobiography in the spring of 1930, when he was fifty-three years old.[4] He admitted to being a rather desultory student of biography. Nevertheless, in his introduction he stressed that in attempting any biographic enterprise one had to consider the way in which childhood shaped the subsequent development of the individual. He also pointed out that childhood had to be viewed as the product of both hereditary and environmental influences, and therefore it was important to know people's ancestry as well as their early experiences.

Family Genealogy

Terman was born on 15 January 1877, the twelfth of fourteen children of a farm family in central Indiana.[5] His family's farm was located in Johnson County, seventeen miles southeast of Indianapolis and eight miles northeast of Franklin, the county seat and largest town in the immediate area.[6]

In recounting his ancestry, Terman pointed out that had he followed his forebears he would have been destined for a life on a farm or as a manager of a small business.[7] His education would probably have gone no further than high-school graduation and might have even stopped at an earlier point. Terman's paternal ancestors had migrated to Indiana from Maryland and Virginia.[8] His paternal grandfather, John H. Tarman, who later took the name John Bunyan Terman, was born in Maryland in 1792.[9] He was of Scotch-Irish descent and his forebears probably arrived in the American colonies in the late 1600s or early 1700s.[10] John Terman was a soldier in the War of 1812.[11] At some point, his parents had moved from Maryland to Virginia, and in 1817 John married Ann Jones, a Virginian, apparently of Welsh descent. In 1831 John and his family migrated from Virginia and started a farm in Muskingum County, Ohio, and in 1847 they moved to start another farm in Bartholomew County, Indiana.

John and Ann had twelve children, seven of whom lived to adulthood. James William Terman, Lewis's father, was born in Ohio in 1834. He was one of the youngest of John and Ann's children. James (or "Jim," as he was called) worked on his parents' farm in Indiana until he was nineteen. At this time, he was employed by William Cutsinger, who had a farm in adjoining Johnson County. It was here that Jim met one of the Cutsinger daughters, Martha.[12] Jim and Martha were married in 1854, a year after they had met. After their wedding, Jim and Martha moved about fifteen miles away to a log cabin that Jim had built, and started their own farm on land that had been given as a wedding present by Martha's father.[13]

Martha's ancestry was German (Pennsylvania "Dutch") on her father's side (the Cutsingers) and French Huguenot on her mother's side (the Deuprees). The Cutsingers had migrated from Pennsylvania to Indiana by way of Kentucky, and apparently had not been in America long before they began their westward travels.[14] The Deuprees traced their lineage in America to around 1700.[15] Martha's maternal great-grandfather was a Virginian who served in the Revolutionary War. Her maternal grandfather, who was opposed to slavery, moved from Virginia to Kentucky and then to Indiana. Terman's name, "Lewis Madison," was a traditional one among the Deuprees.

Lewis Terman's ancestry thus contained Scotch-Irish, Welsh, German, and French Huguenot strains, all of which were representative of the dominant Protestant groups that emigrated to America in the eighteenth century. Among the Termans, there may also have been some native American blood.[16] Among the Termans and Cutsingers, no one before Lewis's generation had graduated from college or belonged to any of the professions.[17] The Deuprees had risen to some prominence before they left France because of the Huguenot persecutions and were somewhat more successful than the other branches of Lewis's family.

Growing Up on an Indiana Farm

Ten months after Lewis's parents, Jim and Martha, were married, their first child, Jane, was born.[18] Thereafter, at approximately two-year intervals, Martha gave birth to thirteen more children. Of the fourteen offspring, three died during childhood. Lewis was the twelfth-born and the youngest of three sons to survive childhood, two other boys having died when they were around age two.

As Lewis was growing up, his place in the family was somewhat unique. The first seven children (five girls, followed by two sons) were all about two years apart in age. Due to the early deaths of the eighth-, ninth-, and eleventh-born, Lewis was ten years younger than his nearest brother, and five years younger than the closest older sibling (a girl). Lewis had two younger sisters and was three years older than the next girl in birth order. That he was the youngest son and further apart in age from his older siblings may have provided him with more visibility and attention than his brothers and sisters. Another characteristic that set young Lewis apart from his siblings was his golden red hair.[19]

It was an active and busy life for the Terman family.[20] Jim was not very social outside of the family, rarely attending church or other neighborhood gatherings. He was very devoted to his children and would always get up with them in the night when they needed help. The Terman children would remember their father as being very patient and kind. Martha was more emotional and socially outgoing than her husband. In the local area, she gained a reputation for being a good nurse and being able to dispense medicines when needed. She made a point of getting the latest medical information on the few occasions when a doctor would come to the farm to take care of one of the family. While Jim and Martha had different dispositions, they seemed to get along very well with each other. Their children considered their parents' marriage to be an unusually happy one. Both shared in the managing of the farm, Martha taking an active interest in the crops and helping Jim decide about selling and marketing.

In rearing their children, Jim and Martha encouraged a cooperative family spirit. Despite having only three sons, Jim did not allow the girls to work in the fields, although one daughter who liked animals was allowed to milk the cow. The girls helped their mother in the house and helped tend to the garden and chickens. As the family grew, Martha saw to it that an older daughter was put in charge of a younger child. The maternal duties were therefore efficiently dispersed among the women.

The Terman farm prospered and grew to include as much as 640 acres. Jim acquired the best farm equipment, and each year he had the latest buggy, which was the envy of his neighbors. Horses were available for riding and work, and among the other farm animals there were cows, hogs, sheep, chickens, and turkeys. In 1885 the original log cabin was replaced by a large frame house, which contained eight big rooms and a front porch. Inside the house was a good library consisting of somewhere between 150 and 200 books.[21] Jim liked to read, though preferring newspapers, magazines, and the Bible to books. The oldest son, John, especially enjoyed books and acquired a complete set of the *Encyclopaedia Britannica*. Among the other avid book readers in the family were Lewis and a younger sister, Bertha. All three of these children eventually became teachers. In addition to reading, a favorite family pastime was playing poker with kernels of corn. Although Jim liked to read the Bible, the family was not oriented toward religion. From time to time, Martha and the children went to the Hurricane Baptist Church,[22] probably as much a social as a religious outlet for Martha.

In 1904 Jim and Martha celebrated their fiftieth wedding anniversary with a family reunion held on the farm.[23] By this time, some of the farm land had been sold; shortly after, Jim and Martha sold the rest of the farm and moved to a house in Franklin. Martha died in 1908, on her fifty-fourth wedding anniversary, at the age of seventy-one. A year and a half later, in 1910, Jim died at the age of seventy-six.

Life for the Jim Terman family had seemed generally happy and was sustained by an atmosphere of warmth and pride. But with the premature death of four children (three during childhood, one at young adulthood), there were also times of tragedy. The year of 1880 was especially sad. In October, Sarah, who was seven, died of scarlet fever. According to the other children it seemed as though their mother never got over her grief, blaming herself for not being able to prevent the death. It is possible that Martha's guilt was also accentuated by the tragic loss of her oldest daughter, Jane, who died the previous April of tuberculosis at age twenty-four. When Jane became ill in the fall of 1879, she and her three small children were taken in by Jim and Martha. Jane's husband had abandoned his family and had gone to California to seek his fortune. Jane's illness was to have a profound effect on Lewis, who was three years old at the time of her death. Some of Lewis's earliest memories related to this incident.[24] He remembered his sister's convulsive spells of coughing and his mother's weeping. In the overcrowded house (the original log cabin at the time), Lewis was exposed to the disease. As a young adult, Lewis was destined to contract tuberculosis. He also learned that his father's family was prone to the disease.

Among Lewis's other early recollections were impressions of his parents.[25] He felt closer to his father and remembered him as devoted to the family, self-sacrificing, persistent, just, kind, and especially fond of children. He perceived his mother as outgoing and rather temperamental. While dedicated to her children, Lewis did not think she understood them as well as his father did. Lewis, who was to become a very strong "father" figure in his role as teacher, as well as in his relations to the sample of gifted children he studied, may well have used his father as a model for his own adult sense of paternal caring and warmth.

A One-Room School

Three months before his sixth birthday, Lewis entered school.[26] The local school he attended (district school number 9, in Clark Township, Johnson County)[27] was a one-room "little red schoolhouse" that contained not a single library book. His teachers were all men and, while none had gone beyond the eighth grade, at the time they seemed to be highly competent. Lewis was obviously an impressive student, for at the end of his first term of six months (the length of the school year) he was promoted to the third grade. He "learned by heart" easily and habitually memorized most of the contents of his textbooks. The school day was long, lasting from 8:15 to 4:00, and there was no other reading material available in school. Fortunately, his quest for reading could be satisfied at home. Among the favorite items in his father's library were Hans Christian Andersen's stories, *Robinson Crusoe*, the novels of Cooper and Dickens, the Bible, the *Encyclopaedia Britannica*, and *Peck's Bad Boy*.

Lewis attended the same school until he was thirteen, although he had completed the eighth grade a year earlier. With no high school nearby, he then proceeded to do "post-graduate" work at another grade school—the school at which his older brother John taught. At this school he worked with more advanced texts during parts of two additional winters. One of Lewis's classmates at this time was Arthur M. Banta, who would become a lifelong friend and like Lewis would go on to a distinguished scientific career.[28]

Until the age of eleven, Lewis's vacations from school (five to six months each year) were spent in unsupervised play. Often he would play alone, engaging in such "introspective" activities as word associations, memory challenges, and reflecting upon such experiences as afterimages and the flight of colors. His neighborhood playmates offered little in the way of intellectual stimulation, but Lewis admired them for their superiority in physical strength and agility. Almost all of the boys Lewis played with were three or four years older. He therefore felt cut off from any possibility of becoming a leader among his peers and had a sense that he did not rate very much in their activities. That he excelled in schoolwork did not fully compensate for his inferior position during play. One area of knowledge that Lewis did acquire from his playmates was sex.[29] From the first grade through the eighth, he heard all sorts of obscenity, including references to sexual intercourse. Such exposure also came from the hired hands on the farm. As a result he developed precocious sexual interests, which he felt may have had some influence on his later career interests in sex and marriage.

Lewis also seemed to develop a childhood interest in personality — an area that was to form the major part of his professional activities. As far back as he could remember, he was impressed with people who had distinctive characteristics.[30] Among his schoolmates or acquaintances, those who stood out included a feeble-minded boy who was still on his first reader at the age of eighteen, a retarded albino boy who was pathetically devoted to his small sister, a spoiled crippled boy, and a boy who had unusual arithmetic skills. Another playmate, he recalled, was an imaginative liar who later gained nationwide media attention as an alleged swindler and multimurderer.[31]

An incident that occurred when Lewis was nine or ten years old also served to direct him toward his career interest in personality.[32] A book peddler had stopped at the Terman house for the night. He was selling a book on phrenology, a pseudoscience in which character and mental development were investigated through the study of the shape and protuberances of the skull. That evening, while the family sat around the fireplace, the visitor gave a discourse on phrenology and "felt the bumps" of each member of the family. The incident stood out for Lewis because when his turn came to be examined, great things were predicted. This prophecy seemed to give young Lewis an added sense of confidence and stimulated ambitions beyond the farm.

In the spring after he reached his eleventh birthday, Lewis began "making a hand" on the farm with team, plow, and wagon. He worked close to ten hours a day, six days a week, from April until September. This schedule continued until he was eighteen. He found the farm work pleasant, for the most part, but his desires lay elsewhere. He wanted to get an education beyond the eighth grade; and for an Indiana farm boy in the 1890s, this meant preparing to teach school.

The die had been cast. Lewis's goals of getting further education and making something of himself, possibly doing even more than teaching school, would lead him far beyond his boyhood roots on the farm. He was destined to be the only one of his siblings to go on to university. Among his peers, he stood out because of his intellectual acumen. As a youth with an interest in personality differences, he must have wondered why he was so intellectually superior. Once he began to study his chosen field of psychology, he would adopt the evolutionary doctrine of the times that weighed heredity over environment as a determinant of ability. Lewis would therefore account for his own intellectual giftedness largely in terms of heredity.

His lifelong adherence to the dominant role of heredity in determining intellectual differences may have blinded him somewhat to the circumstances of his own early environment—circumstances that were favorable toward propelling him to a life of academic and scientific eminence. Terman had the advantages of a warm and stable family. These assets included a father whom he adored and whose intellectual tendencies provided a strong role model, an older brother whose interest in books and a school-teaching career also served as a role model, and as the youngest son and one who showed noticeable intellectual skills, a prominent position in his family. He also had the opportunity of being in the right place at the right time. America in the 1890s was undergoing great economic expansion and social change. Professions, such as teaching, were growing; and new careers were being forged in emerging disciplines, such as psychology. The paths to social mobility were open for bright youngsters coming off the farms—youngsters who also had the advantage of belonging to the mainstream Protestant groups that had settled and shaped the American nation.

CHAPTER 2

Schoolteacher
(1892–1901)

The things I had to do seemed, on the whole, pleasant; my plans to escape from the farm were motivated entirely by my desire to get an education. For the farmer boy of 1890 in Indiana, to get an education meant first of all, that one must prepare to teach school.[1]

In 1890, at age thirteen, Terman was determined to continue his education beyond the eighth grade.[2] With no high school in reach of his home, the only available means to further his education was to attend a normal college—that is, a school set up to prepare students for teaching. Such schools, however, required expenses for tuition and board. Terman's father was sympathetic, but explained that due to the economic depression at the time the family simply did not have the money.[3] Nevertheless, his father offered some financial hope by allowing Terman to try and sell one of their horses, Nelly, who was a fine horse. Terman made the rounds among potential buyers but felt that the best offer he could get was considerably below the true value of the horse. After several days of soul-searching, he decided to keep Nelly and defer school.

It took two years before Terman's family was in a position to afford to send him to normal college. In the interim, he spent his winters studying at his brother's school. Finally, at age fifteen, his parents sent him to Central Normal College in Danville, Indiana.

Central Normal College

Terman spent most of the next six years at Danville.[4] After his first school year (1892–93) of thirty weeks, he returned to the farm for the summer period. Upon completing his second year, he was qualified to teach grade school. At age seventeen, during the winter of 1894–95, he had his first teaching assignment at a rural school much like the one he had attended as a child. After this stint of teaching, he returned to Danville and stayed for forty-eight weeks to earn his B.S. degree in what was called the "scientific course." The next winter, he taught at another country school then returned to Danville to complete an eighteen-week "pedagogy course," for which he received the title of B.Pd. (bachelor of pedagogy). Terman wanted still more education and borrowed money to remain at Danville for another year of forty-eight weeks, completing the "classical course" with the degree of A.B.

Thus, in the summer of 1898, when he was twenty-one, Terman had earned three baccalaureate degrees at Central Normal College. Over the next three years, he added some correspondence courses in German and in the history of education. In the fall of 1898, he became the principal of a township high school (Smiths Valley, Indiana) in his home county. He taught the entire curriculum of a four-year high school to about forty pupils. He remained as principal for three years, resigning in 1901 to further his education at Indiana University.

Terman had pleasant memories of the years he spent at Central Normal College—"C.N.C." as the students fondly referred to it. He admitted, however, that judged against the standards of the 1920s and the 1930s the training offered would appear to have been very shoddy. The teachers at C.N.C. were wretchedly paid and had to put in weekly schedules of heavy classroom instruction, ranging from twenty-five to thirty hours. Thorough work in ten-week courses was therefore out of the question. C.N.C. was one of many private normal schools that sprang up in the Middle West in the 1870s and 1880s. Such schools flourished in much of their original form until the first decade of the twentieth century. As Terman commented: "They took raw country boys fresh from the grammar school and in a few ten-week terms made them into teachers. They asked of the entering student no credentials and they lavished their degrees upon him when he departed."[5]

For many Midwest farm boys (and girls as well), the normal schools provided the only means for educational and social advancement. In the late nineteenth century there were few high schools in the Mississippi Valley, and those that existed were poor and geographically inaccessible. Although the teachers were overworked and poorly paid, the quality of instruction in the normal schools was generally very good. Terman noted that his Danville teachers were among the best classroom teachers he had been exposed to. He pointed to four in particular under whom he learned the most. Charles A. Hargrave, who taught most of the science courses, was a talented, largely self-taught naturalist. Gustave Spillmann, an accomplished linguist, taught Greek, Latin, French, and German. The psychology, philosophy, logic, and ethics courses were taught by Jonathan Rigdon, who had a Hegelian orientation and later took his Ph.D. degree at Boston University. The pedagogy, methods, and history-of-education courses were taught by A. J. Kinnaman, who had been exposed to Herbartian doctrines at the University of Jena and had obtained a doctorate of pedagogy at New York University. Kinnaman later went on to receive an M.A. at Indiana University and a Ph.D. at Clark University.

Among the textbooks in Ridgon's courses, Terman studied James Sully's *Outlines of Psychology* (which he particularly liked), John Dewey's *Psychology*, and *Ethics* by Rigdon's mentor, Borden P. Bowne. At about the same time, Terman took on a program of independent reading, which included several volumes of Herbert Spencer, William James's *Principles of Psychology* (another of Terman's favorites), Charles Darwin's *Origin of Species* and *Descent of Man*, and Ernst Haeckel's *The Riddle of the Universe*. Rigdon was especially scornful of the literary style of James's writings and did not like his students to quote from them, so this reading had to be done more or less surrepititously. Under Kinnaman, Terman studied J. F. Herbart, Jean Jacques Rousseau, and the essays on education by John Locke and Herbert Spencer. At C.N.C. he was barely exposed to the writings of such prominent psychologists of the day as Francis Galton, Wilhelm Wundt, and G. Stanley Hall and had never heard of Alfred Binet or James Mckeen

Cattell. All of these figures, except Wundt, were to become major influences in Terman's professional development.

The fact that two of his favorite teachers, Rigdon (a Hegelian) and Kinnaman (a Herbartian) held such opposite views was a source of intellectual excitement for Terman. At the time, he took sides and became an enthusiastic Herbartian. Herbart's child-centered approach to pedagogy seemed much easier to understand and to relate to than did G. W. F. Hegel's abstract philosophy of idealism. Terman's Herbartian leanings at Central Normal College would soon be reinforced when he continued his education at Indiana University and Clark University. At these institutions, he would come under the spellbinding influence of G. Stanley Hall and his disciples—the leaders of the emerging Child-Study movement in education and psychology.[6]

Friends and Interests

Terman's intellectual stimulation during his stay at Danville was not limited to the classroom. There were many bright young men and women who had come to study at C.N.C., and Terman established a number of friendships.[7] Among these were the men he roomed with at the various times he stayed in Danville. His roommates included Arthur M. Banta, whom he had already known as a fellow student in his brother John's school, and Logan Esarey, who was to become a history professor at Indiana University. He developed especially close friendships with Frederick N. Duncan, who eventually earned a doctoral degree in biology and taught at several southern colleges, and P. C. Emmons, who became a school superintendent in Indiana. After leaving Danville, Duncan and Emmons continued their education at Indiana University. This was one of the reasons Terman was to choose Indiana when he decided on further schooling.[8]

During the five years that Terman taught school—two during his span of time at Danville and three as high-school principal—he furthered his intellectual interests through the Teachers' Reading Circle.[9] This was a state-wide reading program that was required of all teachers. In a given year, two or three books would be chosen, and the teachers would purchase and study these books. The books were actually bought for the teachers, and the cost deducted from their salaries. One Saturday each month, all of the teachers in a township (in Terman's township there were nine) met at one of the schoolhouses for an all-day session. Most of the day was devoted to a discussion of the Reading-Circle books, an assignment having been made to each teacher a month in advance.

As a result of this reading program, Terman had read and studied rather intensively about fifteen books in education and psychology over a five-year span. The two books that interested him the most were James's *Talks to Teachers* and William Lowe Bryan's *Plato the Teacher*. James's book intensified his interest in the psychological aspects of education, and Bryan's attractive presentation of Plato made him want to study philosophy. Terman felt that the Reading-Circle books had a lasting influence on him, and pointed him in the direction of a philosophical and psychological interest in education.

Marriage and Family

In 1896, while attending Central Normal College, Terman met a fellow student, Anna Belle Minton (no relation to the author). Three years later, on 18 September 1899, Lewis and Anna were married.[10] Anna was born on 6 December 1876—thus, she was a month older than Lewis—in Pulaski County, Indiana. She had begun teaching school in her home county a year or two before Lewis started his first teaching job.[11] She and Lewis came under the influence of the same teachers at Danville. As Lewis was to comment later, Anna "had exactly the same objectives for me as were already shaping themselves in my own mind."[12]

Anna's background was similar to Lewis's. She was the second of four children and grew up on a farm.[13] In the division of labor among the children, Anna was the one designated to help with the farm chores. The only son among the four children was the youngest, and he died at about age twelve. Anna's father, Reuben B. Minton, was the dominant figure in the family.[14] Apparently, Anna was the only one who would not let her father overshadow her.[15] Born in Kentucky in 1848, Reuben Minton was raised on a farm in Indiana.[16] During the

Civil War, when he was sixteen, he enlisted in the Union army—his older brother had died the year before of typhoid pneumonia while in the army.[17] His education was limited to the eighth grade, but he was nevertheless able to teach school for several winters to help support his widowed mother on the farm.[18] He then became a successful farmer and businessman in his youth, and at about the time he was fifty established a bank in the small town of Star City, Indiana. While he had no formal training as a banker, he was very successful and was quite well off financially by the time he died in 1927, at age seventy-nine.

After their wedding, Lewis and Anna settled in an old farmhouse near the country high school where Lewis was principal.[19] To help supplement the family income, they took in boarders.[20] This was a practice that would continue through Lewis's student years at Indiana University and Clark. Much of Anna's time during these years was spent in managing the family home and looking after the boarders. Several months after marriage, Anna's time would also be taken up with motherhood. In June of 1900, she gave birth to a son who was named in honor of Lewis's three closest friends—Fred Duncan, P. C. Emmons, and Arthur Banta.[21] Frederick Emmons Arthur Terman (the Arthur was later dropped for convenience) brought a new psychological interest to his father's life—an interest that seemed to kindle a desire to become a psychologist.[22] Such ambitions, however, were soon to give way to health concerns. In August, two months after Fred's birth, Lewis came down with a disabling attack of pleurisy that was diagnosed as tubercular.[23] The previous year he had had his first hemorrhage of the lungs, but there were no complications following the attack and the attending doctor concluded it was the result of an injury to a blood vessel in the throat. This time, however, it was evident that tuberculosis had surfaced. Terman believed that the family strain on his father's side, his childhood exposure to a consumptive sister, and a case of typhoid fever when he was nineteen all contributed to his vulnerability to the disease. Lewis's doctor kept him in bed for about three weeks, until his temperature was normal and the pains of pleurisy had subsided. When he was able to move about, he was told that if he did not want to die from tuberculosis in a year or two, he had better resign his job and move to a warmer climate. Though badly shaken by this advice, Lewis decided to stay at his job since there was no other way to insure that he and his family could remain financially self-sufficient while he recovered. He did obtain a month's leave of absence and steadily improved so that he was back on the job at the end of October, though still worried about the final outcome.

Throughout the subsequent school year (1900–1901), Lewis maintained a strict regimen. He described it (as written in 1953) as follows:

In the autumn, when the days were fairly long, I rose early and took a walk of a half-hour in the near-by fields or woods before breakfast. Throughout the year, as soon as school was dismissed at four in the afternoon, I strolled off again unless it was raining or snowing. On Saturdays and Sundays the walks were somewhat longer though still carefully rationed. I took my temperature every day and counted my pulse at the end of my walks. As a measure of safety to my family I slept in a separate room, which was large and had cross ventilation. All through the winter I slept with doors and windows wide open, often waking to find snow drifted half way across the room. I came to enjoy "outdoor" sleeping and during most of my life since then I have usually slept in open or half-open rooms.[24]

This episode marked the beginning of Lewis's lifelong concern about his health and was a source of his later interest in school hygiene.

By the following spring, Lewis had regained his health. It was at this time that P. C. Emmons, a friend from the Danville days, came to visit him.[25] Since leaving Danville in 1898, Emmons had been a student at Indiana University. He and Lewis had visited each other on several occasions, including a couple of fishing trips that Lewis would fondly recall in later years.[26] Emmons, in a 1959 letter to Lewis's son, Fred, recalled that during his 1901 visit with the Termans, Lewis expressed no desires or plans beyond school teaching.[27] While Emmons talked about the opportunities his Indiana University degree would give him, Lewis seemed to be quite content to remain at his position in the country school.[28] Could Lewis's bout with tuberculosis have aborted his ambitions for further education, with the possible goal of becoming a psychologist?[29] Perhaps so, for a time anyway, but events were soon to prove otherwise.

CHAPTER 3

The Choice of
Psychology (1901–1905)

My introduction to the scientific aspects of intellectual differences occurred when I was a senior in psychology at Indiana University and was asked to prepare two seminar reports, one on mental deficiency and one on genius. The reading for those reports opened up a new world for me, the world of Galton, Binet, and their contemporaries.[1]

Shortly after Emmons's visit in the spring of 1901, Lewis, Anna, and young Fred came down to Indiana University at Bloomington to look things over.[2] Emmons gave them his room while he stayed with one of his Bloomington friends. Apparently, by this time Lewis's health seemed so completely normal that he decided it was worth gambling on the future.[3] He would enter Indiana as a first step toward becoming a psychologist.

Indiana University

Several factors contributed to Terman's choice of Indiana University.[4] Two of his Danville teachers, Kinnaman and Spillman, had recommended it, as had several of his Danville classmates, including Emmons and Duncan. Bryan was there and Terman had read one of his books as part of the Teacher's Reading Circle program. In addition, Bloomington was only about fifty miles from his home and living expenses were not too high. Terman was able to get a loan of $1,200 from his father and brother John. This, plus the income Anna received from taking in boarders, proved to be enough to sustain the family for the two years it would take for Lewis to complete his studies.

Terman's goal at Indiana was to obtain an A.B. degree from a standard university, with the possibility of also obtaining a master's degree. The graduate degree would provide him with the qualifications to teach psychology or pedagogy at a normal school or college. If college teaching did not work out, he could fall back upon a high-school principalship or superintendency of schools. He also had vague dreams of a Ph.D., but this seemed too remote and unattainable to plan for in any definite way.

He earned enough credits from his normal-school training to allow him to enter as a third-year undergraduate. Within a span of two years (including summer quarters), he was able to complete three and a half years of course credits and thus earn both the A.B. and A.M. degrees.[5] Both degrees were conferred in June of 1903.[6] During his two-year stay he took all of the psychology courses offered, a year of neurology, as much philosophy and education as he could schedule, several years of German and French, and some courses in economics, anthropology, and sociology.

The psychology courses were taught in the Department of Philosophy and were offered by William Lowe Bryan, Ernest H. Lindley, and John A. Bergström.[7] All three had taken their doctorates in psychology under G. Stanley Hall at Clark University in the 1890s, Bryan having been among Hall's earliest Clark students.[8] As a student in their classes, Terman recalled the "I became fired with the ambition to become a professor of psychology and to contribute something of myself to the science."[9] He also recalled that Bryan and Lindley were brilliant and inspiring teachers. Bergström, because of his modesty and lack of personal force, was disappointing at first, but his skills as experimentalist and scholar soon reflected his value as a teacher. At the end of Terman's first year, Bryan was made president of the university and Terman had only one more class with him. Lindley and Bergström were to be the major influences in his psychology education at Indiana.

It was Lindley who served as Terman's chief mentor, and Terman was greatly indebted to him both for instruction and personal encouragement.[10] During Terman's second year, while he was doing his master's thesis under Lindley, he would have a weekly conference with his mentor that lasted an hour, sometimes two. Both Lindley and Bergström had spent a post-doctoral year of study and research in Germany. Therefore, in his classes with them, Terman studied the works of Wundt, Hermann Ebbinghaus, Emil Kraepelin, and Oswald Külpe. In addition, he was exposed to French psychology through the writings of Binet, Jean Martin Charcot, Théodule Ribot, and Gabriel Tarde. He was aided in all of this work by his mastery of German and French, which he had acquired by the end of his first year. In his psychology courses, he also studied Galton, C. Lloyd Morgan, Hall, James, Cattell, James Ladd, Edward Bradford Titchener, James Mark Baldwin, William H. Burnham, and Edmund C. Sanford.

In the experimental psychology course under Bergström, the laboratory manuals of Sanford and Titchener were used. Terman worked with various kinds of apparatus, including chronoscopes for reaction-time experiments, myographs for the study of movement, and equipment for memory experiments according to the Ebbinghaus method.[11] While he found the subject matter of interest, he did not like working with apparatus. He was to comment later:

Three years of work in the laboratory at Indiana and Clark universities did not enable me to overcome my mechanical ineptness. The set-ups were always difficult for me and a piece of "machinery" always seemed to be an obstruction between me and the thing I was trying to get at. "Brass-instrument" psychology was all right for the other fellow, but was not intended for me. My dislike of apparatus doubtless had something to do later in turning me to tests and measurements of the kind that make no demands upon mechanical skill.[12]

In his philosophy courses, Terman read the classic writings of Locke, George Berkeley, David Hume, René Descartes, and Emmanuel Kant.[13] Of these, he enjoyed all except Kant. As he had found when reading Hegel in Danville, German philosophy continued to seem unnecessarily obscure. In general, his philosophical interests were waning in contrast with his growing enthusiasm for psychology.

The course that proved to be the most meaningful for Terman was the seminar given by Lindley, which involved individual reports. For the seminar, which he took in his first quarter,[14] he prepared two reports: one on "Degeneracy" and the other on "The Great-Man Theory." He read almost everything he could find in the library (in English, German, or French) on the psychology of mental deficiency, criminality, and genius. He was thus introduced in depth to the work of Binet and Galton. The two seminar reports led to the master's thesis he carried out the following year under Lindley's direction. The thesis was an experimental study of leadership and was based on Binet's recently published book on suggestibility, as well as articles by Hall and his students in the field of child study.[15]

For his master's research, Terman used a sample of 100 white children and 16 "colored" children in the Bloomington public schools.[16] Using some of Binet's measures of suggestibility, in which subjects were asked questions about pictures and objects, Terman studied the children in groups of four. His assessment of leadership was based on several indices, including the number of times a child's reply was first, second, third, or fourth; originality in answering; imitating the answers of others; and suggestibility, in terms of falling into a trap produced by answering certain catch questions. Those children who were the most influential with their peers in the groups were identified by Terman as leaders.[17] He also found that the leaders identified by his measures were generally the same children chosen as leaders by teachers and classmates. When Terman asked the teachers and classmates to account for their choices, he found that intelligence was one of the most important qualities mentioned. Others included congeniality, liveliness, and goodness.

In retrospect, Terman believed that his master's thesis was scientifically worthless, although it was eventually expanded and published in the *Pedagogical Seminary.*[18] Nevertheless, he felt that the thesis had a significant influence on his personal development, for it anticipated future directions. The results suggested a relationship between intelligence and leadership. He would soon be concentrating his efforts on trying to assess intelligence as a means of identifying the intellectually gifted, and he thought that it was such individuals who had the potential to become leaders in society.

As his second busy year at Bloomington drew to a close, Terman regretted the idea of having to leave his studies. It was near the end of that school year, in 1903, that his daughter Helen was born. With a growing family and the imminent completion of his master's work, it was time to look for a job as school superintendent or high-school principal. He had had an offer to teach psychology and pedagogy at Central Normal College, but he turned it down because the salary was too low to enable him to pay off his debts and save for further education.

At Lindley's suggestion, he allowed Lindley to recommend him for a fellowship at Clark University. In writing to Hall, who was the president of Clark, Lindley declared that Terman was decidedly brilliant, possessing a remarkably incisive mind and a great capacity for work.[19] He concluded by stating that he had never recommended anyone to Hall with more confidence. Bergström, though not as effusive, also sent on a very positive recommendation, judging Terman an excellent and well-trained student.[20] Hall offered Terman a stipend of two hundred dollars plus free tuition.[21] Terman was greatly embarrassed by the fellowship.[22] He was already in debt and even with the fellowship he would have to borrow more money to go to Clark. However, Lindley, Bergström, and Bryan all insisted that he should go on for his doctorate if he could possibly arrange it financially. Terman presented the situation to his father and brother John. They loyally offered another loan of $1,200. Anna courageously approved. Lewis's remote dreams of a Ph.D. were going to be realized.

Clark University

For Terman, entering Clark University fulfilled his highest aspirations. As he stated, "when I went to Clark in 1903 it was still the American Mecca for aspiring young psychologists."[23] His Indiana teachers—Bryan, Lindley, and Bergström—were all Clark alumni. His prospective teachers at Clark—Hall, Sanford, and Burnham— were already familiar to him, having read nearly everything they had written and having heard them quoted almost daily in his classes. Terman was therefore well prepared for his Clark experience, though he judged himself otherwise. His trepidation was allayed, to some extent, when in his first conference with President Hall, he was commended for his splendid training and the fine report he had been given by his Indiana teachers. Hall had great expectations for him. Terman left the conference with a sense of some reassurance, but he now had a burdening sense of responsibility to live up to Hall's expectations.[24]

In describing the Clark of his day, Terman noted its uniqueness from other American universities.[25] It was primarily a graduate-level institution, with a small student-body. During the time of his attendance there were only about fifty full-time students, thirty of whom were primarily in the related fields of psychology, philosophy, and education. There was an unusual degree of informality. Registration simply consisted of the student giving his name and address to President Hall's secretary. No formal selection of a major or a minor subject was required. For any course, the student could choose to go to as many or as few lectures as he or she cared to attend. No marks or grades were given, and the only examination was the four-hour doctoral oral.

On entering the university, the student was advised by President Hall to sample all the courses of possible interest, and then drop those judged to be of least value. Students of psychology typically began by taking most of the courses offered by Hall, Sanford, and Burnham, as well as the anthropology courses given by A. F. Chamberlain and a course in neurology or physiology given by Clifton F. Hodge. The courses often started out with an attendance of twenty or thirty, but some would be reduced to ten or less by mid-semester.

The guiding spirit at Clark was its president, G. Stanley Hall. Hall had received his doctorate in psychology at Harvard under James, taught psychology at Johns Hopkins, and became the first president of Clark in 1888.[26] He was an ardent evolutionist who believed that heredity was a more significant determining factor than environment. By 1903 he was acknowledged as a leader of the child-centered philosophy of education, a point of view that emphasized the need for schools to adjust their curriculum to the needs and inherent nature of children. According to Hall, the traditional nineteenth-century emphasis on academic subjects with regimented drill was inappropriate. Instead, he championed industrial training, moral education, physical training, and health. He also favored individualized instruction and believed that gifted children, whom he assumed came primarily from the middle class, should be singled out for academic training by the time they reached adolescence.

Reflecting his varied interests, Hall offered the following lecture courses: "The History of Philosophy During the Nineteenth Century"; "The Development of Mind in Animals, Children and the Race"; "The Psychology of Religion and of Christianity"; "Education"; and "Abnormal" (psychology).[27] As a student in these classes, Terman recalled that Hall talked from notes, "the freshness or staleness of which the student could gauge by the amount of fumbling of papers and by the élan of his delivery."[28] Like his writings, Hall's lectures were broad in scope and contained a wealth of allusion.

For Terman, the most significant contact with Hall occurred at the Monday-evening seminars Hall gave in his home throughout the academic year. In these sessions, which started at a quarter past seven and often lasted until eleven or twelve o'clock, two students would report about their work to the full complement of about thirty students in psychology, philosophy, and education. According to Terman, when each student was finished

Dr. Hall usually started the discussion off with a few deceivingly generous comments on the importance of the material that had been presented, then hesitantly expressed just a shade of doubt about some of the conclusions drawn, and finally called for "reactions." . . . When the discussion had raged from thirty minutes to an hour, and was beginning to slacken, Hall would sum things up with an erudition and fertility of imagination that always amazed us and made us feel that his offhand insight into the problem went immeasurably beyond that of the student who had devoted months of slavish drudgery to it. . . . [At the end of each session] I always went home dazed and intoxicated, took a hot bath to quiet my nerves, then lay awake for hours rehearsing the drama and formulating the clever things I should have said and did not.[29]

In a letter to a fellow Clark alumnus, Henry D. Sheldon, Terman commented: "No other educational experience I ever had was comparable to his [Hall's] seminar."[30]

Two of Terman's other Clark professors—Burnham and Sanford— were also important influences. Both had taken their doctorates under Hall at Johns Hopkins, and they were among the first faculty members appointed by Hall when Clark opened in 1890.[31] Burnham's field was educational psychology, and his well-taught courses in school hygiene had a lasting influence on Terman.[32] Sanford, whose field was experimental psychology, was somewhat of a disappointment as a lecturer, but his ability as a scientist earned great respect. Terman worked under Sanford in the psychological laboratory, and it was Sanford who directed his doctoral dissertation.

In addition to the benefits from his teachers, Terman found the atmosphere and the facilities of the university much to his liking.[33]

I think the Clark situation . . . was of almost crucial importance in my development. I have never worked well under the restraint of rules and regulations, and it is hard to imagine a régime that would have been better adapted to my temperament than the one I found at Clark, if régime indeed it could be called. Because I was placed absolutely on my own responsibility, I was able to give my best with unalloyed enthusiasm.[34]

The library provided rich resources, in terms of its collection of materials, the ease by which books could be borrowed, and the ample work space set aside for students. Although he preferred library work to laboratory work, Terman was also impressed with the laboratory facilities. As in the case of the library, work space for students was plentiful, and apparatus was available for almost any experiment a student wished to conduct.

Rounding out Terman's Clark experience was the stimulation he received from his classmates. With a small enrollment the students got to know each other very well. Terman established close associations with W. F. Book, Edward Conradi, Arnold Gesell, E. B. Huey, Fred Kuhlmann, Josiah Morse, and James P. Porter. Book, Conradi, and Porter, like Terman, were all former Indiana University students. Gesell, who arrived in Terman's second year, would become a colleague of Terman's at Los Angeles State Normal School. Huey and Kuhlmann were particularly influential because they, like Terman, were interested in testing. Huey had received his doctorate under Hall in 1899. He returned to Clark at the end of Terman's first year after spending some time in Europe, where he had contact with Binet and Pierre Janet. Terman spent much time with Huey learning about the European developments in psychology, and especially about the work of Binet and Janet. Kuhlmann was conducting an experiment in the psychology of mental deficiency, which Terman followed with great interest.

Terman's own research at Clark was initially guided by Hall. As Terman stated, "I remained pretty much under his hypnotic sway during the first half year."[35] At Hall's suggestion he made a survey of the literature on precocity, which was published in 1905 in one of Hall's journals, the *American Journal of Psychology*.[36] Precocity was defined by Terman as "development in advance of some assumed norm."[37] What would constitute the norm would vary depending upon the standard of comparison. One could make comparisons between or within racial groups or simply focus on the natural rate of development for any particular individual. Guided by Hall's evolutionary perspective, with its emphasis on the biological basis of growth, Terman chose to concentrate on precocity in terms of "prematuration." By prematuration, he meant any factors that would interfere with, and thus hasten, the natural rate or process of development. To illustrate his point, Terman declared that prematuration would include such facts as

pruning a tree to hasten its fruit, dieting an animal to bring it to early maturity; forcing on a child the activities of the adolescent and upon the adolescent the activities of the adult; the engrafting of mature civilization onto primitive races; of an idealistic religion upon a mind incapable of transcending the concrete; to initiate into the harmonies of Mozart, minds that find more edification in the rattle of tom-toms; in short every conceivable example of forced culture.[38]

This list illustrates that within the Hallian framework the minds of children and primitive races were considered to be the same, and it would be dangerous to impose mature civilization upon such minds. According to Hall, adolescence was the period of life to begin the acculturation process for members of advanced races. In surveying prematuration, in such areas as the education of schoolchildren, religious teaching, and the acquisition of sexual interests, Terman pointed to the dangers of providing instruction or training at too early a period of development.

As an extension to his master's research, which had involved the experimental study of leadership in children, Hall suggested that Terman develop a questionnaire on children's leadership. Such a questionnaire would be filled out by teachers. Terman went ahead with his questionnaire survey, completing it and incorporating the results with his master's research in a publication in another of Hall's journals, the *Pedagogical Seminary*.[39] Such questionnaires, given to teachers and analyzed by researchers, formed the major data base for Hall's Child-Study movement.[40]

However, by the end of his first year Terman did not see much value in Hall's questionnaire method.[41] It was only at Hall's urging that he undertook the development of the leadership questionnaire. Terman was anxious to return to the interests he had developed at Indiana on gifted and defective children. He turned increasingly to reading about the method of tests, including the works of Galton, Binet and his collaborators, Ebbinghaus, Kraepelin, William Stern, Charles E. Spearman, Cattell, and Edward L. Thorndike. By the spring of 1904, he had decided to make his doctoral dissertation an experimental study of mental tests. When he approached Hall, he was disappointed by Hall's emphatic disapproval of tests. After much soul-searching, he concluded that he would have to desert the person who had so inspired him and seek out Sanford as his dissertation supervisor. Sanford agreed to become his advisor, and when Terman informed Hall of his decision, Hall gave him his blessing "and some advice on the danger of being misled by the quasi-exactness of quantitative methods."[42]

In the summer of 1904 when Terman was planning his doctoral study, the development of mental testing in America was at a preliminary stage.[43] The major influence was Galton's use of measures of sensory discrimination. Galton assumed that intelligence was related to sensitivity—that is, the more sensory discriminations one could detect the more one had to draw upon in carrying out mental activities. His approach to measuring intelligence became known in America through the efforts of Cattell, who had completed his doctorate under Wundt at Leipzig. Cattell was interested in the study of individual differences, and therefore spent some time with Galton in 1886 and 1887 on his way back to America. Once he returned, Cattell embarked on a series of investigations with college students at the University of Pennsylvania and Columbia University utilizing sensory measures of intelligence. When such tests were correlated with college grades, the results were disappointing because of the negligible correlations.[44]

Other attempts at measuring intelligence involved surveys of school-children in which memory and sensory tests were administered.[45] Some evidence was reported of a small association between the children's test performance and how they were intellectually assessed by their teachers. In addition to these survey studies of testing,

Thorndike's work on educational measurement first appeared in 1903, and Spearman's and Thorndike's views about a "general intelligence" factor were published in 1904.[46] Terman was especially attracted to the work of Thorndike because of the emphasis on statistical methods and the view that intelligence was reflected in a variety of mental activities rather than by any one general factor.[47]

In his doctoral research, Terman chose to focus on the qualitative rather than quantitative aspects of mental tests.[48] He was interested in discovering the types of mental processes involved in intelligence, and he selected two groups of boys to study, using the following procedure

My subjects were specially selected as among the brightest or most stupid that could be found in the public schools within easy distance of Clark University, in the City of Worcester. Three ward principals, by the aid of their teachers, made out a list of about two dozen boys of the desired age, equally divided between the two groups. . . . These two dozen were selected from about five hundred boys. Out of this list, fourteen were found who were willing to come to the university as often as desired for experimentation—seven bright and seven dull.[49]

The boys ranged in age from ten to thirteen, with the dull group being, on the average, somewhat older. Terman did not consider this to be a problem since the advantage in maturity went to the dull group.[50] He tested each subject in eight types of ability: (1) inventiveness and creative imagination (assessed by problem-solving tests); (2) logical processes (another series of problem-solving tasks); (3) mathematical ability; (4) mastery of language; (5) insight, as determined by the interpretation of fables; (6) ease of acquisition, as reflected in learning to play chess; (7) powers of memory; and (8) motor ability both in general and in the acquisition of bodily skill.[51] He developed some of his own measures and borrowed or adapted others in the test literature.

In devising some of his tests, Terman demonstrated resoucefulness. Many years later, Gesell observed:

He was not perturbed by the almost forbidding immensity of the steep wooden staircase which gave monumental entrance to the main academic building. He was preoccupied with problems of stupidity and intelligence. So why not put this formidable incline to scientific use? The flight of steps could test the motor coordination of the bright and the backward boys who were under comparative study! Accordingly, Terman marshalled the boys and served as timekeeper, recording the performance for speed of climbing and descent. Puzzle books were explored for the testing of more subtle intellectual processes—Binet would soon appear on the horizon.[52]

The results of the testing indicated that the bright group of boys was superior on all of the tests, except the motor tests in which the dull group excelled. Within the bright group, the ranking of the individual subjects across the various tests was markedly consistent, leading Terman to comment that intelligence does not develop along special lines. In his final conclusion, Terman declared: "While offering little positive data on the subject, the study has strengthened my impression of the relatively greater importance of *endowment* over *training*, as a determinant of an individual's intellectual rank among his fellows."[53] His impression of the dominance of nature over nurture as a determinant of intelligence would soon become the guiding conviction of his professional career.

Terman devoted the 1904–05 academic year to his doctoral research.[54] Beginning near the end of 1904, he tested his subjects about five hours a day, completing his testing the following May. His research was an independent effort. He had selected the problem, devised the tests and the procedure, and wrote up the results. Sanford followed Terman's work with interest but could provide little help since the problem was outside of his field. Upon completing his dissertation and passing his four-hour doctoral oral, Terman received his Ph.D. diploma in June from the hands of President Theodore Roosevelt, who delivered the commencement address.[55]

Terman's experience at Clark shaped his subsequent career interests —the psychology of genius, the measurement of intelligence, the nature of individual differences, and problems of school hygiene.[56] Hall remained an inspirational figure. When Hall died in 1924, Terman wrote to Burnham: "I can truthfully say that to no one else have I been as greatly indebted for the inspiration which has led to any little measure of success I have had. His influence has been with me through all the years since I left Clark."[57] Indeed, Hall's evolutionary perspective was to serve as the conceptual basis for Terman's professional work. As we review Terman's contributions through the years, his mentor's influence will loom large. While Hall provided Terman with an intellectual framework, Terman recognized the methodological deficiencies inherent in Hall's scientific thinking.[58] Sanford, like Bergström before him, provided Terman with the model of the methodical empiricist. It was therefore possible for Terman to wed Hall's biological determinism with the empirical methodology of testing, as reflected in the work of Galton, Cattell, and Thorndike—scientists who themselves also favored a biological perspective.

When President Roosevelt handed Terman his doctoral diploma in 1905, the dream of becoming a psychologist had been fulfilled. The future held much promise; but there was also uncertainty. The nemesis of tuberculosis had reappeared the previous summer when Terman suffered a pulmonary hemorrhage.[59] After a rest of several weeks, he was able to gradually return to his studies. Within a month he began working six or seven hours a day, and throughout the fall season he and Anna took long Sunday walks in the country, pushing the baby wagon loaded with Fred and Helen. As his health returned, his financial worries were also laid to rest. The previous June his fellowship had been renewed for another year,[60] and while he was ill Anna had arranged for financial help from her father.[61] No symptoms reappeared during the school year, and Terman was able to devote his time to the dissertation, although he experienced insomnia because of the anxiety he felt regarding his health. With his goal of the Ph.D. in hand, he now had to contend with the worries of obtaining a position in a favorable climate and at a salary that would enable him to pay off the debts he had accumulated.

CHAPTER 4

The Fallow Years (1905-1910)

It was September of 1905 when we arrived at San Bernardino after an unforgettable ride through the Mohave Desert on a Santa Fe train. As we coasted down through the Cajon pass, and the San Bernardino valley opened before us almost encircled by mountains of 4,000 to 11,000 feet, the valley seemed to be truly the paradise that the chamber-of-commerce literature had depicted it. Here, if anywhere, I should be able to rid myself of the threat that had been hanging over me.[1]

In looking for a position in a warm climate, Terman limited his search to the South and the Southwest.[2] He preferred a university position, but the only one he received did not provide the financial support he needed for his family. This was a one-year replacement position at the University of Texas at half salary. At about the same time, he received an offer for the presidency of a small normal school in St. Petersburg, Florida. This was at a fair salary, and fearing that nothing better would come along, he accepted. A couple of days later, he received an offer of a high-school principalship in San Bernardino, California. After two sleepless nights of indecision, he decided to pull out of the Florida position and accept the principalship. Although he did not particularly care for this kind of work, he preferred to live in southern California. At this point in his life, health concerns had a higher priority than professional ambition. He was able to get a release from the Florida normal school by finding someone to take his place. Conradi, his Clark friend and fellow graduate student, accepted the Florida appointment, and Terman was now able to go to San Bernardino.

High-School Principal

Terman and his family were warmly received when they arrived in San Bernardino.[3] By the time school opened, they were settled in a five-room cottage.[4] The townspeople raved about the climate, and Terman felt good about the choice he had made. He was pleased with the competence and cooperativeness of his teaching staff, and his work schedule was not too taxing. With things going so well, he was not prepared for the shock that occurred around the beginning of November. One morning, he awoke around five o'clock with his mouth full of blood. The hemorrhage lasted several minutes and was more copious than any he had experienced. He was in a serious predicament. He later recalled:

No one in San Bernardino knew that I had ever had TB, and to admit the fact now might have serious consequences. Instead of calling a doctor I reported to the school that I was not feeling well and would remain at home the rest of the week. During the following week I was on duty only half of each day. . . . Just eleven days after the hemorrhage I was back at work on a full-time basis. The desperate gamble I had taken paid off, for there was no trouble the rest of the school year.[5]

Shortly after his tubercular attack, Terman began a regimen of short walks into the fields and meadows after school hours and longer walks on weekends. Throughout the rest of the school year, he was able to carry out his duties in a way that was not physically taxing, and each day he got plenty of sleep by retiring early. With his health under control, he began to settle into the demands of his principalship. Though the workload was relatively light, he was experiencing difficulty in making the transition from the intellectual life he had enjoyed as a university student. Midway through the school year, he confided in Gesell who was working on his dissertation at Clark:

Sometimes I am half satisfied; other times I feel I ought to have taken the Texas place regardless of financial considerations. The High School work is pleasant, for High School work. Everything has been running along smoothly

enough, but you know how it goes to engage in a line of work where your
heart is not. . . . After four years of the kind of work I have been doing, where
everything gave encouragement toward interest in a particular line, it is very
depressing to be thrown at once into practical life, with very little time for
reading and with no Library, even in case I had time to use it.[6]

Terman reported to Hall that his work performance was viewed
favorably by the school board, and he personally viewed his work as
good preparation for the field of educational psychology, which he
hoped eventually to pursue. However, as he went on to say, there
were times of desperation.

Blues seize me only when I think of the probability of delayed emancipation.
It is very well now, but if long continued it will become a prison. I get to read
so little it is all I can do to keep up with the journals. I have just subscribed
for five of the leading ones and hope to be able to order soon one-half dozen
more. Have taken this course as the safest assurance against getting stranded
high and dry.[7]

The thought of being stranded apparently led him to apply for a
normal-school position in Montana.[8] It seemed that he was willing to
leave the congenial climate of southern California for an intellectual
oasis, even if in the Northwest. Fortunately, he did not have to pursue
such a geographical change. Rescue came in the form of an offer from
the Los Angeles State Normal School. He had been contacted through
a teachers' agency that the normal school wanted someone in his
specialty.[9] Terman took the next train to Los Angeles, had a conference with the president of the normal school, and in a few days was
offered the position of professor of child study and pedagogy, which
he accepted. This turn of events had developed in the spring of 1906.
He had already been reappointed, with a salary increase, in San
Bernardino. However, there were no problems. As he reported to
Hall, "the Board here offered me very material inducements to stay
with them, but seeing my desire very kindly allowed me to go."[10] For
Terman, the normal-school position not only delivered him from intellectual stagnation; it served as a steppingstone to his ultimate goal of
securing a university position in educational psychology.

To ensure that he was physically ready for his new position, Terman
and the family left San Bernardino as soon as school ended in June and
went off to the surrounding mountains, where they camped out in

tents for nearly three months.[11] They were up at an elevation of four thousand feet, and the cool mountain air was exhilarating. By the time they had to leave, Terman felt so well that he could look forward to his next year's work with confidence.

Normal-School Teaching

For the first year in Los Angeles (1906–07), the Termans lived in Hollywood, then a quiet suburb of about four thousand. Terman was quite satisfied with his new position.[12] His work schedule was light, the library facilities were unusually good for a normal school, and the associations with his colleagues were pleasant and intellectually stimulating. These associations were especially important because with the insecurity of his health he did not want to undertake any more work than the minimum his teaching demanded. He did not engage in any research or writing, but read rather widely and tried to make his teaching as effective as possible. In the summer of 1907, the family returned to the mountains where they had camped the previous summer. Terman's Clark friend, Huey, was a guest for the greater part of the summer. Huey was becoming more interested in clinical psychology, and, as they had done at Clark, Terman and Huey talked extensively about the developments in mental testing.

Before leaving for their summer vacation, the Termans had bought an acre-lot in an orange grove at the foot of the mountains in the San Fernando Valley, north of Glendale.[13] They had drafted plans for an inexpensive but comfortable house, and it was ready in November. The house on Valley View Road would be their home for the remainder of the three years they were in Los Angeles. It was an ideal location, for in the pre-smog years the climate of the San Fernando Valley matched that of San Bernardino. Terman commuted to Los Angeles by interurban trolley, leaving by 8:30 each morning and returning early enough in the afternoon to work an hour or more in the garden before dinner. He also devoted much of his time on weekends to gardening.

Shortly before his second school year began in 1907, he wrote to Gesell to inform him of an opening at the normal school in the area of psychology.[14] Gesell had obtained his Ph.D. from Clark the year before, and Terman had been impressed by his dissertation on jealousy, which had been published in the *American Journal of Psychology*.[15] Terman wrote a glowing report of the normal school and the Los Angeles area, revealing that he was so satisfied that he had just refused a virtual offer of a full professorship of education at the State University of Oregon. The double lure of California and his friendship for Terman led Gesell to accept the position, which began in January of 1908.[16]

When Gesell arrived in southern California, he bought the orange grove across the road from the Termans. With the help of his brother Robert and the Terman family, Gesell built a bungalow. He especially recalled the help of young Fred Terman, then age seven, who in Gesell's estimation showed early signs of the eminence he was to achieve as an engineer.[17] Gesell was a bachelor, and Terman introduced him to a colleague, Beatrice Chandler, who was the director of primary teaching. About a year later Gesell and Chandler were married, and they left the normal school in 1909 when Gesell decided to work for his M.D. degree at Yale.[18] In reminiscing about his Los Angeles years, Gesell was most grateful for Terman's generosity and friendship.[19]

Beginning in 1907, Terman began to write some articles about child study and pedagogy for popular periodicals and education journals. In these various articles, which appeared between 1907 and 1909, Terman espoused the Hallian viewpoint. For example, he cited various sources of educational waste, such as inadequate ventilation and illumination in schoolrooms and the lack of testing for eye defects and adenoid growths.[20] Terman recognized that such conditions were deleterious to the education of children. As Hall had stressed, the health of a child was a prerequisite for educating the child. Terman pointed out that it was the purpose of child study to scientifically investigate the sources of educational waste and to prescribe corrective measures.

With respect to teaching methods, Terman pointed to the waste of regimented drill and stressed that the teacher's role should be primarily one of building moral character: "The old adage that knowledge is power should be replaced by the truer one, character is power. For the formation of character the curriculum is not so important as a teacher who is larger than his subject, who thinks more of instilling ideals than of imparting facts, whose personality touches the life of the pupil and sets it aglow with ambition and worthy desires".[21] Such a view was consistent with Hall's educational philosophy that moral training and the training of feelings were more important than intellectual training. Virtues and feelings were consistent with the natural impulses of the child. Intellectual training required a higher level of development and was therefore the refuge of the university.[22] Hall's devaluation of intellect for preuniversity education is clearly echoed by Terman in the following excerpt from an article on secondary education.

The educational spirit today is becoming highly pragmatic. . . . And likewise we desire a practical criterion by which to estimate the value of the elements that make up the school curriculum. Modern educational theory sees a real danger in divorcing the intellectual and volitional tendencies by a school training which neglects the latter. It would be altogether calamitous were our youth to receive an education so exclusively "disciplinary," or "cultural," that their practical tendencies were thereby blunted. . . . Indeed it would be greatly to the credit of our secondary educational system to bridge even more successfully than has yet been done the chasm that has always existed between school and life. Education for most youths, should be an apprenticeship suitable for a busy practical life.[23]

Terman would soon dedicate his efforts to devising a means of selecting those few youths who were bright enough to profit from the intellectual training of the university.

For the summer of 1909, Terman returned to Indiana University to teach in the area of pedagogy.[24] This gave him the opportunity to renew his relationship with his Indiana mentor Lindley. He was also able to see some of his old friends, such as P. C. Emmons.[25] Moreover, his stay in Indiana provided him with what would be his last opportunity to see his father. His mother had died the year before, and his father would die the following spring.

When Terman returned home, he confided to Hall in a letter that he hoped to take the next year off as preparation for securing a university position.[26] As it turned out, he would land such a position the very next year. In 1909 his former Indiana teacher Bergström had gone to Stanford University to fill a newly created professorship of educational psychology in the Department of Education.[27] However, before the end of his first year he died. The position was then offered to Huey, who turned it down in order to continue his clinical studies with Adolf Meyer at Johns Hopkins. Huey coupled his refusal with a recommendation that the position be offered to Terman.

Terman was not an unknown figure to the head of Stanford's education department, Ellwood P. Cubberley. Cubberley had met Terman about a year before at a teachers' institute in southern California.[28] Both were giving lectures at the same session. In fact, this was Terman's first institute lecture, and he had been recommended for the program by one of his normal-school students, Wilford E. Talbert, who was also a schoolteacher in the district where the institute was held. Talbert later went on to Stanford as a graduate student working with Cubberley and Terman. At the institute, Talbert introduced the two speakers to each other and after the session took them out to lunch. As Talbert recalled, the party went to a crowded little restaurant where the food was pretty bad, but Terman and Cubberley were so interested in what each had to say that they didn't seem to notice the quality of the food. Terman believed it was fortunate that he prepared his institute lectures with considerable care, since one of them seemed largely responsible for his invitation to Stanford.[29] Assuming that Cubberley was already favorably disposed to Terman, the recommendations he received from the Clark people would have reinforced such a disposition. Huey had recommended Terman in his place, and Hall in writing to Cubberley commented:

Terman was here [at Clark] . . . and left a really very exceptional record for power of hard work and rather a unique combination of ability to get hard up against concrete facts as a basis of inductions and ability to think constructively. He puts his whole heart and soul into his work and, if he has the physical strength (and I understand California in this respect has regenerated him), he will keep on growing. He has not published a great deal since he left here, but he has a few minor things which have impressed and really edified me in a high degree. . . . He is a very independent man but nevertheless would be thoroughly loyal and cooperative and works well with others.[30]

Terman was offered the position of assistant professor of education, which he happily accepted, even though the beginning salary was below what he was receiving at the normal school.[31] This is how he described the event.

Nothing could have been more fortunate for me than the call to Stanford at this particular time. I had regained my health and was becoming restless.

Gesell had left for Yale a year earlier, but I was compelled to wait until a call came from the right climatic location; for I was unwilling to risk a position in the East or Middle West. Five years had passed since I left Clark, and I had reached the age of thirty-three. A few more years of waiting and my chances of a good university position would have begun to dwindle.[32]

The steps and timing of Terman's career advancement over the past five years had indeed been propitious. He needed the congenial climate and undemanding work schedule that his southern California sojourn provided. His move to the normal school was a significant stepping-stone to a university appointment. As he noted, the Los Angeles State Normal School, with its unusually good library facilities and above-average faculty, gave him the intellectual stimulation and contacts he needed.[33] The normal school itself would soon undergo a metamorphosis. In 1918 it became the University of California at Los Angeles (UCLA).

Terman's call to Stanford meant the fallow years were over. He was physically and intellectually ready for the challenges that lay ahead. Moreover, his financial concerns were a thing of the past, and he could endure the salary reduction at Stanford. He had been able to repay about half of his debts, and the remainder was settled by an inheritance from his father who had died in May of 1910.[34] Still further financial support came from selling the house on Valley View Road.

In preparation for the Stanford move, Terman was "boning up" for the courses he was to give.[35] Shortly before the Termans left Los Angeles in July of 1910, Huey came for a two-week visit. Terman welcomed the opportunity to learn about Huey's work at Meyer's clinic at Hopkins and about the mental test developments by Binet and H. H. Goddard. Huey urged Terman to begin some work with the Binet 1908 scale for measuring intelligence. This would become Terman's major enterprise when he arrived at Stanford.

CHAPTER 5

Establishing a Reputation (1910–1917)

In 1910, I found myself a member of the faculty of Stanford University, the university that I would have chosen before any other in all the world.[1]

When the Termans arrived at Stanford, they "were lucky to find a charming cottage in the country a mile and a half from the University by bicycle."[2] It had a study, two bedrooms, and a screened sleeping porch where the entire family could sleep. They spent two years in the cottage and Terman, in writing to a former student of that period, shared the following recollections.

My joy of getting to Stanford; my anxiety as to whether I should make good, and another deep seated anxiety . . . for I . . . had suffered several attacks of T.B. with hemorrhages, pleurisy, and all the trimmings. If I could survive in this valley and could hold my job I had an eternity of thirty-two years in which to justify my appointment.[3]

Terman's hope of being able to remain at Stanford through to retirement was given a boost in 1912, when on the basis of his scholarly productivity, he was promoted to an associate professorship.[4] In the summer of 1912, he built a house on the Stanford campus that would serve as the family home for the rest of his life. According to his son, Fred, the house provided Terman with a feeling that he had established himself at Stanford.[5] The house's location on campus also allowed Terman to have close contact with academic colleagues. This was important because had he remained in the country or moved to town (Palo Alto) he would have been more socially isolated. Terman was rather shy, and, although he made friends, he needed the comfortable atmosphere of a university community to develop social relationships.

The home was quite substantial and well situated. It was in the foothills not far from the academic quadrangle and on a lot that was one and one-third acres in size. The two-storey house had three good-size bedrooms, a large study, and two sleeping porches on the second floor. The first floor also contained spacious arrangements. The Termans were able to finance the house through a gift from Anna's father of fifteen hundred dollars, which served as the down payment.

Stanford University

When Terman arrived in 1910, Stanford was a relatively new university. It had opened its doors on 1 October 1891 after six years of planning and building.[6] The university was founded by Leland and Jane Stanford as a memorial to their only child, Leland, Jr., who died in 1884 of typhoid fever at the age of fifteen while traveling with his parents in Italy. Leland Stanford was a prominent figure in California. He played a major role in building the first transcontinental railroad and served as governor of California (1862–63) and as a United States senator (1885–93). In 1876 the Stanfords, who lived on San Francisco's Nob Hill, acquired land on the San Francisco Peninsula. This land was soon developed into the Palo Alto Stock Farm, so named because it was near a landmark redwood tree known as El Palo Alto, "the high tree." The Palo Alto ranch, which consisted of about eight thousand acres, became the cite for Leland Stanford Junior University. The document providing for the endowment, scope, and organization of the university was drawn up on 11 November 1885. The following summer Frederick Law Olmstead, the landscape architect who had designed New York City's Central Park, was engaged to develop the physical plan for the university. Olmstead's design of a double quadrangle surrounded by low buildings with arcades still serves as the center of Stanford's campus.

For the presidency of the new university, the Stanfords chose David Starr Jordan who was president of Indiana University. Jordan's academic field was zoology, and he had a strong interest in Darwinian evolutionary philosophy. He was only forty at the time of his appointment and had already attained a reputation as a gifted administrator. His first task as Stanford president was to assemble a faculty. When the university opened in the fall of 1891, he had recruited a faculty of twenty promising young men, some of whom were former colleagues at Indiana. The university was open to both men and women, and about 250 students were expected. However, on opening day 465 students were present, including a future United States president— Herbert Hoover.

During the first two years of its existence the university coped with such growing pains as an insufficient number of faculty, inadequate housing, and delays in receiving books and laboratory equipment. In the summer of 1893, Leland Stanford died. His widow, Jane, had to contend with severe financial problems that jeopardized the future of the university. The country was in the throes of a financial panic, and Leland Stanford's estate was tied up in probate. Mrs. Stanford and President Jordan worked together to keep the university open. Faculty salaries had to be reduced (by twenty percent), and, where possible, new appointments were canceled. A small monthly allowance to Mrs. Stanford from her husband's estate helped to keep the university going over the next few years. In 1898 the estate was finally released from probate. The following year, after selling her railroad holdings, Mrs. Stanford gave the sum of eleven million dollars to the university trustees. After financial recovery, the university had to endure one more major setback—the great earthquake of April 1906. Fortunately, the campus was spared the fire that destroyed San Francisco, but physical damage was extensive. After several months of reconstruction, the campus opened for fall classes.

Among the first faculty members appointed in 1891 was Earl Barnes, head of the Department of History and Art of Education.[7] This one-man department took on the shorter name of "Education" the following year, and in 1893 a teaching assistant was added. Barnes, who had been a professor of history at Indiana University, initiated courses in the history of education and in child study. In addition, he taught psychology in the philosophy department. Though a historian by training, he was particularly interested in child study and carried out a number of projects following the procedures established by Hall. In 1897 Barnes resigned from Stanford because of his wife's poor health. The headship of the education department passed on to Edward Howard Griggs, a professor of ethics at Stanford.[8] The ethics and education departments were combined, and Griggs was given the authority to add an assistant professor. Griggs recruited Ellwood P. Cubberley, an Indiana University alumnus who graduated at the time of Jordan's Indiana presidency. With Jordan's recommendation, he went on to an academic position at Vincennes University in Indiana, becoming president of the institution if 1893. In 1896 he came to the West Coast as superintendent of schools for San Diego. By the time Cubberley arrived at Stanford in the summer of 1898, the education head, Griggs, had left the university. Cubberley was made acting head of education, and two months after his arrival the appointment was made permanent.

President Jordan gave Cubberley three years to raise the education department to a level of academic respectability. Failure to do so would mean the abolition of the department and the dismissal of its new head. Jordan had supported the inclusion of education in Stanford's curriculum because he believed it was important that new fields be cultivated to keep pace with social developments. Cubberley faced a demanding challenge. The education field had little scientific literature, nor was it clear what the purpose was for education as an academic discipline. When he came to Stanford, Cubberley had had little academic training in education; he had however, taught in a rural Indiana school and been a university president and school superintendent. In addition, since he had majored in physics at Indiana University, he had a scholarly and scientific orientation. Within the three-year probation period, Cubberley had convinced Jordan and the Stanford faculty that the education department was academically sound. As a result, starting in 1901 the staff began to increase, library additions were initiated, and the department was given more space. The department continued to grow steadily, and in 1917 as formal recognition of its progress, the department was given the status of a professional school with a dean as executive head.

At the start of his Stanford appointment, Cubberley formulated his own interests and orientation in education. He taught courses in the history of education and in educational administration. He upgraded his academic credentials by taking leaves of absence in 1901–02 and 1904–05 in order to obtain his M.A. and Ph.D. degrees at Columbia University's Teachers College. There he was exposed to the latest advances in education, psychology, and quantitative methods by teachers who included Cattell and Thorndike. When he returned to Stanford in 1905 as professor of education, Cubberley launched upon a remarkably prolific writing career, which later earned him the title "wizard of Stanford."[9] His major book, *Public Education in the United States*, published in 1919,[10] was highly influential and set the tone for the training of American educators.[11] His basic theme, developed in the context of the Progressive Era (1890–1920), was that the public school was society's major source of social improvement.[12] The aims of education were therefore to serve the state and society at large, as well as the individual child. As we shall see, Terman's interests in developing health and testing programs in the schools were highly compatible with Cubberley's social orientation to education.

With the addition of Terman in 1910, the education department had a permanent faculty of four.[13] The following year another faculty member was added—Jesse B. Sears. Terman and Sears soon developed a close friendship that continued throughout their long careers at Stanford. Their wives also socialized with one another. Terman impressed Sears with his friendly and gentle manner.[14] It also struck Sears that while Terman liked being with people, he seemed just as happy when alone wrestling with ideas and facts.

Terman's teaching load was light—seven to eight lectures a week.[15] He was given free range in the selection of courses within the areas of educational psychology, school hygiene, and child development. His light teaching schedule provided him with the opportunity for research and writing. Between 1910 and 1914 he divided his work between research on mental tests and writing on school hygiene. After 1914 he concentrated his scholarly activity in the area of mental testing.

School Hygiene

Terman was first exposed to the study of school hygiene by Lindley and Bergström at Indiana and then by Burnham at Clark. His own

personal health problem acted as a further stimulant. He wrote literature reviews and conducted school surveys on such diverse problems
as malnutrition, dental defects, adenoids, tuberculosis, childhood neu-
roses, and juvenile suicide. Hall's evolutionary perspective and its
implications for education and society pervaded Terman's writings on
these topics. Hall had stressed physical development and health as
prerequisites for mental development. Disease and pathology were
wasteful and therefore detrimental to the educational goals of training
students to become efficient workers and contributors to the industrial
development of the nation.[16] Referring to the social implications of
school hygiene, Terman commented:

The rapid development of health work in the schools . . . is not to be regarded
merely as an educational reform. . . . The prevention of waste has become, in
fact, the dominant issue of our entire political, industrial, and educational
situation. . . . The evolution concept is doing its work. Having at last con-
sented to look at ourselves from the biological point of view, we proceed to
harness the biological and social forces which will make for the development
of a happier, healthier, and better race.[17]

Starting in 1911 and extending through 1915, Terman published
about twenty articles on health issues in the schools.[18] These were
about evenly divided between articles in professional journals, such as
Psychological Clinic and the *Journal of Educational Psychology*, and popular
periodicals, such as *Harper's Weekly* and *Popular Science Monthly*. He
wrote the popular articles to generate supplementary income and was
quite successful in getting them accepted for publication.[19] After 1916,
as royalties from the Stanford-Binet test began to be significant, he
discontinued such writing.

In 1913 he published his first book, *The Teacher's Health*, a short
monograph of 136 pages.[20] Based on what little information was available, Terman concluded that the rate of tuberculosis and neurasthenia
among teachers posed serious problems for both the welfare of students and school efficiency. He was also concerned about the character
of teachers, since undesirable traits could be passed on to students. For
example, he referred to male teachers, "who so often are characterized
by effeminacy, extreme docility, obsequiousness, and lack of manly
force."[21] Moreover, he was critical of a tendency among female teachers to be dogmatic, exacting, and meddlesome in their relations with

children. He recommended that teacher-training institutions, such as normal schools, should reject physically unfit applicants and withhold graduating students who were psychologically unfit to work with children.

Terman published two books in 1914. The first, *The Hygiene of the School Child*, was a textbook intended for normal-school and college students, as well as teachers and parents.[22] The first third of the book dealt with physical growth and considered the role of heredity and environment, disorders of growth, and the hygiene of posture. The remainder of the book dealt with the various physical and mental health problems experienced by schoolchildren. The book's major goal was to sensitize teachers and parents to children's health problems, and in so doing to facilitate the development of preventive programs in the schools. The ultimate aim was to make the schools effective agencies for the welfare of society at large. Terman summed up the book's message in this way.

No other agency compares with the school in the opportunities offered for contributing to the health of the succeeding generation. We cannot legislate desirable habits of living into men and women, but we may be able to mold after our ideals the hygienic habits of the child.

The most characteristic tendency of present-day education is its progressive socialization, the increasing extent to which society is utilizing the school as an instrument for the accomplishment of its ends. We are coming to believe that it is legitimate to levy upon the school for any contribution it is capable of making to human welfare.[23]

Contained in the preceding quote are two related assumptions that Terman adhered to: first, Hall's biologically rooted view that health was a prerequisite for children and adolescents if, as adults, they were to efficiently contribute to the welfare of society; and second, the view of such Progressive Era educators as Cubberley that the schools should serve the needs of society. Reflective of this latter influence, Terman's book was part of an education textbook series, under the editorship of Cubberley.

Terman's second book in 1914 was coauthored with Ernest Bryant Hoag, a physician who was the director of school hygiene for the Minnesota State Board of Health.[24] This book, entitled *Health Work in the Schools*, was also part of Cubberley's textbook series. It dealt with health supervision, health examination, and hygiene teaching in the schools. The book was primarily intended for teachers, though it was also directed at school superintendents, school nurses, and boards of education.[25] Although Terman was listed as second author, he wrote ten of the eighteen chapters.[26] According to Fred Terman, the collaboration between his father and Hoag was not a very smooth one.[27] Apparently, Hoag did not hold up his end of the partnership, and Terman ended up with more than his share of the work.

Terman wrote most of the chapters on health supervision, and in the first chapter of the book he spelled out the social responsibility for the health of schoolchildren.[28] He concluded that the school must assume this responsibility because in general parents' responsibility for their children's health was not sufficient. Based upon a review of the available data, he estimated that approximately sixty percent of schoolchildren suffered from physical defects, many of which could be cured or prevented. The fact that the percentage of children's health problems was so high pointed to the inadequacy of the parental role in this area. He argued that the school's role in health supervision was not an invasion of the rights of the home. The responsibility for remedial action, once the problem was diagnosed, would still be left to the parents. The school's role as an agent for the interests of society was to provide more expert health supervision than the average parent was capable of exercising. Thus, Terman sounded the same social theme of education as he had in his textbook on school hygiene.

He was also concerned with outlining a distinct role for school health programs, and he therefore dealt with the relationship between school health service and private medical practice. He saw no antagonism between these two spheres of practice because school service was essentially preventive while medical practice was primarily curative. Antimedical groups, such as the Christian Science movement, were attacked for their superstition-based conflict with the welfare of the state and its children.

Within the area of hygiene teaching, Terman wrote an interesting chapter on sex education. Consistent with his theme of the social responsibility of education, he advocated the teaching of sex education in the schools and presented guidelines about how the subject was to be presented in relation to the age and gender of the students. His interest in the study of sex was initially stimulated by some of Hall's lectures at Clark during 1904–05.[29] Hall was one of the earliest American intellectuals to be impressed with Sigmund Freud's theoretical perspective of psychoanalysis.[30] He arranged for Freud and Carl Gustav Jung to visit Clark in 1909, and Terman's first readings on psychoanalysis were the published lectures given by Freud and Jung.[31] In Terman's chapter on sex education, Freud's influence can be detected in the following passage: "The sexual instinct is not to be so much repressed as *sublimated;* its energies directed to secondary channels and transformed into higher values."[32] During the period between 1910 and 1916, Terman also read the writings of Havelock Ellis and Richard von Krafft-Ebing on the psychology of sex.[33] Though his interest in the study of sex was to decline after this period, it reemerged in the 1930s with his research on masculinity-femininity and marital adjustment.

Terman was quite pleased with the combined sales of about two hundred thousand copies for his two books published in 1914 on school hygiene.[34] He also felt that the books had a considerable impact on breaking down the early opposition of physicians to the medical inspection of schoolchildren at public expense. For several years, his lectures on child hygiene continued to be much in demand at teachers' institutes. However, his writing on the subject ended in 1914. As he commented, "I had gotten it 'out of my system'. This crusade in a field that was outside my area of major competence gives point to the old saying that if you scratch a health reformer you are pretty sure to find an invalid."[35] Terman was now ready to devote his full attention to mental testing.

The Stanford-Binet

For his doctoral study at Clark during 1904 and 1905, Terman had drawn upon the available research on mental tests.[36] Cognizant of the disappointing results of Galton's and Cattell's sensory discrimination measures of intelligence, he used a variety of tests—including measures of creative imagination, memory, mathematical ability, and language mastery—to differentiate between "bright" and "stupid" boys. Although he did not become acquainted with Binet's 1905 scale of intelligence until 1907, his multitest approach was consistent with Binet's work.[37]

When Terman began his project in 1910, Binet and his collaborator, Théodore Simon, had published a 1908 revision of their original scale. In contrast with Galton's use of sensory discrimination, Binet argued that individual differences in intelligence had to be detected through measures of such complex processes as memory, imagination, attention, comprehension, and suggestibility.[38] In 1904 when Binet was appointed by the French minister of public instruction to a commission concerned with the problem of retardation among public schoolchildren in Paris, he and Simon proceeded to assemble a scale composed of such measures.[39] Thirty different tests were included in the original 1905 scale. Based on preliminary testing, the tests were arranged in an ascending order of difficulty. Age norms for each of the tests were based on a sample of normal schoolchildren between the ages of three and eleven. The tests were also given to mentally retarded children, some of whom were in the schools and some in institutions for the retarded. On the basis of these samples, it was possible to determine both the tests that average normal children could pass within each age group and how far below these averages retarded children performed. An especially useful aspect of the scale was that it provided for the possibility of expressing a child's level of intelligence in relation to the age group whose performance he or she matched. For example, a six-year-old child who performed as well as the average eight-year-old child would have a "mental level" of eight.[40] In the 1908 scale, the tests were arranged into age levels—that is, tests at the three-year-old level were the tests that three-year-old children, on the average, could pass.[41] This arrangement made it easier to derive mental-level scores.

In pursuing his Binet revision, Terman was in the company of several competitors. Goddard had introduced the original Binet tests in America in an article published in 1908.[42] By 1911 several translations of the second Binet-Simon scale had appeared, including those by Terman's fellow Clark alumni, Huey and Kuhlmann.[43] However, Terman went considerably beyond simply translating the Binet-Simon scale. He methodically gathered extensive normative data on each of the existing tests and based on his data placed many of the tests at different age levels than in the original. Furthermore, he added some of his own tests and borrowed some that had been developed or suggested by other testers. The fact that his Stanford revision proved to be the most successful version of the Binet reflected his thorough and comprehensive approach to test construction. Unlike most of his competitors, he also had the benefit of a university appointment, which allowed him to draw upon graduate students for research assistance. Terman was particularly adept at managing collaborative efforts, and his work on the Stanford-Binet was a forerunner of many ambitious team projects that were to follow.

Terman's university connection provided him with another advantage. Because he was in the department of education, he was able to draw upon the liaisons that had been established with the public schools in the vicinity of Stanford. This would be a significant foundation for generating a standardization sample for his Binet revision. He began his work by administering a translation of the 1908 Binet-Simon scale to a sample of four hundred schoolchildren in the Stanford area.[44] He concluded that the Binet type of intelligence scale was feasible, and with corrections and extensions would prove to be of great practical and theoretical value. However, the scale needed a radical revision because the tests at the lower ages were too easy and those at the upper ages too difficult. He also reported that several tests he had devised could be effectively incorporated in a revision of the Binet. These included a test of the ability to generalize (the interpretation of fables), a vocabulary test of one hundred words, and a test of practical judgment that involved hunting for a lost ball in a circular field.

In 1912, with the assistance of graduate student H. G. Childs, Terman published his first tentative revision of the Binet.[45] Over the next several years, Terman and his team of graduate students continued their work, and in 1915 the final "Stanford Revision" was completed.[46] The test, which came to be known as the "Stanford-Binet," and the accompanying monograph, explaining the test and containing guidelines for its use, were published the following year.[47] The monograph was dedicated to the memory of Alfred Binet.

In constructing the Stanford Revision, Terman systematically reviewed the literature on testing and intelligence from the United States, England, and Germany. In addition to the writings of Binet, he was

particularly influenced by the work of two German psychologists—
Ernst Meumann and William Stern.[48] Starting in the 1880s, several
German psychologists, including Hermann Ebbinghaus, Emil Kraepelin,
Axel Oehrn, and Hugo Münsterberg, developed tests of mental abilities.[49] Consequently, considerable interest existed in Germany when
Binet's scale was introduced in 1905. In 1913 Meumann produced an
exhaustive review of the research on individual differences and testing,
including a critical examination of Binet's work. Terman provided a
summary of this review, and in the Stanford Revision he incorporated
a number of Meumann's suggestions for improving the Binet-Simon
tests.[50] By 1900, William Stern had become the best-known German
psychologist in the field of testing. His work was disseminated in
America largely through Guy M. Whipple's translation of a series of
lectures delivered in 1912.[51] In these lectures, Stern had introduced
the notion of a mental quotient that represented the ratio between
chronological age and mental age (Binet's "mental level"). Terman
incorporated this index in the Stanford Revision, calling it an "intelligence quotient" or "IQ." This was the first use of such a score in an
intelligence test.

Terman's choice of a single index of intelligence—the IQ—was a
reflection of his assumption that intelligence was a unitary trait or
factor. At the time of his dissertation, he was closer to Thorndike's
view of independent elementary abilities than to Spearman's position
of a universal trait of intelligence. However, by the time he began to
develop the Stanford Revision, he had apparently accepted the view
held by Goddard and the other Binet researchers in America that
intelligence was a unitary trait and the Binet-Simon tests were measuring such a trait. In his 1916 monograph, Terman pointed out that
Binet had abandoned the older "faculty psychology" approach of measuring a series of separate faculties or functions in favor of ascertaining
the general level of intelligence.[52] In reality, while Binet did not accept
Thorndike's hypothesis of independent abilities, he also did not accept
Spearman's notion of "general intelligence."[53] The fact that Binet did
not commit himself to a clear definition of intelligence, because he felt
there was not enough evidence to do so, left a conceptual vacuum that
was filled by Spearman's notion of a general intelligence factor. The
other major assumption that the American test developers made, namely

that intelligence was essentially determined by heredity, appeared to appropriately complement the notion of a unitary trait. It seemed far easier to trace the genetic passage of a single trait than of multitraits.

One of the features that made the Stanford-Binet so successful was the size of the sample used to standardize the test. This sample consisted of approximately 2,300 subjects, including 1,700 normal children, 200 children in the retarded and superior ranges, and just over 400 adults.[54] These subjects were tested between the years 1910 and 1914. The children were drawn from public schools in largely middle-class neighborhoods in various communities around the San Francisco Bay area, as well as from Los Angeles, Santa Barbara, and Reno, Nevada. They were primarily from the elementary-school grades, but there were also small samples from kindergarten and high school. Tests were also given to a sample of juvenile delinquents at the Whittier, California State School. The adults tested included a group of businessmen in the Palo Alto area, who had little formal education beyond grade school, and two groups of unemployed men, one in Palo Alto and one in Portland, Oregon. The urban and middle-class slant of the standardization sample would prove to be problematic when other less-privileged groups were compared with it. For example, the World War I recruits, many of whom were relatively uneducated or foreign born, fared quite badly when their test performance was judged on the basis of the Stanford-Binet norms.

The guiding principle for test selection (at the fourteen-year-old level and below) was to obtain a standard of scoring so that the median mental age of the children of each age group would coincide with the median chronological age. In other words, the final version of the scale should result in the average child of five to test exactly at five, the average child of six to test at six, and so on. As finally revised, the scale produced a median intelligence quotient (IQ) closely approximating 100 for the unselected (noninstitutionalized) children of each age from four to fourteen. The extension of the scale above the fourteen-year-old level was based on the expectation that relatively intelligent adults would test at the "average adult" level. Adults who were known to be unusually intelligent, by virtue of extensive education or reputation, were expected to test at the "superior adult" level.

The final number of tests added up to ninety. These included six at

:ach age level from three to ten, eight at age twelve (there were no ests at ages eleven and thirteen), six at age fourteen, and six at the "average adult" and "superior adult" levels. There were also sixteen alternative tests (about one or two at each level) that could be used as substitutes. The total of ninety tests and sixteen alternatives contrasted with the fifty-four in Binet's final 1911 scale. The additional tests included several that Terman had devised, and those that had been initiated by other testers, including Kuhlmann and Meumann. Many of the Binet tests were relocated, and a few were eliminated. Terman pointed out that, as far as possible, the Binet tests were retained in their original form, although in some cases it was necessary to introduce alterations in procedure or scoring.

The Uses of Mental Tests

Going beyond the technical discussion of the Stanford Revision, Terman in his 1916 monograph enthusiastically outlined what he saw as the future benefits and uses of mental tests.[55] This discussion reflected his assumption that the tests were measuring innate ability, a point of view shared by other American translators of the Binet.[56] In contrast, Binet believed that while there were genetically determined upper limits, intelligence could also be significantly affected by environmental influences.[57] This difference in interpretation had significant implications for how mental tests were to be used. If the tests were measuring innate ability, as Terman contended, then it was possible to make long-range predictions based on test performance. On the other hand, if the tests were assessing intellectual functioning that was malleable within limits, as Binet posited, then such functioning could be influenced by environmental intervention. Binet viewed mental tests as diagnostic tools; therefore, in working with retarded children, he developed special training methods, called "mental orthopedics," which were aimed at improving learning skills. Consequently, test performance would also be improved.

One of Terman's goals in revising the Binet scales was to obtain a finer gradation in the distribution of test scores than Binet had himself achieved. Terman accomplished this by lengthening the test and extending the age range in the normative sample. Unlike Binet, who was interested in identifying retarded children for diagnostic purposes, Terman was concerned with generating test scores that would be normally distributed. With a normal distribution of IQ scores, it would be feasible to make specific predictions based on where in the distribution a person's score was located. Since IQ scores reflected native ability, such scores were assumed to be stable. According to Terman, therefore, a child with an average IQ of 100 would be expected to have average success as an adult. A child with a superior IQ of 130 or higher would be expected to excel as an adult, and so on.

Terman cited various applications of mental testing. First of all, the tests would identify individual differences in native intelligence and thus enable the schools to develop specialized programs. Such programs would allow each child to progress at his or her own rate—whether that rate was rapid or slow. With respect to mental deficiency, intelligence tests were already being effectively used to identify the degree of retardation. It was therefore possible to decide upon the type of instruction suited to the training of the backward child. Intelligence tests would also make it possible to detect milder degrees of mental defect. This would correct the tendency of older methods of diagnosis to overlook the majority of higher-grade defectives, the so-called "feebleminded." Terman stressed the value of identifying this group by commenting:

It is safe to predict that in the near future intelligence tests will bring tens of thousands of these high-grade defectives under the surveillance and protection of society. This will ultimately result in curtailing the reproduction of feeblemindedness and in the elimination of an enormous amount of crime, pauperism, and industrial inefficiency. It is hardly necessary to emphasize that the high-grade cases, of the type now so frequently overlooked are precisely the ones whose guardianship it is most important for the state of assume.[58]

Terman's pronouncements on the value of mental tests in detecting feeblemindedness reflected the initial *raison d'être* for the development of mental measurement. In western Europe, Great Britain, and America there had been great concern at the end of the nineteenth and beginning of the twentieth centuries about the "menace of the feebleminded." (The "feebleminded" being the strata of society that did not or could not hold down steady employment.) These drifters and loafers posed a growing threat to property and public safety. Particularly in Britain and America, with the impact of evolutionary thinking, the problem of feeblemindedness was viewed as a symptom of the rising tide of degeneracy. The lower classes with their inferior heredity were reproducing at a faster rate than those of superior breed. At the time, therefore, Galton's eugenics program of selective breeding held great appeal. Binet's methods of testing provided the means for identifying the feebleminded; and when these methods were expanded upon in Britain and America, mental tests could be utilized to control degeneracy by detecting the higher-grade defective.[59]

The Galtonian paradigm also pointed to the value of mental measurement in identifying those at the upper end of the ability distribution. Just as the feebleminded might go undetected without the use of mental tests, so might the genius. According to Terman, it was essential to identify genius because this was the potential resource for leadership. Once children of superior intellect were selected by mental tests, they could be prepared through the right education to fulfill their potential. The progress of civilization would be based on the advances made by creative thinkers and leaders in science, politics, art, and morality.

Terman also believed that through the use of intelligence tests it would be possible to study the effects of heredity and environment on mental development. For example, he posed the following question: "Is the place of so-called lower classes in the social and industrial scale the result of their inferior native endowment, or is their apparent inferiority merely a result of their inferior home and school training?"[60] Based on a sample of about five hundred schoolchildren who were given IQ tests and classified by their teachers into five social-class groups, Terman concluded that children of higher social classes make a better showing on the test primarily because of their superiority in original endowment. While he had some reservations about this conclusion, apparently because of the correlational nature of the data, he went on to suggest that from what was already known about heredity it should be expected that the children of higher social-class parents would be better endowed than those children reared in slums and poverty.

Regarding heredity and environment in relation to racial differences in intelligence, Terman queried: "Are the inferior races really inferior,

or are they merely unfortunate in their lack of opportunity to learn?"[61]
He offered the following response, given in the context of discussing
the low IQ scores of two boys of Portuguese extraction.

> It is interesting to note that . . . [these cases] represent the level of intelligence
> which is very, very common among Spanish-Indian and Mexican families of
> the Southwest and also among negroes. Their dullness seems to be racial, or
> at least inherent in the family stocks from which they come. The fact that one
> meets this type with such extraordinary frequency among Indians, Mexicans,
> and negroes suggests quite forcibly that the whole question of racial differences
> in mental traits will have to be taken up anew and by experimental methods.
> The writer predicts that when this is done there will be discovered enormously
> significant racial differences in general intelligence, differences which cannot
> be wiped out by any scheme of mental culture.[62]

Terman's prognostications about mental testing served as a spring-
board for his own research plans. Now that the Stanford Revision was
completed, there was much work to be done. In January of 1917, he
submitted an extensive set of research proposals to the General Education
Board of the Rockefeller Foundation.[63] This was his first attempt at
securing financial support from an external research agency (an organization outside of his own institutional affiliation at Stanford). The
proposed studies included (1) establishing norms of performance for
one or two existing intelligence scales among large groups of workers
in representative occupations, ranging from unskilled labor to the
higher professions; (2) the development of an intelligence scale that
would be independent of language, so that subjects who had not
spoken English from childhood could be fairly tested; (3) a study of
intelligence and school grading to ascertain, in terms of school performance, the educational potential of each level of intelligence; and (4)
several briefer suggestions for studies, such as identifying potential
delinquents, the heredity of intelligence (parent-child comparisons of
test performance), and a new intelligence scale for general use. Terman
asked for $15,000 for a three-year period ($5,000 per year) and stated
that Stanford would add an additional $10,000 for the period—a
contribution equivalent to two-thirds of his salary. In a follow-up
letter, he stated that with the completion of the Stanford-Binet, "the
necessary next step is to work out an entirely new system of intelligence tests; one which will be free from the imperfections of existing

intelligence scales, convenient to use, and standardized with a thoroughness never before attempted."[64]

Terman learned that Robert M. Yerkes of Harvard had sent a similar grant proposal to the General Education Board.[65] He was not sure whether to let matters take their own course, or whether to make an active effort on his own behalf. He decided on the latter and solicited letters of support from eighteen professional colleagues, including his Indiana mentors, Lindley and Bryan; his Clark mentors, Hall, Burnham, and Sanford; as well as Goddard, Kuhlmann, Gesell, and Whipple.[66] Among Hall's comments to Abraham Flexner, the secretary of the General Education Board, were the following:

Although I have been deeply interested in all the scales and tests . . . I have in the past perhaps had a trifle less enthusiasm as to the scientific soundness, finality and the practical serviceableness of this work. . . . But I am bound to say that when Terman's book appeared, with its larger view, the whole subject seemed to me to be placed in a new light, and I have now come to share pretty fully his enthusiastic belief that with sufficient aid, new and more comprehensive methods . . . could be evolved. Certainly among all the others, some of whom have done excellent work, he is now the one man and looms up, and I think this is pretty well recognized by men like Yerkes, Healy, Goddard, Hollingworth and the rest.[67]

When he received a copy of this letter,[68] Terman must have felt deeply gratified that his foremost mentor was finally convinced of the merits of mental testing. Other letters supporting Terman also indicated that he was the most qualified person to carry out the research.[69]

Terman's hopes for securing a grant from the General Education Board had to be set aside for future consideration. Flexner, in June of 1917, indicated that the reviewing committee was interested in Terman's project, especially if it involved the collaboration of Yerkes.[70] However, with the country now involved in World War I, no commitments could be made until events would clear up. Indeed, America's involvement in the war was to prove a turning point in Terman's career.

The Signs of Success

The praise Terman received in the letters supporting his grant proposal was but one sign of the professional success he had achieved by

1917. Recognition of his accomplishments was acknowledged at Stanford. After his initial promotion to associate professor in 1912, he became a full professor in 1914. His department head, Cubberley, noted that Terman was a "strong growing" man who was likely to be called elsewhere for a higher salary.[71] The concern about Terman being lured away to another institution was voiced two years later by Ray Lyman Wilbur, Stanford's third president who was appointed in 1915. Wilbur reported to Cubberley:

At the meeting of the Board of Trustees . . . the following action in regard to Professor Terman was taken: "That the President of the University be requested to try and arrange his budget so that the salary of Prof. L. M. Terman of the Department of Education can be increased from $3,500 to $4,250 for the year 1917–18, and further increased $250 per year until his salary is $5,000, in order to retain Prof. Terman at the University."[72]

Stanford's fear of losing a rising star did not abate. In 1917 Herbert Hoover, Stanford's prominent alumnus and a member of the board of trustees, sent a telegram to Terman upon learning of his being offered an education deanship at the University of Iowa.[73] Hoover hoped the Iowa offer would not be too tempting, adding that the probability of an increase in Stanford's income in a year or so would make it possible to provide additional assistance and increased space for Terman. Hoover reported his relief to Cubberley when Terman wired back that he would stay at Stanford. In fact, Terman was very grateful for the support accorded him at Stanford[74] and especially from Cubberley.[75]

Another source of support Terman received from Stanford was a special fund that provided research fellowships for the study of "backward children." This was the C. Annette Buckel Foundation, established in 1914.[76] Buckel, who died in 1913, was a physician in Oakland, California, and became a philanthropic supporter of movements advocating child hygiene, home economics, and the education of backward children. Her estate was left in the trust of a friend, with the request that it be used for the benefit of retarded children. Influenced in part by the advice of Goddard, the trustee turned over the endowment to Stanford for administration by the Department of Education. The Buckel Fund enabled Terman to attract graduate students to work with him. He had already attracted a number of student collaborators, but he was now in a position to offer financial support.

The first Buckel fellow was J. Harold Williams, Terman's first doctoral student. Williams completed his dissertation, "The Intelligence of the Delinquent Boy," in 1916. He also collaborated with Terman on a testing survey of delinquent boys at the Whittier State School in southern California.[77] After receiving his Ph.D., Williams served as a psychologist at the Whittier school, and with Terman co-founded the *Journal of Delinquency*.[78] The next Buckel fellow was Samuel C. Kohs, who held the fellowship from 1916 through 1918.[79] Kohs had worked with Goddard at the Vineland Training School for the mentally retarded. With this background, he functioned more as a junior colleague than as a graduate student. For his doctoral dissertation, under Terman's supervision, he developed a nonverbal test of intelligence. This was an interest he had developed at Vineland, but it also coincided with one of Terman's proposals to the General Education Board. The test was a block-design test, which would eventually be incorporated in David Wechsler's 1939 intelligence scale for adults.[80]

Through his various publications and especially with the appearance of the Stanford-Binet, Terman was gaining a reputation beyond Stanford. The growing recognition that he received was also enhanced by the associations he formed with other workers in the mental-testing field. The two most important relationships were with Goddard and Yerkes. Goddard, who held the influential position of research director at the Vineland Training School, was a leading advocate of hereditarian thought about intelligence. He was also a pioneering figure in the attempts to translate the Binet tests, as well as a fellow Clark graduate (though he left Clark before Terman arrived). Both Terman and Goddard were close friends of Huey, who tragically died of a gastrointestinal illness in 1913.[81] Goddard, therefore, took over as Terman's chief consultant for the Binet revision. In 1916 he arranged a summer-school appointment for Terman at New York University.[82] This was Terman's first trip east since 1910 and his first visit to New York.[83] On the way he stopped at the University of Iowa—a visit that led to his being offered the position as dean of education. During his stay in New York he visited Vineland[84] and went to Boston to meet Yerkes.[85] He also made contacts at Teachers College and a few months later was offered a position there starting the subsequent year.[86] Though tempted to accept, he turned the offer down. However, he did accept a summer-school appointment for 1917, and thus spent a second summer in New York.

Terman and Yerkes began to correspond when they became familiar with each other's work on the Binet.[87] Yerkes's major interest lay in comparative psychology (the study of differences along the phylogenetic scale).[88] From this evolutionary perspective, Yerkes sought to trace the origins of human intellectual capacity back through simpler forms of life, such as frogs and jellyfish. Eventually, this interest was directed toward the study of more complex species—primates and humans. In 1915 Yerkes began to work with the mentally ill at the Boston State Hospital. It was in this setting that he started his revision of the Binet. The particular approach Yerkes adopted was the "point scale," in which tests were arranged by order of difficulty and the child given credit for all successes. This contrasted with the standard Binet practice of grouping tests by age and basing test credit on a minimum number of successes, as in passing two out of three items in a given test.[89] The point scale was originally conceived by Huey, but it was Yerkes who made the most complete adaptation of the Binet with this idea in mind. Yerkes, in collaboration with James W. Bridges and Rose Hardwick, published the point scale in 1915.[90]

Between 1915 and 1917, Terman and Yerkes wavered between a relationship of cooperation and competition. For example, they first considered the desireability of the leading Binet workers coming to some agreement as to the best version of the scale.[91] However, by 1917 they were each engaged in trying to improve upon their respective scales.[92] They also learned that they were each applying to the General Education Board of the Rockefeller Foundation for financial support.[93] When Terman became aware of this, he decided to solicit letters of support for his grant proposal. Eventually, he received word from the board that they were interested in supporting a joint effort by him and Yerkes, but this would have to await the end of the war.

One interesting piece of information that Terman and Yerkes shared was their children's test performances.[94] Terman reported that Fred and Helen had tested consistently between 125 and 140. He also noted that he had records of close to 100 children of college professors, and most of them were within the range of 120 to 140. This led him to remark: "The more faculty children I test, the better opinon I have of the intelligence of my professional colleagues!"[95] One child of a faculty member has recalled his experience of being tested by Terman around 1914. Robert R. Sears, the son of Terman's education department colleague, Jesse B. Sears, was tested by Terman when he was about six years old.[96] He remembered Terman's gentle and friendly manner. He also recalled the ball-and-field test, which he felt he had fouled-up, but Terman let his answer go without any comment. Sears liked taking the tests and thought the tester was a very nice man. Looking back, in the context of his own position as a child psychologist (Sears has had a distinguished career), he judged Terman to be a very good Binet tester.

Terman's other major correspondent during his early years at Stanford was Gesell, who was working on his M.D. degree at Yale. Terman attempted to bring his close friend out to California in the hope of having him available as a research collaborator in the area of mental deficiency.[97] Through support from the Buckel Foundation, supplemented by funds provided by the California State Board of Education, a position of "child study expert" was created. Were Gesell to accept the position, one of his major tasks would be to conduct a thorough survey of backward children for the entire state. Terman pointed out that such a survey would demonstrate the need for one or two additional state institutions for the feebleminded—a goal he had stated in several of his writings.[98] Furthermore, the survey would arouse state-wide interest in the broader social aspects of the problem, including the education and treatment of retarded children in the public schools. Gesell initially indicated an interest in the position but started to have some misgivings about the specific nature of the administrative arrangements with the state.[99] Shortly thereafter, Gesell accepted a more attractive offer as a faculty member at Yale.[100] Terman was crestfallen that his old friend would not be joining him again in California and expressed his appreciation that Gesell had earnestly considered his pet project. With Gesell's refusal, no further efforts were undertaken to fill the child-study position.

Terman's first seven years at Stanford had been highly successful. He had fully regained his health and was able to work an average of sixty hours a week, although he was careful to rest in bed an hour or two each day.[101] His ability to carry out a heavy work schedule resulted in a period of great productivity and professional recognition.

He was well established at Stanford, and although often tempted by offers elsewhere, he felt compelled to stay at an institution that consistently supported and encouraged him. Furthermore, the California climate, which was so beneficial to his health, could hardly be matched anywhere else.[102]

The Terman family was prospering as well. Anna, who was highly energetic, developed her own independent activities around campus.[103] Her developing independence reflected Lewis's heavy commitment to his work. Fred showed his intellectual precocity in a variety of ways. He did not actually begin school until he was nine.[104] Apparently, following the guidelines of his mentor Hall, Terman felt no necessity to push his son. As a child Fred had always had many hobbies to keep himself occupied with, and he was therefore not particularly dependent on the companionship of other children. When he was eight, Anna, who had been a teacher, started to teach him to read and also gave him lessons in arithmetic. When he started school in the fall of 1909, he was put in the third grade, one year behind his age. He accelerated and graduated from the eighth grade four years later. In seven more years he graduated from Stanford as Phi Beta Kappa. Once the family moved on campus, Fred became interested in radio and eventually operated a radio ham station. These interests laid the-groundwork for his eventual career as a pioneer in the field of radio engineering.

Helen, three years younger than her brother, began school in the first grade at the normal age. Anna took a much more active role in managing Helen's life than she did with Fred.[105] One event that may have influenced this is the fact that Helen had rheumatic fever during the first year the family was at Stanford.[106] As had been the case with Lewis's tuberculosis, Anna spent much of her time tending to Helen's recovery. However, beyond this it appears as though Terman assumed the more dominant role in bringing up his son. He was extremely proud of Fred's accomplishments from childhood through adulthood. In contrast, he said little about Helen, either as a child or an adult. He seems to have assumed that Helen, like most girls, would not be academically oriented. He wrote to Gesell in 1918: "Your 'nail hander' man [Fred] is now a Stanford sophomore. Although he only learned his letters nine years ago, he ranks first in every one of his classes, according to the reports of his professors. Helen is a happy high school sophomore, getting average marks and living true to her instincts by attending more to the frivolities of adolescence than to academic learning."[107] Also indicative of the parental division of responsibility, Terman went on to add that Anna, at least by this time, would not let him test Helen. Helen, for her part, did go on to graduate from Stanford "with distinction."[108]

On 2 May 1917, upon hearing from the General Education Board about the status of his research proposal, Terman wrote to Yerkes that he was looking forward to beginning their collaboration, and that he hoped this would start during his period of summer teaching at Teachers College.[109] He also indicated that he had heard that the army was interested in having some soldiers tested, and he mentined that one of his graduate students, Arthur S. Otis, had some splendid tests for group application. Little did he realize that later that month he would be called to serve on a committee, chaired by Yerkes, to devise mental tests for the army.

CHAPTER 6

Off to the Army
(1917–1919)

Immediately after the declaration of war by the United States the President of the American Psychological Association appointed a "Committee on the Psychological Examination of Recruits." This committee decided to recommend the mental examination of every soldier, and within six weeks had prepared methods adequate for the huge task of testing millions of men.[1]

In the small hours of Good Friday morning, 6 April 1917, the United States Congress declared war on the German Empire.[2] Later that day, a group of psychologists known as the "Experimentalists" was meeting at Harvard University.[3] At the urging of one of the group's members, Robert M. Yerkes, who was president of the American Psychological Association (APA), a special session was arranged to discuss the contributions psychology could make to national defense.[4] It was decided that the issue should be placed before the council of the APA, and Yerkes therefore called a council meeting to be held on 21 April at the Walton Hotel in Philadelphia.

Although Yerkes later recalled that as APA president he felt duty-bound to organize psychologists for the war effort, he actually started to campaign for the use of psychological testing in the military a year before war was declared.[5] His activities in this regard reflected his view that the advancement of the discipline required sponsorship from corporate and government sources. He was also disposed to seek such support for his own research, which necessitated considerable funding. When Congress was debating military preparedness in February 1916,

Yerkes wrote to the War Department about the relevance of testing for military recruitment. His suggestion was turned down, but opportunity struck when a colleague wrote to him about the applicability of mental tests for evaluating disabled soldiers in the Canadian army.

Between the Harvard and APA council meetings, Yerkes acted on the Canadian query by making a four-day trip, at his own expense, to Montreal, Ottawa, and Toronto, the centers where psychologists were carrying out their military work. This fact-finding mission allowed him to make a case before the council for the use of testing in the military. First, he reported that the Canadian psychologists regretted the fact that their involvement had been limited to the problems wounded soldiers faced when returning from the war.[6] Much more could have been accomplished if psychological methods had been used in the selection and training of recruits. Yerkes then went on to present a plan for the American military that would involve psychologists in the selection process. He recommended the use of a short series of individually administered mental measurements (not to exceed ten minutes), which would result in classifying each recruit as "inferior," "normal," or "superior." The inferiors would then be given a more extended mental examination of some thirty to sixty minutes to determine whether they should be eliminated from the military.[7] Yerkes also recommended that a group of trained psychological examiners would be needed to carry out the testing program, and these examiners should be commissioned officers in the medical units of the army and navy.

Yerkes's plan was not greeted with unanimous approval by the four council members. One of the members, Walter Dill Scott of the Carnegie Institute of Technology, had a different plan in mind for the contribution psychology could make.[8] Based upon the work he and his Carnegie colleagues had undertaken with several large corporations during the previous year, Scott wanted to develop a testing program that would include more than just examining for minimum intellectual functioning. He hoped to evaluate areas of competence similar to those which the Carnegie group had investigated in their research on salesmanship selection—areas such as personal qualities of character and industry, vocational abilities, and higher levels of intelligence.[9] Scott also disagreed with Yerkes's scheme of placing psychology under the medical wing of the military. For Scott, it made more sense for psychology to be organized within the personnel area of military organization. Their different personalities (Yerkes was rather stiff and formal, while Scott was outgoing and aggressive) added to the growing conflict between them. Before the council meeting was over during the evening of 21 April, Scott walked out.

The result of the split between Yerkes and Scott was that each ended up directing their own psychological programs for the military. Scott went on to head the Committee on the Classification of Personnel in the Army, under the office of the Adjutant General; while Yerkes became head of the Division of Psychology in the surgeon general's office of the army.[10] The navy wanted little to do with either of these programs, so the efforts of the psychologists were concentrated in the army.[11] Under Yerkes's general direction, several committees of psychologists were established, including those concerned with selecting recruits for special skills, aviational problems, and psychological problems of incapacity (such as shell shock and re-education).[12] Yerkes chaired the Committee on the Psychological Examination of Recruits —the committee that was to elaborate and refine his original plan for the mental testing of recruits.

Developing the Army Tests

By the middle of May, Yerkes was able to obtain financial support for his test development committee.[13] A private organization concerned with the care of the mentally retarded (the Committee on Provision for the Feebleminded, which operated in Philadelphia) provided Yerkes's committee with working facilities at the Vineland Training School in New Jersey, plus expenses for the work to be carried out. Yerkes then went ahead and appointed a committee consisting of Bingham, Goddard, Thomas H. Haines, Terman, F. L. Wells, and Whipple. The committee gathered at Vineland on 28 May and remained in session until 9 June.

Yerkes, as chair, reviewed the developments that led to the formation of the committee and then outlined his plan for the individual mental testing of recruits.[14] A discussion followed about the possible contributions psychology could make to military efficiency, and it was concluded that intelligence tests offered the most promise. The committee, therefore, defined its work chiefly as "the classification of recruits on the basis of intellectual ability, with special reference to the elimination of the unfit and the identification of exceptionally superior ability."[15]

The second day was taken up with a discussion of the relative merits of brief individual tests and longer tests that could be administered in groups. It was unanimously agreed that all recruits should be tested. Questions were raised about the practicality and reliability of brief individual tests. Some of the committee members reported that they had had encouraging experience with various types of group tests and felt that such tests could be adapted for army use. In this connection, Terman presented the group test that he brought along with him—the test developed by his student, Arthur S. Otis.

Otis had received his undergraduate degree in psychology at Stanford, in the same year that Terman had arrived there.[16] Three years later, in 1913, Otis returned to Stanford for graduate work in education and took Terman's course in the measurement of intelligence. This was Otis's first exposure to the subject, and he quickly became caught up in Terman's commitment to testing. However, Otis saw the practical limitations of tests that could only be administered on an individual basis; he therefore proposed to a somewhat skeptical Terman his desire to develop a group-administered intelligence test for his doctoral dissertation. Otis's group scale was directed at grades four through eight and was primarily derived from the Stanford-Binet.[17] The additional tests that Otis developed for inclusion in his scale were largely based on existing group tests that had been constructed as measures of educational achievement.[18] The items in each subtest of the scale were arranged in order of difficulty, and the overall score was based on the number of correct items (an absolute point system). To determine a student's level of intelligence, the total point score was divided by the average score of his or her age group.

Otis's test battery served as the major source for the development of the army's group tests.[19] By early June a preliminary test battery was ready, and it contained equivalent forms to safeguard against coaching.[20] On 10 June the committee recessed for two weeks to gather data on the preliminary test, which would provide a basis for revision and standardization. About four hundred examinations were given in various parts of the country, primarily to marines and candidates in officers' training camps.[21] On 25 June the committee resumed its sessions at Vineland and completed its revisions on the preliminary group test on 7 July. The committee also devised a tentative individual examination that was deemed necessary for illiterate, subnormal, and foreign-born recruits.[22]

The next phase of the committee's work was to undertake a large-scale trial of the examination under military conditions.[23] Approximately four thousand group tests were administered at four military installations during the month of July, and the results were analyzed at Columbia University. The committee was very pleased with the trial of the tests. Scores on the tests correlated about .50 with officer's ratings, and Yerkes declared that this "justified the belief that the new methods would prove serviceable to the Army."[24] The committee then forwarded a plan to the army surgeon general for the adoption of psychological examining—the primary purpose of the examining to be the elimination of recruits who were mentally unfit.[25]

By the end of July, the surgeon general tentatively approved the plan and authorized the establishment of a psychological section in his office. (This eventually became a division.)[26] Yerkes was given a major's commission and became the psychology division's chief. To Yerkes's regret, his commission and those of the other psychologists in the division were in the Sanitary Corps, rather than in the Medical Corps.[27] This tended to work somewhat against the credibility of the psychologists, as perceived by the army administrators they had to deal with. With the provisional approval of the surgeon general, the committee launched a massive trial of the tests in four army cantonments.[28] On the basis of this final trial, psychological examining for the entire army was approved on 24 December 1917. All newly appointed officers and all drafted and enlisted men were to be tested. The purposes of the testing were threefold: "(a) to aid in segregating and eliminating the mentally incompetent; (b) to classify men according to their mental ability; (c) to *assist* in selecting competent men for reasonable positions."[29]

In January of 1918, Yerkes and his staff prepared for the expanded testing program.[30] On the basis of the trial of the previous fall, the original group examination, which had been identified as "A," was revised and relabeled as "Examination Alpha." This battery of eight tests involved such tasks as solving arithmetical problems, choosing word analogies, and answering items of general information. Explicit militarylike instructions were laid out for the test administrators. For example, in introducing the examination, the following statement was to be read: "Now, in the Army a man often has to listen to commands and then carry them out exactly. I am going to give *you* some commands to see how well you can carry them out."[31] Not all the recruits were capable of following such oral directions or reading the examination booklets. A specially constructed group test, labeled "Examination Beta," was developed for illiterate and foreign-born recruits. The Beta test was administered with pantomine instructions and made up of pictorial problems, such as solving mazes and matching symbols to digits.

In order to carry out the full-scale testing, Yerkes had persuaded the army to establish a school of military psychology at Fort Oglethorpe, Georgia.[32] The school opened in February 1918, and most of the trainees were graduate students in education or psychology.[33] When they finished their training, the trainees were sent to the various army camps to administer the tests. By the beginning of May, the testing program was being extensively carried out.

Terman's schedule during the two years he was involved with the army testing was a busy one. When the testing committee at Vineland adjourned in July 1917, Terman went to New York to fulfill his commitment to teach summer school at Teachers College. In the meantime, he had been made a member of Scott's committee on classification, and when his teaching session was completed he was assigned by this committee to Yerkes's staff in Washington, D.C.[34] From mid-August to the end of September, Terman worked on a revision of the Examiner's Guide—that is, the standardized instructions for administering the tests. The revision was based upon the results of the tests during the summer trial. Terman worked closely with another member of Yerkes's staff, Clarence S. Yoakum. During this period, Terman, as well as Yoakum, stayed in Yerkes's Washington, D.C., home.[35]

At the end of September, Terman returned to Stanford for the opening of the 1917–18 school year.[36] During the fall term, with the aid of a group of graduate students, he administered the army group examination (examination "A") to a sample of some five thousand schoolchildren. This was part of the standardization program for the group tests, and it ran concurrently with the large-scale trial testing in the army camps. At the beginning of January 1918, he was called back to Washington, D.C., to work on the revised Alpha examination. He returned to Stanford early in February to complete the school year.

Terman took a leave of absence for the 1918–19 year to devote full-time service to Yerkes's staff in Washington, D.C.[37] With the exception of Fred, who was attending Stanford, the family lived in Washington, D.C., during this period.[38] Shortly before the armistice in November 1918, Terman was commissioned as a major in the Sanitary Corps. To his relief, he had no problem passing his physical and obtaining the usual ten-thousand-dollar government insurance.[39] From November until his discharge from the army in April 1919, Terman contributed to the official written report of the army testing.[40] The particular section he had the major responsibility for dealt with the development of the tests.

The Results of the Army Testing

In the procedures set up for the army testing, all the enlisted men were given either the Alpha or Beta examination, according to their degree of literacy.[41] Each test required about fifty minutes to complete. Those men who were given Alpha but failed to pass were then given Beta; and if they failed Beta, they were given an individual test—the Stanford-Binet, the Point Scale, or a specially constructed performance scale for foreigners and illiterates. Based on the test results, each man was assigned a letter rating, ranging from A at the upper-most end of the distribution, through C at mid-range, and E at the lowest end.[42] According to the psychologists, a rating of A was indicative of officer material; C was at the level of a good private and a fair noncommissioned officer; and E, reflecting marked mental inferiority, justified special service organizations, rejection, or discharge.

In reality, this sequential protocol of test administration and rating was rarely carried out in any thorough fashion. Buried in Yerkes's mammoth final report were the graphic details of procedures not followed because of woefully inadequate physical facilities for test taking, the failure of military officers to cooperate, time pressures, and even systematic bias on the part of examiners.[43] Stephen Jay Gould, in *The Mismeasure of Man*, has culled these deficiencies from the Yerkes report.[44] For example, while the army mandated special buildings for testing, the typical quarters provided were unfurnished rooms in cramped barracks with inadequate acoustics and lighting. As one tester complained, the men sitting in the rear could not hear clearly enough to follow the instructions. Furthermore, conditions were made more difficult by the friction between the officers and testers. Commanding officers at the camps, with few exceptions, voiced negative opinions about the testing program. Other problems arose because of the rather unrealistic time demands placed on the examiners. After rapidly processing the men, the tests had to be scored immediately so that failures could be given another trial on a different test. Some of the recruits were treated with outright discrimination by the examiners. Because of the press of time, shortcut procedures were applied to black recruits. More often than not, those who failed Beta were not recalled for the required individual test.

These various problems translated into distorted test results. A case in point was the unusually high number of zero scores on subtests within both the Alpha and Beta exams. In some cases, zero was the most frequent score. As Gould points out, such results strongly suggested that the recruits in many cases simply could not follow the instructions because of inadequate and anxiety-provoking conditions. Indeed, even Terman himself acknowledged that the high frequency of zero scores reflected deficiencies in administering the tests.[45] As it turned out, however, the particular vulnerability to poor testing conditions that the illiterate and foreign recruits were likely to have experienced, because of their language and cultural disadvantages, was not accounted for in the psychologists' interpretation of the test results.

Another factor not considered was the cultural bias of the test content. While Yerkes and his staff claimed the tests were measuring native intelligence, such items as the following from Alpha were obviously dependent on cultural background:

The Overland car is made in
    Buffalo
    Detroit
    Flint
    Toledo

Nabisco is a
    patent medicine
    disinfectant
    food product
    toothpaste

Moreover, performance on tests such as arithmetical reasoning and disarranged sentences would be helped by school experience. A related problem that was overlooked was the lack of previous experience in a testing situation, a deficiency that would have particularly affected the illiterate and foreign-born men. Nor did the Beta exam completely control for illiteracy. It still required such recruits to use a pencil and to have a familiarity with numbers and how to write them.[46]

When the testing program came to an end shortly after the armistice of November 1918, Yerkes and his staff began their challenging task of reporting the results.[47] According to the conclusions in these various write-ups, the testing program was a definite success. The litany of procedures not followed, inadequate testing conditions, and examiner biases were mentioned in passing at intermittent points in the official report, which numbered close to one thousand pages.[48] However, these serious problems that might have cast doubt on the validity of the entire program were not cited in the summary statements and conclusions. It would be the summaries and short reports that would be read and in a few years time distilled and disseminated to the public.

Why were the army psychologists so neglectful of the problems? As established scientists they should have known better. Perhaps, from the perspective of the ambitious scope and innovative nature of their project, plus the press of time, the problems seemed insignificant. It may also be that their strong commitment to the testing method and its potential for the real world produced an overeagerness to present a success story. It would take more detached critics to uncover the flawed foundation of the testing data, and this would have to await the passage of several years before the results were generally made available.

The amount of data collected was impressive. The staggering figure of 1.75 million men had been tested.[49] Close to 8,900 men were recommended for immediate discharge because the tests indicated they were mentally unfit for service. Another 10,000 were judged to be at a marginal intellectual level and recommended for labor battalions or other service organizations that required no training. The letter-rating system was deemed to be valuable in appropriately selecting military personnel.[50] Charts showed that officers clustered at the upper ranges (the modal or peak distribution being within the A range), sergeants clustered at the B range, literate enlisted men at C, and illiterate enlisted men at D.[51] Other supporting evidence was provided by the high degree of correlation between test scores and officers' ratings of the military value of the men under their command. The correlation between the tests and the officers' ratings ranged from .50 to .75.[52] Median test scores for various occupational groups in the army were also generally consistent with expectations. Engineer officers, army chaplains, and medical officers were within the high B and A ranges; while common laborers, miners, and teamsters were within the C range.[53]

The army psychologists also campaigned for the use of tests beyond the military. Raymond Dodge, another member of Yerkes's staff, pointed out that the "mental engineering" service developed by the army psychologists was a "permanent contribution to the organization and utilization of human forces and could thus be applied toward reconstruction needed in the post-war period."[54] Yoakum and Yerkes commented that while new tests would have to be devised for specific purposes, the group method of testing established in the army had wide practical application.[55] For example, schoolchildren could be quickly classified according to their level of tested intelligence and then sorted into suitable types of educational treatment. Group tests could also be widely used to detect individuals with criminal tendencies because of mental inferiority. The successful army experience of classifying men into various occupational groups, according to their level of tested intelligence, held great promise for industrial placement and vocational guidance.

Underlying these stated benefits and prognostications of testing, the army psychologists appeared to be working out of an implicit model of what they considered to be the "good society." With the growing industrialization and technical development of America in the twentieth century, it would become important to keep pace with the increasing specialization of skills. Mental testing would provide the means whereby individuals could be most effectively fitted into a society organized according to a hierarchy of skills. When Terman published his Stanford-Binet, he had stressed the contribution that such tests could make in determining the future level of occupational skill for schoolchildren.[56] Furthermore, he pointed out, by identifying the most intellectually gifted children, it would be possible to train the future leaders of society to fulfill their inherent potential.[57]

Such a model, appropriately enough first used in the military, implied a tightly organized social system concerned with efficiency and productivity. Conformity and standardization were needed to accomplish such goals. This kind of model was explicitly identified by one of Terman's former doctoral students, Kimball Young, in his review of the history of mental testing, published in 1923.[58] Young's paper was written in the style of an objective review. However, in his concluding statement, he pointed to what he saw as a major drawback of the testing movement.

The present tendency for statistical and quantitative classification is part and parcel of the general trend toward mechanization and standardization of life, consequent upon the application of science to human endeavor, in industry, in education, in the military. It is an inevitable effect of a materialistic civilization. In this mad rush for mass production, be it in the classroom product or in business enterprise, the trend is ever and anon toward those values which are expressible in quantitative units. We are rapidly losing our older notions of quality, of calm and divergently integrated personalities. . . . The present statistical treatment of . . . [man] in terms of I.Q. and score, buttressed by averages of correlation quotients, tends to make man a psychological robot with no emotion, no quality, no personality.[59]

Young's ability to detect the negative implications of testing reflected his initial graduate training at the University of Chicago under W. I. Thomas and George Herbert Mead. His Chicago mentors were concerned about the quality of relationships among the various constituent groups in American society, as well as the integrated functioning of individuals.[60]

The psychologists' success story of the army testing, with its implicit theme of organizational efficiency, was not necessarily consistent with the army's own view of what the psychologists had accomplished.[61] References to the original army documents point to a different picture than that painted by Yerkes and his staff.[62] Many regular army officers complained that the psychologists were interfering with traditional military practices and prerogatives. They questioned the usefulness of the tests, and the personnel policy of making assignments on the basis of test scores. The officers and the psychologists disagreed particularly in cases of low intelligence ratings. Many of the "D" and "E" men were illiterate or foreign born. However, the army found that once these men were taught to read they became highly capable soldiers.

The fact that the physical facilities provided for testing were often inadequate was another sign of the army's resistance. Much to Yerkes's exasperation, the army general staff never matched his manpower requests for conducting the program. Furthermore, the army's opposition to testing was expressed at lower staff levels. It appears that the personnel officers did not typically use the intelligence ratings in assigning recruits. As for the unit commanders—when they were asked to pass on the soldiers with high intelligence ratings, they kept them for their own units and instead passed on those with low ratings. Such discrepancies between the psychologists' recommended utilization of personnel, based on test scores, and the actual operation of the system made it impossible to obtain any solid evidence for the predictive validity of the tests. Added to this was the impact of the armistice, which gave the psychologists little opportunity to collect validation data from the returning troops.[63] Aside from the lack of predictive evidence, there were the problems of inadequate and inconsistent testing conditions, which undermined the validity of the test scores themselves.

What had the army psychologists accomplished? With respect to military organization, it is fair to say that under the leadership of Yerkes and Scott they at least introduced the basis for a scientific personnel system.[64] While there was much resistance to the testing program by the senior officers, the younger generation did seem to appreciate the contribution such a program could make in the future. On the other hand, there was little to support the psychologists' contentions that the tests were valid measures of native intelligence, or that tests had meaningfully contributed to the efficiency of the military during the war. Yet, the psychologists were convinced that the war was a great boost for the testing movement. In this respect, they were correct. Questions of validity aside, they had demonstrated that large groups of people could be tested and classified within an organizational context. Testing had been made respectable, and, as part of the war effort, it had gained great publicity. While testing may not have made a significant contribution to the war, the war had made a significant contribution to testing and as a by-product to psychology in general.[65]

In the immediate postwar period, the psychologists who had been involved in the army capitalized on the momentum of their program to further the applications of testing beyond the military. Consequently, generations of schoolchildren and college students would become familiar with group tests that could be easily administered and quickly scored.

The Value of Team Research

As a result of working closely together, the army psychologists began to realize that teamwork among themselves was essential. They had been literally thrown together, and with the exigency of the war conditions they had to come up with quick and practical programs if they were going to make any professional contributions. While some antipathy existed in the early stages, as in the conflict between Yerkes and Scott, in the end even these two seemed united by the common thread of the practical contributions psychology could make to the war effort. Within the Yerkes committee on developing the tests, Yerkes's own opposition to group tests soon gave way to the demonstrated evidence that such tests were far more practical than individual tests in accomplishing a hierarchical classification system. If there were a lesson to be learned from the army experience of the psychologists, it was that team effort and pooled resources had higher payoffs than the endeavors of any one individual or competition among individuals working on similar tasks.[66] Dodge, in his conclusions about the army testing program, emphasized the value of group cooperation among the psychologists, by declaring:

To the military tasks the psychologists brought their appreciation of the distinctly human and mental aspects of the problems that were involved, their training in the technic of mental analysis, their laboratory methods for estimating human reactions, and their ingenuity in developing new instruments for special purposes. But in no case was the necessary skill and practical experience in the possession of any one person. The best work of the psychologists was the product of a group cooperation.[67]

For Terman, the army experience made him well aware of the value of team effort. He had had considerable experience with collaborative research while working with graduate students at Stanford, but the army committee work was his first exposure to working directly with professional peers. In his subsequent research career, he often engaged in team efforts and these generally worked out very well. Terman was also very sensitive to the need for leadership in any large-scale group project, and in the case of the army testing he felt that Yerkes had admirably fulfilled his leadership role. Many years later, he commented to Yerkes:

I have long believed that no one else could have done as good a job as you did in getting psychological examining accepted as a standard procedure in the Army. Certainly not the dogmatic and impatient Thorndike, nor the tempermental Whipple, nor the (then) immature Bingham, nor the timid and socially inept Terman! Scott possibly could have if he had known more about mental testing; in the committee work he headed he was superb. You displayed the kind of generalship, and leadership, and executive ability which is conspicuously lacking in me.[68]

At a very personal level, the war experience ended Terman's relative professional isolation.[69] Before the war he had corresponded with a few adherents of the testing movement and had made some direct contacts during his eastern trips. But starting with the Vineland meetings, he was able to establish close working relationships with a large number of fellow psychologists. Some of the associations he formed during his army years were to serve as his closest professional relationships throughout his career—the two most significant being Yerkes and Edwin G. Boring. Boring was a somewhat junior member of

Yerkes's staff; but towards the end of the army period he worked closely with Yerkes in turning out the official report of the testing, and thus had considerable contact with Terman as well. Among the other lasting and close relationships Terman established were those with Thorndike and Whipple, and because they were eventually to become colleagues at Stanford, Truman L. Kelley and Edward K. Strong. Another aspect of Terman's emergence from professional isolation was his realization of the "importance of mental tests as an integral part of scientific psychology."[70] Indeed, he began to identify himself more as a psychologist than as an educational specialist. He joined the American Psychological Association in 1917.[71]

In April of 1919, Terman completed his formal ties with the army. He had become especially close with Yerkes. In the closing weeks of their army service, the two men often walked in Rock Creek Park, near Yerkes's Washington, D.C., home.[72] They talked about their future plans, their professional dreams—for Terman, a large-scale study of gifted children; for Yerkes, a laboratory of primate behavior —dreams that would come to fruition. For the more immediate future, they had already started in January to pursue their earlier collaborative effort (interrupted by the war) to obtain funds for a new intelligence test for schoolchildren. Now that their army work was nearing completion, this goal became the new focus of activity for both men. In fact, Terman would assume a major leadership role in extending the army's group-testing methods to the schools. In his later reflections on Yerkes's leadership skills, he was much too modest about his own executive ability. By 1923, Terman would reach a level of professional leadership.

Lewis M. Terman in 1905, the year he received his Ph.D. in psychology at Clark University. He subsequently became a high-school principal in San Bernardino, California. (Courtesy Department of Special Collections and University Archives, Stanford University Libraries.)

Anna Minton in 1895, the year before she met Lewis at Central Normal College in Danville, Indiana. They were married in 1899. (Courtesy Doris Tucker.)

The Terman garden around 1909 in Glendale, California. Terman was on the faculty of the Los Angeles State Normal School from 1906 until 1910 when he went to Stanford University. (Courtesy Doris Tucker.)

Anna, Fred, Helen, and Lewis, around 1909. The parental responsibilities were divided, so that Anna primarily looked after Helen's development while Lewis gave most of his attention to Fred. (Courtesy Doris Tucker.)

Terman in 1910, the year he arrived at Stanford. He believed that he could not have chosen a better university position. (Courtesy Department of Special Collections and University Archives, Stanford University Libraries.)

The psychologists who constructed the army tests at Vineland in 1917. Upper, left to right: F. L. Wells, Guy M. Whipple, Robert M. Yerkes, Walter V. Bingham, Lewis M. Terman. Lower, left to right: Edgar A. Doll, H. H. Goddard, Thomas M. Haines. (Courtesy Robert M. Yerkes Papers, Yale University Library.)

Terman in 1918, the year he was commissioned as a major in the army. He was on the surgeon general's staff and collaborated on the report of the army testing program. (Courtesy *Stanford Illustrated Review*, March 1919.)

The Terman house at Stanford, around 1920. Lewis and Anna built the house in 1912, and it served as their lifelong home. (Courtesy Doris Tucker.)

Lewis and Anna in the 1920s. By midlife their relationship had become more distant. (Courtesy Doris Tucker.)

Anna and Helen in the 1920s. Although Helen had married in 1925, Anna continued to keep a close watch over her daughter's life. (Courtesy Doris Tucker.)

Lewis with Helen's children, Doris (left) and Anne (right) around 1930. Doris and Anne, as well as Fred's sons, were often given IQ tests by their grandfather. (Courtesy Doris Tucker.)

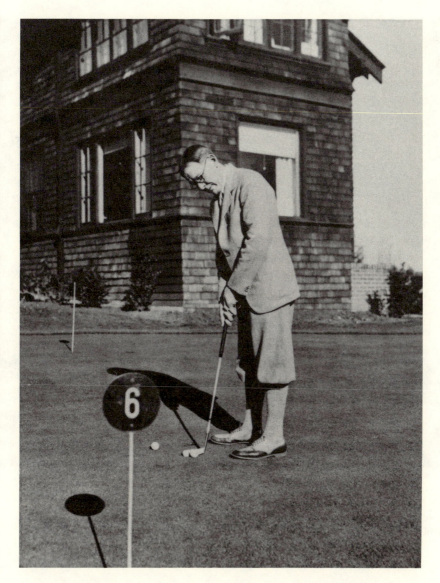

Terman on the putting green in front of his house in the 1930s. At this period in his life, he began to spend more time pursuing avocational interests. (Courtesy Doris Tucker.)

Terman at the time of his retirement from Stanford in 1942. During his retirement years, he devoted himself to the follow-up study of the gifted. (Courtesy Department of Special Collections and University Archives, Stanford University Libraries.)

Terman in 1951. In addition to his involvement with the gifted study, he
spent much of his time reading a wide variety of books and following political
affairs. (Courtesy Department of Special Collections and University Archives,
Stanford University Libraries.)

Lewis and Anna with Fred's family around 1955. Upper, left to right: Terry (Fred's son), Anna, Fred W. (Fred's son), Sibyl (Fred's wife), Fred. Lower, left to right: Sally Briscoe (fiancée of Fred W.), Lewis, Lewis II (Fred's son). (Courtesy Doris Tucker.)

CHAPTER 7

Professional Leadership (1919-1923)

The early experiments with intelligence tests were directed chiefly toward the better understanding of the feeble-minded . . . It is becoming clear, however, that their greatest usefulness will be found in their universal application to school children. . . . The group examination methods now in process of development may be expected to add still further to the popularity of intelligence tests as an aid in the more accurate grading and in the wiser educational guidance of school children. "A mental test for every child" is no longer an unreasonable slogan.[1]

In January of 1919, Yerkes wrote to Abraham Flexner of the General Education Board about his collaborative plans with Terman to develop a group mental test for schoolchildren.[2] Yerkes and Terman had each been in touch with Flexner about such plans before the war. Yerkes now pointed out that the war had completely changed their thinking. The new group methods, in contrast with individual tests, would provide a feasible means of being able to grade large numbers of schoolchildren. Yerkes and Terman were already being "bombarded" by requests from school officials to use the army tests. More suitable tests had to be developed for use in the schools.

Following up this preliminary correspondence, Yerkes and Terman submitted their formal proposal for a grant of $25,000.[3] They proposed that the work be carried out by a five-person committee, including themselves. The General Education Board approved the project with the stipulation that it be sponsored by a research agency.[4] The

National Research Council was suggested, and the council in turn agreed to the sponsorship.[5] M. E. Haggerty, Thorndike, and Whipple joined Terman and Yerkes to form the committee, officially labeled the "Committee on Intelligence Tests for Elementary Schools." Yerkes had wanted Terman to chair the committee. However, because Terman would be returning to Stanford after the committee's preliminary work, Yerkes (who remained in Washington, D.C.) agreed to be chairman.[6]

Developing Group Tests

At the first meeting of the school testing committee in March 1919, it was decided that the group intelligence examination would be applicable to elementary-school pupils from the last months of the third grade through the eighth grade.[7] Multiple forms were to be developed to discourage coaching, verbal and nonverbal (performance) subtests were to be included, quick and objective scoring methods would be provided, and the test battery would take less than an hour to administer. All the potential subtests were adapted from the army tests. In May preliminary forms of the school battery were ready, and test trials were conducted in public and private schools in several cities, including New York, Cleveland, and Richmond.

In October the committee met to review the results of the test trials and to put together the final versions of the test. The decision was made to have two scales, each composed of five different subtests (both verbal and nonverbal items were included). Each scale could be administered in about thirty minutes, and both scales could be given, with a day's interval, to obtain reliability data.[8] The two scales were designated as the "National Intelligence Tests." It was agreed to seek a publisher for the tests and to have test royalties revert to the committee (under the auspices of the National Research Council) for the continuation of test development.

At the October meeting, there was also considerable discussion about how to obtain norms for the tests.[9] General agreement was expressed that rural schoolchildren would score lower than city schoolchildren, but the committee decided to exclude the former because of the extra cost of testing such populations. "Colored" children were also ruled out, though as Yerkes indicated the reason for this exclusion was political.[10] The committee would have trouble getting access to the colored schools in Washington, D.C. (the city had had race riots in July). The committee concluded that obtaining data from white schools in several cities would be representative enough. Each city would provide estimates of "central tendency." Such estimates would overcome the problem of social-class differences in a given city since the scores would be averaged out. Thus, in addition to eliminating separate norms for rural-urban and racial distinctions, separate social-class norms were also ruled out. The exclusion of social-class norms is particularly noteworthy since Yerkes had earlier argued for the establishment of mental-test norms for different social levels.[11] The committee's prime concern was obtaining norms that could be easily reported and be available for the forthcoming test manual. They gave some thought to the idea of supplementing the initial data. As Thorndike commented, "the second edition of the manual can have ten pages of scores of one-legged children and red-haired children."[12] But as the sarcastic tone of Thorndike's remarks suggested, norms based on demographic considerations would not be forthcoming.

White, urban, middle-class children were to set the standard of test performance (the same standard Terman had set for his Stanford-Binet). However, this was not viewed as problematic because the committee had made it clear that it was developing methods for testing "native intellectual ability."[13] Consequently, if poor or black children scored lower on the tests it reflected their lower native intelligence, rather than any disadvantage resulting from a comparison with a more culturally advantaged population.[14]

Following the October meeting, several publishers were contacted. The committee report declared an interest in finding a firm that could effectively sell and distribute the tests to elementary schools throughout the country.[15] It was estimated that the test booklets would be demanded "by the million."[16] Early in 1920 an agreement was reached with the World Book Company, the firm that had published Otis's Group Intelligence Scale two years earlier.[17] During the summer of 1920, one form of each scale was published.[18] With the first edition of the tests, four hundred thousand copies were available for school adoption in the fall. The first edition also included a test manual with preliminary age and grade norms based on four thousand pupils in Washington, D.C., and Pittsburgh. These norms were eventually supplemented to include a standardization sample of thirty-seven thousand children in various cities throughout the country.[19] The National Intelligence Tests gained quick acceptance in the schools. Two hundred thousand copies were sold within the first six months of publication.[20] The tests continued to have wide use even when other similar scales came on the market, reflecting, at least in part, the prestige of the committee that developed them.[21]

When Terman returned to Stanford in the fall of 1919, he began to work on a high-school level group test of intelligence. This battery, which was called the Terman Group Test of Mental Ability, was targeted for grades seven through twelve, and consisted of ten subtests, which, like the National Intelligence Tests, were drawn from the army tests. In January he had made arrangements with the World Book Company for publication, and the test was ready for school adoption in the fall (the same time that the National Tests were available).[22] Grade norms were provided for a national sample of forty-one thousand white, largely urban pupils.[23] Within a few years of publication, sales for the Terman test had reached an annual figure of 550,000.[24]

In 1921 Terman began work on the third test he was to be involved with during the early twenties. This was an educational or achievement test battery, known as the Stanford Achievement Test. Truman Kelley was the senior author, and Giles M. Ruch, a doctoral student in education, also collaborated. Terman had met Kelley during the army testing program and was largely responsible for bringing him from Teachers College to Stanford (in the School of Education) in the fall of 1920.[25] Terman was eager to have Kelley as a colleague because of his expertise in quantitative methods. With financial assistance from the World Book Company, the test battery was published in January 1923.[26] This test was designed to assess the mastery of school subjects from grades two through eight.[27] Achievement tests in individual subject areas had been published before, but the Stanford Achievement Test was the first test battery of its kind and was therefore the first to have a single normative group for different school subjects.[28] Four alternate forms were produced, based on a national sample of close to 350,000 children—quite a pioneering undertaking for its time.[29] Subject-area achievement tests had already become popular in schools, and the Stanford Achievement Test battery became widely used. By the end of 1925, Terman reported that annual sales had reached 1.5 million copies.[30] Several competitors appeared in the 1920s, and the Stanford Test went through many revisions (it is still on the market). For Terman, the Stanford Test was his major source of royalties.

Reorganizing the Schools Through Testing

Before he began his work on the army testing, Terman was committed to the widespread use of intelligence tests in schools. Though the book was not published until after the war, he had written *The Intelligence of School Children* to promote the educational use of the Stanford-Binet.[31] He argued that teachers must learn to use the Binet, though psychologists would be needed to interpret the results.[32] With the test results plus other supplementary data, such as the quality of schoolwork and personal traits like dependability and social adaptability, Terman argued that teachers should be encouraged to classify students into five-fold or seven-fold ability groups, ranging from "very inferior" to "very superior."

With the development of group tests, the task of testing schoolchildren was made immeasurably easier and more efficient. Indeed, Terman could now argue that " 'a mental test for every child' is no longer an unreasonable slogan."[33] During the war he had already taken steps to introduce testing in California schools. In Oakland, Virgil E. Dickson, as part of his doctoral research (under Terman and Cubberley's supervision), arranged to have about one thousand first-grade pupils tested with the Stanford-Binet, and gave about three thousand group tests (the Alpha or Otis) to pupils in grades three through nine.[34] William M. Proctor, one of Terman's school of education colleagues, administered tests to thirteen hundred Palo Alto high-school students, and two graduate students (Margaret Hopewood Hubbard and William T. Root) identified and worked with some sixty gifted children (with IQs above 140).[35] These preliminary investigations had pointed to the applicability of intelligence tests for school grading and vocational and educational guidance. Based on IQs, it would be possible to predict a child's placement on the vocational hierarchy.[36] Conse-

quently, the tests would be of great value in planning a child's education. According to Terman, a child with an IQ of 75 should be
prepared for semiskilled jobs; a child testing above 110 or 115 for
professions or business.

Upon Terman's return from the army, the testing programs were
expanded in Oakland and Palo Alto.[37] In addition, the introduction of
testing to a third California city, San Jose, was carried out by Kimball
Young as part of his doctoral study, under Terman and Cubberley's
direction.[38] San Jose was a city with a high proportion (over half) of
first- or second-generation immigrants from "Latin" countries—southern Italy, Portugal, Spain, and Mexico. Young's major purpose was to
compare the intelligence of "American" and "Latin" elementary
schoolchildren. Regarding the nature of intelligence, Young commented: "The assumption was made that general intelligence is mea-
surable, and that it is to a large extent inherited, and is not greatly
altered by the adventitious character of a particular environment; that
is to say, not altered in form and potentiality, only in content."[39]
Young used the army Alpha and Beta tests and found "extensive
retardation of the Latins as compared to the Americans."[40] He concluded that the retardation of the Latin children was not due to any
language handicap since they were inferior on the Beta (nonverbal) as
well as the Alpha. The retardation of the Latin group therefore reflected native capacity. This was consistent with the conclusion reached
by the army psychologists when they explained the inferior test performance of recruits from southern and eastern European background.[41]
Young, like the army psychologists, failed to consider such cultural
influences as motivation to perform well on tests, or ease and familiarity in dealing with testing situations, or even ability to follow and
understand directions given in pantomime (for the Beta test)—factors
that gave the advantage to the American children.[42]

Based on the test results, Young made several recommendations for
educational programming. The school populations should be regarded
in terms of mental age rather than chronological age.[43] Within each
grade, there should be three levels of schoolwork—in essence, three
ability groups ("superior", "average," and "backward"). Only those
who were average or above should be exposed to the traditional academic curriculum. For those below average—and this would have

included most of the Latin children—the curriculum should be oriented to vocational training. As it turned out these recommendations had an impact. In 1921 San Jose had a new school superintendent who was receptive to Young's suggestions.[44] A year later the San Jose school system had initiated a major reform program based on testing and ability grouping. Similar reorganization programs were taking place at the same time in Oakland and Palo Alto—the other school districts the Terman team had started to work with.[45]

While Terman was making inroads into California schools, he was also beginning to have an influence on educational policy at the national level. This resulted from his chairmanship of a National Education Association (NEA) subcommittee on the "Use of Intelligence Tests in Revision of Elementary Education." The subcommittee worked under the aegis of the NEA Commission on the Revision of Elementary Education, a commission appointed in 1918.[46] This was the year that the NEA had clearly opted for a differentiated curriculum—a policy aimed at bringing order out of the chaos of a burgeoning population of schoolchidlren, swelled by large numbers of recent immigrants.[47] At the high-school level, which was rapidly expanding, vocational education was starting to be emphasized for those pupils who did not have the ability to master the traditional academic curriculum. Thus, the stage was set for the potential use of testing at the secondary level.

At the elementary-school level, from its inception, the new commission viewed testing as an essential part of its mission of revision.[48] When the commission began its work after the war, Terman was invited to become a member and to take the responsibility for reporting on the value of intelligence tests in school reorganization.[49] Terman had hoped to get some funding from the NEA for a detailed investigation of the use of mental tests in school grading.[50] When this was not forthcoming, he chose to present reports of ongoing studies of school testing. He and his subcommittee produced their report in a monograph, entitled *Intelligence Tests and School Reorganization*, published in 1922.[51] This book extolled the use of testing for reorganizing schools so that students could be classified according to ability. In Terman's words "intelligence tests have demonstrated the great extent and frequency of individual differences in the mental ability of unselected school children, and common sense tells us how necessary it is to take such differences into account in the framing of curricula and methods, in the classification of children for instruction, and in their educational and vocational guidance."[52] Among the specific programs presented were Dickson's five-track plan of homogeneous ability groups in Oakland, an individualized instruction method matched to tested ability in Los Angeles, and the use of a tracking system in the schools of a small city in Arizona.

Referring to Dickson's tracking plan, made up of "gifted," "bright," "average," "slow," and "special" groups, Terman recommended the specialized course be continuous through the eighth grade.[53] For the first four groups, who would be going on to high school, the differentiated curriculum should continue, and for the slow group it "should be almost entirely vocational."[54] He did not view the notion of ability groups as undemocratic, arguing "transfers from track to track must always be kept open."[55] However, he failed to realize how difficult it would be for a child to move from one track to another, as illustrated by the stigmatizing effects of being labeled "slow." Terman more aggressively expounded upon the value of ability grouping as an instrument of democracy in his introduction to an expanded version of Dickson's program (now in the Berkeley schools as well as in Oakland). Introducing Dickson's 1923 monograph, he commented:

One of the author's most important contributions is to show that the differentiation of curricula and the classification of school children according to ability, far from being undemocratic measures, are absolutely essential if the public school is to be made a real instrument of democracy. . . . He holds that true democracy does not rest upon equality of endowment, but upon equality of opportunity. . . . Reclassification of children and differentiation of courses of study . . . will go far toward insuring that every pupil, whether mentally superior, average, or inferior, shall have a chance to make the most of whatever abilities nature has given him.[56]

In July 1923, Terman gave an address to the National Education Association in which he predicted that within one or two decades tracking plans like those in Oakland and Berkeley would become standard.[57] His prediction was to come true: by 1923 the new group mental tests were generally welcomed in the schools as an expedient tool for sorting pupils into ability groups.[58] After this early rush of enthusiasm, some school officials criticized the use of the tests, pointing to the dangers of labeling and the difficulties of dealing with parents' objections to testing. However, by 1930 intelligence testing and ability grouping were common practices in elementary schools. Terman had played a notable role in fostering this development, but the schools themselves were ready for a differentiated curriculum. Thus, both the testing advocates and the school administrators agreed that mental tests were the efficient means for sorting pupils.

Terman saw the widespread use of mental tests in the schools as a reflection of how testing could be of use to American society. In this light, it also fulfilled the promise of the army testing program. But school testing was even more important for Terman because it was to be the primary means of achieving his vision of a meritocracy within the American democratic ideal—that is, a social order based on ranked levels of native ability. He presented this vision in a popular article in 1922, arguing as follows:

There is nothing about an individual as important as his IQ, except possibly his morals . . . the great test problem of democracy is how to adjust itself to the large IQ differences which can be demonstrated to exist among the members of any race or nationality group. . . . All the available facts that science has to offer support the Galtonian theory that mental abilities are chiefly a matter of original endowment. . . . It is to the highest 25 percent. of our population, and more especially to the top 5 percent., that we must look for the production of leaders who will advance science, art, government, education, and social welfare generally. . . . The least intelligent 15 or 20 per cent. of our population . . . are democracy's ballast, not always useless but always a potential liability. How to make the most of their limited abilities, both for their own welfare and that of society; how to lead them without making them helpless victims of oppression; are perennial questions in any democracy.[59]

The highest purpose that testing could serve was the identification of children who were intellectually gifted and therefore had the potential to become the leaders of society. It was the responsibility of the schools, once these children were identified, to devote the necessary time and effort to cultivating their potential. As Terman commented, "the school's first task is to find its gifted children and to set them tasks more commensurate with their ability."[60] Such a goal was related to the differentiated curriculum he was advocating, and the notion of grouping pupils on the basis of innate ability was perfectly consistent with the ideals of democracy. Every child would have the same opportunity "to make the most of whatever abilities nature has given him."[61]

Terman's meritocratic model was based on the assumption that success is essentially dependent upon intellect. Like Galton, as well as his fellow mental testing advocates, Terman attributed the hierarchical division of labor to the distribution of native ability. He was unable to entertain the possibility that other factors might account for various levels of achievement, such as differential opportunities for education or the privileges connected with social class. Moreoever, even if one did not question the connection between success and intellect, the priority he attached to heredity led him to disregard the influence of education and social class upon tested intelligence. Terman's thinking on these matters was more ideological than empirical. That is, his assumptions about native intelligence and the connection of success with intellect were not based on unequivocal empirical support.[62] The correlational data (gathered in such settings as the schools and the military) that demonstrated relationships between IQ and social class or IQ and occupation could be interpreted in a variety of ways. Nevertheless, it seems that Terman and the other mental test supporters were so swayed by the natural-science model of a biological foundation for intelligence and its association with achievement that they could not conceive of other explanations as legitimately scientific.

During the early twenties, Terman was making great strides toward accomplishing his goal of reorganizing the schools through testing; and as we shall see, he also embarked on his ambitious longitudinal study of gifted children. However, this was also a time in which he experienced a considerable amount of criticism regarding his work on the army tests and his campaign to spread the use of testing in the schools. Therefore, he felt compelled to direct much of his energy to defense of his meritocratic vision in order to quell the rising tide of opposition.

Debating the Testing Critics

The monumental report of the army testing program was published in the spring of 1921.[63] By early 1922, the major results of this report were communicated in popular magazines and newspapers. Mental testing in America had become a cultural phenomenon. The first article to spread the word appeared in the *Atlantic Monthly* in February 1922 and was written by Cornelia James Cannon, the wife of the well-known Harvard physiologist Walter B. Cannon.[64] It seems likely that Mrs. Cannon got her scoop because Yerkes and her husband had been friends since they were graduate students, training under Charles G. Davenport, the infamous eugenicist.[65] The Cannon and Yerkes families summered together in New Hampshire. In her essay, Mrs. Cannon reported that according to the tests, 47.3 percent of the white draft fell below the mental age of thirteen, and therefore they would be classified as "morons." With this major finding, as well as the reported ethnic and racial differences, she then drew a number of sociopolitical implications, as illustrated by the following:

A democracy is the most difficult form of government to perfect, because it demands of each citizen so much understanding and cooperation. . . . It is to the interest of all to be represented by those possessing the highest abilities . . . . Indeed, we may have to admit that the lower grade man is material unusable in a democracy, and to eliminate him from the electorate. . . . Has not the time come to withhold the privilege and responsibility of citizenship from the majority of the newer immigrants, whose quality shows so marked a falling-off from that of the immigrants of fifty years ago, and whose intelligence is so far below that of the ordinary American, and bestow it only upon carefully selected members of the group? . . . Of the entire Negro draft . . . 89 percent [were] under the mental age of thirteen . . . the education of the whites and colored in separate schools may have justification other than that created by race-prejudice.[66]

Such were the issues of the day that the army testing could shed light on. In the case of immigration policy, the mental testers themselves argued for immigration restriction based on their findings of inferior test performance by draftees of southern and eastern European background.[67]

Cannon's essay set the pace for a number of other popular articles, including one by H. L. Mencken in the *Baltimore Sun* stating that "over 47 per cent of the white draft, and an even larger per cent of negroes are feebleminded."[68] Another influential interpretation of the army tests was presented by the new president of Colgate University, George B. Cutten. In his inaugural address in October 1922, he stated: "With only 13½ per cent. of the population able to get through college well, 15 per cent. able to get through at all, and 25 per cent. unable to comprehend the significance of the ballot, democracy is out of the question."[69]

Were these popular interpretations wrong? They were not refuted by Yerkes or Terman or any of the other psychologists who contributed to the 1921 report. Cannon had drawn her comments about mental age from a section in the last part of this report.[70] As stated therein, in order to obtain a standard index across the various mental tests, the raw scores of a sample of 160,000 cases were converted into mental-age equivalents. With respect to the average mental age of the white draft, the report indicated: "It appears that the intelligence of the principal sample of the white draft, when transmuted from Alpha and Beta Examinations into terms of mental age, is about 13 years (13.08)."[71] Also considered was the discrepancy between this estimate and Terman's estimate of an average adult mental age of sixteen on the Stanford-Binet. According to the army report, "for norms of adult intelligence the results of the Army examinations are undoubtedly the most representative. It is customary to say that the mental age of the average adult is about 16 years. This figure is based, however, upon examinations of only 62 persons."[72] Regarding the percentage of "morons" cited by Cannon, the figure 47.3 was taken from a table showing the percentage of the white draft with mental ages of 12.9 or less.[73] In the case of blacks, the corresponding percentage was 89.

The issue of the average adult mental age proved to be especially significant for Terman in the ensuing controversy that emerged. Starting in the fall of 1922, the influential journalist Walter Lippmann wrote a series of highly critical articles about the army tests in the *New Republic* and *Century Magazine*.[74] Furthermore, in the very first article, he specifically referred to Terman's work on testing and suggested that the discrepancy between the average adult mental ages on the army tests and the Stanford-Binet cast doubt about the validity of the latter because of the small adult sample used. As Lippmann put it, "the army tests had knocked the Stanford-Binet measure of adult intelligence into a cocked hat."[75] Elsewhere in the series, he asserted that the claim made by Terman and the other army psychologists that the tests measured innate ability had no scientific foundation. He voiced his concern that "intelligence testing in the hands of men who hold this dogma could but lead to an intellectual caste system in which the task of education had given way to the doctrine of predestination and infant damnation."[76] It should be noted that Lippman did not simply rely on persuasive argument in challenging Terman. He specifically drew attention to what he believed were faulty interpretations of the data. For example, Terman had argued that the correlation between IQ and social class among schoolchildren pointed to a hereditarian interpretation because the correlation coefficient declined with increasing age, thereby indicating the decreasing effect of the home environment.[77] Lippmann contended that as the child grows up, he or she spends less time in the home and more time in the school and playground. He therefore concluded that Terman's data were "a rather strong argument . . . for the traditional American theory that the public school is an agency for equalizing the opportunities of the privileged and the underprivileged."[78]

Terman was enraged by Lippmann's attack.[79] Despite the technical sophistication of many of the criticisms, Terman in his published reply recommended that Lippmann, as a layman, should stay out of issues he was not informed about.[80] In fact, Terman was quite evasive in responding to the specific criticisms. For example, in dealing with Lippmann's argument that there was no proof that mental traits are inherited, he pointed to Lippmann's clever trick of playing off the opinion of one psychologist with those of another (Cattell questioning Goddard's proof that mental deficiency was inherited). Terman did not debate Lippmann's environmental interpretation of the correlation between IQ and social class. With respect to the question of the average mental age of the army draftees, he pointed to norms demonstrating that on the army tests draftees scored lower than fourteen-year-old schoolchildren. But even here he was less explicit than he was in an earlier article in which he acknowledged such problems as the army norms being unrepresentative of the entire draft, and the poor testing conditions adversely affecting test performance.[81]

Terman received mixed reviews from his colleagues. Cattell thanked him for pointing to Lippmann's quoting out of context (regarding Cattell's views on heredity) and opined that Terman's reply was "admirable" while Lippmann's counterreply showed "bad temper" and an "incoherent point of view."[82] E. G. Conklin, a leading biologist and an advocate of eugenics, considered Terman's reply to be "splendid" in contrast to Lippmann's "shallow" and "partisan" critique.[83] Conklin added his consternation that the "Jew Republic" (an aspersion to Lippmann's Jewish origin) would believe that "all men are essentially equal." Yerkes felt that Terman's reply was good reading for a psychologist but feared that the "layman" would not understand Terman's sarcasm and irony.[84] Another psychologist, Howard C. Warren, while agreeing with Terman, criticized him for being sarcastic in responding to seriously intended criticism.[85] Even more so than Yerkes, Warren feared the casual reader would be prejudiced against Terman. When all was done about the debate, Terman had second thoughts about making any more forays into popular journals. He confided to Jessie Chase Fenton, a former graduate student: "I think that answers in the future will be confined to presentation of data in scientific periodicals. There is no use trying to argue with some people."[86]

In 1922, some months prior to his exchange with Lippmann, Terman engaged in a debate with psychologist William C. Bagley of Teachers College.[87] This marked the beginning of a controversy with fellow psychologists about intelligence testing that would last intermittently through 1940. Bagley, like Lippmann, challenged Terman's assumption that intelligence tests measure native intelligence and branded Terman a "determinist" because of his fatalistic conclusions regarding the influence of education on intellectual performance. Bagley was especially critical of Terman's contention that through IQ tests the limits of a child's educability could be determined by the fifth or sixth school year, and consequently differentiated vocational training could begin at this time. For Bagley, who was committed to a social evolutionary perspective in which mass education could improve the intellectual functioning of children generally and better prepare them to participate in a democratic society, Terman's prescription of equality of opportunity for each child to develop his or her original nature was tantamount to a system of intellectual aristocracy. Bagley (as was also the case with Lippmann) acknowledged the existence of differences in native ability, but he professed that it was the similarities in ideas, ideals, aspirations, and standards that were more significant for social progress. As he stated, "a little more light for the common man this year, next year, a hundred years from now, and the battle for humanity, for democracy, and for brotherhood is won."[88] According to

Bagley, in order to achieve a "pervasive common culture," which was the prime function of democratic education, the significant goal should not be rate of school progress but the ultimate product—in other words, schools should bring forth an equality of results.

Terman, in his response, accused Bagley of relying on sentiment and believing in "miracles" and concluded:

With respect to any issue we should be guided by the preponderence of evidence. From Galton on down to Thorndike and Davenport the scientist has produced a considerable amount of evidence in support of the hypothesis that one's mental traits, especially his intellectual abilities, are pretty largely determined by native endowment. . . . Certainly any definition . . . [of democracy] will have to square with the demonstrable facts of biological and psychological science.[89]

In his response to both Lippmann and Bagley, Terman dismissed his critics as being unscientific. Terman was convinced that the facts of science pointed to a hereditarian explanation of IQ differences. Did the data unequivocally point to such an interpretation, and was it empirically established that the schools could do little to raise the level of pupils' intellectual functioning? These were the questions raised by Lippmann and Bagley. Furthermore, a more basic question alluded to by these critics concerned the assumption that intelligence could be defined by a unitary quality, such as "abstract thinking."[90] Could it not be argued that such a criterion, as reflected in intelligence tests, was a socially constructed one and that it is used as a scheme of social ranking by those who had already achieved the standard of comparison? This line of attack was heralded by John Dewey. Dewey had followed Lippmann's critique in the *New Republic*, and in an essay in that periodical commented:

We accept standards of judging individuals which are based on the qualities of mind and character which win under existing social conditions conspicuous success. The "inferior" is the one who isn't calculated to "get on" in society such as now exists. "Equals" are those who belong to a class formed by like chances of attaining recognition, position, and wealth in present society. . . . Superiority and inferiority are meaningless words taken by themselves. . . . There is doubtless some degree of correlation between traits which promote superiority in more than one direction. But the idea of abstract, universal superiority and inferiority is an absurdity. . . . It was once supposed . . . that the purpose of education . . . was to discover and release individualized capacities so that they could make their own way with whatever of social change is involved in their operation. But now we welcome a procedure which under the title of science sinks the individual in a numerical class; judges him with reference to capacity to fit into a limited number of vocations ranked according to present business standards; assigns him a predestined niche and thereby does whatever education can do to perpetuate the present order.[91]

While Dewey did not make any further forays into the public arena of testing controversy, the Terman-Bagley debate generated considerable discussion in the literature.[92] As in the case of the Terman-Lippmann exchange, as well as in the replays which were to follow in the late twenties and the thirties, both sides often seemed to talk past one another. This is because they were each operating from opposing ideological positions. For Terman and the other army testers, the ideal society was to be organized along vertical dimensions, in which levels of responsibility and skill would match the distribution of native ability. In contrast, testing critics such as Bagley and Dewey sought a society based on equal participation by all of its constituent members and groups.[93] Rather than stressing differences between people, their goal was to insure that all segments of society could be active participants in a cooperative, democratic social system. Each group derived its ideas from Darwinian evolutionary thought—the major intellectual influence in social science during the Progressive Era of 1890 through 1920. However, the testing advocates held to a reductionist view in which the principles of biological evolution determined social evolution. The testing critics, on the other hand, believed that social evolution had its own laws.[94]

Social scientists—like Terman—who were committed to the reductionist view of evolution were the more influential group, at least through the early 1920s.[95] In general, it seemed that biological determinism and a hereditarian explanation of human differnces were compatible with the vertical division of labor necessary for an industrialized society. More specifically, the use of mental tests provided an efficient means of classifying individuals in terms of their potential contribution to the social order of the corporate state. As we have seen, within the context of public education, mental tests were welcomed as an expedient tool for classifying schoolchildren. And yet, by the 1930s the pendulum would begin to shift in the direction of an egalitarian, as opposed to vertical, mosaic as the proper fit for American society. With restrictive immigration in place, the threat of undesirable elements continuing to erode the character of the American population no longer existed. The new concern was creating a harmonious climate out of the diversity of social groups in America. As the decade progressed, the Fascist specter in Europe would give added meaning to the need for America to be a bastion of intergroup cooperation. This intellectual shift would pose increasing difficulty for Terman in his later exchanges with the testing critics—especially by 1940.[96]

Advancing Test Publishing

In furthering his goal of establishing testing in the schools, Terman forged an important alliance with the publishing industry. This alliance also proved helpful in fending off the testing critics. Terman had benefited from having his Stanford-Binet test published by the firm of Houghton Mifflin—the house that had published his monographs on school hygiene. Unlike most of the other competing Binet revisions produced in America between 1910 and 1916, such as those by Goddard and Kuhlmann that were published in professional journals and disseminated and sold by the test authors or their institutions, the Stanford-Binet enjoyed the advantages of being marketed by a publisher. This state of affairs undoubtedly contributed to establishing the Stanford revision as the most widely used individual test by the 1920s.

When Otis had completed his group test in 1918, Terman attempted to interest Houghton Mifflin in publishing it.[97] Upon learning that the firm did not wish to get involved with group tests, Terman turned to the World Book Company, a house which had published a survey he had conducted in 1914 for the Portland, Oregon, school system.[98] World Book agreed to publish the Otis scale and looked forward to the subsequent group tests that would be developed after the war.[99] Indeed, these were forthcoming with the publication of the National Intelligence Tests and Terman's own group test in 1920.

The World Book Company was founded in 1905 by Caspar W. Hodgson, an 1896 graduate of Stanford University.[100] Among his closest friends at Stanford were classmate Ray Lyman Wilbur, later to be a president of the university, and Herbert Hoover, who was in the class of 1895. Hodgson continued his friendship with Wilbur and Hoover after he left Stanford, and both of these prominent figures remained confidants. In 1902 Hodgson became a Pacific Coast representative for the publishing firm D. C. Heath. Through this position he met the superintendent of schools for the Philippines, David P. Barrows. Barrows complained that he was unable to get publishers interested in preparing textbooks suitable for Philippine schools and suggested that Hodgson start a book company for this purpose. Such unorthodox beginnings for the company seemed to portend Hodgson's willingness to pursue new directions in publishing. Thus, when Terman approached him in 1918 about publishing group tests, he sensed the potential market for the fledgling mental-testing movement.

Another instance of the boldness of Hodgson's entry into test publishing was his postwar appointment, with Terman's recommendation, of Otis as the company's editor of psychological and educational tests. Among his many activities, Otis launched the firm's division of test research and service. For twenty years he played a major role in the growth of World Book as a test publisher.

By 1920 Terman's relationship with World Book could best be described as that of a senior professional advisor on test publishing. This role was first manifested by his directing several group tests to the attention of the company. However, his need to do this was lessened as the momentum of the firm's test publishing activities accelerated, and Otis's editorial endeavors became more established. Hodgson shared Terman's goal of achieving mass testing in the schools. For World Book, which had a corner on the market, such a goal meant huge profits as well as influence on school policy—a factor that would bring more business to the company. In 1922 World Book published the monograph Terman produced for the National Education Association about reorganizing elementary education through testing. The previous year Hodgson had proposed a special role for Terman in the company that would advance the leitmotif of the NEA monograph— mass school testing and ability grouping in the schools.

Hodgson invited Terman to become the editor of a series of textbooks on tests and measurement.[101] The series was entitled "Measurement and Adjustment," the latter term reflecting "adjustments to meet the problems of instruction and school administration arising out of individual differences."[102] The textbooks, which were directed at teachers and school administrators, were to deal with such topics as intelligence testing, educational measurement, the effects of individual differences on school organization, and educational and vocational guidance. As Terman commented on the goal of the series, "our education has been mass education. The task of the series is to focus attention on education as adapted to individual abilities and needs."[103] He also saw the series as a way of obtaining a position of leadership for himself in the testing movement. He confided to his Houghton Mifflin publisher: "After spending so many years in helping to initiate the test movement I feel that it is my duty now to do what I can to help give direction to it."[104] The first book published in the series was Dickson's 1923 monograph on the tracking system in the Oakland and Berkeley schools. Over the next ten years, fifteen more books were produced.

In 1922, when Terman became involved in the debates with Bagley and Lippmann, Hodgson and other World Book officials were concerned that the attacks on testing would adversely affect test sales. To counter the critics, World Book reprinted copies of Terman's published replies and widely circulated these to school superintendents.[105] Hodgson applauded Terman's hard-hitting response and asserted that Lippmann "is red, he is Bolshevik, and I am a little uncertain as to his breed but I think I can guess what it is."[106] In replying to Hodgson, Terman ignored the anti-Semitic overtone but picked up on the "red connection," remarking: "When that magazine [the *New Republic*] started I rather liked it, but its turn toward Bolshevism during the war was more than I could stand. Since then it has become redder and redder."[107]

Terman's association with World Book in the early twenties helped to further the cause of establishing mass testing in the schools. By the middle of the decade, World Book was the leading producer of intelligence and achievement tests.[108] Terman continued his active association with World Book through the early 1940s, and the firm continued to be one of the leaders in the test publishing field throughout its separate existence and its eventual merger with Harcourt Brace Jovanovich in 1960.[109]

Launching the Study of the Gifted

Terman's interest in the gifted took root during his graduate-student days at Indiana University and Clark. In his master's research, he had concluded that a high level of intelligence was one of the most important qualities contributing to leadership. The aim of his doctoral research was to identify the mental processes that distinguished "bright" from "dull" boys. In developing the Stanford-Binet, he became aware of the value of the Binet method of identifying intellectually gifted children.[110] In 1911 Terman began to collect data on children with exceptionally high IQs, and in 1915 he reported a study of thirty-one children with IQs above 125.[111] Contrary to his own expectations, as well as popular beliefs, teachers' ratings indicated that these intellectually precocious children were well developed in other spheres of functioning. They were not sickly, eccentric, one sided, or socially inept as he had initially presumed they would be. In 1916, with the collaboration of Margaret Hopwood Hubbard, he collected data on a sample of fifty-nine children with IQs above 140.[112] More extensive ratings and information were obtained from teachers than in the previous study, and similar data were supplied by parents. These precocious children also turned out to be emotionally and socially well adjusted.

In 1919, at Terman's request, Stanford established a research fellowship for the study of gifted children, which provided further opportunity for revising the information and rating forms.[113] Moreover, an interest blank was developed for children to fill out about themselves. The fellowship was set up for a period of ten years and carried an annual stipend of $1,000. Terman agreed to contribute an annual sum of $250 (based on his book royalties), a sum that was matched by a contribution from Cubberley, and the Stanford Board of Trustees agreed to match these two personal contributions by providing $500 in the president's annual budget.[114] By the spring of 1921, with the aid of the annual fellowships, complete data were available for 121 children with IQs over 140. The record of good personal adjustment emerging from these cases supported Terman's earlier findings about gifted children. Terman also pointed to social-class and ethnic-racial differences. With respect to class differences, he concluded that "heredity is superior," since fifty percent of the fathers belonged to professional groups and not one to the unskilled group. Regarding ethnic distinctions, he reported an "excess of Jewish cases and a deficiency of cases from the Italian, Portuguese, and Mexican groups living in the vicinity of Stanford University."[115]

In addition to gathering test, rating, and questionnaire data, Terman carried out several individual case studies. In 1917 he published an intellectual portrait of Francis Galton's childhood.[116] Based on Karl Pearson's biography, which contained letters written by young Galton describing his intellectual accomplishments, Terman estimated that Galton's IQ was near 200. According to Terman, Galton's childhood vocabulary, interests, and educational mastery suggested that his mental age was approximately double his chronological age.[117] Terman also reported a father's account of the training of an infant daughter who by the age of twenty-six months could read as well as the average first-grader.[118] With Jessie Chase Fenton, a recipient of the Stanford Gifted Children Fellowship, Terman described the case of a nine-year-old girl who was an accomplished poet.[119] Five of her poems, as rated by Stanford students in advanced English classes, compared favorably with poems by well-known authors.

As Terman became more involved in studying gifted children, he often took a personal interest. Fenton recalled her experiences as a research assistant during the 1920–21 year.[120] Her major assignment was to check up on all the gifted children that had been studied up to this time. She retested and interviewed the children, visiting their homes and in some cases speaking with their teachers. She remembered Terman's eagerness in hearing about all the details whenever she returned from visiting one of the gifted. Even before this episode, Terman had taken a particular interest in a gifted young musician by the name of Henry Cowell. In 1911, through his first Stanford graduate assistant Harold Williams, Terman met Cowell who was then twelve years old.[121] Cowell worked as a janitor at a local school in order to support himself and his mother (his father had left home). He had dropped out of school at the age of seven because of lack of interest. However, at a young age he had studied the violin, and when Terman met him he had already trained himself to play the piano. Despite Cowell's lack of formal education, his tested IQ was above

140. Terman introduced him to Stanford's music faculty, and through various other contacts Cowell was able to pursue a musical education. Terman continued to take an active interest in Cowell's career, and Cowell eventually developed a reputation as an avant-garde composer.[122]

By 1921 Terman was ready to go beyond the preliminary data he had collected. His goal was to obtain a sample of one thousand cases so that he could claim a reasonably representative sample of intellectually gifted children.[123] In this venture, he was supported by the Commonwealth Fund of New York with a grant of $20,300, which was supplemented the following year by $14,000 plus an additional $8,000 from Stanford. As spelled out in his grant application, Terman intended to obtain at least two intelligence tests for each of the one thousand subjects, as well as measures of school achievement, trait ratings, and social data. He also intended a follow-up of the subjects for a period of at least ten years.

In launching his study of the gifted, Terman began the first psychological investigation involving a longitudinal research design, in which a sample of subjects was followed over the course of several years. The only precedents were brief longitudinal single-case studies based on baby diaries.[124] During the 1920s, several other longitudinal studies of children were begun. Terman's study was also innovative in its scope. Since his aim was to gather as complete an assessment of his subjects as possible, he made use of a wide variety of methods. Moreover, as he was often attempting to measure characteristics not previously assessed, he had to devise many of the instruments he used. For example, as part of the study, the first achievement test battery (the Stanford Achievement Test) was constructed. Another instrument to emerge from the study was the first measure of masculinity-femininity (The Terman-Miles scale).

Upon receipt of the Commonwealth Fund grant, Terman devoted three months to finalizing plans, tests, and information blanks, as well as to securing the necessary research collaborators and assistants. Stanford colleague Truman L. Kelley was enlisted as assistant director and essentially served in the capacity of a statistical consultant. Giles M. Ruch, who was completing his dissertation under Terman, served as an administrative assistant and also took on the major responsibility of developing the achievement and general information tests.[125] In addition, Terman sought four full-time field assistants who would be primarily responsible for the data collection. Writing to various colleagues in the mental-testing field, Terman finally selected Florence Fuller, Florence L. Goodenough, Helen Marshall, and Dorothy M. Yates.

The data to be collected for each child in the first year of the study included two intelligence tests (the Stanford-Binet and National-Form B); an achievement test (the Stanford Achievement Test); a test of general information (science, history, literature, and the arts); a test of knowledge and interest in play activities, games, and amusements; an interest blank; and a two-month reading record kept by the children. Furthermore, Terman enlisted the aid of parents and teachers. He had previously made use of such "lay-experimenters" in his preliminary studies of gifted children, and he now expanded their data input. The parents filled out a home information blank, which asked for a developmental case history, a report on home training, and ratings on twenty-five traits; and the teachers filled out a school information blank, which covered school health records, quality of schoolwork, social adjustment, and the same twenty-five traits that the parents were given.

The fieldwork began early in September 1921. The original intention was to identify the highest one percent (IQs above 140) of all California schoolchildren. However, due to financial limitations, only the larger and medium-sized urban areas were canvassed, and as it turned out, the one percent cutoff was set at an IQ of 135.[126] Goodenough and Fuller were assigned to Los Angeles, Marshall to San Francisco, and Yates to the East Bay (Oakland and Berkeley). Volunteer assistants took responsibility for covering smaller cities, such as Santa Barbara, Fresno, San Jose, and Santa Ana.

In the various cities, the field workers attempted to canvass all the elementary schools (grades three to eight); in the larger cities, they canvassed the high schools as well. For standardization in selecting the sample, the following procedure was adopted in the elementary schools: in each classroom, the teacher was asked to fill out a blank calling for the name of the brightest child in the class, the second brightest, the third brightest, and the youngest.[127] The teacher was also asked to give the name of the brightest child he or she had had the previous year. All the nominated children in a given school were then given a group intelligence test (National-Form B). Those who scored high on this test were given an abbreviated Stanford-Binet, and those scoring high on this short version were in turn given a complete Stanford-Binet.[128] To check on the efficiency of this search method, the entire population of three schools (which had already been canvassed for teacher nominations) was tested. The results revealed that the search procedure was identifying close to ninety percent of all who would have qualified if each pupil had been given the Stanford-Binet. However, there were difficulties in trying to cover all the schools, particularly in the larger cities. Goodenough wrote to Terman about the difficulties in Los Angeles and questioned whether it was worthwhile covering fourteen special schools that handled children who had been found guilty of minor offenses.[129] Terman responded that she should use her own judgment, voicing concern about taking extra time to cover "side lines that do not promise reasonably well."[130] It is likely that these special schools, which apparently did not get included, had a disproportionate share of children from lower social-class backgrounds; it is also likely that social-class bias (in favor of the higher levels) would have influenced teacher nominations in the schools selected. Terman did not appear to be sensitive to these possible sources of bias, which would have worked to the exclusion of lower-class children. His tendency to attribute class differences primarily to heredity would account for his relative neglect of cultural factors that might influence the selection of subjects.

Among the various categories of teacher nominations, the youngest child proved to be the most fruitful in terms of qualifying for the IQ cutoff of 135, followed closely by the brightest child. The systematic search yielded a total of 661 subjects, 354 boys and 307 girls, from an elementary-school population of about 160,000. This group, designated the "Main Experimental Group," was compared with a control group consisting of a random sample of children of comparable age.[131] A second Binet-tested group of 365 elementary-school children, 197 boys and 168 girls, was also included. Some of these children had been tested and followed up prior to 1921; others were discovered with the help of volunteer testers in smaller California communities not covered by the main survey. A third group, made up primarily of junior and senior high-school children, was included in the study of the basis of group intelligence tests. This group consisted of 444 subjects, 273 boys and 171 girls. The total group added up to 1,470 cases, 824 boys and 646 girls.[132] It would seem that through the various nomination and "discovery" procedures, a sex bias in favor of boys may also have been operating.[133]

The remaining data were collected during the 1922–23 year.[134] In an attempt to dispel the popular notion that gifted children were underdeveloped in nonintellectual areas, Terman included medical and physical assessments, as well as measures of personality, character, and interests. The medical examinations of the gifted children (eighty-seven percent of the sample were examined) were carried out by two physicians. Anthropometric measurements, including height, weight, breathing capacity, grip, and body-part dimensions, were obtained for most of the children identified through the systematic search procedure carried out by the field assistants. These physical measures were supervised by Bird T. Baldwin, a psychologist with expertise in this area and director of the Child Welfare Research Station at the University of Iowa. His assistant, Beth L. Wellman, made the actual measurements. Finally, character and personality tests (constructed by A. S. Raubenheimer, a graduate student of Terman's) and a test of intellectual, social, and activity interests (constructed by Jennie Benson Wyman, another of Terman's graduate students) were administered.

The data amounted to close to one hundred pages for each gifted child, two-thirds of which were test and measurement material, while the other one-third were questionnaire items. The IQs for the pre-high-school subjects ranged from 135 to 200, with a mean Stanford-Binet IQ of 151.[135] The IQs for the high-school subjects ranged from 135 to 169, with a mean IQ of 143 on the Terman group test. In terms of racial-ethnic origin, it was estimated that by comparison with the general population of the cities concerned there was about a one hundred percent excess of Jewish ancestry, a twenty-five percent excess of native-born parentage, and an underrepresentation of Italian, Portuguese, Mexican, and Negro ancestry.[136] The social-class breakdown in terms of father's occupation revealed a preponderance of professional, semiprofessional, and business categories (81.4 percent). It was concluded that the typical gifted child was the product of "superior parentage," from the standpoint of both cultural-educational background and heredity (the latter gleaned from genealogical data). This combined advantage was judged to account for the slightly better "physical specimen" among the gifted sample as compared with the average child. Such a comparison was based on the anthropometric measurements, health histories, and medical examinations.

Educationally, the average gifted child was accelerated when compared with his or her age group. With respect to mastery of subject matter, this acceleration was about forty-four percent. This percentage was much higher than the fourteen percent acceleration in grade placement, leading Terman to conclude that the gifted pupils were kept at school tasks two or three grades below their actual level of achievement. The interests of gifted children were seen as many sided and self-initiated. They learned to read easily and read more than the average child. Their play preferences showed a degree of maturity two or three years beyond the norm of their age. On character tests, the gifted were above average on qualities such as trustworthiness, emotional stability, and "wholesome" social attitudes. Trait ratings by teachers and parents confirmed this character portrait.

Terman pointed to two "facts" that stood out in the composite picture:

(1) The deviation of the gifted subjects from the generality is in the upward direction for nearly all traits. . . . There is no law of compensation whereby the intellectual superiority of the gifted is sure to be offset by inferiorities along nonintellectual lines. (2) The amount of upward deviation is not the same in all traits. It is greatest in those aspects of behavior most closely related to intelligence, such as originality, intellectual interests, and ability to score high in achievement tests.[137]

Terman cautioned that this composite portrait reflected central tendencies. He noted that one could find individual examples of almost any personality defect, social maladjustment, behavior problem, or physical frailty. He concluded, however, that among gifted children the incidence of such deviations was lower than in the general population. For Terman's purposes, this last point was most significant for two reasons. First, it demonstrated that gifted children did not conform to the commonly held belief (in the 1920s) that such children were often one sided and neurotic. Second, it suggested that gifted children had the kinds of well-rounded personalities and skills that, given the opportunity, could be harnessed for leadership roles in Terman's meritocratic society. Terman acknowledged that the purpose of his study was to identify and describe gifted children and eventually to follow-up the development of these children. He had no specific recommendations about the educational methods that should be adopted to meet the needs of intellectually superior children.[138] However, he strongly advocated a differentiated school curriculum that would place gifted children in special classrooms where they could accelerate educationally according to their ability rather than their age (as in the traditional curriculum).

One other aspect of the second year of the study needs to be noted. Grant money was also used to support a parallel study conducted by Catharine M. Cox (her dissertation) under Terman's supervision. This was an ambitious extension of Terman's method of estimating Galton's IQ to a representative group of three hundred eminent individuals throughout history. The completed study was published as the second volume of the monograph series on the gifted.[139] Terman described the purpose of this study was to determine whether the childhood traits of individuals who later achieved eminence paralleled the traits that he had discovered among his sample of gifted children.[140] In essence, he concluded that this was indeed the case. As he stated, "we are justified in believing that geniuses, so called, are not only characterized in childhood by a superior IQ, but also by traits of interest, energy, will, and character that preshadow later performance. The ancient saying that 'the child is father to the man' probably expresses a truth far more profound than anyone has hitherto suspected."[141]

Cox's study and Terman's analysis of Galton's IQ represented innovative attempts at using history as a research laboratory of sorts. However, neither investigator was sensitive to the potential biases that could intrude upon the validity of the data. For example, Cox started from a list of the 1,000 most eminent individuals in history compiled by James McKeen Cattell, and narrowed this down to 301 cases, largely on the basis of available biographical material (in English, French, and German). Thus, the selectivity of data could have biased results in favor of the reported connection between childhood signs of giftedness and adult eminence.[142]

Other Ventures in Applied Psychology

As a result of their professional involvement during World War I, American psychologists were generally eager to promote applied psychology in the postwar years. Not only were the new group testing methods directed at schools, but other areas of application were projected, most notably crime prevention (through identifying delinquency) and business and industry.[143] Pervading the psychologists' delineations of specific practicalities were such catch phrases as "mental engineering," "organizational efficiency," and "the proper utilization of human talent." The implication was that psychology could offer services that would achieve order, efficiency, and control to postwar American society. Such accomplishments had been sought as part of the Progressive Reform movement of the prewar years.[144] Psychology now had the methods to bring these goals to fruition.

While Terman's primary focus in the early twenties was to direct the new applied psychology to primary and secondary education, he also became involved in other ares of application, which included business, juvenile delinquency, higher education, and professional affairs in psychology. His activities in the realm of the business world appear to have started just prior to the war when he helped establish the Pacific Coast Bureau of Employment Research.[145] This bureau was staffed by some of his students, including Otis. In 1919 Terman was listed as a member of the technical staff, acting as a consultant in matters relating to applied psychology. For this year and the next, he offered lectures (apparently as part of training programs) on such topics as "Intelligence Tests: How They are Made and Why They Work," and "The Feeble-Minded in Industry."[146] It is not clear whether the bureau continued after 1920, but Terman had no further connection with it.

A somewhat more extended venture in business and industrial application came about through Terman's association with the Psychological Corporation—the brainchild of Cattell.[147] In the fall of 1919, Cattell wrote to Terman about his ideas for a "Psychological Corporation." [148] He noted three chief interests: the advancement of psychology as a "useful science," placing scientific research on an economic basis, and giving psychologists "control" of their own work. Cattell thought very highly of Terman's work, citing it in a letter to President Wilbur of Stanford as "the most active part of the science" at the present time. [149] The Psychological Corporation was incorporated in April 1921, and at the first meeting of the board of directors in New York City, Terman, in absentia, was elected as "Second Vice-President." [150]

Cattell's model of organization for the Psychological Corporation had psychologists involved in teaching, research, or consultation in various parts of the country organizing themselves into branches. Exactly what these branches would do or accomplish was never clearly spelled out by Cattell—a situation that doomed the early development of the corporation. In June 1921, Terman assured Cattell that he would organize a California branch. [151] However, it took almost two years for the California group to get started. The delay was to some extent a consequence of Terman's heavy commitments to his various other projects but was probably also a reflection of the lack of guidance on Cattell's part. When the California branch met in February 1923, Terman invited some of his Stanford associates (Kelley and J. H. Williams, among others to attend), as well as members of the psychology faculty at the Berkeley and Los Angeles campuses of the University of California. [152] Several ideas were discussed, including the possibility of psychological consultation to the "Motion Picture companies," securing private funds for research in delinquency, research on advertising, developing a training system for typewriting skills, and Terman's own intention of opening a clinic for gifted children at Stanford. The group also discussed a free schedule and methods of making contacts with perspective clients. All in all, the California group did not seem to know what their next steps should be. As stated in the minutes of their first meeting, "frequent references were made to the employment of psychology in business and industry, but none of those present seemed in touch with any actual demand in such fields." [153]

Follow-up correspondence between the secretary of the California branch, Warner Brown of Berkeley, and Cattell provided no usable guidelines on Cattell's part. [154] Similar frustrations were expressed by members of other branches. The California branch remained inactive, and by 1926 Cattell resigned as president. The corporation at that point was reorganized. Thus, Terman's involvement in business application was more one of spirit than any concrete accomplishment.

Terman's interest in delinquency had begun in the mid-1910s, when he had supervised the doctoral research of J. Harold Williams. At that time, he had also become acquainted with Fred C. Nelles, the superintendent of the Whittier State School, an institution for juvenile delinquents in southern California.[155] Nelles was instrumental in establishing the Bureau of Juvenile Research at the Whittier School in 1915, and Williams became the bureau's first director. The following year, Nelles and Williams, with Terman's support, founded the *Journal of Delinquency*.[156] In various prewar reports, based on surveys at Whittier, Terman and Williams argued for the close association between innate mental deficiency and delinquency.[157]

However, after the war Terman shifted his position about the causes of delinquency. While not abandoning the role of mental deficiency, he admitted that "the early mental test studies of both juvenile and adult offenders led to an overestimate of the proportion who were feebleminded."[158] Certain emotional and personality traits appeared to have an association with delinquent tendencies, and, unlike the case of intelligence, these traits tended to be the result of early environmental experiences. Citing John B. Watson's conditioning studies of anger and fear, Terman concluded that any personality traits linked with delinquency would become fixed relatively early in life, due primarily to "unfortunate" training in the home. The identification of personality traits related to delinquent tendencies emerged from two doctoral studies competed in 1923. The studies were carried out under Terman's supervision by Vernon M. Cady and A. S. Raubenheimer.[159] Cady found that measures of trustworthiness, honesty, modesty, moral judgment, and emotional stability differentiated between two groups of preadolescent boys—those who were judged by their teachers to be incorrigible in school versus those who were judged to be well adjusted to school requirements. The latter group had the positive character traits. Similar results were obtained by Raubenheimer in his study.

Terman was not very explicit in accounting for his conceptual shift in the area of delinquency.[160] He alluded to the criticisms of the earlier

research by himself and others that argued for the association of delinquency with mental deficiency and agreed with those critics who
pointed to environmental factors and nonintellectual traits as more
promising research directions. Beginning with the work of William
Healy and Augusta Bronner in the mid-teens, there had been mounting criticism of the mental deficiency-hereditarian view of delinquency.[161] One of Terman's own graduate students, Franklin S. Fearing, criticized his professor' hereditarian views on delinquency.[162] While
Terman did accept these criticisms by the early 1920s, his readiness to
do so appears to be connected with his involvement in the gifted study.
One of his goals in studying gifted children was to demonstrate that
they were "well-rounded" and had better-than-average character traits.
He therefore was interested in measuring such traits, and the fact that
Watsonian behaviorism suggested an environmental basis for the development of emotional characteristics helped to provide a place for
"nurture" in the psychology of individual differences. In other words,
it would seem that finding a place for environmental factors in his own
specialty in psychology provided Terman with more credibility. He
would not be judged as a hereditarian extremist. Thus, while intelligence was primarily tied to heredity, personality (nonintellectual traits)
was primarily the result of early environmental influences. Studying
gifted children provided Terman with the opportunity to look at both
intelligence and personality, as well as heredity and environment.
Terman's interest in delinquency per se waned after the early 1920s,
but by 1930 he was interested in other personality-related areas, most
notably masculinity-femininity and sexual adjustment.

With his interest in having primary and secondary schools adopt
mental tests and achievement tests, it seemed natural for Terman to be
interested in the application of testing to higher education. In February
1921, Terman gave an address before a group of Stanford faculty on
the use of intelligence tests in colleges and universities.[163] He reported
findings in other institutions and argued for the adoption of intelligence tests at Stanford, pointing out that Stanford students disquali-
fied for poor scholarship were costing the university, before disqualifi-
cation, about twelve percent of the annual budget for instructional
purposes.

In a related paper, he reported a case study of an "intellectually inferior" Stanford student, identified as "K," with a Stanford-Binet mental age of twelve and a half.[164] While K's "stupidity" was not extreme (Terman judged him to be "intellectually gifted" when compared to the "average American Negro"), his level of intellect was not suited for a college curriculum. Even with Terman's guidance about methods of study and notetaking, K failed all of his courses in his first term and was consequently dismissed from the university. The implication of this case study was that college selection based on intelligence tests would increase the efficiency of institutions of higher education, avoid the heartaches of those who were not college material, and appropriately accept those within the top ten percent of intellectual endowment who had the potential to be college graduates.

Largely through Terman's efforts, Stanford instituted a testing program for all new undergraduate students, commencing with the 1921–22 academic year.[165] The examination selected was the Thorndike Intelligence Examination for High School Graduates. The Thorndike test was given on an experimental basis for two years. Terman chaired the committee evaluating the testing results. After the two-year trial period, the committee recommended that the testing continue to be a requirement and that candidates falling below a minimum cutoff score be denied university acceptance. The committee's recommendation was accepted, and in a follow-up report it was demonstrated how the quality of Stanford undergraduates had been improved. By 1925 Karl M. Cowdery, one of Terman's former graduate students and coauthor of the follow-up report, was appointed director of personnel research. Terman and Cowdery presented a research program that included a continued evaluation of the entrance examination, as well as the inauguration of special aptitude tests, the diagnosis of vocational interests, and future hopes to institute personality testing. In essence, Terman had anticipated what has become common practice in university personnel programs.[166]

Terman's contribution to professional affairs in psychology grew out of his army testing experience. In December 1917 he was appointed to a newly created committee of the American Psychological Association (APA)—the Committee on Qualifications for Psychological Examiners and Other Psychological Experts.[167] The committee made several recommendations, which were subsequently adopted, regarding the certification of psychological examiners and other psychological experts. In addition, minimum requirements for approved applicants were spelled out, which included a Ph.D. in psychology, as well as an apprenticeship in practical work and expertise in such areas as evaluating intelligence, assessing vocational skills, and recognizing indications of abnormal mental conditions. In a related event, Terman was elected to charter membership in 1917 to the American Association of Clinical Psychologists (AACP). This group of some fifty members was formed to establish professional standards in clinical psychology.[168] In general, Terman played a significant role in attempts to establish professional qualifications for psychological practitioners.[169]

Throughout the postwar period, Terman was deeply committed to the advancement of applied psychology. As a result, he was interested in demonstrating the growth of this subfield within the discipline. In 1921 he published a short paper on the status of applied psychology in the United States.[170] The paper was in response to an earlier report by Boring, who was secretary of the APA at the time, which listed the percentage breakdown of APA members in the various areas of research specialization.[171] Boring had divided applied psychology into a number of separate categories, giving the impression of a fragmented and narrow subspecialty.[172] Boring, who had trained under Titchener, could thus demonstrate the primacy of "pure" as opposed to "applied" psychology. Terman attempted to correct this impression by combining all of the applied areas. In doing so, he came up with the following breakdown: 51.5 percent in applied psychology versus 48.5 percent in pure psychology. Thus, he concluded that somewhat over half of the psychological research being carried out by APA members fell in one or another of the fields of applied psychology. He predicted that since applied research had chiefly emerged within the last decade (the 1910s), the trend would continue. Terman opined that this was a healthy trend. "One has only to recall how such sciences as physiology, bacteriology, chemistry, physics, and biology have been stimulated by human needs to realize that a science stands to gain rather than lose, even as pure science, when it enters the lists in the service of mankind. It is unlikely that psychology will prove an exception to the rule."[173]

Professional Recognition

In 1922, only five years after he became a member of the APA, Terman was elected as president of the organization for the 1923 year. In the fall of that year, he began to prepare his presidential address for the annual December meeting to be held in Madison, Wisconsin. Incorporated within his speech, entitled "The Mental Test as a Psychological Method," were the results of a brief questionnaire sent out to twenty-two APA members.[174] The questionnaire contained three questions. The first read: "What are the essential characteristics of a mental test? By this is meant what (if anything) distinguishes it from any other psychological experiment?"[175] The second question dealt with the contributions of the test method, and the third was a rating scale of the "potential value for psychological science" of the test method, as defined by the respondent in the first question.

Terman's sample was selected from two groups of psychologists: the eleven surviving presidents of the association since 1910 (which included Thorndike, Watson, Yerkes, and Scott) and eleven individuals chosen because of their contributions to "test psychology." The latter list was made up of Bingham, Boring, Harold Burtt, Cattell, Goddard, Kelley, Kuhlmann, Rudolf Pinter, L. L. Thurstone, Wells, and Whipple. Terman received responses from each person he had solicited. He chose the two groups so that he could compare psychologists "interested" or committed to the test method with a "random" group (through some in this latter group, such as Yerkes, Thorndike, and Scott, had expertise in testing). Terman reported that six of his respondents had pointed out "the essential methodological identity of the test and the experiment"[176]—a view that Terman supported. He went on to state: "I wish to show that psychologists have too often conceived of the mental test as a mere practical device; that it has a large value as an instrument of research; and that its kinship to other psychological methods is much closer than either the average tester or the average laboratory worker appears to assume."[177]

Terman cited various examples in the history of psychology to support his case, noting that such testing pioneers as Binet, Cattell, and Thorndike were as interested in theoretical as in practical considerations. He also stressed that the mental test developed as a fairly

integral part of experimental psychology and added that "the psychological test is a method of sampling mental processes or mental behavior, and so, in a sense, is any method of psychological experiment."[178]
In summing up, he declared: "I think we may conclude that the
attempt to distinguish between the method of tests and the method of
experiment is not warranted either on logical or historical grounds.
The mental test is part and parcel of experimental psychology."[179]
Moreover, as a part of experimental psychology, testing was throwing
light on new areas of research and application; and as such "it has
broadened and intensified our incentives to research, enlarged the
public support of our science, and attracted new hosts of workers to
the psychological vineyard."[180]

To what extent such sentiments convinced those in Terman's audience who were critical of the testing movement and wary of applied
psychology is difficult to determine. Testing and experimental psychology continued to go their separate ways.[181] There was even some
criticism from among his group of testing experts. For example, Yerkes
opined that mental testing had higher technical than scientific value.[182]
He also felt less inclined to commit himself to brief and seemingly
dogmatic statements about testing in view of the recent experiences
with Lippmann and other testing critics.[183] Thurstone expressed his
view that many, though not all, mental testers had poor scientific
training and overstated the values of testing.[184] While Terman may not
have won over many converts, his APA presidency was an acknowl-
edgment of his pioneering contributions to testing. He seized the
opportunity to legitimize the field as an integral part of the scientific
base of psychology. At the same time, his view of legitimate science
was that it also had to be in the "service of mankind." The mental test
as a psychological method was both "pure" and "applied."

The postwar period was an especially productive and rewarding
time for Terman. He rose from relative professional obscurity to a
position of high visibility and leadership. Developments at Stanford
during this period also helped propel him to a leadership role. When
he first came back after the war he was somewhat disappointed with
the lack of financial support the university could provide for his research.[185] He became very interested in the possibility of a new position that was being created at Yale through Gesell's efforts. However,

as events unfolded, Yale could not meet Terman's requirements for research support, and the matter was not pursued.[186] Other offers were also considered, but by the spring of 1920 Terman wrote Yerkes that he was hopeful that developments at Stanford would make it worthwhile for him to stay.[187] In 1921 Terman received the Commonwealth Fund grant for his study of the gifted, so that he finally had the needed financial support for his research. The following year he was given the opportunity to assume a leadership role at Stanford. Frank Angell, the chairman of the psychology department, was retiring and Terman was appointed to succeed him.

By 1923 Terman had clearly made his mark on the psychology scene. He would now be entering a new career phase. He had the challenge of shaping the psychology department at Stanford, and, having launched his pet project of studying gifted children, he could now focus on the research that would become the major priority for the remainder of his career.

CHAPTER 8

Midcareer
(1923-1932)

The opportunity opened to me when I was appointed executive head of the department in 1922 was one of the rarest in the history of psychology in America. . . . Moreover the field was clear for the new regime inherited only Dr. Coover and was free to move in any direction. There was no local tradition in regard to graduate work because practically none had ever been done in the department. During the preceding history of thirty years there had been only one Ph.D. graduate and three or four M.A. graduates.[1]

Psychology at Stanford in the pre-Terman era could best be characterized as narrow and undistinguished. The department was established in 1892, one year after the university had opened. Frank Angell, who had received his doctorate under Wundt, was appointed department head.[2] Angell did not share his mentor's comprehensive perspective of psychology as both an experimental and a social science. For Angell, psychology was nothing more than experimental, and even his interests within this restricted sphere were narrowly focused in the area of psychophysics. As a result of such orthodoxy, most of the courses offered during Angell's regime were in experimental psychology. The department also suffered because Angell was not a very productive researcher, nor did he have any particular interest in encouraging graduate students to work in the department. His reputation at Stanford was as a gifted teacher and "inspirer of students."

Psychology was a one-person department until 1899, when Lillien Martin was appointed. The selection of a woman for a faculty position at a coeducational institution was quite extraordinary at the turn of the century. However, Stanford was very progressive in this regard. Martin's training and interests were quite similar to those of Angell.[3] Although she never completed her doctoral studies, Martin had spent several years in Germany studying experimental psychology, and her specialty was psychophysics. Martin's tenure in the department ended in 1916 when she reached retirement age. Like Angell, she was more of a teacher than a scholar. However, she was also interested in applied psychology, and to a limited degree broadened the scope of course offerings. After her retirement she worked as a clinical psychologist.

During Angell's thirty-year regime, the department underwent little change. One significant development did occur in 1911. Leland Stanford's youngest brother, Thomas Welton Stanford, presented the university with a gift of $50,000 to support a fellowship in psychical research.[4] The following year, the first Psychical Research Fellowship was awarded to J. E. Coover, who had just completed his Ph.D. in psychology at Stanford. Coover was the one doctorate produced by the department during the Angell years. Other fellows were eventually appointed for one- or two-year periods, but Coover remained a Stanford Psychical Research Fellow until his retirement in 1937. In 1914 he was also given a faculty appointment in psychology. Thus, the area of psychical research was added to the department's course offerings.

In 1918, at Thomas Welton Stanford's death, a second gift was added to the psychical research fund. This was a sum of somewhat over $500,000, and it bode well for the future of psychology at Stanford. It appears that in 1914 President Jordan had persuaded T. W. Stanford to include the phrase "psychological science" in his will.[5] Ray Lyman Wilbur, the university's third president (as of 1915), saw the great potential of the bequest for rescuing the psychology department from mediocrity. With only a few years left in Angell's headship, Wilbur began to take an active role in searching for a replacement as well as adding new faculty.

Developing a Successful Psychology Department

Wilbur relied to a large extent on Cubberley's judgment regarding the future of the psychology department. With Terman's accomplishments in educational psychology, it seemed natural for Wilbur to assume that there would be some subsequent cooperative effort between psychology and education. It was the lack of such cooperation in the past that had been a sore point for both Cubberley and Terman. A case in point was the situation of Maud A. Merrill. As Cubberley pointed out to Wilbur, Merrill had come to Stanford in the fall of 1919 hoping to obtain a Ph.D. in psychology, with the plan of doing much of her work with Terman.[6] She was an assistant to Kuhlmann at the Fairbault, Minnesota, State Home for the Feeble Minded. Before coming to Stanford, she had spelled out her plans in a letter to Angell. According to Cubberley, Angell answered her in a single sentence in which he asked why she wanted to travel so far when there were so many other universities close by. Kuhlmann was apparently so dismayed by this response that he sent a copy of the letter to Terman. Cubberley cited it as an example of the "type of cooperation" psychology had given education for "twenty years."

Merrill did attend Stanford, but she did all of her work with Terman in education, receiving a master's degree in 1920. Much to Cubberley's consternation, Angell then appointed her to an instructorship in psychology in which she taught courses that duplicated those in education. As far as Cubberley was concerned, this was only one instance of the trend of duplication that psychology was engaging in. He went on to suggest that once Angell retired in two years, Stanford should follow the lead of several other universities where psychology had been administratively combined with education. In the meantime, Cubberley recommended that Wilbur inform the psychology department that no new faculty appointments would be forthcoming. Further, he was instructed to point out that all developments in applied psychology would be placed under Terman's direction.

Wilbur also consulted with Angell about the future of the psychology department. Angell's recommendation was that the Thomas Welton Stanford fund be used to expand the department in the area of abnormal psychology or "pathopsychology."[7] Angell distinguished this area from applied psychology and pointed out that the application of psychology to education was adequately handled by Stanford's education department. However, he did profess some misgivings about the extent to which that department dealt with the "theoretical foundation" of testing. In essence, Angell did not perceive that by expanding into abnormal psychology the psychology department was in any way trespassing on the education department's territory. Cubberley, to the contrary, perceived such a trend as "duplicating" his own department's efforts.

From 1920 to 1922, Wilbur diplomatically proceeded to obtain independent proposals and recommendations from each of the two camps. When it came time to consider new faculty appointments for psychology, which would begin in the 1922–23 year, each group forwarded their assessments and rankings of prospective candidates. The two sides saw things very differently in this regard. For example, Angell and Coover were drawn to more established and older candidates, while Cubberley and Terman pushed for young and promising prospects. Furthermore, they differed on whose work was at the core of psychology. Two cases illustrate these differences. Angell and Coover supported Shepherd I. Franz, a forty-seven-year-old former APA president and head of the research laboratories at St. Elizabeth's "Hospital for the Insane" in Washington, D.C.[8] Terman's assessment was that Franz's field was primarily neurology, not psychology, and that he was mediocre in general intellectual caliber, teaching ability, and personality.[9] Opposing views also surrounded the consideration of K. S. Lashley, a thirty-one-year-old assistant professor at the University of Minnesota, who had worked with Watson at Johns Hopkins. According to Angell, Lashley's work was more biological than psychological because he dealt almost exclusively with animal behavior.[10] In contrast, Terman referred to Lashley as "the most promising young man in the field of neuro-psychology."[11]

Predictive of which camp Wilbur was leaning toward, Cubberley, on a trip to the East Coast in February and March of 1922, reported back to Wilbur on his interviews with prospective faculty appointments as well as on his meeting with his former teacher, Edward L. Thorndike.[12] The latter meeting was especially fruitful, as Cubberley asked Thorndike to rate both the candidates for new faculty appointments and department head. In Cubberley's view, Thorndike was the best person to ask, for he knew "the men of the country" and he had "excellent judgment."[13] As Cubberley expected, Thorndike chose Terman as his first choice for department head because he considered him to be one of the "most promising younger men in psychology," and he was applied. Cubberley had heard Thorndike repeatedly say that "psychology must be tied up with its applications." In his assessment of Terman (as reported by Cubberley), Thorndike also cited the candidate's executive qualities, sound scholarship, charming personality, and cooperative ability. Thorndike's other choices for the headship were (in order) Dodge, Boring, Walter R. Miles, and Walter B. Pillsbury.

With respect to new faculty positions in the area of experimental psychology, Cubberley, after his consultation with Thorndike, chose the following three in the order listed: Arthur I. Gates, Boring, and Miles.[14] Gates, who was at Teachers College, was also highly regarded by Terman. However, as Thorndike had predicted, Gates was not available. Negotiations then began in earnest with Boring. After the war, Boring had become professor of experimental psychology at Clark University.[15] Hall retired as president of Clark in 1920 and was succeeded by Wallace W. Atwood, a geographer, who set out to displace the institution's focus on psychology with his own discipline of geography. By 1922 Boring was seriously considering other academic offers.

Terman and Boring had continued their friendship after their army association, and Terman had helped Boring get his appointment as secretary of the APA after the war.[16] In 1921 Terman was instrumental in having Boring come to Stanford to teach during the summer quarter. In the same year, Terman, at President Wilbur's request, had also written to Thorndike, Watson, Robert S. Woodworth, and E. C. Sanford soliciting their recommendations for the "best young men in psychology."[17] Boring headed the list. Terman's own assessment of Boring read: "personality and character splendid, keen, a gifted teacher, and a hard worker."[18] Terman, however, added the reservation that Boring may have been "too much wedded to introspective and brass-instrument psychology"[19]—a reference to his Titchenerian roots. But even this qualification was hedged because Terman pointed out that Boring's army experience had "broadened" him.

Cubberley's opinion of Boring was generally positive.[20] However, he did voice concern that Boring would want to "run the place in time" and would have little sympathy with any connection between educa-

tion and psychology. Based on the feedback from Terman and Cubberley, Wilbur decided to make an offer to Boring.[21] At a meeting in
Boston, Wilbur asked Boring to write up a prospectus about the kind
of psychology laboratory he envisioned for Stanford. Boring responded with an eight-page typed letter setting out twenty-four "suggestions," which included financial conditions, space requirements,
curriculum recommendations, faculty appointments, and his own duties as the "executive head of the laboratory." It seemed as though
Cubberley's concerns about Boring taking over were well founded.
When Terman received a copy of Boring's letter, he expressed his
"disappointment" to Wilbur. "He wants everything in sight and is too
much concerned about getting it all spiked down."[22] Terman added
that Boring's demand for complete control over the introductory psychology course would "head everything toward Titchenerian psychology, [something] I could not agree to." Furthermore, Terman thought
Boring's "conditions" would make his own position as executive head
"entirely nominal." Terman concluded by urging Wilbur to try and
appoint Miles rather than Boring.

Why did Boring make such excessive demands to the point of threatening the position of his good friend and supporter, Terman? The
answer seems to lie in Boring's own concerns that applied psychology
was taking over the discipline at the expense of experimental psychology.[23] In fact, in a 1921 published correction to Boring's APA statistics, Terman argued that more and more psychologists were turning
to applied psychology.[24] Boring may therefore have felt that he had to
be especially sure of his control over experimental psychology in a
department headed by Terman. In a follow-up letter, Boring admitted
to Wilbur that his prospectus was guided by the notion that experimental psychology was to have a position of importance in the new
department.[25] Boring did not receive any assurances from Wilbur that
his suggestions for the laboratory would be favorably agreed to. He
therefore wired Wilbur that he could not make a decision about the
Stanford offer until the matter was clarified.[26] He added that his
ultimate decision would depend on what the Stanford offer was in
comparison with other offers. Wilbur seized upon Boring's indecision,
offering his interpretation that Boring was no longer interested in
Stanford and only wanted to compare the offer with other opportuni-

ties.[27] Wilbur was obviously sympathetic to Terman's and Cubberley's concerns. As it turned out, Boring also had an offer to head up the psychology laboratory at Harvard—an offer that he accepted.[28] In concluding his affairs with Stanford, Boring thanked Wilbur for having been considered for the position and expressed his belief that the psychology department under Terman's leadership might easily become the strongest department in the country.[29] Despite the strains Terman experienced in the negotiations with Boring, their friendship survived and probably prospered more than it would have had they been competitors in the same academic department.

With the Boring negotiations at an end, Wilbur now set about to make an offer to Miles. Miles was trained in experimental psychology at the University of Iowa, where he worked under Carl E. Seashore and received his Ph.D. in 1913.[30] The following year, Miles obtained a position at the Carnegie Nutrition Laboratory in Boston, where over the course of the next eight years he was engaged in alcohol-nutritional research. When Cubberley had met Miles in March 1922, he wrote back to Wilbur that he was not very impressed.[31] He found Miles to be quiet, very sober, wholly devoid of any sense of humor, and a "fairly capable and accurate plodder." Nevertheless, Cubberley felt that he was "much better than he seemed," which apparently suggested that Miles's scholarly qualities were strong enough and outweighed his flat personality. When Wilbur met Miles in Boston, he was sufficiently impressed to make him an offer. Miles accepted it.[32] Indeed, Miles was happy to return to an academic setting, which, according to Wilbur, sounded very promising. Furthermore, Miles was very pleased to obtain such a position through no solicitation on his own part. When Miles officially accepted, Wilbur felt it necessary to point out that Miles's laboratory was only one of the laboratories in the psychology department (Coover's psychic research lab was mentioned as another).[33] Based on the experience with Boring, Wilbur had learned to spell out territories in advance.

There remained a second experimental psychology position to be filled. Lashley, from the University of Minnesota, had been in the running for one of the two positions, and Terman had enthusiastically recommended him to Wilbur.[34] However, Wilbur had visited Minnesota and learned from various people there that Lashley was "a queer

duck and a long hair." This impression was consistent with Thorndike's estimate, as communicated by Cubberley, that Lashley was a
very "little man" physically, about "as big as a pint of peanuts," and
was "effeminate looking" and often affected a monocle.[35] Thorndike,
however, was impressed by Lashley's intellect. Apparently, as far as
Wilbur was concerned, Lashley's personal eccentricities outweighed
his intellect, and Terman proceeded to make inquiries about other
potential candidates. The man Terman set his sights on was Calvin P.
Stone, who had trained under Lashley at Minnesota.[36] Both Lashley
and Haggerty (who was also at Minnesota) highly recommended Stone,
with Haggerty pointing out that Stone had a high army Alpha test
score.[37] When Terman met Stone in Chicago in April, he was favorably impressed, pointing out that Stone, while perhaps not brilliant,
was "solid and substantial" with a good personality.[38] Stone's Ph.D.
thesis was on the sex behavior of the white rat, and animal behavior
was the area Stone concentrated on when he came to Stanford.

On 27 May 1922, Terman received the official word from President
Wilbur—the previous day the board of trustees had approved his
appointment as executive head of the Department of Psychology.[39]
This was an exciting opportunity for Terman,[40] though not unex-
pected. Since 1920 he had worked closely with Wilbur and Cubberley
in making recommendations for the psychology department, once Angell retired. The previous year, he had entertained thoughts about
leaving Stanford because of the limited research support he was receiving.[41] However, by the spring of 1920, he confided to Yerkes that he
was very hopeful that "developments" at Stanford would make it
worthwhile for him to stay.[42]

Wilbur also communicated with Angell on the day that he informed
Terman of his new appointment.[43] Wilber pointed out that the appointments of Miles and Stone would insure the continuance of "fundamental work" in psychology, and he added that the two new faculty
appointments, together with Terman as head, would add strength to a
department already enhanced by the Thomas Welton Stanford funds.
Angell was granted the use of a laboratory room and made a professor
emeritus. Whether he used this research space during his retirement
years is not clear. It is likely that he devoted more of his time to
following and supporting amateur sports on campus. Angell had acted

as director of university sports for more than twenty years and was known as a "sympathetic friend to generations of Stanford athletes."[44] Angell Field, Stanford's track and field stadium, was named in his honor.

When Terman took over as head of psychology in the fall of 1922, his faculty consisted of Miles (professor), Coover (associate professor and research fellow in psychic phenomena), Stone (assistant professor), and two instructors—Maud A. Merrill, his M.A. student who then obtained her Ph.D. with him in 1923, and Gertrude M. Trace, who like Merrill had been appointed by Angell.[45] Merrill went on to become a senior faculty member and a research collaborator with Terman on the revision of the Stanford-Binet in the 1930s. Trace was dropped from the department in 1923 (interestingly enough, this was one of Boring's recommendations). The only Angell holdover who Terman had no power to dismiss was Coover. Coover, until his retirement in 1937, remained an irritant for Terman.[46] As a psychic research fellow, Coover's teaching duties were limited. What teaching he did carry out was mainly in the area of psychic research, hardly an example of mainstream psychology.[47] Furthermore, Coover published little. Thus, he occupied a faculty position that could have been filled by a productive scholar.

During the 1922–23 academic year—Terman's first as department head—he sought further faculty appointments. In the area of vocational and industrial psychology, Terman was able to bring in Edward K. Strong, who started in 1923.[48] Terman had met Strong during his army years, and Strong had built up an excellent reputation in his field during the postwar years when he taught at Carnegie Tech in Pittsburgh. When the Graduate School of Business was established at Stanford in 1925, Strong received a joint appointment. Eventually, most of his time was devoted to the business school. He is best known for the development of the Strong Vocational Interest Blank, which was first published in 1927.

In 1923 Terman was also able to add Truman Kelley, his colleague from education, who thus held a joint appointment in both departments. Kelley had already established himself as a leader in the application of statistical methods to psychology. Kelley left in 1930 for a position at the Harvard School of Education. His successor in the department was Quinn McNemar, who was first appointed as an instructor in 1931. He completed his Ph.D. under Terman in 1932 and, after a year's post-doctoral fellowship in New York with the Social Science Research Council, returned to the department as a permanent faculty member. McNemar became a leading figure in psychological statistics; like Kelley, he served as a statistical consultant for Terman's testing research. Another faculty addition was Paul Farnsworth, who came in 1925. His research and teaching interests were in experimental esthetics and social psychology. The only other change among the regular faculty appointments during Terman's twenty-year tenure as head was the appointment of Ernest R. Hilgard in 1933. Hilgard, who was an instructor at Yale, replaced Miles who had taken a position at Yale the year before.

As head, Terman was also able to appoint some visiting professors for one quarter or for an academic year. Among these visitors were several European psychologists, many of whom were eager to obtain American academic positions. The most notable visitor was Kurt Lewin in 1932–33.[49] Lewin was still formally a faculty member at the University of Berlin, though with the subsequent Nazi takeover he did not return to his post. Initially, Terman was not especially well disposed to the kind of German psychology Lewin represented—a psychology that was strong on theory rather than quantitative methods. He shared these sentiments with Boring, who was also not a fan of the German school of Gestalt psychology. In 1927 Kurt Koffka, one of the leaders of the Gestalt movement, had presented a series of lectures at Stanford. Terman wrote to Boring that he was not impressed, and added: "Koffka I should want to watch for about five years yet and see whether he goes in for scientific psychology or Gestalt propaganda."[50] In a reference to another Gestaltist, Wolfgang Köhler, Boring admitted that he had a "mistrust" of German science.[51] Nevertheless, as political changes were taking place in Germany, Boring and Terman shared their concerns about the plight of German academics like Lewin.[52] In fact, Boring was impressed with Lewin and recommended him to Terman. After Lewin's stay at Stanford, Terman wrote back that Lewin's "work commanded the respect of our students, both graduate and undergraduate, and of our department faculty."[53] Terman was disappointed that it was not possible to keep Lewin on at Stanford.

There was an interesting aside to Terman's efforts in bringing Lewin to Stanford. In order to arrange for the visiting appointment, Terman felt that he had to know about Lewin's personal background, especially the delicate matter of whether Lewin might be Jewish. Therefore, he wrote to Boring and asked "whether Lewin is a Jew. It would not necessarily be fatal to his appointment here if he were, but it would be best for me to know the facts if I were recommending him. The few Jews we have on our Stanford faculty have no trace whatever of the objectionable traits usually attributed to Jews, and against this kind I haven't the slightest prejudice in the world."[54] After some inquiries, Boring reported back to Terman that Lewin was a Jew.[55] As events developed, Terman thought highly of Lewin and tried—unsuccessfully—to obtain a permanent American academic appointment for him.[56] Terman's comments to Boring about Jews reflected his two-sided attitude toward this minority group. On the one hand, he had positive feelings about Jews because of their intellectual accomplishments and was impressed with the proportion of Jewish children in his gifted sample. He was also sensitive to the discrimination and prejudice Jewish academics faced, especially since one of his graduate students, Samuel C. Kohs, had been forced to give up an academic career because of the frustrations he faced as a Jewish instructor in the 1920s. Kohs reported that Terman was very disturbed about anti-Semitism and was completely free of such a "virus."[57] However, it appears that Terman was not entirely free of some prejudice, essentially in the form of commonly held beliefs. Thus, he seems to have accepted the notion that Jewish people could be prone to certain "objectionable" traits. An illustration of this is that on the vocabulary test of the Stanford-Binet "Jewish" was listed as one of the correct responses for the word "shrewd." By the 1950s, however, he regretted having included this association.[58] In general, Terman was not anti-Semitic. By the 1950s (as in the case of his attitudes toward blacks), he regretted the ethnocentric statements he had made earlier in his career.

In addition to faculty recruitment, Terman as department head was active in trying to generate financial support for research. In the late twenties and early thirties, he concentrated on two research areas that would involve collaborative efforts by faculty in the department. These were child development and aging (the latter was referred to as "later maturity"). With respect to child development, he hoped to obtain support from the Laura Spellman Rockefeller Memorial Fund, the agency that had funded several child research centers at a number of universities, including Iowa, Berkeley, and Teachers College.[59] When this attempt failed, he proceeded to try and obtain private funding for a "Bureau of Human Development Research." Proposals were drawn up and submitted through the Stanford president's office, but these attempts did not prove to be successful.[60] Among the specific research projects included were several that Terman and his students were engaged in, such as the gifted study and the relative influence of nature and nurture. However, other research projects involving other faculty members were also spelled out, including musical abilities (Farnsworth), tests of occupational and other interests (Strong), and the development of psychomotor functions (Miles).

Terman had more success in obtaining funds for work in the area of later maturity. In collaboration with Miles, he drew up a proposal in 1928 aimed at establishing a well-endowed research center at Stanford.[61] The research expertise of most of the department members (Coover was the only one not mentioned) was indicated as relevant to the area of later maturity. This proposal led to a Carnegie Corporation grant of $10,000 in 1929, which was renewed two years later.[62] These grants enabled Miles and his graduate students to carry out several studies on developmental changes in adulthood. This work was discontinued at Stanford when Miles left for Yale in 1932.

Because of his position as department head, Terman also became influential in university affairs. Two areas that particularly interested him during the 1920s were the "citizenship course" and superior students. During the early 1920s, Stanford had moved from an educational philosophy of freedom of choice to one of required basic courses. One of these was entitled "Problems of Citizenship" and was instituted in 1923. The course was required of all first-year students and was designed "to present the salient features" of contemporary American society.[63] The course was interdisciplinary, and one of the lectures was given by Terman, under the heading "Intelligence and Democracy." Among the topics covered were intelligence testing, the "heredity of mental ability," racial differences in intelligence, and "intelligence as a qualification for citizenship." The latter topic was further divided into the following subtopics: "justifiable limitations of franchise," "representative versus direct forms of government," and "intellectual leadership in a democracy." Readings included works by Galton and Goddard, plus Carl Brigham's monograph on racial differences in intelligence (based on the army testing) and William McDougall's *Is America Safe for Democracy?*, a monograph highly supportive of eugenics policies. This lecture reflected Terman's vision of a hierarchical society based on native ability that would be led by those at the upper end of the IQ distribution, with justifiable franchise limitations for those at the lower end.[64]

Terman had chaired a committee that recommended an independent study plan in the junior and senior years for superior students at Stanford. This plan was adopted and took effect in 1925–26.[65] Terman also hoped that Stanford would become a specialized institution for gifted students. He shared these thoughts with Caspar W. Hodgson, the World Book publisher who was a Stanford alumnus and friend of President Wilbur. In 1926 Terman predicted that Stanford would soon become a strictly upper-division (junior and senior years), graduate-level university. He believed that Stanford would be able to institute a highly restrictive admissions policy that would result in the admission of only intellectually superior students.[66] While Hodgson did not share Terman's idea of dropping the lower division, he fully supported the notion of making Stanford into a university for the gifted that would "train leaders for a democracy."[67] Furthermore, Hodgson promised to use his influence on Wilbur to bring about such a policy. While entrance requirements based on ability were tightened up during the 1920s and 1930s (with Terman helping to establish a testing program), the lower division was not eliminated, and Stanford was not officially designated as an institution for intellectually gifted students.[68]

Following up the Gifted

In 1927 Terman received a grant of $10,800 from the Commonwealth Fund to carry out his planned follow-up of the intellectually gifted children he had begun to study six years earlier.[69] Terman also received some assistance from the Thomas Welton Stanford Fund, as well as a private donation of about $2,500 from Max Rosenberg, a San

Francisco businessman. He initially had some difficulties in securing funds for his follow-up, and it was Yerkes's suggestion that he contact Rosenberg.[70] During 1927–28, three field assistants retested the children and interviewed parents and teachers. Helen Marshall, who had been one of the assistants on the initial study, collected the data in San Francisco. She was helped in the Bay Area by Melita H. Oden, a Stanford B.A. in psychology who had had considerable experience in clinical psychology and social work. The Los Angeles area was covered by Alice M. Leahy, one of Florence Goodenough's students at the University of Minnesota. Two of Terman's doctoral students, Barbara S. Burks and Dortha W. Jensen, rounded out the research staff. Burks was the senior assistant with primary responsibility in the data analysis and the write-up of the testing results. Jensen reported on her study evaluating the literary productions of a small subsample of the gifted children.

For the most part, the same kinds of tests and ratings that were used in the original data collection were repeated. The follow-up sample consisted of the majority (91.7 percent) of the main experimental group of the initial study.[71] The major finding of the follow-up was that for the group as a whole the composite picture "did not greatly change" over the six-year interval.[72] The intellectually gifted children (some now adolescents and college students) continued to show high academic achievement, varied interests, good personality adjustment, and better-than-average health and physique. The results thus supported Terman's expectations about "the promise of youth" within a group of gifted children.

There were also some new findings of note, among which were the results of a specially constructed measure of "masculinity-femininity."[73] This was another example of Terman's attempt to demonstrate that the gifted were well adjusted in nonintellectual areas of functioning—in this instance, appropriate gender indentification. In the original survey, masculine and feminine interests were derived from questionnaire preferences regarding play activities, games, and amusements. Among the gifted sample, a high masculinity index reflected preferences for activities that were frequently elected by boys in the control group and infrequently by girls; the femininity index was based on similar criteria. The 1921–22 results showed that the gifted sample was similar in gender orientation to the control sample. Terman had secured a National Research Council grant in 1925 to investigate sex differences in nonintellectual traits. With the help of Catharine Cox Miles (who had married Walter Miles in 1927), a masculinity-femininity (M-F) test was devised and ready for use in the 1927–28 survey. This multiple-choice test consisted of a variety of items. For example, there were word-associations consisting of a stimulus word and four response choices from which the subject had to choose one. Based on a normative sample of high-school and college students, the response words were categorized as masculine or feminine. An illustration of this type of item was the stimulus world "jealous." If the subject chose "lover" or "women," he or she received a masculine score; if "angry" or "green" were chosen, the subject received a feminine score. Another type of item dealt with general information—for example, "eggs are best for us when" followed by four responses. The masculine responses were "fried" and "hard-boiled"; the feminine responses were "deviled" and "soft-boiled." Other types of items included preferences for books, objects, and activities, and responses to situations that might arouse emotions, such as anger or fear.[74]

The results showed that gifted girls as a group were significantly more "masculine" then the normative sample of female students. On the other hand, gifted boys were generally similar to the male-student norms. Terman and his coauthors suggested that the "masculine" tendency demonstrated by the gifted girls was a desirable deviation from the norm, citing the historical examples of Queen Elizabeth (the First) and George Sand. They also pointed out that these results lent some truth to Cesare Lombroso's opinion that "there are no women of genius; the women of genius are all men."[75] Yet the authors did express some concern about the future adjustment of gifted subjects who showed extreme gender inversion, such as "Roberta," who liked to dress up in a boy-scout outfit and a naval-officer"s uniform and "Renwick," a boy organist who played with dolls and amused himself by designing feminine garments and acting out feminine operatic roles[76] In the 1930s in his monograph on masculinity-femininity, Terman would have much more to say about the dangers of extreme cross-gender identification.

The question of gender also appeared in the reported finding of the sex ratio among the gifted. In the first volume of the monograph series, it was stated that there was a higher proportion of boys and that this sex difference was even more noticeable at the high-school level. According to Terman and his coauthors, the follow-up study indicated that the larger excess of boys, at least at the upper age levels, was due to the fact that "gifted girls do not maintain their intellectual superiority in adolescence as well as boys do."[77] To account for this, it was suggested that boys have a somewhat greater variability in IQ scores and that girls have an "earlier cessation of mental growth." No mention was made of the social pressures that gifted female adolescents might be subject to if they continued to excel intellectually. On this point, Leta S. Hollingworth, another major investigator of intellectually superior children, was highly sensitive to the selective biases and social pressures working against gifted girls. She shared her concerns with Terman, but he did not assimilate those concerns into his thinking.[78]

Included among Terman's conclusions was a discussion of the socio-political implications of studying and identifying the intellectually gifted.[79] He continued to advocate a meritocratic society, arguing that "genius" was even more important now than it had been historically because of the increasing complexity of civilization and science. He spelled out this notion as follows:

That important scientific discoveries are sometimes made by fairly common-place intellects may be freely admitted . . . It is more reasonable to believe that the mounting quantity and growing complexity of knowledge call more insistently for the masterful genius today than ever before. Disrupted social and economic orders, from England to Japan and from Canada to the Argentine, are calling almost in vain for statesmen of genius and vision . . . Lawmaking in most countries, and perhaps nowhere more than in the United States, is chiefly the product of fourth-rate minds.[80]

Terman was also concerned about the generational continuity of genius; therefore, he referred to the "eugenic aspects" of the study.[81] Terman had some data about the spouses of gifted subjects, reporting that in a majority of cases the spouses were "less well endowed" than the gifted subjects who married them. He hoped that such a trend could be counteracted by eugenic education.

One offshoot of the gifted study during this period was a publication on children's reading. This work had initially been carried out by

Margaret "Peggy" Lima for her M.A. thesis; in 1926 it was expanded into a monograph, coauthored by Terman (a revised edition appeared in 1931).[82] The authors wrote about the reading interests of children and dealt with such factors as children's motivation to read, the influence of intellectual differences, the role of sex differences, and the qualities of a "desirable" book. They then presented a recommended list of children's books, which they pointed out had a generally wider range of material and a larger proportion of nonfiction than was typical of other lists. The data on which the monograph was based came primarily from the reading interests that the gifted children had indicated in the 1921–22 survey. Similar data had been obtained from the group of unselected schoolchildren. Overall, about two thousand children were studied, and some additional information was obtained from parents and teachers.

In completing the first follow-up of his gifted sample, Terman demonstrated his skills as a scientific manager. He was successful in obtaining the necessary financial support for his ambitious project, as well as in efficiently directing a research staff. Many members of his staff were also his graduate students, who in turn carried out their own research in areas related to the gifted study. In reporting his results, Terman was generally able to confirm the expectations he had started with. He did have confirmatory evidence; but his interpretations contained biases, most notably with regard to class and sex. His hereditarian assumptions led him to neglect the intricate ways in which culture worked. Thus, he seemed insensitive to conditions that might exclude lower-class youngsters from a study of gifted children. Furthermore, he failed to consider the kinds of social pressures that might impede bright adolescent girls from excelling in the same way as their male peers.

Mental Inheritance and Eugenics

In the spring of 1924 Barbara Burks, then a Stanford senior, completed her research report, "I.Q. Farming," and submitted it to Terman who was her supervisor.[83] The report was a portrait of the family of Frank B. and Lillian M. Gilbreth, the scientific management pioneers (Lillian was also a psychologist) of "Cheaper by the Dozen" fame. Terman, in addition to his own study of the gifted, was continuously on the lookout for newspaper articles and other materials on child prodigies, as well as for families that had large numbers of gifted children.[84] Most likely at his suggestion, Burks contacted Lillian Gilbreth and sent her the various forms and questionnaires used in Terman's gifted study. At the time, the fall of 1923, Gilbreth had eleven children, ranging from a daughter at Smith College to a fifteen-month-old toddler.[85] By correspondence from her home in Montclair, New Jersey, Gilbreth informed Burks that all of her school-age children had been given mental tests in their schools and gave Burks permission to obtain the scores. With the test scores and the forms the Gilbreth family filled out, Burks was able to amass the same data that was used in Terman's study.

The family portrait Burks presented included parents and children whose IQs were all within the gifted range (above 135), outstanding and accelerated school achievement on the part of the children, outstanding professional success on the part of the parents, an intellectually enriched and efficiently functioning family life, and evidence of good, "substantial" family genealogy.[86] Reflecting the views of her mentor, Burks concluded: "It is from men and women with intelligence like this that our spiritual and material progress has sprung. It is such men and women who have made the great scientific discoveries, written the great books, composed the great music, and served as great statesmen. May their kind increase!"[87]

She compared the Gilbreths and their "crop" of children with another family.

The other crop is being farmed by a South European laboring family living in San Francisco. The mother, whom we shall call Mrs. Jacuzzi because that isn't her name, has just given birth to her twenty-fourth child! Now Mrs. Jacuzzi's crop, with reasonable luck, may never tap the resources of San Francisco charitable organizations. But it is not to be imagined that these children will ever realize the magnificent possibilities for useful citizenship that are so striking in each member of the gifted Gilbreth group. They come of a class of countrymen that are the despair of the truant officers in youth, and the meat of oily-mouthed political rascals all their lives; a class, which taken as a whole, is below par by every social and mental standard. . . . Most unfortunate of all, they come of a racial group so fertile that not even the proposed restriction of its great tide of immigration can prevent its alarming increase.[88]

Burks, who went on to develop a close professional and personal relationship with Terman, zealously captured her mentor's views about mental inheritance in families and races as well as his eugenic concerns.

In connection with his gifted study, Terman had hoped to carry out an investigation on the hereditary basis of intellectual superiority.[89] During 1923 and 1924, Terman tried to obtain funding from several foundations, including the Laura Spelman Rockefeller fund, the Carnegie Corporation, and the National Research Council—all to no avail.[90] With the money that he had received from Max Rosenberg (starting in 1925), he was able to divert some support for a planned study of the intelligence of foster children.[91] Such a study would involve a comparison of foster parent–foster child IQs with natural parent–natural child IQs and would consequently provide a test of the relative influence of nature and nurture on mental development. Burks undertook this research project for her doctoral dissertation, which she completed in 1929.[92] Using the Stanford-Binet for both the children and the parents, Burks found a much closer resemblance between the IQs of natural parents and natural children than for the foster parent–child IQs. Furthermore, the correlations in the foster parent–child group were rather low (.23 for foster mother–child and .09 for foster father–child). The Burks study was one of the first of its kind. The study's support of the greater influence of heredity on IQs was challenged by the results of another study of foster children that was reported in 1928 by Frank N. Freeman and his associates at the University of Chicago.[93] In this study, the environments of the foster homes were shown to have a strong influence on the IQs of foster children. These divergent results on the nature-nurture issue formed a central part of the testing debate of the late 1920s, which Terman became involved in.

With respect to the racial inheritance of intelligence, Terman in his 1916 monograph on the Stanford-Binet had warned about the racial inferiority of Negro, Spanish-Mexican, southern European, and American-Indian groups. After the war, he reiterated these concerns.[94] An interesting example of his views about racial inferiority occurred in 1929. Terman had read about the noteworthy accomplishments of a young African student who had attended his alma mater, Indiana University. Terman wrote to W. F. Book, a former Clark classmate who was on the Indiana faculty, about his dismay that an African could make the transition from a "savage existence" to modern civilization. As it turned out, the student in question was Hastings Banda, who went on to become president of his native African country of Malawi.[95]

In 1919 Terman had been appointed to the Division of Anthropology and Psychology of the National Research Council. In this connection he proposed a study on racial differences that would involve mental and physical measurements of twelve-year-old children of four racial stocks.[96] This proposal was expanded by Walter V. Bingham, the division chair, in a memorandum circulated to the division's members.[97] The primary focus of this project was on "Mexican stock" because of the sharp increase of Mexican immigrants since the war. It was proposed that eleven- and twelve-year-old Mexican-American children be given intelligence tests. It was also proposed that the researchers take anthropometric measurements. The same data would be obtained from children of other racial groups, including native American, Scandinavian, Sicilian, and Japanese. It was hoped that this investigation would shed light on "important racial elements which the American people are under the necessity of assimilating."[98]

For his part, Terman contacted the secretary of the Japanese Association of America in San Francisco.[99] In 1922 Terman had received a grant of approximately $5,000 from this organization, and with the assistance of Marvin L. Darsie, one of his former graduate students, intelligence tests had been administered to some six hundred Japanese-American schoolchildren in California.[100] As in the case of Chinese-American children, the IQs of the this group were generally equivalent to those of white American children.[101] Terman appeared to be pleased that he could point to at least one non-European group that was not intellectually inferior, and he believed that more Chinese and Japanese children would have been included in his gifted sample had the segregated schools that most of them attended been included in the original search for subjects. Regarding the other racial groups to be studied by the Division of Anthropology and Psychology, there appears to be no evidence that these groups were studied by other investigators.[102]

Terman's interest in the familial and racial inheritance of intelligence was not limited to research projects. He was eager to apply scientific data in this area to social policy, and he participated in various eugenics organizations.[103] During the early twenties, he often voiced his concern about the differential birth rate, in which the birth rates of the lower social class and racially inferior groups far exceeded the birth rates of those at the upper end of the IQ distribution.[104] As he stated in a 1923 talk to the Stanford Psychology Club, "with the less intelligent classes reproducing about twice as rapidly as the more intelligent element . . . American civilization is a matter for grave consideration."[105] In 1922 Terman was elected to the Advisory Council of the International Commission on Eugenics.[106] The following year he was on the Advisory Council of the Eugenics Committee of the United States of America—the American body of the international group. Foremost on the American group's agenda was the advocacy of selective immigration legislation—legislation which was passed in 1924.[107] The subcommittee's report on selective immigration referred to the results of the army testing on the relatively low IQs of recruits with southern and eastern European origin.[108] When the American Eugenics Committee became independent as the American Eugenics Society in 1925, Terman was a charter member and continued on its advisory committee.[109] In 1930 he agreed to be listed as one of the "Minute Men"—persons who could be called upon by the society to write to politicians or the media in support of the society's policies on immigration.[110] Apparently, the society feared a backlash against the restrictive immigration policy.[111]

While Terman was not especially active in the American Eugenics Society, he supported its policies on immigration as well as other eugenic matters—at least through the early thirties. He resigned in 1935, claiming he could not afford to continue his membership due to getting only half salary for a sabbatical.[112] By this time, it is possible that he was growing wary of the link eugenic policies might have with the racial propaganda of the Nazi movement in Germany, for he also severed his connection with another eugenics group.[113] However, before the mid-thirties, Terman clearly subscribed to eugenic principals. When asked by the secretary of the American Eugenics Society to make a statement in 1927 on eugenics, he commented: "It is more important for man to acquire control over his biological evolution than to capture the energy of the atom . . . The ordinary social and political issues which engross mankind are of trivial importance in comparison with the issues which relate to eugenics."[114]

In a lecture on Mexican immigration to the Commonwealth Club of California, he noted that "we should carry our civilization into their land, rather than bring Mexicans into our country to raise theirs up."[115] In a brief commentary on the "Norwegian Program for Race Hygiene," he pointed out that "the present differential birth rate is probably the most serious problem facing mankind."[116] He attached this remark to his support of California's state policy of sterilizing the mentally "defective."

Terman was most active as a member of the Human Betterment Foundation, a eugenics organization. This incorporated body was founded by E. S. Gosney, a wealthy Pasadena businessman with a longtime interest in eugenics.[117] Gosney's particular focus was on the sterilization of the insane and mentally retarded. He established and endowed the foundation in 1928 for the "advancement and betterment of human life." Terman was one of the Foundation's charter members, and its board of trustees included former Stanford president David Starr Jordan, a staunch eugenicist. Gosney had first contacted Terman to comment on the program of research Paul Popenoe was conducting on the effects of the sterilization legislation in California, which had been passed in 1909.[118] Popenoe was the secretary of the foundation and had been trained as a biologist.[119] His varied career included journalism, the editorship of the *Journal of Heredity*, and a number of books on eugenics. Popenoe's research plans called for surveys of insane and feebleminded individuals who had been sterilized to determine the psychological effects the operation had on these individuals and an assessment of the attitudes of surgeons, probation officers, and social workers toward sterilization policy. Terman was impressed with Popenoe's plans in general, but especially with the extensiveness of the research.[120]

Popenoe had extensive data to work with. California was one of the first states to pass sterilization legislation. From 1909 to 1929 just over six thousand sterilizations had taken place in the state (about six hundred more males than females, and sterilization of the insane outnumbered the feebleminded by more than two to one).[121] By 1936 the number of cumulative sterilizations in California had jumped to close to eleven thousand, which was almost one-half of the total American figure of just over twenty-three thousand.[122] The report of Popenoe's investigation appeared in 1930. In the same year Gosney and Popenoe coauthoried a book summarizing the results for the general public.[123] As far as the authors were concerned, the findings turned out to be positive. Patients, relatives of patients, state officials, surgeons, probation officers, and social workers were all virtually unanimous in supporting the value of sterilization. The operation produced no changes in sexual feelings or behaviors and reduced the frequency of sex offenses. So successful had the operation become that many mentally retarded or unstable individuals were being admitted to institutions simply to be sterilized and then discharged. The only negative findings reported were four deaths from the operation, three known failures of vasectomies, and four know failures of salpingectomy (pregnancy had occurred after the sterilization operation). Of course, in hindsight other negative results are apparent in terms of the morals and ethics of forced sterilization, and the investigators seemed oblivious to the social pressures sterilized psychiatric and retarded individuals faced when they responded to the survey. That sterilization could have even more ominous consequences was not perceived when the 1934 annual report of the foundation cheerfully and naively reported about developments abroad: "Attention has been aroused . . . based largely on information furnished by the Human Betterment Foundation . . . by the inauguration of eugenic sterilization on a large scale by Germany. The German law is well drawn and in form is better than that of most American states."[124] The Nazis had come to power in 1933.

Terman had been advocating sterilization of the mentally retarded from the time he developed the Stanford-Binet,[125] and he was pleased with the work the foundation was doing.[126] With the depression and the change in political climate, the foundation was facing increasing difficulties. Popenoe resigned in 1937 to devote full time to his directorship of the Institute of Family Relations—a center founded in 1930 that provided genetic and eugenic counseling to marital and prospective couples.[127] In 1938 Terman still supported the foundation's work, citing its valuable service in sterilization research and propaganda.[128]

However, he now expressed disappointment that the foundation was no longer in a position to "finance fundamentally important researches in genetics without regard to their propaganda value." [129]

Resolving the Testing Debate

The testing debate that Terman had engaged in with Lippmann and Bagley in 1922 left matters unresolved. It seemed to Terman that the central issue that needed to be clarified was the relative influence of nature and nurture on tested intelligence. [130] In his words:

It is time to find out whether intelligence quotients earned on the best intelligence tests reflect chiefly the quality and amount of environmental and training factors. If . . . [this] is true, then high intelligence quotients can be manufactured at will by supplying the appropriate stimuli. . . . On the other hand, if children's intelligence quotients depend chiefly on the germ cells of their parents, it is time we are finding that out. . . . If this, or even half of it, should be found true the practical consequences would be well nigh incalculable. Eugenics would deserve to become a religion. Educational effort, while it would deserve to continue, would have to be largely redirected. The first task of the school would be to establish the native quality of every pupil; the second, to supply the kind of instruction suited to each grade of ability. [131]

Terman was putting his adherence to the nature interpretation on the line. In 1924 he announced that a committee had been appointed (at his suggestion) to prepare a yearbook on the subject of "the possibilities and limitations of training," under the auspices of the National Society for the Study of Education. [132] At the same time, it was also announced that grants had been made to the University of Chicago and Stanford University that would enable Terman and Frank N. Freeman of Chicago to carry out their studies of the resemblance of adopted children to their siblings and foster parents. This would be the major research paradigm to resolve the nature-nurture issue. Terman's study was actually carried out by his doctoral student, Barbara Burks.

The National Society for the Study of Education was an organization founded in 1901 to stimulate investigations and discussions of important educational issues through the regular publication of a two-volume yearbook. [133] The secretary of the society was Guy M. Whipple, who had worked with Terman on the army tests and the National Intelligence Tests. Whipple also served as editor for the society's yearbooks. The committee for the 1928 yearbook, the one devoted to the nature-nurture issue, was chaired by Terman and consisted of a membership selected "so as to represent all shades of opinion on the issues involved."[134] The committee members were Bagley, Bird T. Baldwin, Carl C. Brigham, Freeman, Rudolf Pintner, and Whipple. Bagley, Baldwin, and Freeman had environmentalist leanings while Brigham, Pintner, and Whipple were in Terman's hereditarian camp. Terman worked most closely with Whipple both by correspondence and through a Stanford visit Whipple made in May and June of 1927.[135] This reflected the fact that Whipple, as yearbook editor, was primarily responsible for organizing the papers and the annual conference at which the papers were read and discussed.

The 1928 yearbook consisted of two volumes; the first dealing with the influence of nature and nurture on intelligence, and the second with the influence of nature and nurture on school achievement. Most of the ensuing discussion focused on intelligence, and although there were a variety of papers within the volume devoted to this topic, the discussion centered around the papers by Burks and Freeman. Burks's study on foster children supported a hereditarian thesis because the IQ correlations between natural parents and natural children exceeded those between foster parents and foster children.[136] On the other hand, Freeman and his associates found fairly high correlations (ranging from .28 to .50) between the IQs of foster parents and their children, as well as other evidence showing the positive influence of the foster-home environment.[137]

Several yearbook discussion speakers were lined up by Terman for the Boston meeting of the society in February 1928.[138] In addition to himself, the speakers included Bagley, Baldwin, Freeman, Whipple, and noncommittee members Arthur I. Gates and Charles H. Judd.[139] In his invitation to the speakers, Terman expressed the hope that the discussions would be at an objective, scientific level, rather than appealing to emotional bias.[140] Alluding to his previous debate experiences, Terman admitted that he had "sinned" in this respect. Bagley, who along with Lippmann, had been a target of Terman's admitted emotionalism was put off by Terman's invitation. He agreed with

Terman's suggestion that the conference program should be "thoroughly objective."[141] However, in what must have seemed like a reference to Terman's previous charge that Bagley's arguments were based on "sentiment," Bagley confessed that he had acquired the habit of "injecting sentimental issues into educational discussions." In response, Terman went out of his way to appeal for Bagley's participation. Terman was most likely concerned that Bagley's absence would give the impression that as chair he was not being evenhanded to both sides of the nature-nurture issue or, even worse, that he personally alienated those (like Bagley) who disagreed with him. He wrote to Bagley, "I want to assure you that you may feel absolutely free to put whatever warmth of expression into your address you wish to."[142] Terman was relieved when Bagley agreed to remain on the program.[143] Through all the preparations for the meeting, both men had managed to maintain cordial relations.

In his address before the society, Terman emphasized that the yearbook had been devoted to the dispassionate exposition of scientific investigations relevant to the nature-nurture problem.[144] In reviewing the research presented in the yearbook, he concluded that he could not find any evidence that differences in school attendance greatly affected IQ scores. Similarly, language handicap did not seem to be related to IQ since when the home language was German, Scandinavian, or Yiddish, IQ scores were not lower than those for native-born groups —even though IQs were lower if the home language were Italian or Spanish. With respect to the Freeman and Burks studies of foster children, he believed that Freeman's data pointing to the considerable influence of environmental factors were not conclusive, primarily because he and his associates had not controlled for the selective placement of foster children (such as placing brighter children in better homes). On the other hand, Burks's data in support of hereditarian influences had successfully controlled for selective placement. In closing, Terman pointed out that largely because of its failure to eliminate the effects of selective placement Freeman's Chicago study "stands most nearly alone with respect to the influence it finds for environmental factors."[145] For Terman, the yearbook vindicated his hereditarian interpretation of IQ differences. Privately, perhaps, he was less convinced for he confided to Bagley that the yearbook as a whole was less conclusive than he had hoped it might be.[146] However, his opinion in this context may very well have reflected his desire to appear, relatively neutral to Bagley, since the comment was made prior to Bagley's speech.

In his address, Freeman countered Terman (and Burks's charge as well) regarding the issue of selective placement, pointing out that in his study "neither the agents who placed the children nor the foster parents appeared to take the intelligence of the child into account in deciding upon its adoption."[147] He added that the best evidence of the effect of environment was the change in intelligence children manifested after a change in the environmental conditions they were exposed to. As for the other discussants, Whipple, as expected, concluded that the yearbook had strengthened the contentions of the hereditarian proponents.[148] As expected, Bagley championed the cause of mass education in raising intellectual performance and supported Freeman's findings regarding the importance of the home environment.[149] Gates tended to be impartial, providing support for both hereditarian and environmental influences.[150]

The remaining two discussants, Judd and Baldwin, chose to draw broad implications from the yearbook studies. Judd was an influential educational psychologist and head of the University of Chicago's School of Education.[151] Reflecting his Wundtian training, he believed that the historical method was of equal importance to the experimental. He also held the position that being exposed to sociocultural enrichment was a major determinant in the individual's mental development, and therefore the role of education was to provide a superior environment for everyone. With respect to empirical-experimental data, Judd was critical of the "effort of the Stanford investigation to put into numerical terms the relative importance of heredity and environment."[152]

Baldwin was the director of the University of Iowa's Child Welfare Research Station and had overseen the collection of anthropometric measurements in Terman's initial survey of gifted children. By 1924 he had adopted an environmentalist position regarding intellectual development.[153] In his discussion paper, he cited the longitudinal studies of childrens' mental-test performance conducted at the Iowa Station. He concluded that "the IQs fluctuate and usually show improvement. Nature furnishes some of the elements for education, but environment, nurture, and training are the determining factors in the results."[154]

As in the previous exchanges of the testing debate, both sides often seemed to talk past one another. Terman and Whipple were committed to a biologically rooted model of social evolution. Bagley, Judd, Baldwin, and to some extent Freeman (though he focused on data rather than theory) held a nonreductionist perspective of social evolution. It appeared as though an impasse had been reached—but Terman was to be dragged one more time over the coals for his hereditarian position. Baldwin, who died prematurely only a few months after his talk to the society, had already begun to study developmental changes in IQ scores. His successor at the University of Iowa, George D. Stoddard, guided a cadre of Iowa researchers who looked at the effects of various environmental enrichment programs. Fanned by the flames of the New Deal social reconstruction of the thirties, Stoddard and his group challenged Terman to a yearbook rematch in 1940, which was to prove far more acrimonious than any of Terman's previous exchanges.

Friend and Mentor

As a result of their collaboration on the army testing report, Terman, Yerkes, and Boring developed a close lifelong professional friendship. Terman had experienced some strains in his early relationships with both. In the case of Yerkes, there had been the prewar competition for funds to develop their respective mental tests. This situation was resolved during the climate of wartime teamwork, which continued in the postwar period with the development of the National Intelligence Tests. With Boring, there had been the unsuccessful attempt to bring him to Stanford. This effort was doomed because of Boring's insistence on having a controlling hand in running the psychological laboratories—a stand that threatened Terman's position as head of the psychology department. This competitive edge was eliminated when Boring went to Harvard.

After the war, Terman and Yerkes shared their mutual concerns about career decisions.[155] Terman had doubts about whether Stanford could provide the financial and staff support he needed for his research. He seriously considered the possibility of an offer from Yale that Gesell had been working on. However, by 1921 he was starting to get the local support he needed and as he confided to Yerkes, "the plans I have cherished so long will have a good chance of realization. Of course, I shall know the outcome more definitely a year from now."[156] Indeed, the next year Terman was appointed executive head of the psychology department. Yerkes was very "gratified" to hear of Terman's appointment, as well as the fact that the department had been reorganized "to your satisfaction."[157]

Yerkes had decided to stay on in Washington, D.C., after the war. He resigned his position as psychology department head at the University of Minnesota to devote full time to the National Research Council. His long-range goal, however, was to find an academic position that would provide him with the opportunity to carry out his psychobiological research and more specifically to establish a "station" for studying apes, which had become the focus of his research plans. Terman made an attempt to interest Wilbur, Stanford's president, in such a project, but this was not successful.[158] In 1924 Yerkes received an appointment from Yale and communicated his satisfaction to Terman.[159]

During the twenties, when Terman was trying to obtain financial support for his research, Yerkes was quite helpful in providing information and leads. Yerkes, because of his various connections through the National Research Council, was well informed about sources of research funding. It was Yerkes who directed Terman to Max Rosenberg,[160] the San Francisco businessman who provided some financial support for the gifted follow-up as well as for the Burks study of foster children. With Yerkes's help, Terman was also able to obtain a grant for the development of the masculinity-femininity test.[161]

Boring was about ten years younger than both Terman and Yerkes, an age difference that was reflected, to some extent, in the Terman-Boring correspondence.[162] Boring often sought out Terman as a sounding board for conditions at Harvard. For example, one time he expressed his concern about the lack of support for the psychology laboratory.[163] Boring also had more general concerns about what he believed to be Harvard's inadequate support for the psychology department. On one occasion, he described psychology as a very strong department of "young unknown men" who would hopefully develop reputations—a state of affairs that he felt was a consequence of low salaries.[164] Another problem cited by Boring was the fact that the Harvard department included both psychology and philosophy, a situation that was rather anachronistic by the 1920s.[165] Terman fully supported the need for psychology and philosophy to split apart administratively.[166] Indeed, in 1934 a separate psychology department was created with Boring as head.[167]

On matters regarding the nature of psychology as a science, Boring and Terman related as peers. Boring had little regard for philosophy and theory in relation to experimentation, pointing out that he viewed himself as an "ardent experimentalist."[168] In general, neither Terman nor Boring had much regard for those psychologists, such as the members of the Gestalt school, who emphasized theory at the expense of empirical data.[169] Terman was favorably impressed with Boring's *History of Experimental Psychology* but chided him for the relatively meager material on testing.[170] Boring, however, felt that since testing did not as yet qualify as an area of experimental psychology, it was not germane to his history book. While Terman often gave Boring advice about faculty appointments at Harvard, he also came to rely on Boring's appraisals regarding other psychologists. He was particularly grateful for Boring's recommendation of Lewin for the visiting professorship at Stanford.[171]

Starting in the early twenties, Yerkes and Boring became Terman's major professional friends and confidants. Terman continued his friendship with Gesell, but their letters became less frequent by the 1930s, and their share of mutual interests was not as great as in the case with Yerkes and Boring. In the twenties, Terman and Gesell had occasion to review each other's books, and they each wrote highly positive appraisals. In Terman's case, he felt that Gesell's *The Mental Growth of the Child* was a "pioneer and monumental piece of work."[172] Gesell had reviewed the first volume of the gifted study, and Terman was grateful for his "splendid review."[173]

When he returned to Stanford after the war, Terman continued to attract graduate students to work with him, as well as undergraduates to assist him in large-scale projects such as the gifted study. The fact that he had already established a national reputation, based on his testing work and his plans to study the gifted, drew many who came especially to study with him. Perhaps because he felt more secure about his position and work, he seemed to take a greater personal interest in the postwar generation of students than he had with the prewar group.

The majority of students Terman worked with during the twenties were women. This was partly a reflection of the fact that most women thinking of a career in psychology chose testing and child development as areas of specialty because their job marketability was usually limited to clinical and public-school settings. Therefore, Stanford's graduate psychology program had a high proportion of women. This was true for the education program as well. There were also personal factors that contributed to Terman's close relationships with female students. Many women were personally attracted to him, and he in turn had a strong attraction for bright young women. His relationships with female students often continued after they completed their studies with him. In some cases, he was instrumental in getting them established in their careers; for example, he helped Florence Goodenough obtain a position with the newly created Institute of Child Welfare at the University of Minnesota.[174] Catharine Cox was another student who profited from her association with Terman. After completing her dissertation on eminent geniuses in history, Cox went to work at a mental health clinic in Cincinnati. Two years later, Terman recommended her for a position at the University of Minnesota. However, he was sensitive to the discrimination women in academia faced and confided to Cox that he doubted she would be given a "fair chance."[175] Indeed, she did not receive an offer from the University of Minnesota, and it was at this point that Terman invited her to return to Stanford to work with him as his research associate in developing the masculinity-femininity test.

Terman also took an interest in the Stanford students who over the years boarded in his home. It was through one of these students, Cecil Brolyer, that he developed a mentoring relationship with Anne Roe.[176] Roe was married to Brolyer, and they both stayed with the Termans when he returned to Stanford in 1927 to take his doctoral orals. While there, she became quite ill and had to remain at the Terman home for a period of several months after her husband returned east to take up a position. Anna looked after her physical needs, while Terman engaged in long discussions about the work he and his students were doing. She had studied psychology at the University of Denver (she went on to get her Ph.D. from Columbia University in 1932), and her discussions with Terman relieved her sense of professional isolation. After she left Stanford, she and Terman maintained a correspondence, and, particularly in the 1940s, he gave her considerable professional advice and general encouragement. A different kind of mentoring relationship involved Jack Russell, who had boarded with the Termans during the period before World War I. Russell went on to a career in the insurance field, but he continued to exchange letters with Terman about his readings in psychology.[177] Terman made suggestions about what to read and offered his opinions, as well as answered questions about what Russell had read.

Reflections at Midcareer

In 1928 Terman was invited to contribute a chapter to Carl Murchison's newly established series of autobiographies of famous psychologists.[178] Terman was one of fifty who had been selected for this honor; at the age of fifty-one he was one of the youngest.[179] He completed his manuscript in the spring of 1930, and it was published in 1932.[180]

At the close of his chapter, Terman responded to Murchison's suggestion that each author provide a self-appraisal of his or her work. Terman did not believe that his work "contributed very greatly to the theory of mental measurement." On the other hand, he stated:

If I am remembered very long after my death, it will probably be in connection with my studies of gifted children, the construction of mental tests, and the psychology of sex differences. I think that I early saw more clearly than others the possibilities of mentality testing, have succeeded in devising tests that work better than their competitors, and by the application of test methods, have added to the world's knowledge of exceptional children.[181]

Within the context of his own times, his self-appraisal seems quite fair and accurate. He had clearly established himself as a leader in the fields of testing and individual differences. As a reflection of this, he was honored in 1923 with the presidency of the American Psychological Association. Another distinction, which meant a great deal to him, was his 1928 election to the National Academy of Sciences.[182] At that time, the academy typically elected only one psychologist a year and never more than two. Furthermore, these elections were conducted in such a way that for a psychologist to be elected, he or she had to have broad support from the psychologists who were already members.

Writing his autobiography at midcareer was a reflective exercise that called for positive image-making. Nevertheless, the autobiography's self-assured tone of career accomplishment seems consistent with other reflective statements in his correspondence with such confidants as Gesell, Yerkes, and Boring. His autobiography also drew him back to his professional roots, and there were other events over the previous decade that contributed to this as well. In 1924 Hall, who had been his chief mentor, died. Terman conveyed his feelings about the loss to another of his revered Clark professors, W. H. Burnham: "His passing leaves me, as it must every Clark man, with a feeling of deep personal loss. I can truthfully say that to no one else have I been as greatly indebted for the inspiration which has led to any little measure of success I have had. His influence has been with me through all the years since I left Clark."[183]

There were other reminders of Terman's indebtedness to Hall and Clark. He was also saddened to hear of Sanford's death only a few months after Hall's passing.[184] At the occasion of Burnham's seventy-sixth birthday in 1931, Terman was asked to prepare a written statement. He credited Burnham with being one of the four of five teachers who most influenced him.[185] After Hall's death, Terman joined a group of Clark psychology alumni from the Hall era who generated an exchange of correspondence to keep each other abreast of developments at Clark.[186] This group was upset by the decline of psychology under the administration of Hall's successor, Wallace W. Atwood. As they saw it, Atwood, a geographer, pushed his own discipline into prominence at the expense of psychology. (As a member of the Clark psychology faculty in the early twenties, Boring concurred in this.) The group which identified itself as the "Old Clark Psychologists" developed a sense of camaraderie but apparently never developed a clear strategy for trying to change the situation at Clark.[187]

The success of Terman's midcareer period was matched by generally rewarding events in his personal life. By the mid-twenties, the family was in comfortable financial circumstances.[188] For example, in 1925 Terman received about $11,000 from book and test royalties.[189] The following year he and Anna began to invest in property in the resort community of Carmel on the Monterey peninsula. These investments proved to be profitable. After the 1929 stock-market crash, he confided to Keith Sward, a postdoctoral fellow, that it was fortunate that he and Anna had invested in the Carmel property rather than in stocks.[190] Commensurate with the new income level were changes in the household. The family had a live-in housekeeper, thus providing Anna with a degree of freedom she had never had before. In 1929 the Termans had their house remodeled and almost entirely refurnished.[191]

Terman's health was generally satisfactory. However, in the summer of 1928 he had a brief flare-up of tuberculosis.[192] After about ten days in bed, he was gradually able to return to his work schedule. In the twenties, he also started to have recurring bouts of bronchitis, as well as frequent colds and some attacks of influenza.[193] Often these health problems would develop after his long train trips to various professional meetings and conferences. As a result, he reduced the number of these trips, especially to the East Coast. Once he became sick, he would take to his bed for several days, sometimes weeks, until he was sure that he was back to normal health. During these periods he would carry on his research and writing at home. At times his Stanford colleagues felt that he used his health problems as an excuse to avoid social and recreational gatherings so that he could use the time for work.[194] This may well have been true, but it also seems that he was often genuinely worried about his health and thus was cautious both in preventive and recuperative measures. Anna, in her diary entries during the 1920s, recorded times when Lewis seemed quite depressed over his health.[195]

Health problems also plagued another family member. A life-threatening case of tuberculosis struck Fred in 1924.[196] He had just returned home, after completing his work for a doctorate in electrical engineering at the Massachusetts Institute of Technology. The spread of infection progressed rapidly, and the specialist called in on the case told Lewis and Anna that their son had, at the most, only a year to live.

However, a second opinion brought a verdict that Fred's situation was not hopeless. The regimen for recovery involved an eight-month period in which Fred was not allowed to leave his bed and had to lie flat with sandbags over his left chest. Anna hired a housekeeper and took over the entire job of nursing under the attending physician's direction.

According to his father, Fred never doubted his ultimate recovery. However, he began to brood (as Lewis had done) about his chances of ever getting a job in a medically safe climate. He had a position as an instructor at MIT but was afraid of the risk of returning there. Fortunately, a message came from President Wilbur indicating that there would be a position for him in electrical engineering at Stanford, as soon as he was ready for it. This put an end to Fred's brooding and seemed to clearly hasten his recovery. By September 1925 he was able to take on a half-time appointment as an instructor, and the following year he assumed full-time duties. Fred had no further recurrence of tuberculosis, but even when he assumed full-time teaching during the 1926–27 year he had to continue to rest a few hours each day. In 1927, in order to help Fred's research, Terman initiated an annual contribution from his royalties to the electrical engineering department so that Fred could hire a research assistant.[197] This practice persisted through the 1930s. Terman continued to take a very active interest in his son's career. This interest had intensified before Fred's illness. In 1920 Terman suggested that Fred obtain a doctorate in engineering from a university other than Stanford—something which at the time was very unusual. Fred was grateful to his father for this suggestion, for when he started his professional career at Stanford, his MIT background made him a "senior faculty" member from the beginning.[198]

Helen graduated from Stanford in 1924. Terman, in a rather rare reference to her intellectual achievements, noted that she had graduated "with distinction."[199] Helen taught for a year at a one-room country school near San Luis Obispo.[200] However, she had no desire for a career and was anxious to marry and have a family. In 1925 she married a Stanford law graduate, Albert Mosher, who set up his law practice in Los Angeles. Lewis was very pleased with the marriage because he assumed that Al, being partly Jewish, had superior heredity. In 1927 the couple satisfied Lewis's and Anna's great desire for grandchildren with the birth of a daughter.[201] A year later a second girl was born.

In 1928 Fred married Sibyl Walcutt, a psychology graduate student who had come from the University of Arizona to work with Terman.[202] A year later Sibyl gave birth to the first of three sons. The story behind Fred's marriage, as handed down through the family, was that he had asked his father to find a girl with a "high IQ."[203] In response, Lewis and Anna invited Sibyl to the house to meet Fred. Lewis's role as a matchmaker for his son was also known among the students in the psychology department. Roger G. Barker, a graduate student at the time, recalled that Terman's commitment to IQ was mildly ridiculed by some students because he looked up the IQs of certain female students on behalf of Fred.[204]

By the mid-twenties, Terman found a little more time for leisure activities. He had built a cabin in the mountains to the west of Stanford and periodically spent a day or two there, often by himself.[205] His favorite avocational pastime was reading, but he also began to take up golf and had a little putting green set up on his front lawn.[206] Anna became increasingly involved in the faculty women's organization and other university social functions.[207] She continued to play a significant role in furthering Lewis's career. When the children were young, she had taken over the responsibility of looking after them and managing the household.[208] She provided Lewis with the working conditions he needed—freedom from interruptions and from the daily demands on his time and energy. She maintained an interest in Lewis's work and at times helped him in the construction of test items.[209] Moreover, she was well informed about his various projects—a characteristic that impressed former graduate student Lowell Kelly, who saw her frequently during her month's visit to Hawaii in 1930.[210] As wife of the department head, Anna frequently hosted student and faculty gatherings and entertained visiting scholars and research colleagues. Ernest R. Hilgard, who joined the faculty in the early thirties, remembered her as a well-liked hostess who easily mixed with people.[211] With her social skills and the knowledge she had about her husband's work, it was also possible for her to serve as his representative on certain occasions. The best example of this was her trip to Copenhagen in the summer of 1932 to attend an international congress of psychology. Terman had been invited to attend; but with his growing aversion to travel, he sent Anna instead. With her love of travel, Anna enjoyed the trip and took the opportunity to visit England and to make several stops on the Continent on her way to Copenhagen.[212]

Anna was becoming more independent of Lewis, though this was not entirely of her own choice. For one thing, their interests, commitments, and personalities were very different. Lewis was extremely work oriented and, being rather shy, was not particularly interested in social events that had no connection with his work. In contrast, Anna was very outgoing and energetic. She socialized to a considerable extent in the Stanford community and often took short trips to Carmel as well as frequent jaunts to San Francisco for shopping, dining, and entertainment. The city visits were often in the company of another faculty wife or Maud Merrill.[213] In Carmel she looked after the real-estate investments, but she also spent time with friends or drove by herself along the nearby coastal roads. She liked to travel, especially by car. In fact, having her own car and taking motor trips seemed to be a significant way for her to express her freedom. She made several motor trips by herself to visit relatives in Indiana, apparently unphased by any problems that might confront a woman driving alone.

Anna's independence, however, also represented a means of coping with an emotionally disturbing situation. Starting around 1925, and persisting for about ten years, rumors circulated about Lewis's sexual relationships with other women.[214] These brief liaisons appeared to be drawn from the many women students Terman worked with. They supposedly took place at hideaways, such as the mountain cabin or the little study Terman had built at the nearby golf course.[215] It was also suspected that they took place at the Terman home when Anna was away. The Stanford house had a number of side entrances, making it easy for visitors to discretely slip in and out. While the rumors persisted among the psychology faculty and graduate students, Terman never made any comments about these alleged encounters. No public criticism was voiced around the department. Harry F. Harlow, a graduate student at the time, recalled that the students explained the affairs as Terman's need to combine social with intellectual ties.[216] It was assumed that a high level of personal warmth was involved; therefore, according to Harlow, none of the students were critical.

It seems fairly evident that Terman's extramarital activities did actually occur. Anna was certain of their existence and confided this to Helen, who in turn divulged the information to her two daughters as they were growing up.[217] Anna, however, chose not to impart such information to her son. Fred and his sons learned about the affairs from May V. Seagoe's biography of Terman, published in 1975. Fred found the revelations very difficult to accept.

Anna's initial reaction seems to have been one of depression. In her diary entries during April 1926, there are references to feeling sad and lonely and spending sleepless nights.[218] At one point, she went off by herself to the mountain cabin to get away from the house until the "air" cleared. By mid-May the depression subsided. She noted that "care" had "dropped away," and she caught herself returning to her cheerful habit of humming a song. While she does not identify the source of her depression, its onset in the spring of 1926 is closely timed with the start of the rumors the previous year. It's possible that it took several months before she became aware of such revelations. Whether she was depressed or not, it is clear that resentment over Lewis's affairs did develop. Her diaries contain some snide comments, such as hearing about the "fun" Lewis had while working at Carmel (apparently with a student) and being "pepped up" by a certain caller who visited him one evening while he was recovering from a tubercular attack.[219] Moreover, Helen confided to her daughter Doris that Anna was very bitter, feeling that she had sacrificed much to help Lewis establish himself and was now being displaced by Lewis's middle-aged need for younger women.[220] Some of this bitterness was recorded in other diaries that Helen destroyed after her mother's death. Unfortunately for Anna, it does not appear that she received much sympathy from her daughter. Helen resented her mother for being so domineering with her and apparently felt that Anna was getting what she deserved. Helen thought it was all rather amusing. Though not close with her father, she greatly admired him and felt that more often than not he was the one who was being chased.[221]

As for Lewis's needs and justifications regarding extramarital liaisons, there are no personal sources of evidence to draw upon since he kept such reflections to himself. From the comments of various women students, we get the impression that he had the facility to charm and attract them. For example, Helen remembered having lunch, sometime in the forties, with her father and Peggy Lima, a student he was close to in the early twenties.[222] Peggy laughed about how all of his female students were "in love with him." Helen also observed that her father was always attractive to women and liked them as long as they were interested in what he was interested in. As Seagoe hypothesizes in her biography, it is also possible that being shy Terman had a need for intimacy, which he could express with relatively young and attractive women who shared his interests and were intellectually stimulating.[223]

Another dimension needs to be added. Lewis and Anna seemed to have been drifting apart for some time, perhaps from the time Lewis had arrived at Stanford and began devoting himself increasingly to his work. The actual strains in their relationship may have started by the end of World War I, when they resettled at Stanford. With the children grown, Anna had less to do. By the early to mid-twenties, with full-time domestic help, she had still more free time on her hands. Anna had two personal qualities that seemed to stand out—a high degree of energy and a need to dominate those close to her. With her increasing freedom, it may be that as an expression of her need to dominate she placed more demands on Lewis's time or in some ways began to interfere with his career activities. This possibility has to be weighed against the fact that she was also very protective in managing household affairs so that Lewis would not be disturbed. Nevertheless, when it came to her family she tended to be critical and overbearing.[224] With the children grown, Lewis may have become more of a target for her control. Such a pattern might well have alienated him and directed him to seek intimacy elsewhere.

Anna's domineering ways continued to impact upon her children even when they started their own families. When Helen got married and moved to Los Angeles, Anna went down to find a house to rent for the newlyweds.[225] She felt that Helen was incapable of making such arrangements. Anna continued to make frequent visits, keeping her daughter closely in line. Helen who had been very shy as a child

remained so as an adult and also continued to be dependent on her
mother. With Fred, Anna established a pattern whereby Fred made
weekly visits to his mother to report about the domestic affairs of his
family. Not surprisingly, this pattern greatly irritated Fred's wife,
Sibyl. Anna's continued dominance with her children may well have
been exacerbated by her growing distance from Lewis. She had a need
to hold on to the family, and she keenly felt the empty-nest syndrome.
When Fred and Sibyl married, she wrote in her diary: "Depression
grips me. The last child [is] gone and new adjustments [are] ahead."[226]

In undertaking an analysis of the family dynamics of the Termans
at midlife, it would be unfair to conclude that it was only Anna who
might have alienated Lewis and then suffered because she had driven
him away. Anna was also a victim of the conventional gender roles of
her time, which in turn were reinforced by her husband. Apparently,
she had learned to be a controlling force in her own family. She had
had a dominant father, but she was the only member of her family
who learned how to stand up to him.[227] Her managerial skills fitted in
well with the needs of Lewis and the children in the early years of the
marriage. However, like so many women of her generation (and several generations to follow), her identity was defined entirely in terms
of her role as wife and mother. In his 1932 autobiography, Terman
made the comment that when they were married Anna had the same
objectives for him as were already shaping themselves in his own
mind.[228] Her life was to be subordinated to his career goals. It is
probably this chauvinistic attitude on Terman's part that prevented
him from ever expressing any concern about the strains his sexual
affairs might have had on the marriage. From his perspective, how
unhappy could Anna be if she were sharing the rewards of his career
success. In fact, despite the strains and distancing the marriage was
sustained.

One final comment is relevant to Terman's family life. In the 1930s
one of Terman's major research projects dealt with marital adjustment.
He was to conclude that sexual compatibility was not closely related
to marital happiness.[229] If he had any guilt feelings about his extramarital affairs, his own research findings would provide a means of salving
his conscience.

CHAPTER 9

New Directions
(1932-1942)

I have been wishing there were some possibility of getting you here to go partners with me in a rather extensive bit of research on sex differences in non-intellectual mental traits, (chiefly interests). For the last year the National Research Council has been financing my study on masculinity-femininity tests. . . . To me it has become extremely fascinating. If it can be put through I think it would be a land-mark, like Genetic Studies.[1]

During Terman's professional career each decade was highlighted by a major project. In the 1910s, it was the development of the Stanford-Binet; in the 1920s, it was the gifted study. In each case, the seeds for the idea had taken root in the previous decade. So it was that the 1930s would see the culmination of Terman's plans, begun in the mid-twenties, for a study of masculinity-femininity. This area represented a new direction in Terman's interest in individual differences. Stemming from his study of gifted children, he was now focusing on nonintellectual traits. Catharine Cox Miles accepted his invitation of collaboration, and in 1936 their coauthored book, *Sex and Personality: Studies in Masculinity and Femininity*, was published.[2]

Masculinity-Femininity

The psychological study of masculinity-femininity grew out of the investigation of sex differences. In 1894 Havelock Ellis published his comprehensive review and analysis of the available evidence on the

differences between men and women.[3] By 1910 many American psychologists had conducted empirical studies of sex differences in such
areas as motor, sensory, and intellectual abilities.[4] Over the next two
decades, hundreds of studies appeared examining sex differences in
various abilities as well as a myriad of other phenomena, including
memory, fear responses, stammering, and handwriting. By 1930 the
earlier enthusiasm psychologists directed at sex-difference research
faltered somewhat due to the inconclusiveness of research results, as
well as the professional difficulties of women psychologists—the group
that had undertaken a good part of the research. Little consistent
differentiation between the sexes could be deduced from mental ability
measures or even in other special ability dimensions. Some psychologists, most notably Joseph Jastrow, turned to a depth psychology
orientation and pursued ideas such as the "feminine mind."[5] Consequently, there was an emerging interest in the notions of masculinity
and femininity.

   In the introduction to their study, Terman and Miles conceded
sexual equality in general intelligence and the majority of special tal-
ents.[6] Their purpose was to explore the commonly held belief that the
sexes differed in instinctual and emotional traits, such as sentiments,
interests, attitudes, and modes of behavior. They used the concept of
"masculine and feminine personality types" to represent these kinds of
sex differences. For both practical and theoretical reasons, they opined
that it was highly desirable that the notions of masculine and feminine
types—as they existed in contemporary American culture—should be
clarified and given a more factual basis. To accomplish this goal, a
measure was needed in which an individual could be compared to the
mean of either sex. Thus, the range and overlap of the sexes could be
more accurately determined than was possible by observational and
clinical methods.

   In the gifted study, a masculinity-femininity (M-F) test had been
constructed for the 1927–28 survey. After the initial survey, additional
data were collected on male and female groups, ranging in age from
early adolescence to late adulthood. Based on this extended sample,
test items which successfully differentiated male and female respondents were selected for a revised measure. The final version—labeled

the "Attitude-Interest Analysis Test" to disguise its purpose—was composed of about 450 items, each of which was responded to by checking one of two, three, or four multiple responses. Two "parallel" or equivalent forms of the test were also developed. As in the preliminary test, the items were grouped into several subtests, including word associations, information, interests, and emotional and ethical responses. (See Chapter 8 for some examples of these subtests.) It was thus possible to obtain a total score as well as subscores (masculinity scores were positive; femininity scores were negative). Norms for each sex were developed at three age levels: high-school juniors, college sophomores, and the general adult population (though because of the relatively small samples, norms for this group were limited to the subscores).

It was expected that the M-F test would provide clinicians and other investigators with an accurate and objective rating of those aspects of personality in which the sexes tended to differ. More specifically, as it was possible to determine the amount of direction of an individual's deviation from the mean of his or her sex, quantitative comparisons could be made for groups differing in age, intelligence, education, occupation, interests, and "cultural milieu." The subscore patterns would also provide a basis for the qualitative as well as quantitative investigation of sex differences. The authors claimed that they made no assumption about the causes that might determine an individual's score—that is, physiological, biochemical, psychological, and cultural influences. However, they felt that the availability of their test would lay the groundwork for investigating such influences.

Comparisons between total M-F scores and other variables were carried out.[7] The pattern of results clearly fitted in with the cultural expectations of the times. For example, high-scholarship men were more feminine and their interests were more cultural. On the other hand, low-scholarship men were more masculine and their interests were more mechanical and athletic. Athletes of both sexes tended to be strongly masculine. Occupational comparisons for males revealed engineers, lawyers, and salesmen as the most masculine, with clergymen and artists the least (they were barely within the range of masculinity scores).[8] Among women, there was not much of a distinction between housewives and working women (the areas represented were traditional female occupations).[9] Female high-school and college teachers did stand out by having markedly lower femininity scores.

Terman had hoped that his investigation with Miles would be a scientific "land-mark" and that it would lead to a book that would have popular as well as professional appeal.[10] Therefore, he was disappointed to learn that the book had very limited trade sales.[11] As reviewers remarked, the book was light on theory and heavy on data, and much of the latter was insignificant and wearisome.[12] Did the authors contribute anything beyond documenting the obvious cultural stereotypes about gender?[13] To counter such a verdict, Terman and Miles in their conclusion pointed out that ratings of masculinity-femininity by teachers and psychologists were often erroneous when compared with M-F scores.[14] This justified the need for an accurate measure that could overcome the biases and unreliability inherent in observations of overt behavior (or rankings of occupational groups, the task the psychologists were given). Assuming an accurate measure, it would then be possible to attend to the significance of masculinity-femininity differences. For example, was it desirable to have the child attracted to two relatively distinct patterns of personality and yet, because of social pressure, have to accept the gender-appropriate one and reject the other? On the other hand, the opposite extreme of cross-gender identification could lead to the following scenario: "The less aggressively inclined males will be driven to absurd compensations to mask their femininity; the more aggressive and independent females will be at a disadvantage in the marriage market; competition between the sexes will be rife in industry, in politics, and in the home as it is today."[15]

Terman and Miles seemed to hedge on matters in this respect. They wanted to demonstrate that developing accurate and objective measures of something as significant as masculinity-femininity could shed light on the kinds of issues they were raising. Nevertheless, they went on to say that it was not the task of the scientist to condemn or praise any particular type of behavior but rather to understand it. It would be the social reformer who would apply scientific findings to social betterment, once there was a substantial body of knowledge. This was what Terman and Miles saw as their major contribution—establishing facts where there was only opinion. But could they really separate fact from opinion? In the comments cited above they seemed close to stating an opinion that some deviation from sex-role norms might be desirable, but too much deviation suggested serious problems and consequences. That they could not separate fact from opinion emerges more clearly when we consider how they applied their work on masculinity-femininity to the study of homosexuality.[16]

Homosexuality

In order to validate the M-F test, Terman and Miles compared the scores obtained from their general population samples with those obtained from male and female homosexual groups. To establish validity, the investigators felt it was necessary to go beyond sex differences in the general population.[17] Within each gender group they had to demonstrate differences between "normal" samples and homosexuals—a group alleged to be inappropriately gender identified. Indeed, the researchers obtained the comparative data they were looking for, but it took some conceptual stretching for the results to match their expectations.

Terman had to face the challenge of trying to get data from a group that was not readily identifiable or available. In America, homosexuals had been typically studied by psychiatrists for forensic or clinical purposes.[18] Terman and Miles met with their two male graduate assistants working on the M-F project, Quinn McNemar and E. Lowell Kelly.[19] Terman looked at both assistants and said one of them would have to go to San Francisco and locate a sample of male homosexuals, while the other would stay at Stanford to carry out the statistics. McNemar spoke up first and firmly said that Kelly was going to San Francisco. Kelly admitted that he knew practically nothing about homosexuality, but he and Terman agreed that the most likely places male homosexuals would turn up would be jails, prisons, and reform schools.[20] Kelly found a subject in the San Francisco County Jail who agreed to cooperate in lining up more cases by approaching others he knew in San Francisco. Through this source and other network contacts, a sample of fifty-nine noninstitutionalized subjects was found. In addition, twenty-nine other subjects were recruited by Kelly from the San Francisco County Jail and San Quentin State Prison.

Terman and Kelly were particularly interested in locating male homosexuals who were "passive" as opposed to "active." According to Terman and Kelly (they coauthored the chapters on homosexuality), a male homosexual "is said to be an *active* homosexual if he plays the male role in the copulatory act, and a *passive* homosexual if he plays the role of female."[21] The latter group thus fit the criterion of a male group with cross-gender indentification. Kelly deduced the active-passive classification of the subjects by interviewing them about their sexual practices. On this basis, seventy-seven subjects were categorized as "passive" (these included all of the noninstitutionalized subjects). The remaining eleven were rated as "doubtful" and were not included in any further data collection. Terman and Kelly also wanted an "active" group. Such a group was recruited through the efforts of Captain G. E. Hesner, a staff psychiatrist at the Army Disciplinary Barracks at Alcatraz. Thus, the active group consisted of forty-six army prisoners, all of whom were serving sentences for sodomy. According to Captain Hesner, who interviewed them, "in practically every case the prisoners in question were supposed to have played the active part."[22] Everyone in this group was therefore categorized as "active."

The masculinity-femininity (M-F) scores revealed that the group of passive homosexuals, who ranged in age from seventeen to forty-four, had the most feminine scores of any of the male groups tested. In fact, they were more feminine than a group of "outstanding" college women athletes. Based on the interview data, the researchers characterized the passive group as having been markedly feminine in their interests and activities since early childhood, and their occupations were generally viewed as the kind that "tend to attract effeminate men."[23] In addition, ten men among the noninstitutionalized subjects were known prostitutes; a greater number were believed to engage in prostitution. For the passive group as a whole, Terman and Kelly concluded: "They are far lazier than any persons of similar age with whom we have come in contact, being inclined to shun any occupation which promises even a small amount of hard work."[24]

Another reported impression of this group was that

the passive male homosexual . . . takes advantage of every opportunity to make his behavior as much as possible like that of women. . . . Practically every subject had adopted a "queen" name by which he is known among his associates. They constantly refer to themselves as "the girls." Their behavior often seems exaggerated and ridiculous, although in some cases the inversion of behavior is remarkably complete.[25]

Nevertheless, Terman and Kelly concluded: "The 'pansy' type of behavior of adult inverts is not primarily an affectation or the result of 'abnormal' or 'perverted' sexual practices."[26] Since the inversion of interests, attitudes, and activities existed from early childhood on, the causes had to be biochemical or "psychological conditioning." As physical measurements revealed no differences between the passive group and "normals," the explanation seemed to point to psychological conditioning as the "cause" of homosexuality.[27] As Terman had determined in the case of delinquency, nonintellectual differences were more the product of nurture than nature.

The results with the active males revealed that their average scores were slightly more masculine than a comparison group of unselected soldiers of comparable age and background. The active group also had a somewhat bimodal distribution of scores, prompting the investigators to conclude that some of those classified as "active" must actually have been "passive."[28] The marked differences in M-F scores between the two homosexual groups, as well as the information that the active homosexuals preferred masculine activities as children, led Terman and Kelly to reason that active and passive homosexuality had different causes. Borrowing from Havelock Ellis's distinction between sexual invert and pervert,[29] they argued as follows:

Passive male homosexuals are typically true inverts . . . active male homosexuals seem not to be. The latter are masculine in their responses, but the stimulus which provokes their sexual responses is a male instead of a female, though preferably a male of feminine personality. . . . In the making of active male homosexuals it is probable that chance circumstances often play an important role . . . [as in] a willingness to experiment in search of new types of sexual gratification. The active male homosexual is rather a pervert, in the primary and nonmoral connotation of the term.[30]

This explanation was extended to women, though it was the passive women homosexuals who were the "perverts" and the active women homosexuals who were the "inverts."[31] Terman and his research team had little data on which to base any conclusions about female homosexuality, so they turned to another kind of abnormal sample—institutionalized delinquent girls—and through testing identified a masculine and feminine group.[32] As in the case of the male homosexuals, they found in each of these groups gender interests to be well established in early childhood. In addition, through contacts with the New York–based Committee for the Study of Sex Variants, Terman and Miles were able to include a small sample of eighteen female homosexuals, which they broke down into "passive" and "active or mutual" subsamples.[33] Consistent with their findings with male homosexuals, they reported tested differences on M-F. The active-mutual women were more masculine than the passive women.

What Terman and his team were getting at by the invert-pervert distinction was that the invert was the homosexual with the inappropriate gender identity, mentality, and emotionality—all apparently psychologically conditioned by parents in such a direction from early childhood. The pervert was the homosexual whose gender characteristics were "appropriate" but who, by chance and possibly through curiosity, turned to a form of sexuality that went against his or her natural gender adjustment. The implication seemed to be that the pervert was not really a bona fide homosexual. Therefore, their conclusion was that true homosexuality reflected gender-role deviation.

One other analysis in the Terman and Miles study needs to be considered to complete their portrayal of homosexuality. Terman and Kelly noted that the M-F differences between the passive homosexual and normal males were most pronounced on the subtest measuring interests.[34] To specify the divergencies between the invert group and normal males, Terman and Kelly selected the norm group of junior-high-school boys and compared their item responses with those of the invert group. Those responses which most discriminated between the two groups were given the highest scoring weights. On the basis of the distribution of scoring weights, a scale of "Sexual Inversion" was developed. Contrary to the expectations of the researchers, the correlation between the "I" scale and the M-F scale for the invert group was only .09. In essence, there was only a negligible correlation.[35] However, this did not prevent Terman and Kelly from proceeding to depict the "feminine personality" of the inverts based upon their "I" scale responses. The following composite picture of the invert personality was presented.

The interests, attitudes, and thought trends of this invert group are more or less typically feminine throughout the test. . . . The feminine personality of the inverts appears in their fastidiousness with respect to dress, cleanliness, and care of person; in their preoccupation with domestic affairs; in their preferences for feminine types of occupations_ their fondness for sentimental movies and romantic literature . . . in their liking for literature, art, music, and dramatics. . . . by their repudiation of everything that is characteristically masculine: aggressive leadership, energetic activity . . . interest in warfare, adventure, outdoor sports, science, and things of a mechanical nature.[36]

Beyond this feminine profile, the following was added.

The inverts show evidence of an excessive amount of sex consciousness, especially consciousness of the forbidden nature of their sex lives. . . . One of the most marked differences between the two groups appears in the lax ethical standards of the inverts. . . . The introvertive and psychoneurotic tendencies of the invert group are reflected in . . . social maladjustment, nervousness . . . and a marked tendency to worry and anxiety.[37]

Judged by the conventional frame of reference that Terman and his team operated from, this was indeed a pathological portrait. In reality if we accept this description at face value, it reflects a group of male homosexuals who seemed psychologically healthy in their pursuit of a lifestyle that was normative within their own subculture, though audacious to the male subculture at large. Furthermore, in the context of the times (the late twenties to the early thirties), they appeared to be realistically vigilant and concerned about the "underground" nature of their lives.[38]

Terman's conclusions about homosexuality and its relation to masculinity-femininity mirrored the norms and beliefs of American society. His own conventional outlook would hardly allow him to entertain the possibility of a sexually pluralistic society in which homosexuality and bisexuality were acceptable options. In a rather contradictory way, he credited Havelock Ellis "as one of the most civilizing influences of the last hundred years."[39] Yet he seemed to miss the point that although Ellis (like himself) championed the study of sex differences, Ellis valued a pluralistic society with respect to gender roles and sexual-object choice.[40] In the introduction to his *Sex and Personality* monograph, when Terman placed himself in the role of the objective scientist who could not "condemn or praise" any particular type of behavior, he failed to realize how his own heterosexist bias distorted the facts that he accumulated with the unintended consequence that he could not, despite his claim to the contrary, separate fact from opinion. Furthermore, when he claimed that his role was to understand the behavior he studied, he was unable to realize how his own biases distorted and misconstrued the very thing that he studied—in this case homosexuality. His penchant for empirical-data gathering, so typical of the American psychologists of his generation, seemed to lead him to the false belief that he was an "objective" scientist. This raises the question as to whether or not psychology (and social science in general) can be the same kind of objective science and can use the same methods as employed in the natural sciences. For Terman and the majority of his American psychology colleagues, it was simply assumed that for psychology to be a science it must follow the course of the natural sciences.

Not only did Terman impose his values on the study of homosexuality, he did the same with respect to masculinity-femininity. In this regard, it is worth observing that masculinity scores were positive while femininity scores were negative. Particularly revealing was his conclusion that marked deviations from sex-appropriate behaviors and norms were psychologically unhealthy. Such deviations could very likely lead to homosexuality. Even if this abnormality did not develop, other problems could arise. Referring to those with cross-gender identifications, Terman and Miles commented: "One would like to know whether fewer of them marry, and whether a larger proportion of these marriages are unhappy."[41] Specifying this point further, they observed that "aggressive and independent females" could very well be at a disadvantage in the "marriage market."[42] They also feared that too much competition between the sexes would not be desirable in industry, in politics, or in the home. In essence, they supported the status quo relationship between the sexes—a relationship based on male dominance. (It is difficult to determine the extent to which Catharine Cox Miles concurred in all of this. Terman acknowledged prime responsibility for the concluding chapter. However, he also stated that the authors collaborated in the final revision.)[43]

After the publication of *Sex and Personality*, Terman continued to be interested in homosexuality. As a touching outcome of the book's appearance, he received several letters from young males concerned about their possible homosexuality.[44] To one high-school boy he wrote back that it was too early to worry yet, but if in two or three years he was still infatuated with boys he should see a psychiatrist. In the meantime, he should do "nothing overt." At a personal level, he became a confidant for those members of his gifted sample who revealed their homosexuality to him. About fifteen to eighteen males did so.[45] To learn that some members of his gifted sample were homosexual must have been especially troubling for Terman. He had hoped to demonstrate that a gifted sample was relatively free of pathology. That they might not make a successful heterosexual adjustment also meant their loss to the genetic pool for superior intelligence.

As a direct consequence of his M-F scale, Terman was invited in 1935 to become a member of an interdisciplinary committee on the study of homosexuality.[46] The Committee for the Study of Sex Variants was privately funded by an anonymous donor.[47] The anonymity of the donor and the committee's inability to obtain funds from any other source reflected the stigmatization attached to the scientific study of homosexuality in the 1930s.[48] Catharine Cox Miles was also invited, and other members included psychologists Carney Landis and K. S. Lashley, psychiatrists George W. Henry and Adolph Meyer, as well as representatives from sociology, anthropology, corrections, gynecology, and endocrinology. Henry, who was on the staff of Cornell's Payne Whitney Psychiatric Clinic, was the director of research. He worked closely with Jan Gay, a woman who over a ten-year period had collected three hundred histories of homosexual women. She was able to recruit a New York City sample of fifty male and fifty female homosexuals who were followed up by Henry and other research associates. In fact, Gay, and most likely the donor as well, was a member of the homosexual community.[49] It seems highly improbable, however, that the committee would have even suspected such a possibility. The donor, Gay, and the homosexual subjects might well have been motivated to cooperate with the committee in the hope of attaining tolerance and understanding through scientific investigation. With the heterosexist bias of the researchers, what the homosexual community received was sympathy for a group of unfortunate deviants.

Henry and his team conducted psychiatric interviews, medical and physical examinations, and the administration of the Terman-Miles M-F test.[50] The M-F scores proved to be highly similar to those reported in the Terman-Miles monograph. All of the data were put together in a case-study format and published as two volumes in 1941 (one on men, the other on women). Henry, who authored the volumes, came to the same conclusion as Terman. Homosexuality was related to cross-gender identification. Henry's message was even more explicit than Terman's—any significant deviation from the prescriptive gender roles in society was a pernicious force in the development of overt homosexuality.[51]

Terman planned to revise the inversion scale he had presented in his M-F monograph. In the early forties, Robert Ross, who was an instructor at Stanford, worked on a revision in conjunction with case histories he had collected in the navy.[52] However, there is no indication that a revision was ever successfully completed. Terman would have one more involvement in the area of homosexuality. In 1948 he published a review that was critical of the Kinsey study of male sexual behavior.[53]

Marital Happiness

Terman's interest in studying marital adjustment began through his association with Lowell Kelly, the graduate student who had worked with him on the masculinity-femininity project. During one of the weekly evening seminars held in Terman's home, Kelly reviewed a book that had been published in 1929, which dealt with a large-scale study of marital adjustment.[54] During the same year, the results of two other similar studies became available.[55] Kelly was impressed that all three of these studies pointed to the same conclusion—marital happiness was primarily a function of sexual compatibility. It seemed to him, however, that while sexual maladjustment was associated with marital problems, the basic difficulties were due to the personality or

temperamental incompatibility of the spouses, which in turn was manifested in sexual symptoms. Kelly proposed this hypothesis to Terman
along with a plan for a longitudinal study of adjustment in marriage,
which he hoped would be his dissertation project. Terman, however,
pointed out that such a study would take several years and suggested
that Kelly pursue it once he had his Ph.D. Kelly took Terman's advice
and instead conducted an experimental study with Walter Miles for
his doctoral research.

Apparently, Terman was interested in the area of marital adjustment because he worked on plans that he hoped would enable Kelly to
carry out the research. After completing his doctorate in 1930, Kelly
received a faculty appointment at the University of Hawaii. Terman
expressed the fear that Kelly would become a "lotus eater" if he
remained in Hawaii. In order to ensure that Kelly would get a solid
academic position, where he would be able to conduct his marital
research, Terman obtained a post-doctorate award for Kelly that involved a year of study in Germany. Thus, Kelly spent the 1931–32
year abroad. Terman continued to lay the groundwork for Kelly's
academic and research career by applying for a grant for the marriage
study through the National Research Council's Committee for Research
on Problems of Sex (the committee was chaired by Yerkes). Terman
had assumed that with the depression and Kelly's being abroad such a
grant would provide Kelly with the opportunity, upon his return, to
carry out his study as a research associate at Stanford. As it turned
out, Terman obtained the grant, but Kelly was able to obtain a faculty
appointment (with Terman's strong recommendation) at Connecticut
State College (now the University of Connecticut). The end result was
that Terman now had a grant for a marriage study which he would
have to undertake on his own.[56]

Terman and Kelly agreed that their specific interests in marriage
research were complementary.[57] Terman's project would be a short-
term cross-sectional comparison among different levels of marital adjustment, while Kelly's study (begun in the late 1930s) would be a
long-term longitudinal follow-up of marital couples. Although Kelly
played a significant role in directing Terman's interest to research on
marital adjustment, Terman himself was undoubtedly interested in the
area. He had set aside one of his seminar sessions (the one in which

Kelly reported) for discussion about research on marriage. Marital
research was an area of increasing interest in the late twenties (two
books had appeared and a third was forthcoming). With Terman's
involvement on the masculinity-femininity project, he most likely saw
marital adjustment as a promising extension of his new commitment to
study nonintellectual aspects of individual differences.

Terman also had a good source for obtaining marital data. Through
his association with the eugenics-oriented Human Betterment Foundation
he knew Paul Popenoe, the director of the Los Angeles–based Institute
of Family Relations. The institute, which was based on the marriage
clinics developed in Europe in the 1920s, claimed that it was the first
American institution of its kind when it was founded in 1930.[58] Marriage counseling and public education were provided, as well as a
limited research program. The organization had a biological orientation as reflected in the background of its director, Popenoe, who was a
specialist in heredity and eugenics. There was also a medical director
and several medical consultants. Among the psychological consultants
were several of Terman's former students—Barbara Burks, Jessie Chase
Fenton, and J. Harold Williams.

Terman began his study in 1934, and the complete results were
reported in a monograph, *Psychological Factors in Marital Happiness*,
published in 1938.[59] As with his other large-scale projects, the marital
study was a collaborative effort. Paul Buttenweiser and Leonard W.
Ferguson were graduate assistants; Donald P. Wilson, a Ph.D. psychologist, was associated with the Institute of Family Relations and
acted as a field assistant; and Winifred Bent Johnson, also a Ph.D.
psychologist, collaborated on much of the write-up. In introducing the
study, Terman pointed out that most of the previous research on
marital adjustment had been carried out by physicians or social workers.[60] This led to an excessive emphasis on the importance of sexual
factors with a corresponding neglect of psychological factors. While
there had been some corrective for this inbalance by recent sociological
studies, Terman stated that his was the first major investigation of
marital happiness along psychological lines.

A preliminary study of some 350 married couples and 100 divorced
couples from the San Francisco area demonstrated that particular attitudes expressed by the subjects were related to scores of marital hap-

piness. The marital happiness scores were obtained from a specially constructed questionnaire, assessing such items as commonality of interest, amount of spousal agreement, subjective estimates of happiness, and a checklist of domestic grievances. The attitudes were reflected in responses to individual items on the Strong Vocational Interest Blank (the test developed by Terman's Stanford colleague, E. K. Strong) and the Bernreuter Personality Inventory. The latter instrument was developed by Robert G. Bernreuter for his dissertation under Terman in 1931.[61] The Bernreuter test measured four personality traits: neurotic tendency, self-sufficiency, introversion, and dominance. However, rather than any of these "traits" or any of the interest patterns, it was the responses to individual items across both tests that were associated with the marital happiness scores.

The final study included a much larger sample and also added background factors and information about sexual adjustment in the marriage. About eight hundred married couples, mostly from the Los Angeles Institute of Family Relations with a small group from a San Francisco center, filled out the information schedules in the presence of a field assistant. This procedure was used to prevent any collaboration between husband and wife in responding to the questionnaire. The group studied consisted primarily of urban and semiurban couples at the middle and upper-middle "cultural" levels. It was noted that such a sample appeared to be somewhat biased in the direction of "superior marital happiness." According to Terman, the major finding of the study was that the combination of personality and background factors was more influential than sexual compatibility in predicting marital happiness. This conclusion was contrary to previous marriage studies, which held that sexual compatibility was the key to marital happiness.

The personality characteristics that differentiated the happy from the unhappy of both sexes reflected the extent to which each spouse was tolerant, sensitive, and accepting of the other's needs and feelings. For example, unhappy subjects tended to be touchy or grouchy, lose their tempers easily, fight to get their own way, and chafe under discipline or rebel against orders. There were also some specific patterns that characterized wives and husbands.[62] Happily married women had "kindly attitudes toward others," did not easily take offense, were cooperative, and did not "object to subordinate roles"—in essence, the traditional role that was set for American women before the feminist revolution of the 1960s. This conventional idea was not questioned by Terman and his collaborators. In fact, consistent with the admonitions raised by Terman and Catharine Miles in their masculinity-femininity book, unhappily married women were aggressive, ambitious, and not interested in "benevolent and welfare activities"—in other words, the traditional feminine areas of interest. In Terman and Winifred Johnson's words (Johnson collaborated on this section), unhappily married women "give evidence of deep-seated inferiority feelings to which they react by aggressive attitudes rather than by timidity."[63] It was also reported that these women were more radical in politics, religion, and social ethics than their happily married counterparts.

It seems unfortunate that the happiness scores were only analyzed with respect to individuals—that is, data for couples were not reported. This deficiency makes it difficult to interpret the distinguishing characteristics of happy and unhappy husbands in relation to their wives. For example, happily married men tended to have "equalitarian" attitudes toward women, while their unhappily married counterparts tended to be domineering and took pleasure in assuming "commanding roles" over women and business dependents. One wonders if unhappy domineering husbands had rebellious wives, or were the rebellious wives the spouses of happy husbands who deluded themselves in their equalitarian attitudes? Terman reported that the happiness scores between the group of husbands and wives correlated about .60, which he interpreted as follows: "the happiness of one spouse is to a surprising degree independent of the happiness of the other."[64] This suggests that there was a fair degree of diversity between the happiness scores of spouses. Consequently, wives might rebel from their husbands for a variety of reasons.

The background factors that were most predictive of marital happiness reflected childhood happiness and a good relationship with one's parents during the premarital years.[65] Other background factors included the "superior happiness of parents," parental frankness about sexual matters, and a positive premarital attitude toward sex. As for sex factors themselves, Terman reported that there were only two that correlated markedly with happiness scores: the husband-wife difference in strength of sex drive and the wife's orgasm adequacy. The relative strength of the sex drive was assessed by the ratio (computed for each subject) between actual and preferred number of copulations per month and each spouse's ratings of his or her relative passionateness. Equality or near equality of sex drive was an indicator of happiness. This sex factor, however, was less important than the background factors of parental happiness, childhood happiness, and the amount of conflict between child and mother. On the other hand, the wife's orgasm adequacy was the one sex factor more important than any of the background factors. Orgasm adequacy was related to the happiness score for the wife and the husband.

Terman was perplexed by the findings on orgasm adequacy. He reported that a third of the wives fell into the inadequate group (defined as "never" or "sometimes" as opposed to "usually" or "always"), and he noted that these figures were in close agreement with those found by other investigators in Europe and America. The clearest picture that emerged from the questionnaire analyses (the Bernreuter and Strong items) was that orgasm inadequacy was associated with "neurasthenic tendencies, diminished responsiveness, and lack of zest, vigor, or colorfulness of personality."[66] On this basis, Terman concluded that orgasm inadequacy in women was biological rather they psychological and was perhaps largely of genetic origin. Apparently, another influence underlying his biological conclusion was his expectation that the more liberal climate of the 1930s would have reduced the amount of orgasm inadequacy among the younger wives, but the data did not support this. Terman's biological interpretation of orgasm inadequacy also seems to have reflected his insensitivity to such cultural factors as the dominant role that men have traditionally played in sexual intercourse—that is, the sex act reaches its conclusion when the man achieves orgasm. Furthermore, he seemed to be carried away by the questionnaire pattern of "lack of zest" as a cause, when it is possible that such a pattern could alternatively have been the result of the orgasm inadequacy experienced by females.[67]

Terman's monograph on marital happiness attracted considerable attention. The reviews were generally positive, acknowledging that Terman's psychological approach was a pioneering effort that would provide the basis for further research along similar lines.[68] He was also pleased to receive letters of praise from other writers and investigators in the field of marital relations, such as Havelock Ellis, Robert L. Dickinson, and G. V. Hamilton.[69] However, there was one review by fellow psychologist Harry L. Hollingworth that displeased Terman. In writing to his publisher, Terman commented that it was a "nasty review," which "contained some personal innuendo which one could not stoop to answer."[70] Though he did not cite any particular passage in Hollingworth's critique, he was probably disturbed by the following statement, which appeared within the first paragraph of the review (Hollingworth was referring to Terman and his collaborators).

Periodically they urge the reader to remember that mere correlates, if any, have no causal implications; whereupon they feel free to indulge in exclamatory conclusions concerning the causal effects and influences of such correlates. But what is sauce for the reader ought to be sauce for the authors. The procedure followed is that of the pious man who hopes to win salvation on the installment plan, interspersing spasms of wickedness between his recurrent confessionals.[71]

Hollingworth was caustic in his introductory comments, but this tone was not apparent throughout the article. His major criticism was that Terman was prone to draw cause-and-effect conclusions based on correlational data—a criticism that was also echoed by other reviewers, albeit in less colorful terms and matched with more positive evaluations of the work as a whole.[72] Hollingworth also pointed to the limitations of a psychometric approach that assessed hypothetical rather than actual events, as in the case of "marital infidelity."[73] Terman published a response to Hollingworth; but unlike his earlier responses to Lippmann and Bagley, he refrained from any personal attack.[74] Instead, he pointed to the predictive value of his study by referring to Kelly's marital research. Kelly, using the same questionnaire, was able to demonstrate that the personality and background items correlated with happiness as assessed two years later. Aside from the specific research issues involved, Terman's private reaction to Hollingworth's review reflected his difficulty in dealing with criticism. As in the case with Lippmann and Bagley, he overreacted. Fortunately, in the episode with Hollingworth he was able to control his anger at what he perceived as a personal insult.

One other instance of strained personal relations emerged from the marriage study. Lowell Kelly wrote to Terman about his surprise at finding no reference to his own preliminary work in Terman's monograph, especially since he felt he had played an influential role in the project's birth.[75] Terman replied that he was appalled to learn of the omission and appreciated Kelly's "restraint" in the way he brought the matter up.[76] Terman explained that he now realized that his discussion of Kelly's research had appeared in a methodological chapter of the book, which eventually had been discarded because of the publisher's limitation on the book's length. He assured Kelly that he would try to publish the omitted chapter as a journal article. Indeed, the paper (with a discussion of Kelly's work) appeared a short time later.[77] With his own former student, Terman was appropriately sensitive to the slight he had unintentionally committed and made immediate restitution.

Test Revisions

In 1931, fifteen years after its publication, Terman could justifiably boast that the Stanford-Binet was the most widely used instrument for testing the intelligence of individual subjects.[78] Although group intelligence tests provided the means for mass testing in the schools and in the military, individual tests were utilized by psychologists in such clinical settings as child guidance centers and institutions for the retarded. The adoption of the Stanford-Binet was not limited to the United States, for it had been translated into several languages and was available in nearly all of the "leading countries of the world." The Stanford-Binet had several advantages over the various other individually administered Binet revisions that appeared in America.[79] In terms of test content, the Stanford-Binet was the most thorough and extensive revision of the Binet-Simon scales. The standardization procedure proved to be the most ambitious attempt of its time to obtain a representative sample (although it still fell short of modern standards). The test's introduction of IQ as an overall index won quick recognition and was incorporated into other individual tests, as well as into group intelligence tests. Furthermore, the Stanford-Binet had a comprehensive examiner's guide, and its publication by Houghton Mifflin, a leading educational publishing firm was advantageous with respect to marketing and sales.

Nevertheless, as Terman himself admitted, there were problems with the 1916 scale.[80] It was not adequately standardized, some of the individual test items did not reveal satisfactory validity, the ability range of the scale was inadequate below the four-year level and above the average adult level, and only one form of the scale was available (which provided no control for coaching effects). With a series of grants from Stanford's Social Science Research Council, starting in 1927 Terman embarked on a thorough revision of the Stanford-Binet, which was published in 1937.[81] Over a seven-year period he received a total of $33,300 from the council, which was supplemented by about $10,500 from the Thomas Welton Stanford Fund and his own personal contribution of $3,600.[82] Maud Merrill was initially employed by Terman (at his own expense) to assist him. However, beginning in 1930, she became the co-director of the project. One of the aims of the revision was to construct two alternate forms—composed of different items but equivalent in such test characteristics as difficulty, range, reliability, and validity. The existence of alternate forms would provide a safeguard against coaching and would also minimize practice effects when a subject was retested. Representing the joint authorship, one form was labeled L for Lewis (Terman); the other was labeled M for Maud (Merrill).[83]

The 1937 revision included several major changes.[84] In contrast to the 90 items or subtests of the original, each of the alternate forms was composed of 129 items. The increase in items contributed to the wider sampling of abilities, especially at the upper (adult) and lower (preschool) levels. Other content changes reflected a greater weighting of nonverbal tasks at the lower ages and less reliance on rote memory at the higher ages. Directions for test administration were more carefully standardized, and scoring was made more objective. The most time-consuming change involved the new standardization sample. Approximately thirty-two hundred native-born, white subjects between the ages of one and a half and eighteen were included. In order to achieve a representative sample (within the restriction of the white population), steps were taken to obtain adequate geographical and socioeconomic distribution. The sample was drawn from seventeen communities in eleven widely separated states, and several indices of socioeconomic status were utilized. Despite these procedures, the sample was somewhat biased toward the higher social-class levels and toward urban as opposed to rural subjects.[85]

With respect to interpreting the findings of an association of higher IQs with higher socioeconomic status, Terman and Merrill noted that such data did not "offer any conclusive evidence of the relative contributions of genetic and environmental factors."[86] This was a marked departure from Terman's 1916 conclusion that social-class differences were primarily the result of native endowment.[87] By the late thirties, Terman appeared to be less dogmatic about hereditarian explanations.[88] And yet, as we shall see, the reopening of the nature-nurture issue in 1940 resulted in his reaffirming a hereditarian stance in interpreting IQ scores.

When the 1937 revision was on the market, it led to an unanticipated political protest. At the preschool levels, German-made toys were utilized. When the standardization began in 1928, this presented no problem. However, by the time the test was produced in 1937, the Nazi regime was in power. Several protests were communicated to Terman, as well as the publisher, Houghton Mifflin. These protests, which demanded the removal of the German materials, were mounted by several groups located in New York City, including the American Jewish Congress, the Graduate Psychology Group of City College (an organization of graduate students), and the Psychologists' League (a socialist-oriented group of professional psychologists).[89] In writing to the secretary of the graduate-student group, Terman commented: "Your group can't dislike the Nazi government any more than I do."[90] He added, however, that unless identical objects were found it would not be possible to replace the German-made objects. Substituting different materials would invalidate the standardization norms, which were based on the original materials. As it turned out, Houghton Mifflin was unable to locate duplicate toys, and it was decided to make no changes.[91] The matter was not closed, for with the outbreak of World War II the German materials could no longer be imported, and the relevant test items had to be deleted. Terman and Merrill sent out a new set of directions to test-users. These involved using some of the "alternate" items available in the scales, as well as changing the scoring system in the age levels affected.[92]

In general, the 1937 revision was judged to be a significant improvement over the original edition, especially in the care taken to obtain a representative sample and the thoroughness used in the selection and placement of test items.[93] Some problems remained, such as the lack of assessing separate abilities, the unsuitability for adult testing (because of an insufficient ceiling for superior adults), and the inefficiency of the all-or-none scoring system. With the appearance in 1939 of an individual test for adults, the Wechsler-Bellevue Intelligence Scale,[94] the 1937 Stanford-Binet became more clearly identifiable as a scale for children. The sales of the Stanford-Binet continued to reflect widespread use for the 1937 scale even after a major competitor appeared in 1949, the Wechster Intelligence Scale for Children.[95] In the 1950s Merrill took most of the responsibility of revising the Stanford-Binet for its third edition. The 1960 revision (again coauthored by Terman and Merrill) did not involve a restandardization.[96] The major change was the selection of the best items from the 1937 test for inclusion in one form, labeled Form L-M. A fourth edition was published in 1985.[97] This revision, coauthored by Robert L. Thorndike, Elizabeth P. Hagen, and Jerome M. Sattler, retains many of the item types in the previous editions but has been restandardized and includes several new scoring features.

The Terman Group Test of Mental Ability for grades seven through twelve, first published in 1920, was revised in 1941. The revision was a collaborative effort with Quinn McNemar; hence it was retitled the Terman-McNemar Test of Mental Ability.[98] The original test had proven to be popular—eleven million copies were distributed between 1920 and 1941.[99] The revision involved some changes in the content and organization of the subtests, as well as an extensive nationwide standardization procedure. The Terman-McNemar, like its predecessor, was a widely used high-school ability test.[100] However, because there were no further revisions, it eventually went out of print.[101]

The Stanford Achievement Test, being closely associated with educational curriculum content, required more frequent revisions than the ability tests. The original 1923 test was revised several times during

Terman's lifetime (in 1929, 1940, and 1953), and with three subsequent revisions continues to be one of the major achievement batteries on the market.[102]

During the 1930s, Terman experienced two sources of difficulty connected with the Stanford Achievement Test. First, there was a problem in obtaining royalty payments (for the 1929 revision) from the publishing firm, the World Book Company.[103] Second, a conflict emerged between Terman and one of his two coauthors, Truman Kelley, which resulted in Kelley's not participating in the 1940 revision. The problem regarding royalty payments reflected the financial difficulties World Book faced in the early thirties. The depression had cut into book sales, although test sales continued to do relatively well.[104] However, the major financial difficulty stemmed from the management of the company. In 1931 the publisher, Caspar Hodgson, had taken some of the company's profits and diverted them for his own use (apparently to pay off a blackmail threat involving an alleged "domestic situation").[105] Some years later, Hodgson justified his actions by stating that he fully intended to replenish the company coffers; but as he lamented to his former Stanford classmates, Ray Lyman Wilbur and Herbert Hoover, the New Deal legislation so added to his financial woes that he was unable to carry out his intentions.[106] In 1933 the firm was placed under the aegis of creditors, and test authors, such as Terman and Kelley, were realistically concerned about the future of their royalty returns.[107] The financial crisis was resolved the same year when Hodgson was forced out of the company. He died a broken man in 1938.[108] The firm was reorganized from within its management ranks, and all the royalties owed Terman and his test coauthors were fully restored.[109]

Terman's problems with Kelley went back to 1934. It was at this time that plans were under way for the third revision of the Stanford Achievement Test. According to Terman, Kelley's "ego was injured" over their disagreement about how to proceed with the revision.[110] Terman felt that Kelley was too technical in his approach to test construction, as illustrated by Kelley's insistence upon "statistical methods that teachers and even test users would not know how to use."[111] Terman's judgment of Kelley receives some confirmatory support from another source. Apparently, as a statistics teacher Kelley was also considered too technical. McNemar, who was a student in several of Kelley's classes, stated that even though he received "A" grades he was unable to follow much of what was going on.[112] As a consequence of their disagreement, Kelley insisted that Terman sell out his interest in the Stanford Achievement Test.[113] When Terman did not agree to do so, Kelley refused to take any part in the revision. It took some time for the rift to heal, for it was not until 1944 that the two men began to communicate with each other. What had been a close professional relationship was never reestablished.[114]

With Kelley out of the test collaboration, Terman turned to his other coauthor, Giles M. (Murrel) Ruch. Ruch had been involved with the achievement test from the start as a graduate student working with Terman. Ruch apparently shared Terman's misgivings about Kelley,[115] and the successful completion of the third revision was based on the ability of Terman and Ruch to work well as a team. Terman had thought highly of Ruch as a student and expected him to have a successful academic career in educational psychology.[116] After receiving his Ph.D. from Stanford in 1922, Ruch taught at the University of Iowa for several years and then went to the University of California at Berkeley. Unfortunately, while at Berkeley he unwittingly became involved in a grafting scheme carried out by a county school superintendent.[117] Although innocent of any wrongdoing (no legal charges were ever brought against him), his connection with the affair led to his dismissal by the university in 1933. A promising academic career was thus prematurely ended, and he never fully recovered either physically or emotionally from the episode. In 1938, when the test revision began, Ruch was working for the United States Office of Education.[118]

The 1940 revision of the Stanford Achievement Test was largely the work of Ruch and his wife, Verness. Terman's contribution was limited by his commitment to other writing projects; however, through correspondence he remained in close contact with Ruch.[119] In 1940, at the time the revision was completed, Ruch's physical health was declining, and the following year he had an emotional breakdown.[120] The tragic spiral of events ended with Ruch's suicide in 1943.[121] Terman lamented, "It seems a pity that one so able and valuable should have taken this way out."[122] Ironically, only a few months before another of Terman's most promising students, Barbara Burks, had ended her life (see Chapter 11).[123]

The events surrounding the 1940 revision of the Stanford Achievement Test were atypical with respect to Terman's collaborative efforts. Kelley appears to have been the only colleague with whom Terman was unable to maintain a working relationship.[124] One of the keys to Terman's high rate of professional productivity was his ability to collaborate with various graduate students and colleagues on a wide variety of projects.

The Reopening of the Testing Debate

In 1928 Terman had chaired the yearbook committee of the National Society for the Study of Education (NSSE). He had proposed the yearbook theme of the nature-nurture issue (regarding intelligence) in order to resolve the debate about the army tests that had erupted in the early twenties. The 1928 debate did not lead to a détente between the hereditarians and the environmentalists. On the contrary, each side felt that they had successfully supported their respective positions, as exemplified by Terman's conclusion that the evidence continued to point to a hereditarian interpretation of IQ scores. Nevertheless, with the airing of the nature-nurture issue within the scholarly confines of the NSSE, Terman must have experienced some personal relief from any further pressures to publicly resolve matters. The course of events was to prove otherwise, for in 1940 Terman was forced to return once again to the scene of the battle. George D. Stoddard of the University of Iowa had proposed a second yearbook on the nature-nurture issue. As chairman of the committee for the 1940 yearbook, he naturally invited Terman to be a member.[125] Having chaired the previous yearbook, Terman was hardly in a position to refuse.

Stoddard was the director of the University of Iowa's Child Welfare Research Station. He had obtained his doctorate at Iowa in 1925, working under Terman's former student G. M. Ruch.[126] In 1928 he succeeded Bird T. Baldwin (who had died of a streptococcus infection) as the director of the station. Baldwin had given an address at the 1928 NSSE meeting that was critical of the hereditarian position.[127] During the 1920s, Baldwin collected longitudinal data on IQ tests and was interested in demonstrating the role of environmental factors in shaping intellectual development. This work was carried on by his close associate, Beth L. Wellman.[128] In a series of studies begun in 1932, Wellman reported that mental growth, as reflected by increases in IQ scores, was facilitated by school experience at both the preschool and elementary-school levels.[129] Other Iowa researchers investigated the effects of institutional environments (such as orphanages) and foster homes on tested intelligence.[130] The major conclusion stated in these studies was that IQs could be increased if children were exposed to environmentally stimulating conditions. An especially dramatic illustration of this effect was the reported gain, over a two-year period, of 27.5 IQ points by a group of preschool children who were transferred from an orphanage to an institution for the mentally retarded, where they received more intellectual stimulation.[131] In contrast, a group of the same-aged children who remained at the orphanage showed an average loss of 26 IQ points.

Stoddard was not directly involved in the research. However, in his capacity as the director of the station, he acted as the intellectual leader.[132] He also took on the role of spokesperson—both as author and as lecturer—and in this role emphasized the implications of the findings. For example, he favored restricting the use of intelligence tests to research and clinical purposes.[133] In this fashion, IQ tests could be used as indices of environmental change. He was, therefore, opposed to the standard procedure of widespread testing in the schools for the purposes of educational placement and long-term vocational prediction. Such a position was in direct opposition to Terman's views on the hereditary basis of intelligence and the use and purposes of testing. The Iowa research program and Stoddard's articulate leadership rocked the very foundation of the testing movement that Terman had been so instrumental in shaping. Terman reacted to the Iowa challenge as a personal threat to his career accomplishments; it was a threat that proved far more irksome to him than his earlier encounters with Lippmann and Bagley. Unlike the earlier debates, Terman had to contend with an ongoing research program that ran counter to his views. Furthermore, he had to confront a group of investigators who were propelled by their own sense of creating an intellectual revolution in the testing field. It seemed inevitable that the events surrounding the 1940 yearbook would be tinged with deep emotion, as well as considerable ego investment on the part of the participants.

Preparations for the yearbook began in 1937.[134] Stoddard made an effort to have a balanced steering committee. He and his colleague Wellman were balanced by Terman and Florence Goodenough. Rounding out the committee were two other environmentally inclined members, Frank N. Freeman (who had been involved in the 1928 yearbook) and Harold E. Jones, plus two other members disposed to hereditarian views, Leonard Carmichael and Leta S. Hollingworth.

The NSSE meeting at which the yearbook was presented and discussed took place in St. Louis on 24 and 26 February 1940. By early 1939, the committee members were able to look at the manuscripts being submitted for inclusion in the yearbook. Regarding the reports of the Iowa studies, Terman commented to E. S. Gosney of the Human Betterment Foundation (the eugenics-oriented group that Terman helped found): "I am amazed by the propaganda from the Child Research Institute at Iowa University by Stoddard, Wellman, and Skeels. They seem to think they have demonstrated that feeble minds can be brought up to average by their nursery school program and that the average can be made into the exceptionally brilliant. These preposterous contributions are not backed up by data at all convincing."[135]

These sentiments were echoed in Terman's published reactions in the yearbook, in which he stated: "It appears characteristic of the Iowa group of workers that they so often find difficulty in reporting accurately either the data of others or their own."[136] In her yearbook contribution, Goodenough supported Terman by arguing that the evidence from the Iowa research offered no meaningful validity for the impact of environmental stimulation upon IQ scores.[137] For their part, Stoddard and Wellman were critical of the studies supporting the Terman-Goodenough position of the primacy of heredity as a determinant of IQ.[138] In a subsequent book on intelligence published in 1943, Stoddard remarked about Terman's Stanford-Binet: "The Iowa workers . . . feel that, over the years, the Stanford revisions have offered not very reliable measurements of functions not very close to intelligence."[139]

Before the yearbook was discussed at the NSSE meeting in February 1940, a series of confrontations took place between various mem-

bers of the Terman and Stoddard camps. In November 1938, Goodenough and Wellman met in Iowa City as part of a planning session
for the yearbook.[140] Goodenough anticipated "something of a knock-
down, drag-out fight." While no written description of this meeting
survives, Goodenough was troubled by what she perceived as intran-
sigence and self-deception on Wellman's part.[141] She confided to Leta
S. Hollingworth, her former teacher and fellow committee member,
that she was a close friend of Wellman's (they had worked together in
the 1920s on the gifted study) and that she was entirely convinced of
Wellman's sincerity.

Terman thinks that she has deliberately attempted to present her data in a way
calculated to deceive the reader. I cannot agree with him in this. . . . I am
personally entirely convinced of her sincerity. What has happened is, I am
confident, that she has deceived herself . . . the situation is entirely comparable with that of a religious fanatic who hears the wings of angels in every rustle
of the dishtowels on the family clothes line.[142]

In May 1939 the yearbook committee met in Chicago, the first
meeting that Terman was able to attend.[143] As preparation for the
meeting, Terman had asked McNemar to prepare a critical examination of the Iowa studies.[144] As a result of this exercise, McNemar came
up with so many faults that Terman suggested the review be published. As McNemar's criticisms touched points not covered by Terman and Goodenough in their yearbook evaluations, Terman further
suggested that the paper be published elsewhere. It appeared in 1940
in the *Psychological Bulletin* paired with a rejoinder by Wellman and her
Iowa colleagues, Harold M. Skeels and Marie Skodak.[145] This exchange contained some rather invective phrasing on McNemar's part,
and he was chastised by Wellman and her coauthors for embarking
upon a mission of "demolishing," "destroying," and "exploding" the
conclusions of the Iowa researchers.[146] Matters were not helped when
Kurt Lewin attempted the role of peacemaker at the September 1939
APA meetings, which were held prior to the paper's publication.[147]
Lewin had a dual allegiance since he had been a visiting professor at
Stanford in the early thirties, and he was now at the Iowa Research
Station. He brought McNemar and Wellman together for a dinner
meeting. The meeting itself proved congenial, but at its conclusion

when they were alone, Wellman told McNemar: "You should realize that Lewis Terman has poisoned your mind."[148]

The two principals, Terman and Stoddard, confronted one another publicly at Stanford in July 1939. The previous March Stoddard had invited Terman to join him on a National Education Association–sponsored panel to discuss the forthcoming yearbook.[149] It seems that plans for this summer meeting did not work out. Instead, in conjunction with Stanford's School of Education Terman arranged for a similar panel to be held at Stanford on 7 July.[150] Stoddard was invited to be on the panel, but Terman was scheduled as the featured speaker. Thus, instead of the original plans for a panel discussion on the yearbook in which Terman and Stoddard would be on equal footing, Terman was now given the dominant position. In fact, Terman was allotted a full hour while Stoddard was given ten minutes.[151] Stoddard later recalled that he felt the whole affair had been "rigged."

Not only was the conference schedule slanted in Terman's favor, but he also took advantage of the situation to publicly discredit and insult the Iowa investigators. In his memoirs, Stoddard gave the following description of what occurred: "Terman was scornful of the reports of Harold Skeels and Marie Skodak, whose researches clearly established that children of dull parents, if placed early in good foster homes, would show IQs well above the average. Invariably he pronounced 'Skeels' and 'Skodak' explosively, lip curled, as if these two young Iowa researchers were a species of insect that had crept under his collar."[152] While Stoddard's reactions at the time and his later recollections were not those of a neutral observer, there is independent evidence of Terman's performance. Robert Sears was in the audience that night and felt that Terman had been extremely rude to Stoddard.[153] Furthermore, Sears reports that at the time Terman's friends at Stanford had the same reaction. Another corroborative report comes from Edgar Z. Friedenberg who, as a Stanford student, attended the conference and thought Terman made a fool of himself.[154]

Stoddard's metaphoric reference to insects getting under Terman's collar seems an apt description for the chain of events following the Stanford encounter. From Terman's perspective the Iowa team continued to act as pests and as such had to be contained. Stoddard and his group persisted in spreading their ideas throughout academic circles and beyond. Two examples illustrate the extent to which the Iowa cause spread beyond the confines of scholarly debate. At about the time of the Stanford conference, Terman learned, much to his disappointment, that A. E. Wiggam, the journalist who had interviewed him in the 1920s about the gifted study, was going to write an article for the *Ladies Home Journal* that would be sympathetic to the Iowa conclusions.[155] Terman could not prevent the Iowa message from seeping into the public media. With the help of his former student, Barbara Burks, he was more successful in holding off the opposition at the level of the federal government. It seemed that Stoddard had tried to obtain support from a fellow Iowan, Secretary of Agriculture Henry A. Wallace.[156] Burks had a Washington friend, geneticist Robert Cook, and the pair saw to it that Terman's Stanford speech was circulated in the Agriculture Department. Burks happily reported that although Secretary Wallace was enormously impressed with the Iowa publications and other publicity "blurbs," she and Cook were able to turn the tide and prevent a national movement from occurring. Burks proclaimed, "Wallace is no longer ready to 'buy' IQ's, i.e. to try to manufacture them by given dosages of nursery school, [or] moron nursemaids."[157]

Terman's attempts to hold the Iowa forces at bay also had to be carried out in more traditional arenas. He was invited to give an address in October 1939 at Columbia University to the Joint Educational Conference, a group that had invited Stoddard to speak the previous year.[158] Terman was unable to appear, but he thought the occasion an important one and recommended Goodenough as a substitute.[159] Goodenough accepted and in response to her request for suggestions for the talk, Terman answered: "Don't mince words . . . I think you know I was none too polite in my address here July 7. . . . Polite methods simply don't accomplish the job in this sort of situation."[160] Goodenough reported back that her talk had been well received and that there had been a large audience of around eight hundred.[161] She added that the "other side" was at the New York World's Fair listening to Stoddard who was talking to the "masses" at the same time. One further organizational battlefield had to be dealt with before the forthcoming St. Louis yearbook meeting in February

1940. Stoddard and Wellman were presenting their research at the annual meeting of the American Association for the Advancement of Science (AAAS) in December, and Terman was invited to participate.[162] This time Terman sent another of his former students, Lowell Kelly, who successfully fended off the opposition.[163]

With the series of encounters that preceded it, the St. Louis yearbook conference was somewhat of an anticlimax. The fact that Terman had no plans to attend (he had given up winter trips to the East) deflated some of the event's emotional edge.[164] Stoddard presented the Iowa side and Goodenough's colleague, John E. Anderson, the director of the University of Minnesota's Institute of Child Welfare, held the fort for the opposition. Benjamin R. Simpson, who attended the conference, provided Terman with a description of the events. Simpson had published a rather caustic critique of Wellman's studies on the effects of schooling on tested intelligence.[165] He had no connection with Terman's Stanford circle; but as a result of his article, Terman wrote him an unsolicited letter of praise, stating: "You have not put things too strongly, for their [Iowa] reports present the most appalling mess I have ever worked over."[166] In conveying the events of the yearbook meetings, Simpson recounted to Terman that the "house was full" for both Anderson's and Stoddard's addresses.[167] However, there was no discussion from the floor, and Simpson was especially impressed with the care taken by everyone to avoid any emotional utterances in public.

Simpson had one other noteworthy impression to communicate. He was surprised that in his talk Stoddard continued to "stick to his guns" in the face of all the criticism he had already received. Simpson was concerned that Stoddard was out to win popular support for his claims; therefore, he would be more of a force to "reckon" with than Simpson had expected. He added that another attendee, Horace B. English of Ohio State University, opined in private that Stoddard was a "dangerous man" and that those educators who opposed him would have a "stiff fight" on their hands. Terman in his reply to Simpson wrote: "I am inclined to agree with English that Stoddard is a dangerous man."[168] Terman's inclination soon gave way to conviction. In May, he wrote to Goodenough about his reaction to Stoddard's published address to the National Society of College Teachers of Education, given in

St. Louis a few days after the yearbook conference. In this address, Stoddard put forth his recommendation for the restrictive use of intelligence tests for research and clinical purposes, rather than the widespread use of such tests in the schools.[169] Terman communicated to Goodenough: "I have just read with considerable exasperation Stoddard's St. Louis speech . . . I have completely lost confidence in his intellectual integrity; it looks to me as though he is willing to go any distance in the direction of distancing data to suit his ends."[170]

Stoddard had become the bane of Terman's existence. Mass testing —the foundation of Terman's meritocratic edifice—was threatened. Terman was not alone in his concern about Stoddard's address. William C. Ferguson of the World Book Company expressed his fears of the widespread dissemination Stoddard's ideas were receiving, in both educational quarters and among the general public.[171] He urged Terman and other advocates of mental testing to make their positions known. Terman replied that he had lined up Benjamin Simpson to write a book for the Measurement and Adjustment Series, which would deal with the nature-nurture controversy as well as the proper use of mental tests.[172] Terman expressed his opinion that this book would serve the purpose of counteracting the Stoddard attack on testing. Simpson's book, which was expected to take a year to complete, was never produced. After almost ten years of working with the author, Terman as series editor was still doubtful about the manuscript when he submitted the final revision to World Book.[173] He was, therefore, not surprised to learn about its rejection.

As the course of events unfolded, Simpson's book was not really needed. There was no groundswell for discontinuing the use of IQ tests in the schools, though the Terman circle did receive at least one report of such an attempt.[174] By October 1940 Terman believed that the controversy was over and that few psychologists competent enough to judge the Iowa studies took "any stock in them"[175] The following year, Terman was heartened to learn that Stoddard was leaving Iowa to accept an appointment as the state commissioner of education for New York.[176] Both Terman and Goodenough were convinced that Stoddard had received so much criticism about the IQ studies from his Iowa colleagues (outside of the Research Station) that he was virtually forced to leave.[177] However, there seems to be no basis for such an interpretation. Ronald Lippitt and Marie Skodak Crissey, who attended the University of Iowa at the time, have indicated that Stoddard continued to be well thought of in the university community.[178]

Terman, however, persisted in his belief that the Iowa studies were worthless.[179] Nor did he believe that the Iowa graduate students were properly trained in administering tests. In the 1950s when Maud Merrill was preparing the third revision for the Stanford-Binet, she wanted to make use of test data that had been collected at the University of Iowa.[180] Terman strongly objected, but finally gave in because Robert Sears assured Merrill that the Binets given at Iowa were completely trustworthy. Sears, before he came to Stanford, had replaced Stoddard as director of the station. Regarding the nature-nurture issue, by the 1950s Terman had changed his views about the genetic basis of racial intelligence. He had told a number of people, including his Stanford colleague, Paul Farnsworth, that he wished he could have erased some of his earlier statements about racial differences.[181] Nevertheless, Farnsworth felt that when it came to individual intelligence, Terman believed to his "dying day" that every individual has a genetically determined intelligence that is stable over time. This belief was at the heart of his debate with Iowa.

How should the Stanford-Iowa debate of 1940 be evaluated? This exchange involved a clash between two groups of scientists, each committed to a very different set of underlying assumptions. For the Iowa group, tested intelligence was very malleable and sensitive to environmental intervention. Nevertheless, the Iowa position did not rule out heredity. Rather, what was assumed was an interactive process between internal (genetic) and external (environmental) influences on mental growth. Stoddard and Wellman stated this clearly in the yearbook: "In the life space of the child these two are never separated: he is a flexible, changeable, responding organism within wide limits set by heredity and other organic conditions, and within other wide limits set by environmental stimulations and opportunities."[182] In contrast, the Stanford group assumed that tested intelligence primarily reflected native ability and therefore should be stable over time. Long-term predictions could be made and an educational curriculum, geared to native individual differences, was the most efficient and democratic means of insuring that each child would fulfill his or her potential in society.

As in the earlier testing debates, these basic assumptions were often bypassed by a plethora of discussion about empirical data. The Stanford group raised criticisms about sampling issues, statistical problems, lack of replication, bias on the part of the testers, and so on. Indeed, some of these criticisms were valid (for example, the sampling problems and statistical regression effects).[183] What is noteworthy is that the Iowa researchers were in the forefront of generating studies on the relationship between environment and intelligence. Although their results did not conclusively demonstrate the impact of environmental stimulation upon intelligence, they were suggestive of such a relationship. Furthermore, the Iowa findings were not isolated ones. Evidence in support of environmental effects had already been presented in the 1928 yearbook, and subsequent research, especially in the 1960s, would provide additional support.[184] Stoddard's recommendation that IQ tests be used to assess environmental changes became a widely used practice in assessing compensatory education programs during the 1960s.

The fact that the Iowa group was embarking on relatively new waters resulted in its being doggedly scrutinized by those committed to the shibboleths of the testing movement. It should be recalled that the earlier criticisms of testing had challenged the issue that the tests were measuring innate intelligence. Indeed, Terman never provided unequivocal evidence that IQs reflected native ability. Based on his weddedness to Hall and Galton's biological determinism, he simply assumed that IQs were genetically determined. Moreover, his critics could be easily dismissed because they were outside of the testing field and, as in the case of Lippmann, outside of academia. In view of Terman's influence and connections (he had quite an army of willing and active supporters to turn to), it was quite an accomplishment that Stoddard and his small band were able to go as far as they did. Stoddard's power base was virtually limited to the state of Iowa, though he was able to reach Iowans in high places such as Agriculture Secretary Wallace. But even this was counteracted by Terman's Washington connection.

The 1940 Stanford-Iowa debate is also a critical incident in revealing

Terman's character. He does not emerge in a very positive light. When challenged, as in his previous exchanges with Lippmann and Bagley as well as his private reaction to Harry Hollingworth's review of his marriage book, he overreacted. The fact that the Iowa challenge was the most protracted and threatening incident that he had to face in his career makes it a bellwether marker in assessing Terman's personality. First of all, it reflects how ego involved he was in his commitment to testing—or more accurately, his prescription of how testing could serve as the means to creating a meritocratic society. Stoddard's program was viewed as a direct threat to Terman's career commitment. From Terman's perspective, how useful could IQs be as a selection device for choosing the most intellectually gifted if they were subject to changing conditions?

In fairness to Terman, he genuinely believed that Stoddard and his group were poor scientists, jumping to unwarranted conclusions. Nevertheless, as best evidenced by his performance at the Stanford conference, Terman chose unprofessional and heavy-handed tactics to suppress the opposition. Stoddard was placed in the humiliating position of listening to Terman's cynical attack of his Iowa colleagues and was then restricted to a brief rebuttal period. Terman appears to have purposely set up this situation. Apparently, Terman thought that if he browbeated his challenger, he would settle the issue. Just as in his ill-conceived cynical reply to Lippmann of two decades before, he showed poor judgment. In both cases, even Terman's friends were appalled by his behavior. Unfortunately, the pattern of his debates with those holding opposite views reveals a major flaw in Terman's personality. He was basically unable to accept criticism.

Political Involvement

Events leading to America's involvement in World War II set the stage for Terman's participation in an episode of political action. In the summer of 1941, he became one of the leaders of a group of Stanford faculty who sought to issue a public statement condemning isolationism. The motivation behind this compaign lay in the fact that Stanford trustee Herbert Hoover and Stanford president Ray Lyman Wilbur were among a group of fifteen prominent Republicans who issued a statement critical of Roosevelt's policy of aid for America's European allies.[185] The Stanford connection in this isolationist manifesto was particularly upsetting to many faculty because they feared it might lead to the impression that Stanford, as an institution, supported such a policy.[186]

The particular event that had sparked the isolationist forces to speak out was President Roosevelt's June 1941 announcement of aid to Russia, which had just been attacked by Hitler (breaking the Nazi-Soviet pact of 1939). During the summer of 1941, a group of nine Stanford faculty, including Terman, met and drafted a statement entitled "Our Nation's Foreign Policy."[187] This position paper advocated unified support for President Roosevelt in a period of national "emergency," as well as support for a "more dynamic policy of action" as opposed to "passive defense." The statement was in the form of a circular with space for a signature, and it was distributed among the faculty. Terman seems to have had an influential hand in drafting the paper since a few days before he had prepared a "letter to the editor," which contained the same points outlined in the circular sent to the faculty.[188]

The faculty circular was distributed on 21 August. By 5 September, it had been endorsed by 176 Stanford professors (close to eighty percent of those responding).[189] These results were reported in several newspapers in the Bay area, and the *Palo Alto Times* included the names of the 176 signers. When Hoover learned about these events, he sent out a questionnaire of his own to about 800 individuals connected with Stanford, including not only full-time faculty but also visiting and part-time faculty, instructors, librarians, secretaries, and clerks. Enclosed with the questionnaire was an individually typed covering letter indicating that everyone could agree with the expression "dynamic policy" as opposed to "passive defense."[190] However, Hoover added that he wanted a more specific survey of opinion; therefore, he requested that each recipient fill out the enclosed questionnaire. The six-item questionnaire, which was to be filled out anonymously, included such queries as "Do you think we should carry munitions to England in American Flag Ships?" and "Do you think we should send a land force to the Continent against Hitler?"[191]

The day after Hoover's questionnaire was circulated, seventy-five of the signers of the original faculty circular met.[192] In an open letter to his Stanford colleagues, Terman summed up the consensus of the meeting. It was generally felt that Hoover's call for categorical yes or no answers would not clarify the faculty position and could well be misleading. It was decided to draft a new statement, which would be more specific than the original one. In order to frame the proposed document, respondents to Hoover's questionnaire were requested to send copies of their responses to Graham Stuart, the chairman of the new committee charged with producing a revised faculty position paper.

The results of Hoover's questionnaire were announced in *The Stanford Daily* on 2 October.[193] Hoover concluded that sixty percent of the respondents opposed the "dynamic defense" policy advocated by the 176 faculty signers. The following day Terman issued a statement to the press stating that the Hoover poll was misleading because the questions could not be meaningfully responded to in a categorical yes-no fashion.[194] He concluded that little significance could be attached to any of the precise figures (to each question) reported in the Hoover poll.

The results of the Hoover poll also received national coverage, and the editorial opinions generally questioned Hoover's judgment as a university trustee canvassing his own faculty.[195] Many Stanford faculty members questioned the way the poll was conducted. There was also some suspicion that the results may have been rigged by Hoover's supporters at the Hoover library, which was located on the Stanford campus.[196] Hoover's personal integrity, however, was not questioned.

On 22 October the second faculty position statement was ready for distribution.[197] Terman was a member of the committee that drafted this revision, and because of his expertise he played a leading role in the polling procedures. Three questions were included that were specific enough so that they could be meaningfully responded to in a yes-no format. They dealt with past and proposed policy regarding the Axis powers. While working on the October statement, Terman and the committee had to fend off pressure from President Wilbur to drop the matter. Terman responded to Wilbur that, aside from the issue at hand, they could both agree that "the greatest peril that could confront a university would be the discouragement of free expression of opinion among the faculty."[198]

The results of the second faculty poll were released to the news media on 23 October. Terman concluded that more than eighty percent of the 341 faculty responding approved the Roosevelt administration's current foreign policy and that seventy-five percent endorsed the use of even stronger steps if needed. Terman forwarded a copy of the committee report to Hoover, who replied to Terman that it was useless to engage in such discussion with friends who were uninformed about what they were doing.[199] He added that he would file away all the papers dealing with the controversy and have them examined ten years later to determine the wisdom of the committee's proposals. It did not take long for the committee's wisdom to be vindicated—the attack on Pearl Harbor was only a little more than a month away.

Terman received widespread praise from the faculty for his handling of the poll, as well as for the forbearance he showed in his correspondence with Hoover.[200] He was also cited by the chief editorial writer of the *Oakland Tribune* for his leadership in injecting some intelligence into the controversy. One episode of acrimony did emerge from the poll. Terman's department colleague Calvin Stone, who was a staunch isolationist, embellished his questionnaire with caustic statements about the questions and the questioners.[201] Terman returned the questionnaire to Stone, saying that he could not turn in such a thing to the rest of the committee. A heated exchange took place, with Terman accusing Stone of being stubborn and woefully uninformed about public affairs. In recalling the episode, Maud Merrill felt that neither Terman nor Stone could respond reasonably to each other's bias. Generally, Terman did seem to handle the Hoover controversy well. The conflict with Stone seems to have reflected the tendency of both men to become overly emotional when directly confronted with opposing views.

Terman's involvement in the Hoover affair reflected his dedication to the cause of insuring that sloppy empirical research should not go unchallenged. However, beyond his career-long concern with proper science, the affair seemed to spark an interest in political and social issues. Throughout his retirement years (which began in 1942), he took an active interest in politics. More specifically, the encounter with Hoover sensitized him to the issue of academic freedom; and this became an issue of great concern to him during the McCarthy era.

A Gift from Students

On 15 January 1942 Terman reached his sixty-fifth birthday. When he entered his office he was pleasantly surprised to find a book sitting on his desk.[202] The book, entitled, *Studies in Personality*, contained the following preface.

Lewis M. Terman, servant of psychology, has labored untiringly to extend the boundaries of our knowledge of human behavior. His achievements and personality have been an inspiration to psychologists everywhere and especially to those who have had an opportunity for work and study under his guidance. It is fitting, therefore, that this series of papers on a topic about which so much of his own research has centered should be prepared for the occasion of his sixty-fifth birthday.

The authors of this book are but a small proportion of his many former graduate students who have been quickened by his leadership and who join with us and with his colleagues everywhere in the hope that his work may be continued for many years to come.[203]

A committee of seven former graduate students, chaired by Goodenough, had worked to put the volume together. Two of the committee members, McNemar and Merrill, took on the added responsibility of acting as editors. Sixteen authors contributed chapters describing their own research in the field of personality. Some, such as Burks, Goodenough, Lowell Kelly, Catharine Cox Miles, and Kimball Young, had worked closely with Terman as both students and colleagues. Others, including Roger G. Barker, Harry F. Harlow, Robert R. Sears, and Miles A. Tinker, had contact with Terman as a teacher. At the end of the book there was an annotated bibliography of Terman's publications.

The volume was introduced by Columbia University's Robert S. Woodworth, a prominent experimental psychologist.[204] Such an introduction was a great honor since it was written by a highly esteemed professional colleague who was outside of Terman's area of specialty. Woodworth began by noting that "none of our contemporary psychologists, it is safe to say, is more widely known by the general public."[205] This was a reference to Terman's work on intelligence tests. Woodworth then proceeded to review Terman's life and work, drawing largely upon his autobiography. He pointed out that much of

Terman's research was cooperative, something that he felt character-ized the man. He concluded with the following: "No one can say that Terman has picked out the easy tasks, and no one can deny that he has succeeded nobly in his early ambition to establish a direct relation between scientific psychology and the life of the people. He is truly to be numbered among the pioneers, whose example is an inspiration to the younger generation and whose work and influence will long en-dure."[206]

This introduction, as well as the book as a whole, was a great tribute. Understandably, Terman was very moved. In an open letter to the contributors, he expressed his feelings.

Studies in Personality was as big a surprise as Pearl Harbor. No suspicion had crossed my mind. I was caught completely off the alert. Like Pearl Harbor too it left me overwhelmed and speechless.

There the parallel ends, for the after effects are as pleasing as the event itself was surprising. No other conceivable token of your appreciation could have meant so much to me. . . . In accepting your splendid memorial I must beg leave to think of it as more than a personal tribute to me . . . Both in scientific and literary merit *Studies in Personality* is vastly creditable to its authors and to Stanford.[207]

The sixty-fifth birthday gift reflected a salutary quality about Terman. Throughout his Stanford career as a teacher and as department head, Terman had been influential; and, in several instances, he had been a source of inspiration to his students. Examples of this have already been touched on during Terman's career in the twenties. The pattern continued in the thirties and early forties. However, one change did take place. In the later period, Terman's influence was exercised more in the role of advisor than as a research supervisor.

Largely due to increasing commitments to his own research and writing, he supervised only seven psychology graduate students from 1930 to his retirement in 1942.[208] This contrasts with the twenty-one theses (M.A. and Ph.D.) he directed in psychology from 1922 (the year he moved to that department) through 1929. Another factor accounting for this change is the fact that by the 1930s he had already trained a cadre of former students to carry out the kind of research he was interested in; and many of these students continued to work closely with him, most notably Merrill, Cox-Miles, Goodenough, Burks, and G. M. Ruch. Thus, by 1930 he had less of a need to attract graduate students as research apprentices. In this later period only one of the Ph.D. students he directed continued as a research collaborator. This was McNemar, who as a graduate student impressed Terman because of the statistical competence he demonstrated in Truman Kelley's courses.[209] When Kelley left Stanford, Terman was able to rely on McNemar as a statistical consultant.

Several of those who were graduate students during the thirties have reported recollections of Terman. Roger Barker, who completed his Ph.D. under Miles, described the kind of department "atmosphere" Terman fostered.[210] For example, Terman strongly supported the slogan of the university at that time—"Let the Winds of Freedom Blow." Hence, in the department there was a minimum of bureaucracy. Faculty and students were free to teach and study what they desired. Terman had achieved the same atmosphere he depicted at Clark when he was a graduate student (see Chapter 3). Another characteristic Barker noted was Terman's espousal of empiricism and "hard practical work." The generation of data was a highly prized objective. At the interpersonal level, Terman conveyed his interest in students—though he was not especially friendly with them.[211] This mode of interaction supported his emphasis on task accomplishments and enabled him to take objective actions on students' behalf.

All of the graduate students were directed (usually in their first year) to take Terman's year-long course sequence in educational psychology. This was not a lecture course. At the first meeting, Terman outlined the subject matter and then passed out a list of topics of current interest.[212] The students were instructed to choose a topic, search all the library sources, and be prepared to orally present a written report at least an hour in length to the class four months later. The class was then dismissed. McNemar has observed that the delivery of these reports was typically a traumatic experience for students because they felt that their candidacy for the doctorate was going to be determined by their performance.[213] And indeed this was an accurate perception. Terman made few comments during the oral presentation, but with his editorial red pencil the written reports were filled with suggestions and critical comments. In McNemar's case, he had received encouraging feedback from Terman at the end of his class presentation. He was asked to revise his manuscript because it was deemed worthy of publication. Several weeks after turning in the revision, Terman called McNemar into his office, calmly looked up from his desk, and said: "How can a person think if he can't write?"[214] McNemar's ego was deflated, but he was determined to improve his writing and sought help from his wife Olga, as well as from a fellow student who had an M.A. in English. Terman's high standards were an important influence in shaping McNemar's career. This was with respect not only to writing ability but also to injecting a critical attitude. McNemar has stated that "I honestly believe my emergence as a critic had its roots in Terman's insistence that the literature of psychology should be approached with skepticism and a critical eye."[215]

Another significant exposure to Terman took place at the weekly evening seminars at his home. This was a gathering of both graduate students and faculty. In atmosphere, time, and place it carried on the tradition Terman had been exposed to when he attended Hall's seminars at Clark. For the faculty, the seminars served as an integrative force in the department.[216] For the students, it was another setting in which they would be evaluated.[217] The seminars were held in the congenial confines of the Terman living room, usually with a fire going in the fireplace. Chairs were arranged in a single-row circle to accommodate about twenty-five. Thee was one speaker, usually a graduate student, but sometimes a faculty member. The reports typically described completed research or proposals for research; occasionally books or monographs were reviewed. The emphasis was on data and methods. Theories or general issues were rarely seminar topics. The exchanges between the speaker and other seminar members were usually for more information or clarification about the research reported on. Terman set the tone by listening attentively, making some contributions, and at times asking searching questions. In recounting his reactions to the seminars, Barker felt that what he got most out of the experience was a socialization into the language, mores, and ethos of the "psychology tribe."[218] However, he disliked what he believed to be the focus of the seminars—namely, that the individual's personal worth was being judged by others. Neal E. Miller, a master's degree student at the time, recalled the seminars as extremely lively and stimulating sessions.[219] He credited Terman with creating a warm and friendly atmosphere, but one which was also intellectually competitive and highly critical.

Terman's impact on the graduate students went beyond the classroom and the seminar. In many specific cases he had a profound influence on their careers. Sometimes this could be at a very paternalistic level. He was not reticent to offer personal criticism on career-related characteristics, such as writing style or patterns of speech.[220] Another instance of Terman's paternalism affected Harry Harlow, whose original name was Harry Israel. Harlow was less than 1/64th Jewish.[221] After he received his Ph.D., Terman called him into his office and pointed out that if he wanted an academic career a Jewish-sounding name would pose a considerable hardship. Terman recommended that Harlow choose a name in his family. He presented Terman with two names—Harlow and Crowell. Terman chose Harlow, and Harry Israel thus became Harry Harlow. Harlow later commented that he was probably the only scientist to be named by his major professor. Beyond being renamed, Harlow credited Terman with being a prime influence in his career. About twenty years after he left Stanford, Harlow wrote to Terman, expressing his feeling that Terman's kindness and faith in him were primary factors in his professional achievements (among which were the presidency of the American Psychological Association).[222]

In general, Terman maintained an active interest in the careers of his former students and was typically alert to congratulating them on their many professional accomplishments. He set the tone of Stanford's psychology department and imparted a theme of high standards for intellectual achievement and productivity. Therefore, it is not surprising that a high proportion of the students—especially in the 1930s and 1940s—were subsequently high achievers.[223] Three alumni from this period, Harlow, Kelly, and McNemar, eventually became presidents of the American Psychological Association. Moreover, Terman often took an active role in promoting and placing former students, as in the case of Lowell Kelly.

Terman's influence was also felt by some undergraduate psychology majors. A high proportion of them (about three out of five) went on to graduate study in the discipline, and Terman took an active role in trying to place them in good departments at other universities.[224]

Terman would typically select a senior he considered especially promising and invite the student to sit in on the weekly evening seminars. One such student was Robert Sears, who at Terman's urging went on to Yale to study with Clark L. Hull.[225] Sears did not find Terman a stimulating teacher in his undergraduate course on biography, but he was grateful for the continuing interest Terman expressed in his career development.[226]

At the end of the summer quarter of 1942, Terman retired as teacher and department head.[227] However, when interviewed by a reporter for the *Palo Alto Times*, he emphasized that retirement did not mean an interruption in his work and added that he probably would be "pursuing gifted children" for the rest of his life.

CHAPTER 10

Retirement from Teaching (1942–1956)

Although it is possible for a superior department to lose prestige about as rapidly as it gained it, I look forward with confidence to the future of psychology at Stanford. Trends and problems of any science change with the passing of time, but I think that certain basic traditions have been established here that will carry forward.[1]

Terman looked back with pride on his accomplishments during his two decades as department head at Stanford.[2] He pointed to recruiting the ablest appointees available, the adoption of democratic administrative procedures, encouraging teamwork within the department, fostering close relationships with other departments, and guaranteeing academic freedom combined with personal responsibility. This self-appraisal is matched by Ernest Hilgard's characterization of Terman as a "remarkable" head, who was supportive, unobtrusive, and encouraging in his relationships with the department faculty members.[3] In turn, the faculty were generally "delighted" with him as head. The exception was J. E. Coover, the one Angell holdover, whose relationship with Terman was rather cool.

Terman had good evidence to support his assertion of recruiting appointees of high caliber. Including himself, five of the twenty presidents of APA between 1922 and 1942 were either members of the Stanford psychology department (Terman, Miles, and Stone) or had been nominated for a department position (Boring and Lashley).[4] These same five individuals were also elected to membership in the National

Academy of Science. (They constituted one-third of the psychologists so elected between 1922 and 1942.)

Terman noted that with such a successful faculty (he also lauded the accomplishments of his other appointees), it was not surprising that the department had developed an excellent reputation. In the late thirties, the American Council of Education ranked psychology as one of the four "outstanding" departments at Stanford.[5] As another index of the department's success, Terman referred to the subsequent performance of the Ph.D. graduates. On this account, he believed Stanford's psychology department was among the top few in the country. In support of this, he pointed to the high percentage of those awarded post-doctorate fellowships and also the high percentage elected to full membership in APA, which during the 1920s and 1930s required considerable evidence of research productivity. Terman had clearly established Stanford's psychology department as one of the best in the country. His legacy continued—in 1957 the department was ranked fifth in national ratings; in 1964 it was second;[6] and it has since continued to be among the top two or three.[7]

In his assessment of the department, Terman by no means excluded the contributions of others. He attributed the department's accomplishments to the quality of the faculty, the teamwork within the department, and the "unfailing" support of President Wilbur. In a letter to Wilbur, Terman expressed his feelings in this way: "I figure that during my twenty years in the Psychology Department the total of our annual departmental budget amounted to something like a million dollars. And in the allocation of those funds I never had reason to mistrust your judgment. No one could have had more loyal support and the department could not possibly have accomplished what it has done without your backing."[8]

As his tenure as head was nearing an end, Terman was concerned about the choice of a successor. Therefore, he engaged in a thorough canvass of the leading psychologists in the country below the age of fifty.[9] His recommendation was Hilgard.[10] As early as 1937, in a letter to Boring, Terman had predicted that Hilgard's strong qualities as a teacher, researcher, and individual would lead to his future appointment as an administrator.[11] Hilgard was appointed to succeed Terman, but because he was in Washington, D.C., during the war, he did not assume his duties until 1945.[12] Paul Farnsworth was acting head during the interim period.

In preparing for retirement, one of the things Terman decided on was to donate his extensive professional library. He felt that Stanford, being a well-endowed institution with a good library, did not need his collection. Instead, he wanted to give his books to a university with limited economic resources and a graduate psychology program, so that students could profit from technical books that they might not otherwise have access to. With the help of the director of Stanford Libraries, he chose the Joint University Libraries in Nashville. These libraries were used by students from Vanderbilt University, George Peabody College for Teachers, and Scarritt College for Christian Workers.[13] The first shipment of books, which numbered about one thousand volumes, was sent in January 1941. The remaining three thousand volumes were sent over the years, with the last being received in 1956.[14]

When he retired in August 1942, Terman moved to a new office and began to devote his energies to the follow-up of the gifted. The continuation of his professional work was now guided by a set of "ten vows" that he had set down in writing and circulated to his fellow "Stanford Emeriti Graduates of 1942."[15] Among these ten commandments were not feeling sorry for oneself; maintaining a reasonable degree of philosophical detachment; keeping an open mind to new trends in one's field; not dwelling upon past accomplishments; not cultivating the illusion that one's most important accomplishments lie ahead; keeping a sense of humor; and as the last vow, not allowing "ourselves to be beguiled by the flattery of friends who tell us that we look as young as we did twenty or thirty years ago."[16] Thus, Terman anticipated his retirement years with characteristic optimism and wit. Unfortunately, the reoccurrence of health problems was to present serious obstacles to the goals he set for himself in retirement.

Health Problems

Terman's health during his teaching years at Stanford had been relatively good, considering his history of tuberculosis.[17] He did experience, from time to time, attacks of pneumonia and bronchitis; but he suffered only two bouts of tuberculosis, one in the 1920s and a more serious episode in the summer of 1936. In the latter case, he spent close to two months in bed trying to recover from daily occurrences of fever and a general physical weakness.[18] Finally, his physicians insisted that he go to a TB sanitarium for a period of complete rest. He stayed for six weeks at the Bushnell Sanitarium in the foothills of the Sierra Nevada Mountains. During the fall he regained his health; however, he was not able to return to teaching until January 1937 and had to cancel a series of lectures he had been invited to give at Yale.[19]

When Terman retired in August 1942 he was in good health and looked forward to the opportunity of devoting his time to the gifted follow-up and other professional activities. Three months later, during the night of 22 November 1942, he suffered burns from a fire.[20] He was at home, alone and resting in bed. Despite his history of respiratory problems Terman was a heavy smoker, and it was not uncharacteristic of him to be smoking in bed. He fell asleep, and the mattress caught fire. He was rescued and carried out of the house, but he suffered extensive second-degree burns on his back, right leg, and right arm. The house itself was considerably damaged.

Terman's recovery lasted almost three years because of various complications. Anna described the slow, often torturous period of recovery in a series of letters to Fred's wife Sibyl. During the war Fred and his family were in Cambridge, Massachusetts, where Fred directed the Harvard Radio Research Laboratory.[21] Terman was initially hospitalized for just over two months at the Stanford University Hospital in San Francisco, where he went through an extensive series of skin grafts.[22] Toward the end of January 1943, he was able to sit up and walk short distances. When he returned home Anna hired a nurse, who for several weeks came daily during the daytime hours to change the dressings. By the time he returned home, the house repairs were for the most part completed. Anna had also begun to replace some of the clothes he lost in the fire, though this was difficult because of the wartime shortages of fabric. By April Terman was experiencing arthritis and had difficulty sitting up for more than an hour.[23] He was back in the hospital for a period in May, under traction to "unfreeze" his joints.

Anna reported in July that Lewis was improving.[24] He was able to take his bath without help and could shave himself; he was even able to putt in the yard every day. On weekends he received physiotherapy, and Anna felt that this was of great help. But there were also new difficulties. With the bandages removed, Lewis now had great discomfort in wearing clothes. His new skin over all of his back was so sensitive that everything hurt, even wearing pajama tops. Anna complained that Lewis sometimes got very "blue and discouraged" and really had "no reason" to feel this way because she felt he was making progress—though it was very slow to be sure. She also observed (as she had previously in her diaries) that Lewis was "pessimistic by nature," and this came to the foreground when he was physically incapacitated. This is an interesting comment, because in so much of Terman's personal correspondence there is a flavor of optimism with respect to both his own goals and those of others. However, in light of Anna's observations, it seems that when he was struck with physical problems, he became depressed over the obstacles such problems presented in relation to his ability to work and thereby achieve his goals.

Another problem Anna had recounted was Lewis's difficulty in being able to write. However, by September he was able to write a handwritten letter to Sibyl.[25] He was still experiencing considerable pain from the sensitiveness of his new skin. Furthermore, handwriting was still difficult because his fingers were quite stiff. On the positive side, his shoulder had regained most of its mobility.[26] In March 1944 Anna reported that Lewis's pain had become more severe than the previous summer.[27] He was very discouraged because he found it more difficult to work. In the summer, he had been able to go down to his campus office for a few hours about four times a week and work on the gifted follow-up report. Now he had to "drive" himself to sit at his desk and work for a half hour at a time. There was also another physical problem. His good eye was failing, and he would have to have a cataract operation on his other eye. The operation took place in early May and was successful.[28] However, it was a difficult period of recovery because Terman still had his back pains and he could not read. His only diversion was to listen to the radio.

For the next year, Terman continued to suffer with pain.[29] The problem apparently was due to the persistent tightness of the new skin. Finally, by August 1945 he was experiencing some relief. He was able to sleep better and could now drive down to the university and work in the afternoons. Anna wrote that his morale had improved and being able to drive made him feel much more independent. All in all, it had taken him close to three years to reach this point. Over the next several months, he was able to return to a more active work schedule. However, in December he suffered yet another setback. One night, while in his unlighted study, he stumbled over a displaced wastebasket.[30] This resulted in a broken hip that required two operations, and it took him almost a year to recover.[31]

Thus, after about a four-year hiatus, Terman was able to resume his full-time work schedule in the fall of 1946. There would be further pauses, though these were relatively brief. He had a cataract operation on his other eye in the spring of 1947, which resulted in considerably improved vision.[32] Two years later he had a prostate operation.[33] Fortunately, the four-year period of relative inactivity did not impose a serious delay on the follow-up report of the gifted study. Most of the data had been collected before the 1942 fire. With Melita Oden as coauthor, the volume was completed in January 1947.[34]

The Gifted Child Grows Up

The fourth volume of the gifted study was a twenty-five-year follow-up of the survey begun in 1921 and reported the follow-ups conducted in 1936, 1940, and 1945.[35] The 1936 survey was limited to a mailing of two questionnaires: the first, an information blank to be filled in by the subjects, regarding educational and occupational history, avocational interests, general health, and marital status; the second, a home information blank to be filled in by the parents that included personality ratings of the subject and the parents' own accomplishments and activities. These items of information were what had previously been recorded in the 1921 and 1928 surveys. This mail follow-up was more successful than had been anticipated, for about ninety percent of the subjects were located.

In 1939, a grant of $20,000 was obtained from the Carnegie Corporation. Other supplemental grants were added, so that by 1945 a total of about $49,000 was available for the collection of new material. During 1939–40 the subjects were both interviewed (for the purpose of updating the case histories) and given a battery of tests and information blanks by a team of three field assistants. The three assistants were Helen Marshall, who had assisted in the two previous field surveys; Nancy Bayley, a research associate at the University of California at Berkeley; and Ellen Sullivan, a former Terman student who was a UCLA faculty member. The questionnaires included an extended information blank, a specially constructed personality test, the Strong Vocational Interest Blank, the Concept Mastery Test (a specially constructed measure of abstract intelligence), and a marriage blank designed to yield a numerical index of marital happiness. Approximately ninety-eight percent (a total of 1,434) of the living subjects were included in the 1940 survey, an unusually high rate of subject cooperation. The average age of the sample was thirty. In 1945 a follow-up information blank was mailed out, and the returns showed only a small attrition—the sample totaling 1,418 subjects.

The major results revealed that the intellectual level of the group continued to be within the upper one percent of the general population.[36] Vocational achievement was well above the average of college graduates. Furthermore, as the earlier reports had indicated, personal adjustment for the group was good. There were several demonstrations of this. Such "serious maladjustments" as insanity, delinquency, alcoholism, and homosexuality showed a normal or below-normal incidence. Marital adjustment was equal to or superior to that of groups less highly selected for intelligence. The sexual adjustment of married subjects was as normal as that found in a less-gifted and less-educated group of married couples.

There were also some interesting findings derived from comparisons of subgroups within the gifted sample. Those gifted children who tested above 170 IQ were more rapidly promoted in school, did better schoolwork, attained more education, and were more successful in their later careers than lower-testing members of the group. Jewish subjects differed very little from non-Jewish subjects in ability and personality traits but displayed a stronger drive to achieve, formed more stable marriages, and were a little more liberal in their political and social attitudes.

In another comparison, the male sample (in 1940, when the men were twenty-five years old or older) was divided into three groups based on a rating of "life success." The criterion of success was defined as "the extent to which a subject had made use of his superior ability."[37] The three groups constituted approximately the highest fifth, the middle three-fifths, and the lowest fifth.[38] The highest and lowest groups, designated A and C, each consisted of 150 men of comparable mean age and range of age who were almost equally successful during the elementary-school years. However, in high school the two groups began to draw apart as the C group's grades began to drop. During college the grades of the C group were strikingly lower. By 1940 this group showed increasing social maladjustment (fewer marriages, higher incidence of divorce) and a poor employment record (frequent unemployment and job turnover). What appeared to account for the sharp differences between the A and C groups was the stronger tradition of education in the families of the A group. Three times as many A fathers as C fathers had graduated from college, and more than twice as many A fathers were in the professional classes. Another difference was the lower emotional stability and poorer social adjustment of the C group when rated as children in the initial survey. It was concluded that environmental factors and personality adjustment were significant determinants of the extent to which "potential genius" would be successfully expressed. In reaching this conclusion, Terman seemed to be giving more weight to the role of environment than one would have expected based on his initial assumption regarding the genetic foundation of intellectual superiority and the consequent importance of the early identification of giftedness. While not refuting these assumptions, he acknowledged on the basis of his follow-up data that "intellect and achievement are far from perfectly correlated."[39] It thus became important to understand how environment could facilitate or stifle the expression of giftedness.

Various grants from the Carnegie Corporation, the Rockefeller Corporation, and the Office of Naval Research provided for the next follow-up, which ran from 1950 to 1952 and was reported in the fifth volume of the study, published in 1959.[40] Although the fifth volume appeared three years after Terman's death, Terman had written initial drafts of some of the chapters; Oden completed the manuscript. The subjects were again given the Concept Mastery Test (slightly revised from the previous follow-up), an abbreviated version of the marital happiness test, and information blanks about themselves, their spouses, and their children.[41] Those living in California were interviewed, and their offspring of appropriate age were given a Stanford-Binet (the testing of offspring had begun in the 1940 follow-up). In 1955 an information blank was mailed out to obtain updated data. At this time, the average of the subjects was about forty-five, and the total sample was somewhat over thirteen hundred (ninety-three percent of those living).[42]

The gifted group at midlife were found to have maintained their intellectual superiority and, at least in the case of the men, to have attained a high level of career success.[43] Some of the men had achieved notable distinctions in their fields. For example, somewhat over one hundred were listed in such prestigious biographical sources as *American Men of Science*, the *Directory of American Scholars*, and *Who's Who in America*. The career situation for the women was quite different. For the most part they were housewives, though some had achieved career distinction. But as Terman and Oden pointed out, even for women with a career, decisions were based more on such external factors like gender-role conformity and job discrimination than on talent, training, or interest.

The midlife survey also contained a question about what the subjects perceived life success to be. Vocational achievement was frequently listed, but other indices frequently mentioned included a happy marriage and family, contributions to the welfare of others, and emotional maturity. As in the previous follow-up, the gifted sample as a whole continued to portray a well-rounded picture of personal satisfaction and effectiveness.[44]

Terman's involvement in the gifted study included more than overseeing data collection and writing up results. Particularly in his retirement years, he engaged in a number of related activities. One example of this was that from time to time he was called upon to write about the education of the gifted.[45] His ideas about education were most notably spelled out in an address he gave at the University of California at Berkeley in March 1954.[46] This was an occasion of personal achievement for Terman since he was selected to give the first annual lecture honoring the memory of Walter Van Dyke Bingham.[47] Bingham had been a pioneer in applied psychology and had worked with Terman in the World War I testing program.

In his talk, which was an overview of the gifted study, he stressed the importance of the early discovery of exceptional abilities. This could readily be accomplished with the wide availability of intelligence and achievement tests. Early identification of giftedness was important because it would allow for acceleration by grade skipping, a practice that was most feasible in the lower grades. In the gifted study, he reported that those who had accelerated were about equal to gifted nonaccelerates in childhood IQ, as well as health and general adjustment; but those who had accelerated did better schoolwork, continued their education further, and were more successful in their later careers. Terman felt that acceleration was the most feasible approach to educating the gifted. Referring to the postwar conditions of teacher shortages and overcrowded classrooms, he did not see much opportunity for segregating the gifted into special classes or for placing them in fast-learning tracks as part of a tracking system of homogeneous ability groups. With his advocacy of grade skipping, he was critical of what he perceived to be a general trend in the schools to oppose acceleration in favor of an educational lockstep, in which the gifted child was kept with others of his or her own age.

Terman's ideas about the education of the gifted were also reflected in his interest about age and creative achievement. He believed that the early identification of superior ability was important because a person's most creative years came relatively early in adult life. Thus, youths of high achievement potential should be well prepared for their life work before too many of their most creative years had passed. For support of this view, he relied on the results of an extensive study on age and achievement by Harvey C. Lehman.[48] Lehman's investigation was limited to men, and he found that across a variety of different fields the peak period of creative output was between the ages of twenty-five and thirty-five. Terman played a key role in fostering the publication of Lehman's work. In 1945, having read some of his articles in *Scientific Monthly*, Terman wrote to Lehman and urged him to put together his work on creative productivity in the form of a book.[49] Terman hoped that such a book could be included in his edited series for World Book. Unfortunately, Lehman's limitations as a writer created difficulties in getting the book published.[50] With considerable editorial help from Terman, Lehman's book was finally published in 1953, under the sponsorship of the American Philosophical Society. The fact that Terman was willing to write a forward to the book helped.[51] Boring's influence in the society was also a contributing factor to the book's publication.[52] Coincidentally, in 1953 Terman was elected to membership in the society.[53]

Terman also sought out ways to expand the opportunities for identifying and educating the gifted. In 1946 he became involved in a project oriented toward such goals, called the Marsden Foundation for Gifted Youth. The foundation was developed by a New York physician, Elizabeth M. Bonbright, who was interested in setting up a scholarship program along the lines of the Cecil Rhodes scholarships; but in this case foreign students would study at American universities.[54] Bonbright was introduced to Terman by Winifred Johnson, who had worked with Terman on the marriage study.[55] The charter of the foundation was placed under the sponsorship of Stanford. According to the provisions of the charter, an annual grant of $2,000 (starting in 1947) was set aside as a research fund for the gifted study, and a scholarship fund was established for study at American universities, including Stanford.[56] The foundation appeared to be an auspicious asset for both Terman and Stanford. Terman believed that the annual grants would continue for a period of twenty years and would thus be of considerable help in extending the follow-up of the gifted.[57] The university stood to gain at least one-half of the foundation's endowment of around $250,000.[58]

Johnson served as the director of the foundation, and in this capacity worked closely with the young people who were chosen as scholars. Bonbright was the assistant director, and Terman and Fred Terman were among a group of six "university advisors" from various American universities. The scholarship program was in operation by 1947. About six scholars were chosen each year, and Americans were also included; for example, in 1948 the scholars were American, Canadian, and Scandinavian. That year, Stanford agreed to accept one of the scholars with a tuition waiver.[59] Each year the Marsden scholars, who were at various colleges around the country, spent their summer vacations at a Santa Barbara mansion where Johnson was in residence and their winter vacations at the Palm Springs ranch owned by Johnson and her husband Raymond Cree.[60] Terman kept in close contact with Bonbright and Johnson through correspondence and was pleased that the scholarship program was providing educational opportunities for gifted youth who might otherwise be passed by.[61] The research grants and scholarship program ended in 1953, when the monies of the foundation were diverted to medical research.[62] The foundation's change in direction seems to have been related to Johnson's declining health. She died of cancer at the beginning of 1955.[63]

In carrying out his gifted study, Terman was always eager to have the results disseminated in newspaper and magazine articles. Over the years, a number of articles about the study appeared in local newspapers in the San Francisco area. Furthermore, in the 1920s he had granted an extensive interview to A. E. Wiggam (a journalist who specialized in popularizing scientific research), and this interview was written up and included in a book published by Wiggam in 1928.[64] In 1941, through a journalist acquaintance, Frank J. Taylor, Terman interested *The Reader's Digest* in making a financial contribution to his gifted study.[65] The publisher, DeWitt Wallace, sent a contribution of $4,500. Terman, in turn, agreed to provide material for articles that would be written up by Taylor for the *Digest*. However, Taylor was unable to produce any articles, even though Terman had sent him the relevant material.[66]

Another example of popularizing his work occurred in 1947 when he made a guest appearance on the radio show the "Quiz Kids."[67] His appearance on the show coincided with the publication of the twenty-five-year follow-up. In introducing Terman, the program director gave Terman's new book a plug.[68] Terman was interested in the program because he believed it performed a major function in informing the public that highly gifted children were well adjusted and versatile.[69] In his remarks, he commented:

I have devoted a good part of my life to research on children of high I.Q. . . . But despite all my investigations, and those of others, many people continued to think of the brainy child as a freak—physically stunted, mentally lop-sided, nonsocial, and neurotic. Then came the Quiz Kid program, featuring living specimens of highly gifted youngsters who were obviously healthy, whole-some, well-adjusted, socially minded, full of fun, and versatile beyond belief. . . . Result: the program has done more to correct popular misconceptions about bright children than all the books ever written.[70]

His appearance on the "Quiz Kids" provided a means of populariz-ing his own work; but perhaps even more importantly, he was able to lend his name to what he saw as a significant vehicle for changing the public myths about gifted children. Terman's efforts to reach out to the general public represent interesting examples of the interconnect-edness of science and social context. His research was both shaped by and helped to shape social thought. Unfortunately, in the case of the "Quiz Kids," some years after his death the show turned out to be a somewhat dishonest enterprise.[71] It was discovered that some of the children were fed questions in advance.

An aspect of the work with the gifted that Terman found especially satisfying was the opportunity for personal contact with many of the subjects under study. He kept up a correspondence with many of them over the years and in some instances received them as guests in his home. Thus, to many of the gifted children who "grew-up" (and came to be identified as "Termites"), Terman was a benevolent father figure and psychological counselor. After pouring over the files of the gifted subjects, one comes away with the image of Terman as someone who was deeply concerned with and personally interested in the lives of the gifted men and women he studied.[72] For some, his personal interest had a significant impact on the direction of their lives. Part of the psychological dynamic underlying Terman's personal involvement seems to have been his identification with them. In his autobiography, he had revealed his childhood awareness of being gifted and as a result, a feeling of standing apart from his peers.[73] Early in his career, he was sensitive to the need for the early identification and encouragement of gifted children. In the era and in the agrarian environment in which he grew up, such identification and encouragement were not available (though in his own case he credited his family with supporting his desire for more schooling). Terman, in his interactions with the gifted in his study, was able to provide the personal guidance and encourage-ment that he had, for the most part, missed when he was growing up.

Moreover, through his role as "guardian angel," he attempted to effect the outcomes he sought to achieve in his study—that is, to foster the expression of potential giftedness.

Terman's impact upon the gifted was also felt in other ways. Lee J. Cronbach was a gifted subject who met Terman only once when he was given the Concept Mastery Test in 1940.[74] However, being a member of the study had a marked effect on his educational development and career choice. He was "discovered" by a Fresno school psychologist, and this prompted his rapid school acceleration and an interest in the psychology of individual differences—the field he eventually specialized in. Being a member of the gifted group also made him feel the pressures associated with achievement, especially because the label "genius" was attached to the study. Cronbach, who has since become one of the directors of the gifted follow-up, feels that a limitation of the study was the sense of inadequacy it created for the sample because of the high expectations connected with being in a study of "genius." Terman had initially chosen this term, not with the expectation that all of the subjects would prove to be geniuses, but in advertising the study in this way he hoped to include some number of embryo geniuses.[75]

By the early 1950s, with plans developing for the continuation of the gifted follow-up for some years to come, Terman was eager to find a successor who would take over the direction of the study upon his death. When Robert Sears, a member of the gifted group, came to Stanford in 1953 as psychology department head, Terman approached him and Sears agreed to take on the directorship.[76] In his will in 1948, Terman had laid out the groundwork for the gifted follow-up. Custody of the gifted files was transferred to the university with the promise that only highly qualified persons could have access to the materials.[77] It was also stipulated that upon Terman's death one-half of the royalties from the World Book Company (primarily based on the Stanford Achievement Test) were to be applied toward the "expenses of continuous follow-up study." According to Fred Terman in 1974, this fund had a balance of around $70,000 even after substantial expenditures, and the annual amount from royalties was still substantial.[78]

When Terman died in 1956, Melita Oden took over the responsibility for completing the write-up of the midlife follow-up.[79] Sears also made arrangements for Oden to continue the analysis of developmental trends, and a mail follow-up was conducted in 1960.[80] By 1968 Oden had retired from active involvement in the study, and Sears began to make arrangements for the subsequent follow-ups.[81] In 1970 Lee J. Cronbach and Pauline S. Sears (Robert's wife) joined him as collaborators.[82] Follow-ups have since been conducted in 1972, 1977, and 1982; and the study will probably continue for another ten years.[83] The gifted subjects are now in their seventies.[84]

Terman deserves to be credited with pioneering an ambitious and thorough study of children with high ability. In terms of the amount of data generated, the sample size, the financial and staff support, and the fact that it's sixty-year span represents the longest developmental investigation ever attempted, it ranks as a seminal longitudinal study. It also stands as a testament to Terman's tenacity and dedication in carrying through what he defined as his primary mission in life: to change the public's negative image of gifted children and to demonstrate how significant their contributions to society could be when they became adults. Indeed, the public attention and the largely confirmatory conclusions that derived from his study appeared to contribute to attitudinal changes. By 1947 he was satisfied that prejudicial myths about the gifted, such as "early ripe, early rot," were far less common than they had been half a century before.[85] On a related note, it appears that the gifted subjects themselves were generally positive about being a part of the study.[86]

In carrying through his mission, Terman was sensitive to the need not only to detect intellectual giftedness at an early age but once identified to provide proper encouragement for its development. Therefore, he was highly critical of the tendency of some parents to exploit their gifted children by seeking publicity and putting them on display. As far as he was concerned, such practices contributed to the negative image of child prodigies and "burned" them out before they could reach their potential. One of the most publicized examples of this kind of burn-out was the case of William James Sidis, son of a Harvard psychology professor (Boris Sidis), who at four could write French and English on a typewriter.[87] He had a nervous breakdown at the age of twelve and, although a Harvard law graduate, ended up as a clerk with a passion for collecting trolley-car transfers and committed

suicide in 1944 at the age of forty-six. At the time, Terman commented
to a *Time* magazine reporter: "I think the boy was very largely ruined
by his father, giving him so much bad publicity."[88] One of his motives
in launching the gifted study was to dispel such images.

The gifted study must also be appraised in terms of Terman's aim
that it be a demonstration project for a meritocratic society. When his
Stanford-Binet test was published in 1916, he stated: "The future
welfare of the country hinges in no small degree upon the right education of . . . superior children. Whether civilization moves on and up
depends on the advances made by creative thinkers and leaders in
science, politics, art, morality, and religion. Moderate ability can follow, or imitate, but genius must show the way."[89] Terman also consistently supported the view that "mental abilities are chiefly a matter of
original endowment."[90] Thus, individuals endowed with superior ability and given the appropriate educational environment had the potential to be leaders in society.

Was Terman able to validate such a model of meritocracy? The
answer is essentially negative, largely because his basic assumption
that superior intellect was innate was never tested. Indeed, he uncov-
ered evidence that environmental opportunities made a difference in
achievement. Among the men, success was related to being exposed to
intellectual stimulation and emotional support. Such facilitative conditions for achievement were generally not available to the women because, as Terman acknowledged, they were constrained by the force
of the traditional feminine role. However, while acknowledging the
role of environment in fostering or impeding the realization of the
potential for the gifted to excel, he appeared to maintain his view that
intellect itself, as assessed by mental tests, was primarily genetic in
origin. As a result, he failed to consider the ways in which the environment could influence test performance and consequently IQ scores.
This neglect is especially significant for the interpretation of his study
because an IQ cutoff was used to determine the composition of the
sample. Environmental opportunities worked in favor of including
children from middle- and upper-class homes. These were the children
best prepared to be evaluated in test situations, as well as the ones
most familiar with the kinds of materials included in the mental tests.
Consequently, this was the group most likely to be represented in the

sample Terman was constructing. His study is, therefore, most accurately interpreted as an investigation of giftedness among a group of relatively privileged children.[91]

During his retirement years, Terman devoted the larger part of his professional work to the gifted study. However, he also continued to write book reviews and literature-review articles and chapters in his other areas of research expertise, such as sex differences and marital adjustment.[92] In his role as research critic, he became involved in a particularly significant enterprise—an evaluation of the Kinsey study of male sexual behavior.[93]

The Kinsey Critique

The 1948 appearance of the first volume of Alfred C. Kinsey's studies of sexual behavior was a much publicized event.[94] Its impact on the social consciousness of American society, at the time it was published, is captured in the following comment by a team of reviewers: "The Kinsey Report has done for sex what Columbus did for geography. It makes a successful scientific voyage to explore an unknown world which had been open only to speculation and suspicion—the sex life of human beings."[95]

The Kinsey study was not the first of its kind in America. In his 1938 book on marital adjustment, Terman had dealt with sexual practices; and his work was guided by several similar surveys conducted in the 1920s and 1930s.[96] However, the Kinsey volume was by far the most ambitious, and as a result it stimulated the interest of both the general public and the scientific community. Terman's interest in sexual practices was also reflected in his study of masculinity-femininity because he had included a sample of male homosexuals as well as some data on female homosexuals.[97] With his background, it was quite appropriate for Terman to embark upon a review of the Kinsey study. Kinsey was, in fact, familiar with Terman's work and had consulted with him during the course of the study.[98]

Terman began his review by stating that he was "deeply impressed by the magnitude and potential significance of Kinsey's research."[99] However, after careful reading, he felt obliged to point out several "shortcomings" and "inadequacies," which he hoped would have a beneficial effect upon future research. One of Terman's major criticisms was Kinsey's use of the interview, a method that Terman felt suffered from the possible effects of suggestion and did not control for memory distortion.[100] In his own work Terman had used questionnaires that he felt were more valid. Another objection raised had to do with the validity of the sampling procedures, especially the issues of a representative sample and the statistical treatment of the sampling data. Terman also criticized Kinsey for making many sweeping factual statements that were only weakly supported by the data. Finally, Terman took issue with Kinsey's tendency to make value judgments, which as Terman put it were often slanted "in the direction of implied preference for uninhibited sexual activity"[101] and could "impress the youth who is in search of authoritative justification for the unrestrained satisfaction of his sexual urges."[102]

Terman's generally negative review reflected a change of attitude, for when he first learned that Kinsey's volume would be published he was most supportive. In a letter to Kinsey, he declared: "I can hardly wait to see your first volume and shall be just as much interested in the second one. From all I have learned about your investigation I feel sure your data will be by far the most valuable that anyone has published."[103] Kinsey warmly replied that he was honored by Terman's interest and hoped that they would have a chance to meet each other in person.[104] When Terman's review appeared, some two years after this cordial exchange, Kinsey was quite concerned about it. In fact, it appeared to worry him more than any of the other numerous reviews.[105] This was due in part to Kinsey's feeling that a friendly relationship had been breached, but he was more distressed because Terman's critique especially symbolized for him a moralism and prudery that was wrapped in the protective blanket of professional criticism—most of which was directed at statistical issues. In his own copy of the review, he wrote the word "moral" in the margin next to Terman's statement criticizing him for making slanted evaluations "often in the direction of implied preference for uninhibited sexual activity."

In order to obtain some objective opinion about the Terman review, Kinsey turned to Robert M. Yerkes, the chairman of the National Research Council's Committee for Research on Problems of Sex, the group that had funded his research as well as Terman's.[106] Yerkes replied that it was the first review he had seen that contained useful adverse criticism, and he felt that Terman had been objective and fair.[107] He pleaded with Kinsey to accept the criticism and not to reply in print, further suggesting that Kinsey write Terman a conciliatory letter. Kinsey followed Yerkes's advice, at least with respect to writing Terman and not publishing a reply. His note to Terman was terse, simply requesting Terman's recommendation regarding statistical consultants.[108] Terman felt that Kinsey's letter was rather "grumpy," and, as he confided to his friend Yerkes, he did not believe that Kinsey was very willing to profit from criticism.[109]

Kinsey remained convinced that Terman had betrayed him and attributed this betrayal to Terman's basic prudery as well as professional jealousy.[110] Kinsey's charge of jealousy was based on his belief that Terman was hurt by his own criticisms of Terman's marital study.[111] There may have been some validity to Kinsey's interpretation of jealousy, but Terman did not resort to a defense of his own work and compared to his responses to other critics, such as Lippmann and Stoddard, his response to Kinsey was restrained. On the other hand, it seems that Kinsey was quite accurate in accusing Terman of moralism and prudery. The one occasion that Terman and Kinsey met one another is rather revealing about their different attitudes toward sexuality. This meeting took place in 1952 when Kinsey gave an address at Stanford.[112] During the speech, Terman was displeased to hear Kinsey joke about how prevalent homosexuality was in the navy. Unlike Kinsey, Terman could not joke about something that he did not accept. He was also incensed at Kinsey's cavalier attitude. As he confided to Yerkes, "I reacted unfavorably . . . because of my intimate knowledge of the homosexual histories of some fifteen or eighteen men in my gifted group, nearly all of whom have been wrecked in one way or another and three of whom have been blackmailed."[113] Terman could identify with the sufferings of his gifted homosexuals, but he could not accept their sexuality.

As in the case of his attitudes toward gender roles, Terman held conventional views about sexuality. Moreover, in contradiction to his perceived role as an objective scientist, his traditional values intruded upon his scientific judgment. In his own study of homosexuality, he uncritically accepted the established view that such a sexual orientation was pathological, a position which matched his own personal feelings about the subject. His inability to separate fact from value reflected his assumptions about the scientific nature of psychology. He was committed to an empirically based psychology that patterned itself on the methodology of the natural sciences. (In his APA presidential speech he had argued that the mental test was methodologically equivalent to the experiment.) Implicit in his thinking were such natural-science assumptions as the need to arrive at causal explanation in terms of unidirectional antecedent-consequent conditions, the establishment of universal laws, and the role of the scientist as a value-free, objective observer. From this natural-science model, when it came to studying groups of individuals out of the mainstream of society—such as homosexuals—these groups were judged to be pathological whenever they deviated from the universalistic norms and beliefs set by the dominant culture. Scientists wedded to such a perspective, as Terman was, could not conceive of how their so-called "objective" observations were in fact reflections of the conventional norms and beliefs of those powerful segments of society that determined the standards of comparison. Without necessarily intending to do so, these scientists consequently contributed to a perpetuation of the existing social order—in essence, they became "servants of power."[114]

Kinsey's dispute with Terman and more generally his break with traditional medical and scientific thinking about sexuality was the product of a number of factors. His own personality and background were contributors.[115] Kinsey tended to be a maverick, and he was trained as an entomologist who rather late in his career entered the field of human sexuality. As a result, he was not beholden to established thought. Furthermore, he began his work on sexuality during the relatively progressive period of the 1930s, a time in which popular attitudes about sexual practice had become relatively liberated from their Victorian origins. Beyond personal and sociohistorical influences, Kinsey's revolutionary views about sexuality reflected an intellectual shift that was taking place in the sciences. In the physical sciences, the Newtonian version of a cause-and-effect, mechanistic universe (the natural-science model Terman was schooled in) was being replaced by Einstein's notion of a universe of dynamic forces reciprocally affecting one another. In the biological and social sciences this new mode of thinking was translated into an "organismic" model.[116]

In contrast with the mechanistic natural-science model's focus on unidirectional causality, the organismic model conceived of the living organism as dynamically interacting with its environment. In his training as a biologist, Kinsey was exposed to this new viewpoint. Moreover, in his entomological fieldwork on the gall-wasp, he was concerned with ecological issues—that is, the dynamic interplay between organism and environment. When Kinsey turned to the study of homosexuality, he maintained his organismic orientation. In his first publication on human sexuality, he was critical of approaches that sought to discover the causes of homosexuality.[117] In place of causal explanation, he viewed homosexuality as a universal human capacity.[118] The variations across individuals regarding the choice of sexual partner reflected the particular experiences of each individual. The problem of sexual preference was part of the broader problem of choices in general, whether it be the road one takes, the clothes one wears, or the food one eats. As he stated, "a choice of a partner in a sexual relation becomes more significant only because society demands that there be a particular choice in this matter."[119]

Kinsey's discovery of the wide variety of human sexual experience was related to a fundamental tenet of his sexual ideology—acceptance.[120] As a scientist investigating sexual behavior, his role was to understand the diverse experiences of the people he was studying. With understanding came acceptance. He declared: "Understanding something of their satisfactions and heartaches, and the backgrounds of their lives, has increased our sympathetic acceptance of people as they are."[121] With the exception of sexual violence, Kinsey was committed to sexual tolerance.[122] Homosexuality was a part of the diversity of sexual outlet, even though it deviated from accepted sexual standards.[123] In marked contrast with Terman, Kinsey viewed homosexuality as a universal human capacity, and as such it was *not* pathological.

In conclusion, Terman's critique was primarily informed by an uncritical acceptance of conventional moral standards. Working from a scientific ideology that took social convention to be objective reality, Terman could not view homosexuality within the realm of acceptable sexual expression. This is not to say that he had no legitimate criticisms about scientific method. However, he seemed particularly upset over Kinsey's stated tolerance for "uninhibited sexual activity." For Terman, this essentially meant homosexuality. In fact, Terman seemed to go out of his way in his criticisms of method—perhaps he felt obliged to in order to discredit Kinsey's findings. For example, his criticisms of sampling were unfair because he failed to note that Kinsey himself acknowledged these problems.[124] For a more objective evaluation of the methodology of Kinsey's volume on male sexuality, we need to turn to the American Statistical Association's report. This assessment, published in 1954, was generally favorable. Though problem areas were pointed to, these authors felt that the statistical and methodological aspects of the Kinsey study were "outstanding" in comparison with the sex studies that preceded it.[125]

CHAPTER 11

Reflections
(1942–1956)

From my point of view, the wholehearted dedication of one's life to the promotion of social justice, mutual understanding, racial tolerance, and equalization of opportunity, is as good evidence of a truly religious spirit as any beliefs one might hold about miracles, immortality, or a personal God.[1]

The period of late adulthood is typically a time for personal reflection. Looking back over one's life enables a person to integrate his or her experiences, to search for the purpose and meaning of life, and finally to accept and prepare for death. Such a process was very much a part of Terman's retirement years. He expressed his social philosophy about science and religion and voiced his opinion on politics and social issues. He reflected about the events in his life, often in the context of the personal relationships he had developed over the years. With the loss of some of these relationships and with his own advancing age, he revealed his feelings about death.

Social Values and Political Views

In his 1932 autobiography, Terman declared: "I rate as a rather extreme radical in my attitude toward the church and toward most problems of social ethics, but as merely a liberal on political and economic issues."[2] By the 1940s he had more opportunity to express himself in these areas. In 1947 he was asked by the science editor of

The American Weekly to write an article on the religion of a scientist.[3] This was to be part of a series that included among other scientists Albert Einstein, Alfred L. Kroeber, Leonard Carmichael, and Ray Lyman Wilbur. The article, entitled "My Faith," was apparently written in the summer of 1948. Several months later, Terman received word that the manuscript was not accepted because the editor "was afraid the readers of the *Weekly* would not find enough positive religious attitude in it."[4] In the article Terman identified himself as an agnostic, and he was, therefore, not surprised about the rejection. True to his autobiographical statement, he was a radical on religion.

In a letter to Yerkes, written about this time, Terman confided that he had lost complete interest in organized religion when he was around eighteen or nineteen.[5] This change coincided with his enthusiasm for Darwin, Huxley, and other modern scientists. For Terman, his commitment to science had replaced any need for religion. He essentially expressed this point in the article by stating, "indeed, science itself is almost a form of religion, one that commands the highest type of sacrifice and devotion."[6] He went on to suggest that scientists are guided by a concern for social progress; and since scientific discoveries have freed "man from material bondage," they have contributed to the life of the spirit.[7] Science thus brings society closer to God than blind faith. The particular task of psychology and the social sciences should be to civilize humankind's impulses and emotions so that all could live together in peace, justice, and good will. Always sensitive to the application of science in relation to the needs of the times, Terman added that such a goal was especially imperative with the advent of the atomic age.

In contrast to his radical stance on religion, Terman identified himself as a liberal in the realm of political and economic affairs. Over the years, he consistently expressed his faith in such democratic values as individual freedom and equality.[8] However, the version of the democratic ideal he advocated had to be consistent with the facts of science —in particular, the biological facts of individual differences. Thus, freedom was couched in terms of insuring that each individual had the maximum opportunity to develop his or her inherent capacities, and in so doing to attain the greatest possible happiness that was consistent with the "common good."[9] Terman expressed equality in terms of the opportunity for each individual to develop "whatever abilities nature has given him."[10] Democracy was based on equality of opportunity, not equality of endowment. Terman's meritocratic vision that those of superior intellect should lead those of inferior capacity also meshed with democratic values. His rationale was that moral qualities were highly correlated with superior IQ; therefore, as leaders the gifted would look out for the welfare and interests of those at the lowest end of the ability distribution.[11] His advocacy of a hierarchy based on intellect was also democratic in another sense. As he saw it, such leadership would act against the traditional systems of bestowing leadership by such methods as seniority.

There were times when Terman was skeptical about the future of democracy. As a result of the low intellectual ability revealed in the army testing of World War I, he feared where the "ignorance" of "the common people" would lead.[12] However, based on a book he read about popular opinion, which appeared near the end of World War II, he gained more confidence about the viability of democracy. He commented to Boring that despite their ignorance, "the common people have been on many if not on a majority of social issues nearer right than either Congress or the President. Perhaps Abe Lincoln's opinion of the people was not so far wrong."[13] Another instance of his concern over the future of democracy was expressed in the context of the growing threat of totalitarianism during the early forties. He concluded that World War II was a conspiracy of a few ruthless adventurers.[14] With the increasing mechanization and technology of the twentieth century, totalitarianism was not inevitable. The study of potential genius bode well for the future of democracy. Through such study we could learn not only how to foster responsible leaders but also about the nature of the personality distortions that could make potential genius dangerous.[15]

Essentially, Terman identified himself as a liberal because he was wedded to the democratic values and institutions of American society. Furthermore, he viewed social science as a positive force in shaping the social progress of the post–World War II period of international reconstruction. Therefore, he was quite disconcerted when in 1948 he learned that Nicholas Pastore, a doctoral student at Teachers College, had labeled him a conservative by reason of his hereditarian position.[16]

Pastore's thesis was that a relationship existed between the outlook of scientists on nature-nurture problems and their outlook on social, political, and economic issues.[17] Specifically, Pastore argued that hereditarians assume a conservative orientation and environmentalists a liberal orientation. He selected twenty-four scientists from various disciplines who were well known for their views in nature-nurture discussions and had expressed themselves on sociopolitical problems. Among those included were hereditarians Francis Galton, Karl Pearson, Edward L. Thorndike, William McDougall, H. H. Goddard, Leta S. Hollingworth, and Terman. The environmentalists included William C. Bagley, James McKeen Cattell, Frank N. Freeman, George D. Stoddard, Franz Boas, and John B. Watson. In Pastore's initial analysis, all of the hereditarians were classified as conservative, while with the exception of Watson (a conservative) all of the environmentalists were classified as liberal.[18]

Pastore sent a draft of his analysis to Terman, who in response took great exception to being categorized as a conservative.[19] Terman criticized Pastore for misinterpreting his views on testing, education, and leadership, and thereby arriving at the erroneous conclusion of a conservative label. As a corrective, Terman reiterated his views on equality of opportunity. Moreover, he spelled out at length his social, economic, and political attitudes. He identified himself as an independent voter (he had voted for Franklin Roosevelt in 1932, 1936, and 1944 and for Wendell Willkie in 1940). Regarding political ideology, Terman had opposed every form of national totalitarianism, including the regimes of Stalin, Hitler, Mussolini, and Franco; and he had contributed money to the Spanish loyalist cause. Though not a socialist, he was not afraid of the partial socialism then operating in Britain, Sweden, and Norway. He emphasized his fervent support of civil liberties of the kind presumably guaranteed by the Bill of Rights. Therefore, he detested such threats to civil rights as the Dies Committee and other "witch-hunting" activities of the emerging McCarthy era. He concluded with the following: "I am more of a New Dealer than I am a 'social and political conservative'. You can see too . . . that belief in mental inheritance, individual differences, and the value of intelligence tests . . . gives no safe basis for inference regarding one's social and political liberalism or conservatism."[20]

In reply, Pastore revised his chapter on Terman by concluding that Terman was a conservative until the beginning of the depression. Since Terman had subsequently addressed himself to those questions that became dominant in American life during the depression years, he must now be categorized as a liberal. Thus, he represented the one contradiction to the hereditarian-conservative equation.[21]

There were several flaws in Pastore's overall analysis, though it should be acknowledged that it was a rather creative attempt to investigate the link between social context and science—in other words, an example of the sociology of knowledge. As Anne Anastasi pointed out in her review of Pastore's book, his sample was limited to those scientists who had expressed themselves on both nature-nurture and sociopolitical issues.[22] There were other scientists who wrote on the nature-nurture controversy but did not express their sociopolitical views in writing. The attitudes of this latter group were more typical of the members of the scientific community between 1919 and 1940. Scientists who wrote on both nature-nurture and social issues typically represented an older generation who expressed their views in both areas between 1900 and 1918. These scientists may have been especially motivated to refer to the practical implications of their scientific views, in order to gain acceptance at a time when knowledge about the nature-nurture issue was in its infancy.

The most serious limitation of Pastore's analysis was the way in which he assigned the scientists in his sample to political categories. He relied on his own definitions, which in themselves agreed with commonly held views. The conservative was identified as an advocate of the status quo and pessimistic about the ability of the average person to participate in the political process.[23] The liberal was defined as someone who believed in the necessity of change and the democratic concept of political participation by the average person.[24] The problem was not necessarily the definitions themselves, but the fact that Pastore missed the historical context within which his group of scientists expressed their sociopolitical views. This flaw becomes apparent in the case of Terman. As we have seen, Terman consistently identified himself as a liberal. The roots of his sociopolitical orientation were situated within the liberal reform movement of the Progressive Era, which lasted from about 1890 to 1920.[25] As part of the spirit of reform,

Terman was committed to advancing psychology as a science that
could contribute to the social progress of American society. In other
words, Terman believed in the necessity of change *not* in the status
quo. Like so many psychologists of his generation, he viewed science
as a means of producing social change; therefore, he was swept up by
the promise of applied psychology, as demonstrated in the army testing program of World War I.

Terman was committed to social change and also wedded to democratic values. Of course, from his perspective, democracy had to square
with the facts of science. Not everyone was equal in genetic endowment; therefore, a meritocratic society had to be created in which those
of superior intellect would lead and take into account the best interests
of those of lesser ability. Pastore was correct in pointing to Terman's
pessimism about the ability of the average person, but Terman did not
view this "fact" as antithetical to democracy. For Terman the bottom
line of a democracy was an equality of opportunity, whereby each
person could participate within the limits of his or her native ability.
Such a social system also provided the basis for an efficient and ordered
society. "Prediction and control," "human engineering," and "social
efficiency" were the catch phrases of post–World War I American
psychology. Moreover, American society was receptive to these ideas.
Efficiency and order had already become the established themes of the
Progressive movement.[26]

Social science during the Progressive Era was dominated by Darwinian
evolutionary thought. The concept of evolution served as a metaphor
for social change, thus providing social scientists with a rationale for
the relevance of their work to the reform spirit of the times. However,
there were two interpretations of evolution; and this placed social
scientists in one of two camps. There were those who were committed
to a biologically deterministic point of view regarding social progress,
while the alternative view held that social evolution had its own laws.[27]
It was out of these two schools of thought that the debate on mental
testing arose—the meritocratic view of Terman and the other testing
advocates reflecting biological determinism and the egalitarian view of
the testing critics, such as Bagley and Dewey, reflecting nonreductionist social evolution. The biological position would eventually be seen

as anathema to liberalism; but during the Progressive Era, hereditarian explanation was often interpreted as a scientific advancement that could be used for social progess. The mental-testing movement, with its hereditarian foundation, was one example of what might be termed a biologically oriented form of liberalism. Another example during the same time period was the eugenics movement. Terman had been active in eugenics organizations. Most eugenicists sympathized with progressive goals, and many regarded themselves as progressive reformers.[28]

During the 1920s, a shift began to occur in social science. Social progress based on environmental (as opposed to biological) factors came to ascendancy.[29] A number of factors played a role in this intellectual change of direction. Biology no longer had a monopoly on providing explanations for human functioning. By the 1920s sociology and cultural anthropology had established themselves as viable disciplines, and the behaviorist revolution with its radical environmentalism became the dominant school of thought in psychology. With the passing of restrictive immigration legislation, more attention was focused on ways of creating a climate for cooperation among the various strands of American society. Economic and political events during the 1930s gave increased impetus to the changing trend. The Great Depression focused attention on the impact of economic change, and the rise of fascism in Europe pointed to the dangers of accounting for racial differences along biological lines.

By the 1930s liberal social scientists were by and large espousing environmentalism and cultural relativity. Terman and the mental testers were caught in the middle of a conceptual shift. Their brand of liberalism with its biological determinism was no longer in fashion. Their hereditarian explanations of IQ differences, especially regarding racial differences, had come under increasing attack in the 1920s. Some, such as Brigham and Goddard, publicly recanted their earlier views.[30] Terman also began to move in new directions. While still holding to his hereditarian views about intellectual differences, he took an environmentalist position on such nonintellectual characteristics as delinquency, masculinity-femininity, and homosexuality. Even within the realm of intelligence, he no longer adhered to his hereditarian view of racial differences. In sum, Terman was a committed liberal throughout his adult life. To keep in step with changing times some of his scientific views changed, but he never lost faith in his belief that science was an instrument for social progress.

Terman's liberalism also turned more to the realm of political and social issues and was often expressed with strong conviction and deeply felt emotion. His involvement just prior to World War II in the Hoover controversy sparked an active interest in politics. In the early forties, Terman began to write down some of his thoughts about sociopolitical affairs.[31] At the outbreak of the war, as part of a university network, he organized a morale seminar at Stanford.[32] His plans were to develop a book that would contribute to the war literature of the time, but this was not realized because of his recovery from burns in the fall of 1942.

When Terman recovered his health by 1947, he once again took an active interest in politics and social issues. One issue that he followed closely was civil liberties. He was distressed by the postwar international scene of growing "Russian aggression," with the consequence that individual freedom would be crushed.[33] However, he was even more alarmed about the domestic trend of "witch-hunts" for Communists and the reactionary attitudes of many members of Congress.[34]

By 1950 Terman became more concerned about the anti-Communist hysteria of the emerging McCarthy era. He set down his thoughts about this in a letter to Boring: "Since World War II the conduct of the Un-American Activities Committee has seemed to me one of the greatest threats to liberalism in this country, a threat that is far more serious than anything that can be accomplished against us by the one-twentieth of one per cent who are Communist Party members."[35] He went on to refer to the Hollywood purge that had begun in 1948. One of the victims of this purge was a member of the gifted group, Edward Dmytryk, who Terman described as one of the most brilliant movie directors. He had been jailed and fined for his contempt of the Un-American Activities Committee in refusing to tell them if he was a Communist. The witch-hunts were spreading and were now directed at university professors who were forced to sign anti-Communist oaths. Terman was angered over the recent decision by the University of California regents on this matter. His reaction was "the U.C. regents' attitude of sign-or-get-out seems to me motivated largely by the desire to show who is boss. I often wonder whether I would have signed such an oath thirty years ago. I certainly would not now, and would not tell the Congressional Committee whether I am or ever was a Communist if they should ask me. They could send me to jail for the rest of my life." [36]

Terman had strongly approved of psychologist Edward C. Tolman's refusal to sign the University of California loyalty oath, an act which led to his dismissal from the university. [37] In 1952, when Tolman regained his academic position as a result of the California Supreme Court overruling the legality of such oaths, he sent a note of congratulations to Tolman. Terman was now caught up in the presidential election and commented: "I imagine that you are about as reluctant as I am to vote for the Republican ticket this year in view of the fact that Nixon, the smear artist, is on it and Eisenhower has approved McCarthy." [38] A few days later he wrote again to Tolman and mentioned that he had listened to McCarthy's speech "even though I felt like throwing the radio at him." [39]

For Terman, as for liberals in general, Joseph McCarthy represented a threat to civil liberties and American democracy; nor did Terman like Richard Nixon. Although Nixon had come out against the loyalty oath, Terman viewed him as a political opportunist who used the anti-Communist hysteria to unseat congressional representative Helen Gehagan Douglas. [40] Terman was displeased when Dwight Eisenhower added Nixon to the 1952 Republican ticket. When the Democrats chose Adlai Stevenson, Terman began to see some hope for the future of American democracy. He commented to Boring that Stevenson's "acceptance speech was a gem that will go down in history." [41] Shortly after Stevenson's defeat in the election Terman sent him a letter of support for the campaign he had conducted, though he doubted if Stevenson would actually have an opportunity to see the letter. [42] Some months later Terman wrote to Yerkes about his reaction to a speech Stevenson gave over the radio. Terman stated: "Did you listen to the address Stevenson gave in New York City recently? I do love that man!" [43] In the 1956 campaign, Terman again supported Stevenson; and to an old Indiana friend, Fred Jackson, Terman pointed out that Stevenson had a high IQ. [44] It seems that Stevenson represented to Terman the meritocratic ideal of a leader—that is, a person of high intellect and character who would have the best interests of the citizenry at heart.

Personal Relationships

Throughout his professional life, Terman maintained an extensive correspondence with colleagues and former students. During retirement he devoted more time to these exchanges, and they provided a vehicle for reminiscing and sharing his feelings. Some of these thoughts were communicated in the context of condolences or memorials for colleagues who had passed away. When Guy Whipple died in 1941, Terman wrote to his widow lamenting the passing of someone with whom he shared common interests. As he noted, he and Whipple "saw things largely the same way."[45] Indeed, Whipple shared Terman's hereditarian position and in the testing debates was a consistent supporter of the "nature" side. A few years after Leta Hollingworth's death, Terman reviewed her biography by her psychologist husband, Harry Hollingworth.[46] Terman mourned the passing of a fellow colleague in the study of the gifted, commenting that if she were a man her overall productivity would have been rewarded by election to the presidency of the American Psychological Association. In 1943 one of Terman's former students, Barbara Burks, committed suicide. She had worked closely with Terman on the gifted study and the 1928 nature-nurture debate. He was shocked by the loss of one of his most promising students, [47] and in an obituary article, he noted the tragic loss of someone who at age forty had already established an outstanding record of creative productivity.[48]

Terman continued to correspond most frequently with Yerkes and Boring. Yerkes had retired from teaching in 1944. In response, Terman extended his best wishes, commenting that Yerkes deserved his retirement on the strength of his psychological contributions.[49] In their correspondence during the post–World War II years, the two men shared their views on a number of topics, including politics and the many books they read.[50] Their attitudes on politics and their taste in literature ran along similar lines. They also kept each other abreast of their professional work and shared reflections about their own careers. For example, Terman noted that they were both fortunate in being able to see their major research projects come to fruition (Terman's gifted study and Yerkes's primate lab).[51] In 1951 Terman wrote extensive comments on Yerkes's unpublished autobiography, offering a number of criticisms of both style and content that he felt could lead to improvements.[52] In reply, Yerkes pointed out that he and Terman lived in the "same professional world" and should therefore be able to clearly understand and sympathize with each other.[53] Terman confided to Yerkes that he could not see himself writing a book-length autobiography. (He had written a single chapter for the Murchison series in 1932.) His mind was directed to the present and future, while his memory of things past was fragmentary and unreliable. Furthermore, he noted that if he did write about himself it would be devoted to "the larger aspects of my life and my personal philosophy, and that in my honest opinion would not be worth publishing."[54]

In 1954 Yerkes was seriously ill due to heart problems.[55] He recovered but had a relapse the following year. When Terman was informed, he wrote Yerkes's wife, Ada: "The older one gets the more one cherishes the long-time friends who still survive, and the more one regrets not having kept in closer touch with them in the earlier years. If I could live my life over I would give less of my time to writing books and more to my family and friends."[56] A few months later Yerkes passed away.[57] In expressing his condolence to Ada Yerkes, Terman declared that Robert had been the closest friend of his generation. He added: "My indebtedness to him over many years was very great."[58]

Terman's exchange of letters with Boring was somewhat less reflective than was the case with Yerkes. Boring was nine years younger and was still teaching during Terman's retirement years. The two men did share their views about psychology. For example, they both placed more value on empirical data than on theory or philosophy.[59] In describing himself Terman stated: "I am in no sense a philosopher, and lord knows that as a psychologist I am not outstanding either for scholarship or for originality."[60] On another occasion, he commented: "In all my books I have stuck pretty close to my data . . . I guess I just don't have a theoretical mind."[61] In one instance, Terman was critical of Boring's attempt to stray from "demonstrable facts." This was in relation to Boring's autobiography in the series of volumes initiated by

Murchison. Terman did not convey his opinions to Boring but confided to Yerkes that Boring wrote "too much about his frustrations, subconscious motivations, resulting from childhood insecurity and inferiority feelings. Supposed influences of childhood on his later motivations are inferences rather than demonstrable facts."[62] Although Terman and Boring did not always see things the same way (Boring was critical about applied psychology), they had great mutual respect for one another. For example, Terman stated: "I have long been aware of your affectionate friendship, but I know that I don't deserve half the admiration which I have always felt for you both as a person and as a psychologist."[63]

Among the many others whom Terman corresponded with, the most revealing exchanges were with Edward L. Thorndike, Godfrey Thomson, and Florence Goodenough. In these communications, Terman expressed the importance that he attached to professional relationships. Thorndike had been an influential figure in shaping Terman's ideas about quantitative methods and testing during the Clark years.[64] They had worked with each other during the army testing and the subsequent development of the National Intelligence Tests. Thorndike had also played a significant role in Terman's being appointed as psychology department head (see Chapter 8). Over the years, they continued to consult with one another. In 1941 Terman wrote a review of Thorndike's mammoth book, *Human Nature and the Social Order*.[65] Like Terman, Thorndike argued for a hierarchical society based on native ability. However, Terman was rather critical of Thorndike's dismissal of democratic institutions in favor of a benevolent aristocracy. During Terman's convalescence from his burns, Thorndike sent wishes for recovery.[66] In 1946 Terman reciprocated to an ailing Thorndike. Thorndike, in turn, described himself as a "tired old man" who still kept at his writing.[67] Thorndike also identified Terman as a kindred spirit by expressing his wish that the two of them live next door to each other so that they could "discuss the universe." When Thorndike died in 1949, Terman wrote to his son Robert: "As I look back over my own career I can think of only one other man (Binet) who had so much influence on my psychological thinking; this despite the fact that I often disagreed with your father's conclusions."[68]

Terman's lengthy correspondence with Thomson, a British educational psychologist, was rather unusual because they had met each other only once (at the 1923 meeting of the American Psychological Association).[69] There was a brief exchange of letters in 1941, and in 1947 they started to write regularly to each other.[70] They discussed their own work to some extent, but they focused on their personal affairs. Perhaps because they had not worked with one another they felt especially free to talk about their personal experiences. They shared their reading interests, wrote about their families, and kept each other informed about the political and economic conditions in their respective countries. In fact, Terman was quite concerned about the food shortages in Britain and generously sent Thomson and his wife a food parcel.[71] When Thomson died in 1955, Terman communicated to his widow: "I can't tell you how greatly I miss the correspondence with Godfrey. I think of him on so many occasions when I would like to mention a book he would be interested in or when I would like his opinion about some psychological matter. The older one gets the more profoundly one misses the friends who have passed on."[72]

Terman maintained an especially close professional relationship with Goodenough. Their written exchanges reflected the lasting influence of Terman, the mentor, on his former student. They had worked with one another during the 1940 nature-nurture debate. Due to health problems, Goodenough retired from the University of Minnesota in 1947 at the age of sixty.[73] She settled on a farm in New Hampshire with a sister and brother-in-law and looked forward to more time for writing. In extending his best wishes to her, Terman wrote: "I have had more than my share of research assistants whose competence and devotion to the task at hand left me deeply in their debt, but I believe the others would unanimously agree with me in acclaiming you the most fortunate choice I ever made."[74] Terman was referring to Goodenough's work as a field assistant in the initial stages of the gifted study, and he went on to extoll her career contributions to child psychology. Goodenough, on another occasion, expressed how much she was indebted to Terman, noting that he was the person who most influenced her.[75] In 1949 she wrote a book about mental testing, with the following dedication: "To Lewis M. Terman, a worthy successor to Alfred Binet."[76]

Family Ties

In 1948 Terman attended the April meeting of the National Academy of Sciences in Washington, D.C. On the way back to California, he stopped off to see his relatives in Indiana.[77] He had not been there since 1931, and this was to be his last visit. He spent four days in and around Indianapolis visiting some forty relatives, as well as some boyhood friends and acquaintances. He was sad to see signs of deterioration among his peers, but his two brothers and two surviving sisters were in relatively good health for their age. What he saw of the younger generation pleased him and led him to observe that "the nephews and nieces seem more intelligent than their parents, the grandnephews and grandnieces seem even better."[78] One of his nieces later recalled how much she enjoyed seeing her uncle during his Indiana visits.[79] She was impressed by the fact that he was never "big headed," and she fondly remembered the twinkle in his eyes.

Over the years Terman continued to take an interest in his siblings and their offspring, often in the form of financial assistance. He contributed to one niece's college education,[80] and he offered to finance another niece at Stanford, though this did not come about.[81] One of Anna's nieces also lived with the Terman's from 1923 to 1925 while attending high school.[82] In 1954 Terman's oldest brother, John, was in difficult financial circumstances. This was the brother who had been so helpful to him when he was pursuing his normal-school and university education.[83] Terman had sent some funds to John's daughter, Ethel Perry, to take care of her father's financial needs. Unfortunately, Ethel mismanaged the money to some extent but was able to eventually settle her father's affairs. Terman expressed his wish to provide more help but explained that he could not do so because of his own medical expenses. He pointed out that he had spent more than twenty thousand dollars since 1942 and that within the last year and a half had spent an additional twelve hundred dollars because of Anna's declining health. In view of these expenses, Terman revealed to P. C. Emmons, his Indiana friend, how grateful he was to have a royalty income.[84]

Retirement provided Terman the opportunity to spend more time with his immediate family. During the war, Fred was at Harvard where he had been appointed to organize and direct the Radio Re-

search Laboratory.[85] The major mission of the laboratory was to develop countermeasures against enemy radar. As a result of its success,
Fred was decorated by both the American and British governments.
When he returned to Stanford in 1946, Fred was made dean of engineering. During the time that he was away, Terman corresponded
with his son, though this activity was severely limited after November
1942 when Terman was recovering from his burns. In one letter, at
the beginning of Fred's tenure, Terman inquired how Fred was coping
with his heavy workload.[86] He expressed his and Anna's concern that
Fred might overtax his physical stamina, an allusion to Fred's history
of tuberculosis. In his letters, Terman kept Fred abreast of developments at Stanford.[87] From time to time he also referred to Anna's
concerns about Fred's children. This followed the prewar pattern in
which Fred would meet with his mother to go over family affairs in
the Fred Terman household; it was a practice that irritated Fred's wife
Sibyl. For example, in one letter Terman wrote that Anna was "a bit
disturbed" over the rather dull summer and apparent feeling of loneli-
ness the oldest grandson, Frederick, had experienced. Terman cautioned: "If you take any of these things up with Sibyl you will of
course not quote us."[88] On another occasion, when the two oldest
grandsons were staying with their grandparents toward the end of the
war, Terman himself offered some child-rearing advice to Fred.[89]

Terman's correspondence with his son reflected the close bond between them. Fred looked upon his father as a significant influence on
his own career. He expressed the feeling that his father was also his
teacher,[90] and that he was fortunate to have had the guidance of an
"understanding" father.[91] Terman was proud of his son's accomplishments. One niece recalled this pride, as well as Terman's insistence
that Fred was more famous in his own field than his father was in
psychology.[92] In 1930 Terman wrote a vignette of Fred. Fred had been
included in the gifted sample, and under the pseudonym of "Francis"
he was described as one of the examples of a "youthful zealot."[93] After
reviewing his history Terman noted: "We are informed on the best
authority that he is one of the country's most promising young men in
his research field."[94] Among his personal characteristics, Terman noted
that "Francis" was independent in his thinking, highly regarded by
those who knew him, and "perhaps a little too inclined to live to

himself." This last trait was alluded to by Fred's two oldest sons when they characterized their father as reserved and work oriented and therefore rather removed from his children.[95]

In his career accomplishments Fred validated his father's portrayal of him as a promising young researcher. Beginning in the 1930s, he played a pioneering role in establishing the computer industry in the Palo Alto/San Jose area, the region that is now called "Silicon Valley."[96] The impetus for this was to help talented engineering students establish their own companies near Stanford. Two of his former students were William Hewlett and David Packard, who went on to found the Hewlett-Packard Company. As engineering dean, Fred propelled the Stanford Engineering School into national prominence. Terman was pleased to receive Stanford president Wallace Sterling's enthusiastic praise of Fred's contributions as engineering dean.[97] In 1955 Fred was appointed as provost of Stanford, the second-ranking academic position. Working with President Sterling, he helped to develop Stanford into a position of national prominence and prestige. He retired in 1965, and his greatest honor was accorded in 1976 when he personally received the National Medal of Science from President Gerald R. Ford for his contributions to the creation of modern electronics.[98] Fred died in 1982 at the age of eighty-two.

In 1941, at age thirty-eight, Helen separated from her husband in Los Angeles and moved back to the Stanford area with her two daughters.[99] Two years later she was divorced. Although she had taught school for a year before marriage, Helen did not feel confident enough to return to teaching.[100] She found employment as a switchboard operator in one of the women's dormitories at Stanford. Her older daughter Doris expressed astonishment that her mother could be satisfied with such unchallenging work, but Helen was simply content to be associated with the university in some capacity. She even worried about her competency in handling the job. With Fred and his family away and her two daughters at high school, the war years were a lonely time for Helen. She had little company except for her mother, who tended to be critical most of the time. Eventually, Helen obtained a more responsible position as the administrative assistant to the university director of women's housing.[101] She held the job until the early sixties, when Fred in his capacity as provost was asked if she would step aside for a replacement.[102] He approved her "early retirement" without consulting her (she was on a trip at the time). However, this incident typified Helen's position in the family. She was timid and quiet and consequently was ignored. When her father died in 1956, his royalty income went to Helen. (Fred and his family were financially secure from his patents and royalties.) As a result, Helen had financial security until her death from a massive stroke in 1973 at the age of seventy.

The Terman grandchildren have described the relationships they had with their grandparents, who they called "Daddy Lew" and "Nana."[103] They characterized their grandfather as easy to get along with, friendly, and gentle. He spent most of his time at home working in his study. When they were teenagers, he would talk to them about politics and his work on testing and the gifted. When they were younger, he had given them the Stanford-Binet. Terman remarked to a newspaper reporter in 1937 that every time he saw his grandchildren they came running and begged for another test.[104] Some of his nieces also recalled being given IQ tests by their Uncle Lewis.[105] For the two oldest grandsons, Frederick (as Fred W. was called to distinguish him from his father) and Terence, their grandmother seemed a somewhat more distant figure.[106] On the other hand, Helen's daughters, Doris and Anne, remembered their grandmother as domineering. Anna would scrutinize their table manners.[107] Doris had some "fun" when she went shopping with Anna, but Anne could not recall good times with her grandmother.

Doris has identified a sexist bias underlying the way the grandchildren were treated. She felt that her grandmother cared more about the grandsons. One incident brought this out very forcefully. When she was a child, Doris and the other grandchildren had an Easter egg hunt on the lawn of the Terman home. Being the oldest, she found the most eggs; but Anna made her stop hunting before the event was over so that Frederick could get the prize for finding the most eggs. Anna would not allow a girl to win over a boy. Doris also described her grandfather as being chauvinistic. Even though he worked professionally with many women, he expressed the view that women should concentrate on having a family. He liked pretty women and was critical if they had unattractive features. Doris stated that neither she nor her sister was encouraged to seek a career, an attitude that was reinforced by their mother. Doris's impression of her grandfather's male chauvinism is matched by the partiality he showed in his personal correspondence. Whenever he referred to his children and grandchildren, he proudly referred to Fred's accomplishments but barely mentioned Helen. With his grandchildren, he tended to focus on how gifted his grandsons were. Though probably unintentional, there was even an implicit male bias in the telegram Terman sent Doris on her wedding day in 1952: "May all of your children be handsome and gifted and may they be listed in Who's Who in Science."[108]

Related to the sexist bias there was another kind of favoritism that ran through the Terman family circle. Individuals were valued according to their presumed intellectual ability. In other words, the family was a microcosm of the meritocratic society Terman envisioned. This pattern was best revealed when the extended family would gather together for dinners at the Terman house. In hindsight, such occasions had a humorous side to them, for each of the three grandchildren interviewed referred to Sibyl's (Fred's wife) perennial complaint, in private, about the overcooked turkey the Terman maid had prepared.[109] Doris has recalled the table arrangement at the gatherings.[110] She sat next to Anna, who had a deaf ear; and she was specifically seated on the side of Anna's deaf ear. This was the position Helen had occupied when she was younger, and Helen continued to sit near Anna. The "brighter people" sat further down the table near Lewis and Fred, both of whom dominated the dinner conversation. Doris's position reflected the fact that she helped the maid, since she had "domestic inclinations." It was clear that Anna and Helen were at the bottom rung of the family hierarchy of intellect with Lewis and Fred at the top. However, when it came to domestic affairs, Anna assumed the dominant position. The familial meritocracy did not necessarily place all of the women at the lowest level. Sibyl, who completed some graduate work with Terman before she married Fred and subsequently continued professional work in the area of remedial reading, seems to have been respected in the family for her intellect. Coincidentally, Sibyl also confided to Doris that she found the family dinners to be dull, tedious, "unfun affairs."

Terman's male chauvinism was superseded by the value he placed on intellectual ability. If a woman was bright and chose a career over marriage, he was sensitive to the sexist obstacles she faced. This seems to explain how he could be so insensitive to the discriminatory way he treated his wife and daughter, and to some extent his granddaughters, and yet be so sensitive to the problems his female students and colleagues faced.

With advancing age and declining health, Lewis and Anna developed a closer relationship than they had in the period before his retirement. While Lewis had various health problems beginning in 1942 with his recovery from burns, Anna remained in good health until 1954. In May of that year, she suffered a mild stroke.[111] She had a partial paralysis in one leg, which cleared up in a few weeks. However, what especially concerned Lewis was the fact that Anna had been failing mentally, and this decline had begun several months before the stroke. In addition, there was also a marked decline in her hearing.[112] Toward the latter half of 1955, Anna experienced frequent spells of dizziness. In December she had a second stroke. Again she overcame the partial paralysis. However, Terman reported to his sister Jessie that Anna was becoming quit forgetful; and in a letter to Yerkes, he expressed his fear about what Anna's future would be.[113]

The Last Year

With his history of tuberculosis, Terman had to confront the threat of death when he was a young man. Because of this he had learned to conquer his fear of death. His early confrontation with mortality also appears to have contributed to his drive and commitment to scholarly productivity. He felt that he had to devote himself to his career and accomplish as much as he could in what little time he might have left. Before he completed any one project, he was caught up with the anticipation of the next one. As it turned out, his major project—the gifted—was one of long duration. There was always another follow-up to be completed and another volume to be written. When he had major health problems, especially in the early forties, he would become quite depressed because his work was interrupted. There was also the fear that he would be unable to return to it.

In 1953 he was asked to contribute a case history about his tuberculosis.[114] It was to be included in a book about eminent men and women who had been afflicted by tuberculosis. He completed his chapter in December 1953, but the book was never published.[115] Terman's thoughts about death were captured at the end of the manuscript.

Approaching 77 now, I have lived more years than I ever dared hope for a half century ago and have accomplished more than I ever dreamed of, probably as much as I would have accomplished if I had never had tuberculosis. From this distance it is possible to look back upon the threats of those earlier years without reviewing the raw anxiety they caused me. Though I long ago lost my fear of death from tuberculosis (or anything else), I still find myself occasionally counting my pulse or reaching for the clinical thermometer that lies on the table by my bed—perhaps out of habit, perhaps because I want to finish another book and watch the development of our five grandchildren. Besides, there are my 1400 gifted "children," now at mid-life, who were selected by mental tests in 1922; I have now followed their careers for thirty years and should really like to follow them for another thirty![116]

In 1956—his last year—Terman had to face Anna's death and his own failing health. After her second stroke in December 1955, Anna recovered from the mild paralysis; but she was not well either physically or mentally, and a nurse was with her on a full-time basis.[117] She passed away suddenly from a heart attack on 26 March. Terman was not present at the time of her death. A couple of weeks earlier he had been hospitalized because of a back injury produced by convulsive coughing during a flu attack.

In the newspaper account of Anna's death, a statement was included about her relationship with her husband. It was an expanded version of the comments Terman himself had written about her in his autobiography in 1932.[118] The newspaper version read as follows: "Her contribution to her husband's success was summed by Dr. Terman in his autobiographical sketch. He wrote that his wife had the same ambitions for him that he had for himself and that she contributed to his success by valuing the things for which he was striving and making it easier for him to achieve his goals."[119] Indeed, this reflected what their relationship was based on. However, it did not make for a very satisfactory relationship—particularly for Anna during the twenties and thirties (see Chapter 8).

After Anna's death, Terman often expressed how much he missed her.[120] He shared some of his thoughts about her to Godfrey Thomson's widow: "We had been married almost exactly 56½ years. There are so many memories of those years that they make it easier to overlook the deterioration she suffered during the last few months. Even so, the big house still seems very empty without her. . . . Her life was largely one of service to others. She loved looking after people and made a host of friends among the faculty and students."[121] He went on to relate her role in nursing Fred back to health in the 1920s and himself in the 1940s. Undoubtedly, throughout their married life Terman appreciated Anna's help to him, and he was grateful that he could leave family matters and social obligations essentially in her hands. He did not feel that she could share much with him intellectually. For such stimulation he had his colleagues and students, as well as his son. For his emotional and sexual needs, he had other women.

Among the many letters of sympathy he received, the most touching one came from Florence Goodenough.[122] The letter was typed,but it was filled with typographical errors and misspelled words. The reason was that she was disabled by diabetes and was almost totally blind.[123] She expressed her wish that she could be a companion for him in his lonely hours, and if it were not for the long hard trip she would hope he could visit her and share a delightful New England summer. He thanked her for her "lovely" letter, and added: "I know how much you loved Anna and how much at home you were in our seminars and on other occasions when you were here."[124]

Terman returned home from the hospital at the end of March.[125] In order to recover from his back injury, which involved a vertebra, he had to wear an orthopedic corset. By the middle of April, he was able to be out of bed a good part of the time, though he had a practical nurse to look after him. He enjoyed his favorite activity of reading and finally gave into Fred and Sibyl's insistence that he get a television set. He reported that his doctor indicated he would be back to normal in a few months, and he was grateful for the fact that Fred's and Helen's families were nearby. By the middle of May, he was able to work at his campus office for about three to four hours a day.[126] At the beginning of the summer, a graduate law student took up residence in the house, and he was pleased to have the company.[127]

In September Terman had a cerebral thrombosis, but by early November he wrote to Jennie Thomson that the prospects for a complete recovery seemed good.[128] He noted that he would be eighty in January and was doing quite well considering his age. On 21 November he had a second thrombosis.[129] For the next month he was in the hospital, paralyzed on the left side with only brief interludes of consciousness. Melita Oden reported to Jennie Thomson that when conscious his remarks indicated that his mind was not affected. She added that because of his record of remarkable recoveries in the past, she had hoped he would also weather this crisis. However, on 21 December 1956, he died of a cerebral hemorrhage.[130] On the following 15 January, he would have been eighty years old.

Melita Oden, who had been Terman's research assistant on the gifted study for thirty years, expressed her own sense of his loss. She, the secretary, and "our beloved LMT" were like a family at the "gifted office."[131] They shared each other's joys and sorrows and friends. In the Memorial Resolution drafted by the Stanford University faculty, it was stated:

Happily, it can be recorded that Lewis Terman's accomplishments brought him the respect and fame he so fully earned. . . . But perhaps the symbol of success that gave him the greatest pleasure of all was the fact that after 36 years of research with his cherished group of gifted subjects, over 90 percent of those still living were in close and continuing contact with him and were still enthusiastically helping him to fill the picture of what happens to the lives of those whom nature and experience have placed in the upper one percent of ability.[132]

At Terman's request, no funeral rites were held for him at the Stanford Memorial Church on campus.[133] However, as a memorial, a conference on the gifted child was held at the university on 13 April 1957.[134] Oden reviewed his work and previewed what was to be reported in the next volume of the gifted monograph series. Family, friends, colleagues, and some of his cherished "Termites" (the gifted subjects) attended. His gifted study still continues under the direction of two of his "Termites"—Robert Sears and Lee Cronbach.

Epilogue

Terman was a man with a mission. Through his work as a psychologist he believed that he could contribute to the shaping of an American society based on the principle of meritocracy—that is, the establishment of a hierarchical division of labor that would be commensurate with the distribution of ability in the population. The most responsible positions, which also carry the highest social status, would be held by those individuals with the highest levels of intellect, assuming they are industrious enough to make use of their inherent talent. The class structure of inequalities in wealth,power, and status would thus reflect individual differences in ability and insure that each person's place in the social hierarchy would be based on his or her merit.

The idea that the social order should be based on individual merit, rather than any preexisting system of wealth, power, and status, was consistent with the democratic ethos of American society. But it was the growing industrialization of America toward the end of the nineteenth century that made the concept of meritocracy so salient. The developing specialization of the labor market required a system in which individual differences in ability could be identified. Furthermore, those individuals with high ability needed highly specialized training to prepare them for the more responsible occupational positions they would assume. Terman viewed mental tests as the most efficient means of achieving a meritocratic social structure. Such tests would identify native intelligence and, if administered at school age, would appropriately sort pupils into educational tracks according to ability level. Terman was especially committed to the identification of children at the highest level of native intelligence—the gifted. If such children were accurately identified by tests and then provided with special educational opportunities to challenge their intellects, they could assume the positions of leadership necessary for social progress in the emerging age of industrialization. They would also have the moral character to look after the welfare of those individuals at the lower levels of ability.

It was the development and application of psychological testing in the service of this meritocratic vision that shaped Terman the man and Terman the scientist.

Terman the Man

As a boy growing up on an Indiana farm, Terman was sensitive to individual differences. While somewhat inferior in physical prowess to his schoolmates, he excelled in intellectual pursuits. Although he had no available label at his disposal, he had a sense of being intellectually gifted. This vague sense of self-definition sparked ambitions beyond the confines of the farm life he knew. An older brother who was a teacher provided a role model, in terms of both fulfilling intellectual desires and as a means of upward mobility. With the support of an understanding father, young Lewis was able to prepare for the teaching profession. Being pragmatic, he was initially satisfied in fulfilling his commitment to school teaching. However, the more he delved into scholarly pursuits, the more he dared dream of something more challenging. With his entry to university-level studies, the die was cast. The dream for post-graduate study became a reality. At Indiana University he was exposed to the ideas of Hall, Galton, and Binet— writers who translated his own experiences and interests about individual differences into legitimate scientific endeavor.

The opportunity to go to Clark University brought Terman under the direct influence of Hall. As was true with Hall's other disciples, Terman was mesmerized by the personal magnetism and intellectual stimulation of this gurulike figure. At Indiana, Terman had already been socialized in Hall's evolutionary perspective; but at Clark he became imbued with it. Like his other classmates, he was committed to Hallian ideology, but he needed to put these ideas into practice— and it was practice that was Hall's weakness. Terman was astute enough to see the possibilities of using the methods of mental testing, first developed by Galton, as the means of carrying out Hall's ideas. His doctoral research on "genius" and "stupidity," though crude by his own standards, set the tone for his life's work on individual differences.

With a doctoral degree, Terman aspired to an academic career in the areas for which he was trained, pedagogy and child study. His struggle with tuberculosis put a hold on this goal for several years. At one point, his dream of an academic career seemed hopeless—as a high-school principal he felt trapped. However, he was able to enter normal-school teaching and this provided the steppingstone he needed for university teaching. In 1910 his dream came true with an appointment at Stanford University. With his health regained, he started his life's work on individual differences at the point that he had been forced to stop while completing his doctorate at Clark.

Throughout Terman's adulthood his career had top priority. Therefore, his family life was organized to facilitate his work-oriented focus. The woman he married, Anna Minton, had already adopted an energetic and managerial style in handling her father's affairs. She easily fitted into her role of managing domestic affairs in the Terman household. When Terman was a graduate student, she supplemented the meager family income by taking in boarders. With two young children, she saw to it that they did not disturb their father. When Lewis had to deal with tuberculosis and the rehabilitation his illness required, the pattern of taking prime responsibility for the children and the household was reinforced. By the time Lewis's career took off at Stanford, the division of labor in the Terman household was set. Lewis's time and energy were devoted to his work, while Anna looked after the children and domestic management. There also seemed to be some tacit understanding between Lewis and Anna that Fred needed a close relationship with his father. Lewis's own relationship with his father had been important in his development. As a result, he was willing to devote some of his highly valuable time to his son. The time they spent together was not devoted to shared activities, but was rather in terms of Lewis's support and encouragement of Fred's developing interests in radio and electronics. Helen was clearly Anna's responsibility. Although she wished otherwise, her father remained a distant, though admired, figure.

Fred modeled himself closely after his father. Apparently, in his adult life he outdid his father's preoccupation with work. Like his father, Fred left domestic affairs to his wife Sibyl. Like Anna, Sibyl was frustrated once she fulfilled her maternal responsibilities. Helen was never able to escape her mother's domination and remained in the shadow of her parents and brother. Although Helen was bright, she had little encouragement other than to get married and pass on the familial gene stock to her children. Terman basked in the intellectual promise of his grandchildren, though for the granddaughters this promise was to be fulfilled through marriage and reproduction. The Terman family circle was a microcosm of the meritocratic social order Terman devoted himself to. Each family member was valued according to his or her level of intellect. Fred and his sons were encouraged to fulfill their gifted potential by aspiring to high levels of career achievement, while Helen and her daughters were restricted to the fulfillment of domestic roles.

The familial pattern that Terman fostered reflected the intrusion of his priority to career—that is, most of his time and Anna's management of household affairs were in the service of furthering his career goals. Not only did his work prevail time-wise, but his ideology of meritocracy affected the nature of the relationships and expectations within the family circle. Anna, with her high level of energy and her penchant for management, actively reinforced these patterns. In the end, she suffered because the efficient family organization brought about estrangement from Lewis. Furthermore, with her children grown, she had few outlets to satisfy her high energy level and organizational skills. Campus women's clubs, faculty entertaining, and looking after family financial interests helped keep her busy, but much of her need to have a place in the family was now directed at overseeing her grown children's domestic affairs.

In his family relationships Terman seemed to place more stress on "people as things," rather than intrinsically valuing them as persons. It was what the members of his family could do and accomplish that seemed to have more precedence. This is not to say that a sense of love and closeness was missing. In fact, in relating to his grandchildren, his acceptance and benign gentleness were manifest. With Fred, there was a strong bond and rapport. On the other hand, in relating to his wife and daughter this closeness was missing (though it was there with Anna in the early years of their marriage). At some point the merito-cratic ideology intruded—Anna and Helen could not share his enthu-siasm for intellectual pursuits. Seemingly at some unconscious level he could not value them as much as those with intellectual giftedness. His estrangement from Anna appeared to reflect his need to turn to other women who were bright, as well as attractive. With such women, he must have felt the emotional intimacy that he lacked with Anna. With these women he could also express his sexuality, and he apparently had the charm and warmth to attract many of his bright and attractive female students. Anna, for her part, may have unwittingly alienated Terman by her need to dominate, thus reinforcing his search for other women to satisfy his emotional and sexual needs.

The intrusion of his meritocratic ideology into family life and rela-tionships stands in contrast with the pattern of his relationships with friends, colleagues, and students. Once he left Indiana, his circle of associations was almost exclusively within the academic world. It was thus natural for him to choose close relationships with people that he could respect for their intellect. With this as a given, Terman's inter-personal qualities revealed themselves in a positive way. Among the colleagues that he was close with, such as Yerkes and Boring, there was mutual respect and an exchange of support. In the case of these two, there had been a competitive edge in Terman's early association with each of them, but once the circumstances underlying the compe-tition were removed the relationships developed into close ones. With students, Terman proved to be a fine mentor. He maintained an appropriate degree of emotional distance, communicated high stan-dards, and above all provided the nurturance and encouragement nec-essary to bring out the potential of the student. If he could be faulted in this role, it might be that in some cases he assumed a paternalistic attitude that was expressed through his rather forceful approach in dispensing advice and influencing career decisions. He was not an especially good or stimulating classroom teacher; but on a one-to-one basis, he was a revered mentor.

His close associations outside of the family seemed generally free of any prejudices he might have had, other than the fact that these relationships were restricted to the intellectual class. Such a restriction, in his generation and probably even at the present time, is not atypical of academics. Of course, in Terman's time, he would have had little opportunity to associate with members of racial minorities within academic circles. He did, however, have some contacts with Jews. He formed a close relationship with a Jewish graduate student at Stanford, Samuel Kohs. He continued to be supportive of Kohs after Kohs left Stanford, and he was sensitive to the discrimination Kohs was subjected to in the academic world. Kohs was appreciative of his mentor's support in these instances and commented on Terman's open-mindedness and freedom from religious and racial prejudice.[1] Furthermore, Terman was most impressed by the disproportionately high representation of Jewish children in his gifted sample. He was convinced that Jews had an intellectually superior gene pool and was, therefore, pleased when his daughter married someone with Jewish ancestry. In contrast to these positive feelings, he also tended to accept stereotypical depictions of Jews as shrewd and clannish.[2]

Terman's attitudes toward women were rather complex. On the one hand, he was chauvinistic. This determined how he evaluated the women in his family. It also influenced his thinking about the different spheres men and women should function within, as evidenced by his work on masculinity-femininity and sex and marriage. But once again, meritocracy intruded in a positive way. Assuming he could respect a woman for her intellect, he went out of his way to be supportive and, as in the case of Jews, he was sensitive to the prejudice and discrimination women faced in the academic world. In considering his relationships with women, the question arises as to whether the sexual escapades with some of his students represented instances of exploitation. The evidence is lacking to answer this. We do not have any personal documents or statements about these affairs from any of the women involved. It is, nevertheless, a troublesome aspect of Terman's character. He cannot be exonerated from the responsibility of using his powerful position to satisfy his sexual and affectional needs, however enjoyable and exciting this may have been for the female students involved.

There seems to be a dominant quality about Terman that pervades his close relationships with colleagues and students, despite the foibles that have been pointed to. His warmth and caring are clearly indicated in the correspondence that exists bearing on these relationships. Terman often wrote touching and compelling letters that resonated with sincere concern and support. Interviews and correspondence with former colleagues and students lent further support to these qualities. It is apparent that Terman was well liked and appreciated by those who knew him. Besides his warmth and support, he had other endearing qualities. He was gentle and rather low-keyed, relatively approachable and unassuming, and with a twinkle in his eyes he had a elfish sense of humor. In some contradiction to these qualities, he was also quite reserved in face-to-face situations and therefore not demonstrative. There could be a distance and reticence about him.[3] Keith Sward, a post-doctoral associate in Terman's department, has advanced an insightful analysis of the way Terman directed his expressions of warmth. In keeping up by letter with scores of former students, as well as many of his gifted subjects, he could express his warmth and affection from a position of safety. His shyness made it difficult for him to convey such feelings in direct interpersonal contact, but he was able to demonstrate them clearly from the safety of written correspondence.

In contrast to the positive side of Terman's personality, there was a major fault. He could not easily accept criticism about his own work. Such "attacks" threatened his mission. With the drive to fulfill his professional life's work, he viewed objections about testing and the biological basis of intelligence as obstacles. He had little doubt that his work was scientifically sound; therefore, he tended to perceive his critics as relatively incompetent scientists. He was willing to engage in debates with students who opposed his hereditarian position, and, despite this opposition, he remained on friendly terms with them.[4] He had enough other evidence of their ability and friendship. However, for professionals who criticized him in the scientific literature, he had little respect for their ability. Probably the occasion that brought out the worst in him was his personal confrontation with George Stoddard, who represented the "devil incarnate." More than any of the other critics, Stoddard mounted an offensive that Terman perceived as a threat to the very foundation of his career accomplishments. By publicly humiliating Stoddard, he thought he could keep the threat in check.

The other source of hindrance to his career was his health problem.

There were times when he felt defeated and depressed. His dogged determination, as well as the help of Anna, carried him through the various crises. Particularly in the early 1940s and toward the end of his life, he struggled against overwhelming obstacles with his health. One anecdote captures the extent to which he pursued his goals against great odds. In the mid-forties, when he was still recovering from his burns and had to deal with impaired vision, he managed to keep his driver's license so that he could drive down to his campus office to work. At this time, he could not see the eye chart well enough to pass the test. However, he had already committed the eye chart to memory and in that way passed the test and retained his driver's license.[5]

Terman was a modest man, and he was generous in acknowledging the contributions of others who assisted him in his work. Reflecting the coterie of graduate students working with him, he dubbed his Binet revision the Stanford-Binet. The man who more than any other psychologist was responsible for "making the IQ a household word"[6] did not leave his own name on the first test to use this index. Despite his own modesty, he was confident that his life's work would leave a lasting legacy on the framework of American society. He lived long enough to see the fruits of his labor. His meritocratic vision became a reality. Psychological testing in the schools became standard practice. Personality testing was coming into its own. The gifted study had won him wide recognition and adulation. Among the many awards and honors that he received, one of the most significant for him was the honorary doctorate of science he received from the University of Pennsylvania in 1946.[7] The occasion was the fiftieth anniversary of the founding of the first psychological clinic at that university. Terman was one of six to receive the award (the others were Boring, Dewey, Goddard, Köhler, and Woodworth). Thus he was identified as one of the pioneers of American psychology.

Terman the Scientist

Terman was, by his own admission, not an especially original thinker. He was adept at translating the ideas and perspectives of others into scientific practice. Thus, he could take the impressionistic evolutionary framework of his mentor, Hall, and put it into practice in terms of the mental measurements first suggested by Galton and then later in terms of the testing procedures developed by Binet. In entering the testing field, he was one of many investigators in America who saw the promise of Binet's methods. That he was the most successful is due to the particular skills he had as a scientist. It is true that once he arrived at Stanford he probably had better resources and institutional support than most of his competitors. However, he was an especially thorough investigator who had a penchant for collecting large amounts of empirical data. He also had very good administrative skills, which were manifest not only in his departmental headship but also in his ability to work with and organize the efforts of others. In developing his Binet revision, he had the assistance of many graduate students who then went on to carry out projects that complemented his own work. When he went to work on the army tests, he easily adapted to the teamwork pattern that was being established with colleagues and carried on this pattern in developing tests for the schools. His organizational skills as a scientist were at their best in the gifted study, and he was among the first psychologists in the 1920s to successfully obtain large research grants from the private foundations that were being set up for this purpose. He also went out of his way to choose the best research associates and assistants that he could find. Almost all of his research from the twenties on was collaborative in nature. His particular strengths as a scientist enabled him to successfully carry out his career goals and to leave a prodigious record of published writings and psychological tests.

His seminal contributions to the development of psychological testing and the study of the intellectually gifted ensure his position as one of the pioneers of American psychology. Perhaps more than any of the other early advocates of the testing movement, he was successful in devising a wide variety of methods assessing individual differences. His interest in the gifted led him to go far beyond the measurement of ability. As a result, he was in the forefront of developing indices of school achievement, gender identity, interests, marital adjustment, and sexual behavior. He was also innovative in enlisting the services of teachers and parents as assessors of gifted children. The tests he developed have generally been the most successful of their kind. In fact, revised forms of the Stanford-Binet and the Stanford Achievement Test are still being widely used. In listing Terman's various accomplishments, credit should also be given to his impact on American popular culture. His introduction of the IQ score on an intelligence test made the IQ a household word. With his student Arthur Otis, he played a major role in establishing the multiple-choice test, which itself has had a profound effect on American education.

Aside from these personal accomplishments, Terman has left us with an unfulfilled legacy. What he wanted to accomplish with his psychological tests and identification of the intellectually gifted was a more socially just and democratic society. His "faith" was that science could serve the purposes of humanistic social evolution so that a more democratic, tolerant, and just society could be created. His particular accomplishments in the field of individual differences hold promise for such purposes. If used carefully, tests can be a helpful aid in individual decision making and planning, as well as in selection and placement for organizational purposes. The problem has been that a considerable part of Terman's own use of and recommendations for testing have had an unintended dehumanizing effect. For racial and ethnic minorities and lower-class individuals, his recommendation of a differential educational system based on IQ scores has, until challenged in the 1960s, served as an obstacle for personal growth and equal opportunity. His views on masculinity-femininity and homosexuality worked against the creation of a more pluralistic society with respect to gender roles and sexual orientation. Once again, it took liberation movements of the 1960s to confront this kind of scientific thought. Thus, Terman's work has often perpetuated and rigidified the social status of individuals, rather than liberating them from social constraints so that they could fulfill their potential.

Terman's shortcomings as a scientist can in part be understood within the context of the historical conditions that gave birth to and shaped the mental-testing movement. The accelerating rate of industrialization and urbanization in North America and western Europe in the late nineteenth and early twentieth centuries created a need for increasing administrative control over the population. Particular concern existed about controlling the undesirable strata of society at the bottom of the social order—that is, the vagrants and paupers who could not fit into the new industrial work force. The development of mental measurements provided a technology for identifying those who were physically normal but presumed to be intellectually inferior or "feebleminded." The impact of Darwinian thinking, especially in Britain and America, equated feeblemindedness with genetic defect. Mental tests could, therefore, stem the tide of degeneracy by detecting the intellectually inferior and thereby selecting them for institutionalization and eugenic programming. The expansion of public education directed particular attention to sorting schoolchildren, with the initial goal of separating the retarded from the normal. Terman's major contribution to testing in the schools was to establish a fine gradation of measured ability so that schoolchildren could be placed in educational tracks commensurate with their tested level of intelligence. In essence, what Terman and the other testing advocates accomplished was to provide a scientific mode of thought and practice that served the interests of maintaining social order and organizational efficiency. With few exceptions, the distribution of tested intelligence reflected the opportunity structure of the social hierarchy. Those identified as most meritorious came primarily from the most privileged strata; those judged to be least meritorious, by virtue of tested IQ, were disproportionately members of the lowest rungs on the social ladder—often racial minorities or recent immigrants. Terman's work in developing measures of nonintellectual traits also served to reinforce existing social relations. The measurement of masculinity-femininity buttressed the conventional notions of separate spheres for men and women.

What Terman failed to understand was the intricate way in which scientific knowledge interacts with social power. As the French social historian Michel Foucault illustrated in his analyses of deviance and sexuality, scientific discourse in these areas emerged out of a need to rationalize and maintain social control.[8] In turn, scientific discourse and related practices produced a body of knowledge that was utilized to support and extend the mechanisms of power and administration. In similar fashion, Terman, and the mental testing movement in general, produced scientific knowledge and technology that was utilized to maintain social control at a time of changing economics and demographics. Mental measurement fulfilled the increasing demands for selecting a more diversified division of labor. In the new industrial age, potential ability and specialized training became more significant attributes for those who were to occupy the highest positions in the social order.

Although Terman did not comprehend the way in which science could become subservient to vested interests, he was quick to seize the initiative in attempts to gain acceptance for the new technology of mental measurement. He was a part of the first generation of psychologists trained in America. This was a group that made excessive claims about the applicability of psychological knowledge and methods. The mental-testing advocates, in particular, mounted an aggressive campaign to sell their product in a wide variety of markets, including the schools, the military, and business. They even tried to sell their tests as a tool for determining social policy, as illustrated by their attempts to influence the passage of restricted immigration legislation. Such zeal undoubtedly contributed to the scientifically unwarranted conclusions arrived at by Terman, Yerkes, and the other authors of the massive army testing report of World War I. The success story of the army testing program was not in reality supported by the data or by the way in which the data were collected and utilized.

However, aside from professional opportunism, Terman had some personal qualities that made him vulnerable to instances of poor scientific practice. He possessed a missionary fervor surrounding his identity with the gifted. Having been a gifted child, he seemed to believe that as a scientist he was destined to liberate the gifted from exploitation, ostracism, and lack of recognition. This singularity of purpose was accompanied by a tendency toward dogmatism. He held strong beliefs about the nature of intellectual giftedness. These were beliefs he had initially assimilated from the hereditarian thinking of his mentor, G. Stanley Hall. In fact, Hall's own missionary zeal appears to have served in part as a role model for Terman. Yet, he was well aware of Hall's methodological deficiencies as a scientist. Unlike Hall, Terman devoted himself to empirical method. But underlying his empiricism was a set of assumptions—a hereditarian belief system that was held with strong conviction. Thus, especially in his earlier work, there were instances of interpreting the data to fit his preconceived notions or of going beyond the data by excessive claims regarding what tests could accomplish. Also indicative of going beyond the data was his tendency, at times, to draw causal conclusions from correlational findings.

His intolerance of accepting personal criticism was another characteristic that worked against his scientific accomplishments. It is not clear what the source of this problem was. Whether the problem stemmed from some form of childhood insecurity or was more directly a reflection of the devotion to his major aims as a scientist is unclear. Nevertheless, throughout his career he spent considerable time and energy in various debates with colleagues that often involved overreactions on his part. In these instances, he seemed driven more by a need to prove himself than to settle a scientific issue.

In appraising Terman's merit as a scientist, it should be emphasized that beyond his particular strengths and despite some personal failings he was very much a product of his times. His zealousness was related to his pioneering status as a testing advocate. His devotion to empirical data gathering and quantification was in keeping with the style of American psychology that had been established when the discipline shed its philosophical trappings by the time of World War I. His concerns with objectivity, empiricism, scientific thinking, and methodology were all reflections of the natural-science, mechanistic world view that has pervaded Anglo-American psychology. His deeply held conviction that science should be in the service of social progress also tapped a central tenet of American psychology. Indeed, this concern with the application of data for social betterment remains a significant part of American psychology. However, there are increasing doubts as to whether or not the natural-science world view that Terman was committed to is the best means of accomplishing psychology's social objectives. A growing recognition now exists that the subject matter of psychology cannot be divorced from its political or social context; nor can it be separated from an underlying set of humanistic values. Therefore, alternative models of psychology as a humanistic or social science have been proposed.[9]

Notes

Abbreviations

AGP   Arnold Gesell Papers, Library of Congress, Washington, D.C.
ECP   Ellwood P. Cubberley Papers, Stanford University Archives, Stanford University Libraries, Stanford, California
FET   Frederick E. Terman
FGP   Florence L. Goodenough Papers, University Archives, University of Minnesota Libraries, Minneapolis
FTP   Frederick E. Terman Papers, Stanford University Archives, Stanford University Libraries, Stanford, California
GHP   G. Stanley Hall Papers, Clark University Archives, Worcester, Massachusetts
HGP   H. H. Goddard Papers, Archives of the History of American Psychology, University of Akron Library, Akron, Ohio
LMT   Lewis M. Terman
LTP   Lewis M. Terman Papers, Stanford University Archives, Stanford University Libraries, Stanford, California
MSP   May V. Seagoe Papers, Archives of the History of American Psychology, University of Akron Library, Akron, Ohio
RWP   Ray Lyman Wilbur Papers, Stanford University Archives, Stanford University Libraries, Stanford, California
RYP   Robert M. Yerkes Papers, Yale University Library, New Haven, Connecticut

Preface

1. For example, see Leon J. Kamin, *The Science and Politics of I.Q.* (Potomac, Md.: Lawrence Erlbaum, 1974); and Clarence J. Karier, Paul C. Violas, and Joel Spring, *Roots of Crisis: American Education in the Twentieth Century* (Chicago: Rand McNally, 1973).

1. *Hoosier Roots (1877–1892)*

1. LMT, "Trails to Psychology," in *A History of Psychology in Autobiography*, vol. 2, ed. Carl Murchison (Worcester, Mass.: Clark University Press, 1932), p. 297.

2. LMT, *The Stanford Revision of the Binet-Simon Tests* (Boston: Houghton Mifflin, 1916).

3. Carl Murchison to LMT, 20 August 1928, LTP.

4. LMT to Murchison, 8 May 1930, LTP.

5. LMT, "Trails to Psychology," p. 298.

6. LMT to Elmer Davis, 13 February 1950, LTP.

7. LMT, "Trails to Psychology," p. 298.

8. Arvel Crouch, Gertrude Tearman, Edna Tearman, and Goldie Tearman, "A Tarmen, Terman, Genealogy," 1968, FTP (typed).

9. The family name was variously spelled by different family members and included the following: Tarmen, Tearman, Terman, and Turman. According to Frederick E. Terman, these variations reflected the circumstances of frontier life when the Middle West was being settled (FET to Terman Bela, 24 February 1965, FTP).

10. LMT to Louis A. Terman, 23 January 1956, LTP.

11. Crouch et al., "A Tarmen, Terman, Genealogy."

12. Annabelle Spencer, "Martha Cutsinger Terman," 1977, p. 1, FTP (typed).

13. Helen Terman Mosher to May V. Seagoe, [1967], MSP.

14. LMT, "Trails to Psychology," p. 299.

15. W. E. Deupree to LMT, 26 January 1924, LTP; Susan Deupree Jones to FET, 5 January 1979; and Jones to FET, 25 January 1979, FTP.

16. LMT to James A. Turman, 6 September 1956, LTP.

17. LMT, "Trails to Psychology," p. 299.

18. Family record of James W. Terman and Martha Cutsinger Terman, compiled by LMT, 26 October 1950, LTP.

19. LMT to Turman, 25 April 1956, LTP. With respect to red hair, Terman refers to only one of his siblings, a sister who had auburn hair.

20. Spencer, "Martha Cutsinger Terman." A portrait of Terman family life is provided by Anabelle Spencer, a niece of Lewis Terman. Her unpublished manuscript draws upon the oral history handed down to her by her mother (Bertha) and aunt (Jessie), Anabelle Spencer to FET, 21 June 1976, FTP. Bertha and Jessie were Lewis's two younger sisters, Bertha being next to Lewis in birth order.

21. LMT, "Trails to Psychology," p. 299.

22. LMT to Davis, 13 February 1950, LTP.

23. Spencer, "Martha Cutsinger Terman," p. 6.

24. LMT, "I Was Lucky" (first draft), 1953, p. 1, LTP (typed).

25. LMT, "Trails to Psychology," p. 300.

26. Ibid., pp. 299–305.

27. LMT to Judge Harry Olsen, 2 February 1925, LTP.

28. Banta became a biologist. As in the case of Terman, he was included in James McKeen Cattell's list of distinguished ("starred") American scientists. Terman was struck by the highly improbable likelihood of two starred scientists coming from the same one-room school. LMT to Arthur M. Banta, 9 November 1945, LTP.

29. LMT to Robert M. Yerkes, 13 November 1951, LTP.

30. LMT, "Trails to Psychology," p. 300.

31. This was William Darling Sheperd who was brought to trial in Chicago in 1925. LMT to Olsen, 2 February 1925, LTP.

32. LMT, "Trails to Psychology," p. 303.

2. *Schoolteacher (1892–1901)*

1. LMT, "Trails to Psychology," in *A History of Psychology in Autobiography*, vol. 2, ed. Carl Murchison (Worcester, Mass.: Clark University Press, 1932), p. 302.

2. Terman had actually completed the eighth grade a year earlier but stayed on at the same school for another year. LMT, "Trails to Psychology," p. 301.

3. FET, "Special Comments" (Notes) to May V. Seagoe, [1974], p. 28, MSP.

4. LMT, "Trails to Psychology," pp. 305–08.

5. Ibid., p. 306.

6. Hall's Child-Study movement was an outgrowth of Herbart's pedagogy. Hall, like Kinnaman, had studied under Herbartian disciples at the University of Jena. However, Hall, like Herbart's disciples at Jena, tended to read evolutionary meanings into Herbart's ideas—ideas that were absent in the master's teachings. See Dorothy Ross, *G. Stanley Hall: The Psychologist as Prophet* (Chicago: University of Chicago Press, 1972), p. 125.

7. LMT, "Trails to Psychology," p. 308.

8. Ibid., p. 309.

9. Ibid., pp. 308–09.

10. "Mrs. Terman Passes Away at Age 79," *Palo Alto Times*, 27 March 1956.

11. LMT, "Trails to Psychology," p. 309; and LMT to Davis, 13 February 1950, LTP.

12. LMT, "Trails to Psychology," p. 309.

13. Helen Terman Mosher to Seagoe, [1967], MSP.

14. No mention is made of Anna's mother, Sarah Jane Murray, in the records of the Minton family other than the fact that Sarah Jane Murray married Reuben B. Minton in April 1873 (Notes on the Genealogy of the Minton Family, FTP).

15. Helen Terman Mosher to Seagoe, [1967], MSP.

16. Notes on the Genealogy of the Minton Family by Anna Minton Terman, FTP.

17. Nephew (unnamed) to Armenia Troutman Minton, 25 September 1854, FTP.

18. FET, "Special Comments," p. 1.

19. LMT, "I Was Lucky," 1953, pp. 2–3, LTP (typed).

20. "Mrs. Terman Passes Away." Among the first boarders was Daniel Zaring who moved into the Terman house in 1899, paying three dollars a month for rent (Daniel Zaring to LMT, 18 September 1952, and 20 May 1954, LTP).

21. LMT to Lloyd C. Emmons, 5 March 1942, LTP.

22. LMT, "Trails to Psychology," p. 309.

23. LMT, "I Was Lucky," pp. 2–4.

24. Ibid., p. 3.

25. P. C. Emmons to FET, 14 September 1959, FTP.

26. FET to Lloyd C. Emmons, 21 March 1942 and 3 February 1949, LTP.

27. P. C. Emmons to FET, 14 September 1959, FTP.

28. These recollections go back about sixty years, so they may not be very accurate. Yet, it seems significant that Emmons could recall that Terman was so seemingly lacking in ambition. In the same letter he contrasts Terman's lack of ambition at this time with the determination he was to show once he went to Indiana University.

29. Another possibility is that Terman liked teaching and was indeed quite content to remain a country-school teacher-principal. However, in none of his recollections is there any mention of his actual liking for school teaching. Teaching is generally men-

tioned in the context of a means for further education and professional advancement, such as teaching at the college level. One exchange of letters exists between Terman and a former pupil. Terman does not refer to his teaching. The former pupil does point to her memories of the sparkle of mischievous joy in her teacher's eyes. Stella Stewart Clark to LMT, 9 November 1926; and LMT to Clark, 19 November 1926, LTP.

3. *The Choice of Psychology (1901–1905)*

1. LMT to Dennis Flanagan, 17 November 1954, LTP.
2. P. C. Emmons to FET, 14 September 1959, FTP.
3. LMT, "I Was Lucky," 1953, p. 4, LTP (typed).
4. LMT, "Trails to Psychology," in *A History of Psychology in Autobiography*, vol. 2, ed. Carl Murchison (Worcester, Mass.: Clark University Press, 1932), p. 309.
5. Ibid., p. 310.
6. *Indiana University Academic Bulletin, 1904*, pp. 251–56.
7. Ibid., pp. 129–35. Bergström was actually in the Department of Education, but as the director of the psychological laboratory he offered psychology courses in the Department of Philosophy.
8. LMT, "Trails to Psychology," p. 312; and Dorothy Ross, *G. Stanley Hall: The Psychologist as Prophet* (Chicago: University of Chicago Press, 1972), p. 269.
9. LMT, "Trails to Psychology," p. 310.
10. Ibid., pp. 310–12.
11. *I.U. Academic Bulletin*, pp. 129–31.
12. LMT, "Trails to Psychology," p. 311.
13. Ibid., pp. 310–11.
14. Student Record of Lewis Madison Terman, Indiana University, Office of the Registrar.
15. LMT, "Trails to Psychology," p. 311.
16. LMT, "A Preliminary Study in the Psychology and Pedagogy of Leadership," *Pedagogical Seminary* 11(1904):413–51. The "colored" children were drawn from a segregated school and thus tested separately (ibid., p. 427). Terman did not analyze race differences.
17. Ibid., pp. 432–33. Terman found that the leaders had a high average suggestibility. He interpreted this as indicating that for a leader it is more important to lead than to be correct.
18. LMT, "Trails to Psychology," pp. 311–12.
19. E. H. Lindley to G. Stanley Hall, 13 June 1903, GHP.
20. J. A. Bergström to Hall, 15 June 1903, GHP.
21. LMT, "I Was Lucky," p. 4.
22. LMT, "Trails to Psychology," p. 312.
23. Ibid., p. 312.
24. In his autobiography (LMT, "Trails to Psychology," p. 313), Terman noted that Hall's use of praise was a pedagogical device that Terman was only to become cognizant of later. However, from the recommendations Terman received from Lindley and Bergström, Hall may genuinely have had high expectations for him.
25. LMT, "Trails to Psychology," pp. 313–21.
26. See Ross, *G. Stanley Hall*; and Merle Curti, *The Social Ideas of American Educators* (Patterson, N.J.: Littlefield, Adams, 1959), pp. 396–428.

27. *Clark University Catalogue, 1904*, p. 59.

28. LMT, "Trails to Psychology," p. 314.

29. Ibid., pp. 315–16.

30. LMT to Henry D. Sheldon, 27 August 1945, LTP. Sheldon had completed his studies at Clark in 1900. For a description of his recollections of Clark, see Henry D. Sheldon, "Clark University, 1897–1900," *Journal of Social Psychology* 24(1946):227–47. Other published recollections of Clark and Hall by former students are Arnold Gesell, "Arnold Gesell," in *A History of Psychology in Autobiography*, vol. 4, eds. Edwin G. Boring, Herbert J. Langfeld, Heinz Werner, and Robert M. Yerkes (New York: Russell and Russell, 1952), pp. 126–27; and Lawrence A. Averill, "Recollections of Clark's G. Stanley Hall," *Journal of the History of the Behavioral Sciences* 18(1982):341–46. In each of these memoirs, the impact of Hall's personality and his Monday-evening seminars looms large.

31. Ross, G. Stanley Hall, pp. 167, 180.

32. LMT, "Trails to Psychology," p. 320.

33. Ibid., pp. 314–18.

34. Ibid., p. 314.

35. Ibid., p. 319.

36. LMT, "A Study in Precocity and Prematuration," *American Journal of Psychology* 16(1905):145–83.

37. Ibid., p. 145.

38. Ibid., p. 147.

39. LMT, "A Preliminary Study."

40. See G. Stanley Hall, "The Contents of Children's Minds," *Princeton Review* 11(1883):249–72; and Ross, *G. Stanley Hall*, pp. 128–29, 290–92.

41. LMT, "Trails to Psychology," p. 318.

42. Ibid.

43. See Kimball Young, "The History of Mental Testing," *Pedagogical Seminary* 31(1923):1–48; and Joseph Peterson, *Early Conceptions and Tests of Intelligence* (Yonkers, N.Y.: World Book Company, 1925), pp. 72–116.

44. See Clark Wissler, "The Correlation of Mental and Physical Tests," *Psychological Review Monograph Supplements* 3(1901): Number 6, Whole Number 16. For Cattell's contributions to mental testing, see Michael M. Sokal, "James McKeen Cattell and Mental Anthropometry: Nineteenth-Century Science and Reform and the Origins of Psychological Testing," in *Psychological Testing and American Society, 1890–1930*, ed. Michael M. Sokal (New Brunswick, N.J.: Rutgers University Press, 1987), pp. 21–45; and Raymond E. Fancher, *The Intelligence Men: Makers of the IQ Controversy* (New York: Norton, 1985), pp. 44–49.

45. Thaddeus L. Bolton, "The Growth of Memory in School Children," *American Journal of Psychology* 4(1891–1892):362–80; and J. A. Gilbert, "Researches on the Mental and Physical Development of School Children," *Studies of Yale Psychological Laboratory* 2(1894):40–100.

46. Young "History of Mental Testing," p. 34.

47. LMT, "Trails to Psychology," pp. 319–21.

48. See LMT, "Genius and Stupidity: A Study of Some of the Intellectual Processes of Seven 'Bright' and Seven 'Stupid' Boys," *Pedagogical Seminary* 13(1906):307–73.

49. Ibid., p. 314.

50. Ibid., p. 317.

51. Ibid., pp. 317–71.

52. Arnold Gesell to Ernest R. Hilgard, 18 April 1957, quoted in Ernest R. Hilgard, "Lewis Madison Terman: 1877–1956," *American Journal of Psychology* 70(1957):472–79, quote p. 473.

53. LMT, "Genius and Stupidity," p. 372.

54. LMT, "Trails to Psychology," p. 320.

55. LMT, "I Was Lucky," p. 5.

56. LMT, "Trails to Psychology," p. 321.

57. LMT to William H. Burnham, 2 May 1924, LTP.

58. Nevertheless, Terman never held Hall's negative stand toward testing against him. LMT to Joseph Peterson, 14 January 1925, LTP.

59. LMT, "I Was Lucky," pp. 4–5.

60. Hall to LMT, 7 June 1904, GHP.

61. FET, "Special Comments," [1974], p. 2, MSP.

4. *The Fallow Years (1905–1910)*

1. LMT, "I Was Lucky," 1953, p. 6, LTP (typed).

2. Ibid.; and LMT, "Trails to Psychology," in *A History of Psychology in Autobiography*, vol. 2, ed. Carl Murchison (Worcester, Mass.: Clark University Press, 1932), p. 322.

3. LMT to Nora Parker Coy, 4 April 1956, LTP.

4. LMT, "I Was Lucky," pp. 6–7.

5. Ibid., p. 7.

6. LMT to Gesell, 19 January 1906, AGP.

7. LMT to Hall, 29 January 1906, GHP.

8. LMT to Hall, 26 February 1906, GHP.

9. LMT, "Trails to Psychology," p. 322.

10. LMT to Hall, 23 June 1906, GHP.

11. LMT, "I Was Lucky," p. 7.

12. LMT to Gesell, 30 November 1906, AGP; and LMT, "Trails to Psychology," pp. 322–23.

13. LMT, "I Was Lucky," p. 8.

14. LMT to Gesell, 3 August 1907.

15. See Arnold Gesell, "Jealousy," *American Journal of Psychology* 17(1906):437–96.

16. Arnold Gesell, "Arnold Gesell," in *A History of Psychology in Autobiography*, vol. 4, eds. Edwin G. Boring, Herbert J. Langfeld, Heinz Werner, and Robert M. Yerkes (New York: Russell and Russell, 1952), p. 127.

17. Gesell to Hilgard, 18 April 1957, cited in Seagoe's notes of an interview with Paul Farnsworth, December 1967, MSP.

18. LMT to Ada Yerkes, 11 August 1955, LTP.

19. Gesell to Hilgard, 18 April 1957, MSP.

20. LMT, "Child Study: Its Reasons and Promise," *University of California Chronicle* 11(1908):145–58.

21. Ibid., p. 152.

22. See Dorothy Ross, *G. Stanley Hall: The Psychologist as Prophet* (Chicago: University of Chicago Press, 1972), pp. 312–14. Hall's views on development and its implications for education are best represented in his magnum opus, *Adolescence*. See G. Stanley Hall,

Adolescence: Its Psychology and Its Relations to Physiology, Anthropology, Sociology, Sex, Crime, Religion and Education, 2 vols. (New York: Appleton, 1904).

23. LMT, "Commercialism: The Educator's Bugbear," *School Review* 17(1909):193–95, quote, pp. 194–95.

24. LMT to Hall, 16 September 1909, GHP.

25. P. C. Emmons to FET, 14 September 1959, FTP.

26. LMT to Hall, 16 September 1909, GHP.

27. LMT, "Trails to Psychology," p. 323.

28. Wilford E. Talbert to LMT, 2 June 1923, LTP.

29. LMT, "I Was Lucky," p. 8.

30. Hall to Ellwood P. Cubberley, 16 February 1910, GHP.

31. LMT, "I Was Lucky," p. 9.

32. LMT, "Trails to Psychology," p. 323.

33. Ibid., p. 322.

34. LMT, "I Was Lucky," p. 9.

35. LMT, "Trails to Psychology," p. 323.

5. Establishing a Reputation (1910–1917)

1. LMT, "Trails to Psychology," in *A History of Psychology in Autobiography*, vol. 2, ed. Carl Murchison (Worcester, Mass.: Clark University Press, 1932), p. 323.

2. LMT, "I Was Lucky," 1953, p. 9, LTP (typed).

3. LMT to Robert L. Duffus, 10 February 1944, LTP.

4. FET, "Special Comments," [1974], p. 5, MSP.

5. Ibid., pp. 6–7.

6. There are several histories of Stanford University, including the following: Peter C. Allen, *Stanford from the Foothills to the Bay* (Stanford, Calif.: Stanford Alumni Association and Stanford Historical Society, 1980); Orrin Leslie Elliott, *Stanford University: The First Twenty-Five Years* (Stanford, Calif.: Stanford University Press, 1937); and J. Pearce Mitchell, *Stanford University 1916–1941* (Stanford, Calif.: Stanford University Press, 1958).

7. For a biography of Earl Barnes see Edward Howard Griggs, *Earl Barnes: A Life-Sketch and an Address* (Croton-on-Hudson, N.Y.: Orchard Hill Press, 1935). A discussion of Barnes's career at Stanford is also contained in the biography of Ellwood Patterson Cubberley. See Jesse B. Sears and Adin D. Henderson, *Cubberley of Stanford: And his Contribution to American Education* (Stanford, Calif.: Stanford University Press, 1957), p. 56.

8. For the history of the education department at Stanford, see Sears and Henderson, *Cubberley of Stanford*.

9. Lawrence A. Cremin, *The Wonderful World of Ellwood Patterson Cubberley: An Essay on the Historiography of American Education* (New York: Bureau of Publications, Teachers College, Columbia University, 1965), p. 4.

10. Ellwood P. Cubberley, *Public Education in the United States* (Boston: Houghton Mifflin, 1919).

11. Cremin, *Ellwood Patterson Cubberley*, pp. 1–2.

12. Ibid., p. 47; and Sears and Henderson, *Cubberley of Stanford*, p. 63.

13. Sears and Henderson, *Cubberley of Stanford*, p. 84.

14. Jesse B. Sears to Seagoe, May 1967, MSP.

15. LMT, "Trails to Psychology," p. 324; and LMT "I Was Lucky," p. 9.

16. See G. Stanley Hall, "The Ideal School as Based on Child Study," *Forum* 32(1901):24–39; and G. Stanley Hall, *Educational Problems*, vol. 1 (New York: Appleton, 1911), pp. 627, 634, 639. See also Dorothy Ross, *G. Stanley Hall: The Psychologist as Prophet* (Chicago: University of Chicago Press, 1972), pp. 417–19.

17. LMT, *The Hygiene of the School Child* (Boston: Houghton Mifflin, 1914), pp. 1–2.

18. These publications can be found in the bibliography of LMT publications.

19. FET, Notes on a manuscript draft of May V. Seagoe, *Terman and the Gifted* (Los Altos, Calif.: William Kaufmann, 1975), p. 58, MSP.

20. LMT, *The Teacher's Health* (Boston: Houghton Mifflin, 1913).

21. This quote is taken from a chapter Terman wrote summarizing his monograph on the teacher's health. Ernest Bryant Hoag and LMT, *Health Work in the Schools* (Boston: Houghton Mifflin, 1914), p. 279.

22. LMT, *Hygiene of the School Child*, p. ix.

23. Ibid., pp. 10–11.

24. Hoag and LMT, *Health Work in the Schools*.

25. Ellwood P. Cubberley, "Editor's Introduction," Hoag and LMT, *Health Work in the Schools*, pp. vii–viii.

26. Hoag and LMT, *Health Work in the Schools*, p. xiii.

27. FET, Notes on Seagoe manuscript, p. 56, MSP.

28. Hoag and LMT, *Health Work in the Schools*, pp. 1–14.

29. LMT to David Rapaport, 24 February 1956, LTP.

30. See Ross, *G. Stanley Hall*, pp. 368–94.

31. LMT to Hall, 27 April 1910, GHP; and LMT to Rapaport, 24 February 1956, LTP.

32. Hoag and LMT, *Health Work in the Schools*, p. 260.

33. LMT, "Trails to Psychology," p. 325.

34. LMT, "I Was Lucky," p. 9.

35. Ibid.

36. LMT, "Genius and Stupidity: A Study of Some of the Intellectual Processes of Seven 'Bright' and Seven 'Stupid' Boys," *Pedagogical Seminary* 13 (1906): 307–73.

37. Terman first learned about Binet's 1905 scale from Huey's visit to southern California in the summer of 1907 (see Chapter 3). Terman, however, was familiar with Binet's ideas about mental and motor tests (LMT, "Genius and Stupidity," p. 311). In 1906 Terman sent Binet a copy of his dissertation (cited in Joseph Peterson, *Early Conceptions and Tests of Intelligence* (Yonkers, N.Y.: World Book Company, 1925), p. 189).

38. Alfred Binet and Victor Henri, "La Psychologie Individuelle," *Année Psychologique* 2(1896):411–65; see also Theta H. Wolf, *Alfred Binet* (Chicago: University of Chicago Press, 1973), pp. 145–49.

39. Alfred Binet and Théodore Simon, "Méthodes Nouvelles Pour le Diagnostic du Niveau Intellectuel des Anormaux," *Année Psychologique* 11(1905):191–244. Some of the items that Binet and Simon developed were based on the work of two French physicians, Drs. Blin and Damaye. See Wolf, *Alfred Binet*, pp. 173–76.

40. Theta Wolf points out that Binet used the term "mental level" rather than "mental age." The latter term was used when Binet's writings were translated. Binet preferred "mental level" because it reflected the uneven performance he observed among school-children in which successes and failures were averaged out. In contrast, "mental age" implied an ordered developmental progression. See Wolf, *Alfred Binet*, pp. 201–03.

41. Alfred Binet and Théodore Simon, "Le Dévelopment de L'Intelligence Chez les Enfants," *Année Psychologique* 14 (1908): 1–90. Binet's final revision was published in 1911, the year of his death. With some refinements, the 1911 scale was similar to the 1908 version.

42. H. H. Goddard, "The Binet and Simon Tests of Intellectual Capacity," *The Training School* 5(1908):3–9. For an analysis of Goddard's development of the Binet tests see Leila Zenderland, "The Debate over Diagnosis: Henry Herbert Goddard and the Medical Acceptance of Intelligence Testing," in *Psychological Testing and American Society, 1890–1930*, ed. Michael M. Sokal (New Brunswick, N.J.: Rutgers University Press, 1987), pp. 46–74.

43. See Peterson, *Early Conceptions and Tests of Intelligence*, p. 227.

44. LMT, "The Binet-Simon Scale for Measuring Intelligence," *Psychological Clinic* 5(1911):199–206.

45. LMT and H. G. Childs, "A Tentative Revision and Extension of the Binet-Simon Measuring Scale of Intelligence," *Journal of Educational Psychology* 3(1912):61–74, 133–43, 198–208, 277–89.

46. LMT, Grace Lyman, George Ordahl, Louise Ordahl, Neva Galbreath, and Wilford Talbert, "The Stanford Revision of the Binet-Simon Scale and Some Results from Its Application to 1000 Non-Selected Children," *Journal of Educational Psychology* 6(1915):551–62.

47. LMT, *The Measurement of Intelligence* (Boston: Houghton Mifflin, 1916).

48. LMT, "Trails to Psychology," p. 325.

49. See Peterson, *Early Conceptions and Tests of Intelligence*, pp. 79–82; and Kimball Young, "The History of Mental Testing," *Pedagogical Seminary* 31(1923):1–48.

50. LMT, "Review of Meumann on Tests of Endowment," *Journal of Psycho-Asthenics* 19(1914–15):75–94, 123–34, 187–89.

51. William Stern, *The Psychological Method of Measuring Intelligence*, trans. Guy M. Whipple (Baltimore: Warwick and York, 1914).

52. LMT, *The Measurement of Intelligence*, pp. 42–43.

53. See Wolf, *Alfred Binet*, pp. 216–18; and Read D. Tuddenham, "The Nature and Measurement of Intelligence," in *Psychology in the Making*, ed. Leo Postman (New York: Knopf, 1962), pp. 469–525.

54. LMT, *The Measurement of Intelligence*, pp. 51–64; and LMT, Grace Lyman, George Ordahl, Louise Ellison Ordahl, Neva Galbreath, and Wilford Talbert, *The Stanford Revision and Extension of the Binet-Simon Scale for Measuring Intelligence* (Baltimore: Warwick and York, 1917), pp. 7–15.

55. LMT, *The Measurement of Intelligence*, pp. 3–21, 65–104.

56. For example, see H. H. Goddard, *Human Efficiency and Levels of Intelligence* (Princeton, N.J.: Princeton University Press, 1920); E. B. Huey, "The Present Status of the Binet Scale of Tests for the Measurement of Intelligence," *Psychological Bulletin* 9(1912):160–68; and Fred Kuhlmann, "The Results of Grading Thirteen Hundred Feeble-Minded Children with the Binet-Simon Tests," *Journal of Educational Psychology* 4(1913):261–68.

57. Alfred Binet, *Les Idées Modernes sur les Enfants* (Paris: Flammarion, 1909). Also see Wolf, *Alfred Binet*, pp. 204–208.

58. LMT, *The Measurement of Intelligence*, pp. 6–7.

59. For the connection between mental retardation and mental measurement in America, see Peter L. Tyor and Leland V. Bell, *Caring for the Retarded in America: A History* (Westport, Conn.: Greenwood Press, 1984). For the connection in Britain, see Nikolas

Rose, "The Psychological Complex: Mental Measurement and Social Administration," *Ideology and Consciousness* 5(1979):5–68. On eugenics, see Mark M. Haller, *Eugenics: Hereditarian Attitudes in American Thought* (New Brunswick, N.J.: Rutgers University Press, 1963); and Daniel J. Kevles, *In the Name of Eugenics: Genetics and the Uses of Human Heredity* (New York: Knopf, 1985).

60. LMT, *The Measurement of Intelligence*, p. 19.

61. Ibid., p. 20.

62. Ibid., pp. 91–92.

63. LMT to Abraham Flexner, 31 January 1917, with attached memoranda: "Certain Proposed Researches in Mental Measurement," LTP.

64. LMT to Flexner, 22 March 1917, LTP.

65. LMT to H. H. Goddard, 29 March 1917, LTP.

66. The complete list of names can be ascertained from the following: LMT to Goddard, 29 March 1917; and LMT to W. L. Bryan, 30 March 1917, LTP.

67. Hall to Flexner, 5 April 1917, GHP.

68. Hall to LMT, 5 April 1917, GHP.

69. W. F. Book to Flexner, 4 April 1917; Kuhlmann to Flexner, 4 April 1917; and Edmund C. Sanford to Flexner, 5 April 1917, LTP. These are the only surviving letters in the Terman papers.

70. Flexner to LMT, 26 June 1917, LTP.

71. Cubberley, memorandum to the president of Stanford, 15 January 1914, ECP.

72. Ray Lyman Wilbur, memorandum to Cubberley, 4 December 1916, ECP.

73. Herbert Hoover to Cubberley, 4 July 1917, ECP.

74. LMT to Goddard, 22 December 1916, HGP.

75. LMT to Cubberley, 26 May 1933, LTP; and LMT, "Trails to Psychology," p. 324.

76. Ellwood P. Cubberley and LMT, "To Help Backward School Children," *Stanford Alumnus* (April 1914); and LMT, *Research in Mental Deviation Among Children: A Statement of the Aims and Purposes of the Buckel Foundation* (Stanford, Calif.: Research Laboratory of the Buckel Foundation, Department of Education, Stanford University, Bulletin No. 2, 1915).

77. J. Harold Williams and LMT, *Whittier State School Biennial Report: Psychological Survey of the Whittier State School. Preliminary and Final Reports* (Whittier, Calif.: Whittier State School, 1914).

78. "Dr. L. M. Terman at the University of Stanford *[sic]*" (undated, but covering the period of 1911–30), MSP (typed).

79. Samuel C. Kohs to Seagoe, [1967], MSP.

80. David Wechsler, *The Measurement of Adult Intelligence* (Baltimore: Williams and Wilkins, 1939).

81. LMT to Goddard, 14 July 1913; and Goddard to LMT, 22 July 1913, HGP.

82. H. H. Goddard to LMT, 14 December 1915. Goddard was in charge of the summer program for training teachers of the mentally defective. Terman was a replacement for Gesell who was recovering from tuberculosis in California.

83. LMT, "Trails to Psychology," p. 324; and LMT to Gesell, 17 July 1916, AGP.

84. LMT to Goddard, 11 September 1916, HGP.

85. LMT to Yerkes, 1 September 1916, RYP.

86. LMT to Goddard, 22 December 1916, HGP.

87. LMT to Yerkes, 9 December 1915, RYP.

88. See James Reed, "Robert M. Yerkes and the Mental Testing Movement," in *Psychological Testing*, Sokal, pp. 75–94.

89. See Young, "The History of Mental Testing," pp. 38–39.

90. Robert M. Yerkes, James W. Bridges, and Rose Hardwick, *A Point Scale for Measuring Mental Ability* (Baltimore: Warwick and York, 1915).

91. LMT to Yerkes, 9 December 1915; and Yerkes to LMT, 14 July 1916, RYP.

92. Yerkes to LMT, 12 February 1917; and LMT to Yerkes, 19 February 1917, RYP.

93. LMT to Goddard, 29 March 1917, HGP.

94. LMT to Yerkes, 18 September 1916, RYP.

95. Ibid.

96. Interview with Robert R. Sears, 16 March 1984.

97. LMT to Gesell, 10 April 1914, AGP.

98. Cubberley and LMT, "To Help Backward School Children"; LMT, *Research in Mental Deviation Among Children;* and LMT, "Feeble-Minded Children in the Public Schools of California," *School and Society* 5(1912):161–65.

99. Gesell to LMT, 26 April 1914; and 14 June 1914, AGP.

100. LMT to Gesell, 20 July 1914, AGP.

101. LMT, "I Was Lucky," pp. 9–10.

102. LMT to Goddard, 22 December 1916, HGP.

103. FET, "Special Comments," p. 10.

104. Ibid., pp. 8–9.

105. FET, "Supplementary Notes," attached to correspondence of FET to Seagoe, 20 March 1974, MSP.

106. Helen Terman Mosher to Seagoe, [1967], MSP.

107. LMT to Gesell, 22 March 1918.

108. Helen Terman Mosher to Seagoe, [1967], MSP.

109. LMT to Yerkes, 2 May 1917, RYP.

6. Off to the Army (1917–1919)

1. LMT, "The Use of Intelligence Tests in the Army," *Psychological Bulletin* 15(1918):177–87, quote p. 178.

2. Samuel Eliot Morison, Henry Steele Commager, and William E. Leuchtenburg, *The Growth of the American Republic*, vol. 2, 6th ed. (New York: Oxford University Press, 1969), p. 376.

3. The "Society of Experimentalists" was an informal group of experimental psychologists that met periodically. The originator and leader of this group was Edward Bradford Titchener. Titchener, who was chairing the meeting, turned the chair over to Yerkes, claiming that as a British citizen he did not want to be involved in presiding over a meeting dealing with national defense. Titchener was also an advocate of "pure" as opposed to "applied" psychology and did not want to be identified with any professional efforts connected with practical concerns. See John M. O'Donnell, "The Crisis of Experimentalism in the 1920s: E. G. Boring and His Uses of History," *American Psychologist* 34 (1979): 289–95.

4. Robert M. Yerkes, "Psychology in Relation to the War," *Psychological Review* 25(1918):85–115.

5. James Reed, "Robert M. Yerkes and the Mental Testing Movement," in *Psychological Testing and American Society, 1890–1930*, ed. Michael M. Sokal (New Brunswick,

N.J.: Rutgers University Press, 1987), pp. 75–94. See also Thomas M. Canfield, "Psychologists at War: The History of American Psychology and the First World War" (Ph.D. dissertation, University of Texas), Ann Arbor, Mich.: University Microfilms, 1970, No-70-10766.

6. Yerkes, "Psychology in Relation to the War."

7. The superior group, if time permitted, would also be given a more extensive examination, the purpose of which would be to evaluate the specialized contributions they could make to the military organization.

8. Richard T. von Mayrhauser has researched Scott's contribution to the development of group testing in World War I, as well as the basis for the conflict between Scott and Yerkes. See Richard T. von Mayrhauser, "Walking Out at the Walton: Psychological Disunity and the Origins of Group Testing in Early World War I," in *Psychological Testing*, Sokal, pp. 128–57.

9. Scott's ideas were shared by his Carnegie colleague, Walter V. Bingham, who was also an APA council member. Bingham, however, was also interested in intelligence testing and did not get involved in the Yerkes-Scott conflict. See von Mayrhauser, "Walking Out at the Walton."

10. Some psychologists were involved in both programs. For example, Terman was a member of both Scott's committee and one of the committees under Yerkes's supervision (the Committee on the Psychological Examination of Recruits that Yerkes himself chaired). However, Terman's primary involvement was with Yerkes's committee.

11. The navy dealt with a much smaller number of recruits than the army and was, therefore, not interested in any large-scale testing or classification program. See Daniel Kevles, "Testing the Army's Intelligence: Psychologists and the Military in World War I," *Journal of American History* 55(1968):565–81. One of the committees under Yerkes's jurisdiction (the committee on visual problems) did devise tests of special abilities for use in the navy. See Yerkes, "Psychology in Relation to the War," p. 112.

12. Twelve committees had been initially recommended at the APA Council meeting of 21 April 1917. Several of these committees were subsequently accepted as subcommittees of the psychology committee of the National Research Council and eventually came under the jurisdiction of the army's surgeon general's office.

13. Yerkes, "Psychology in Relation to the War."

14. Robert M. Yerkes, ed., *Psychological Examining in the United States Army*, vol. 15, *Memoirs of the National Academy of Sciences* (Washington, D.C.: Government Printing Office, 1921), p. 299. This is the official report of the army testing. Terman was primarily responsible for writing the section on the development of the tests ("Part II—Methods of Examining: History, Development, and Preliminary Results," pp. 293–546).

15. Ibid.

16. Roger T. Lennon, "Foreword," in *Intelligence Perspectives 1965: The Terman-Otis Memorial Lectures*, eds. Orville G. Brim, Jr., Richard S. Crutchfield, and Wayne H. Holtzman (New York: Harcourt, Brace and World, 1966), pp. vii–x.

17. Arthur S. Otis, "An Absolute Point Scale for the Group Measurements of Intelligence," *Journal of Educational Psychology* 9(1918):239–61, 333–48.

18. For the history of educational achievement tests see Murray Levine, "The Academic Achievement Test: Its Historical Context and Social Functions," *American Psychologist* 31(1976):228–38.

19. Yerkes, *Psychological Examining*, p. 299; and LMT to O. S. Reimold, 18 May 1920, LTP.

20. Yerkes, *Psychological Examining*, pp. 300–304.

21. Yerkes, "Psychology in Relation to the War," p. 98.

22. Yerkes, *Psychological Examining*, p. 306. This scale proved to be disappointing and was soon abandoned in favor of the Stanford-Binet and Yerkes-Bridges scales. Eventually a group test for illiterates was also developed (the Beta examination).

23. Ibid., pp. 9–10, 313–23.

24. Yerkes, "Psychology in Relation to the War," p. 100.

25. Ibid., pp. 100–103.

26. Kevles, "Testing the Army's Intelligence," pp. 568–69.

27. Yerkes, *Psychological Examining*, p. 98.

28. Yerkes, "Psychology in Relation to the War," pp. 104–05. About eighty thousand men and five thousand officers were tested.

29. Yerkes, *Psychological Examining*, p. 19.

30. Ibid., pp. 327–45, 363–95.

31. Instructions for Group Examination Alpha, LTP.

32. Kevles, "Testing the Army's Intelligence," p. 572.

33. Several of the graduate students in Terman's department at Stanford participated in this program. See Frank A. Scofield, "Stanford's Share in New Profession," *Stanford Illustrated Review* 20(1918–1919):278–81, 306.

34. Yerkes, *Psychological Examining*, p. 325.

35. LMT to Mrs. Clarence S. Yoakum, 15 February 1946, LTP.

36. LMT to Gesell, 22 March 1918, AGP.

37. "Dr. L. M. Terman at the University of Stanford," MSP (typed).

38. FET, Notes on Seagoe manuscript, p. 85, MSP.

39. LMT, "I Was Lucky," 1953, p. 10, LTP (typed).

40. Yerkes, *Psychological Examining*, pp. 293–546; and LMT to Goddard, 19 November 1918, HGP.

41. *Army Mental Tests: Methods, Typical Results and Practical Applications* (Washington, D.C.: National Research Council, 1918), p. 4. This publication was prepared by Terman and Mabel R. Fernald (though their names did not appear) and later incorporated into a monograph compiled by Yoakum and Yerkes: Clarence S. Yoakum and Robert M. Yerkes, *Army Mental Tests* (New York: Holt, 1920). Terman and Fernald's authorship of the 1918 publication is cited on page 12 of the 1920 monograph.

42. *Army Mental Tests* (1918), pp. 4–7; and Yerkes, *Psychological Examining*, pp. 421–24.

43. Yerkes, *Psychological Examining*.

44. Stephen Jay Gould, *The Mismeasure of Man* (New York: Norton, 1981), pp. 201–14.

45. Yerkes, *Psychological Examining*, p. 340. This was within the section of the report written by Terman.

46. Gould, *The Mismeasure of Man*, p. 204.

47. Despite Yerkes's hopes to the contrary, the division of psychology was abolished on 21 January 1919. See Kevles, "Testing the Army's Intelligence" p. 578.

48. Yerkes, *Psychological Examining*.

49. Yoakum and Yerkes, *Army Mental Tests*, p. 12.

50. *Army Mental Tests* (1918), p. 7.

51. Ibid., p. 8; and Yoakum and Yerkes, *Army Mental Tests*, p. 27.

52. Yoakum and Yerkes, *Army Mental Tests*, pp. 20, 30.

53. *Army Mental Tests* (1918), p. 23.

54. Raymond Dodge, "Mental Engineering During the War," *American Review of Reviews* 59(1919):606–10, quote in Yoakum and Yerkes, *Army Mental Tests*, p. 185.

55. Yoakum and Yerkes, *Army Mental Tests*, pp. 188–203.

56. LMT, *The Measurement of Intelligence* (Boston: Houghton Mifflin, 1916), p. 17.

57. Ibid., p. 12.

58. Kimball Young, "The History of Mental Testing," *Pedagogical Seminary* 31(1923):1–48.

59. Ibid., p. 48.

60. Henry L. Minton and Christopher A. O'Neil, "Kimball Young's Social Psychology: A Precursor of Social Constructionism," *Personality and Social Psychology Bulletin* (in press).

61. Joel H. Spring and Franz Samelson in their analyses of the army testing program have also pointed to the theme of intelligence testing in the service of social efficiency and social control. See Joel H. Spring, "Psychologists and the War: The Meaning of Intelligence in the Alpha and Beta Tests," *History of Education Quarterly* 12(1972):3–15; and Franz Samelson, "Putting Psychology on the Map: Ideology and Intelligence Testing," in *Psychology in Social Context*, ed. Allan R. Buss (New York: Irvington, 1979), pp. 103–68.

62. See Kevles, "Testing the Army's Intelligence"; and Samelson, "Putting Psychology on the Map."

63. Samelson indicates that only a single set of such data was collected for a small fighting unit, and the results were not promising (correlations of .457 and .485 between intelligence test results and officers' ratings of the military value of the men under their command). These findings were not reported in Yerkes, *Psychological Examining*.

64. Kevles, "Testing the Army's Intelligence," p. 580.

65. This is the conclusion Thomas W. Canfield reached in his study of the army psychologists. See Canfield, "Psychologists at War." For other similar conclusions see Kevles, "Testing the Army's Intelligence," pp. 580–81; and Samelson, "Putting Psychology on the Map," pp. 152–58.

66. James Reed discusses the significance the army psychologists attached to team research. See Reed, "Robert M. Yerkes."

67. Dodge, in Yoakum and Yerkes, *Army Mental Tests*, p. 203.

68. LMT to Yerkes, 13 November 1951, LTP.

69. LMT, "Trails to Psychology," pp. 325–26.

70. Ibid., p. 325.

71. LMT to Yerkes, 13 November 1917, RYP.

72. LMT to Ada Yerkes, 7 February 1956, LTP.

7. *Professional Leadership (1919–1923)*

1. LMT, "The Use of Intelligence Tests in the Grading of School Children," *Journal of Educational Research*, 1(1920):20–32, quote p. 20.

2. Yerkes to Flexner, 17 January 1919, LTP.

3. Yerkes and LMT to Flexner, 23 January 1919, LTP.

4. "Report of the Committee on Intelligence Tests for Elementary Schools," 17 March 1921, p. 4, LTP.

5. Yerkes became a member of the National Research Council in 1917 and held various executive positions in the agency for the rest of his career. See Robert M. Yerkes, "Psychobiologist," in *A History of Psychology in Autobiography*, vol. 2, ed. Carl Murchison (Worcester, Mass.: Clark University Press, 1932), pp. 381–407.

6. Yerkes to LMT, 29 July 1920, LTP.

7. Report of the Committee on Intelligence Tests"; and Guy M. Whipple, "The National Intelligence Tests," *Journal of Educational Research* 4(1921):16–31.

8. For the purpose of discouraging coaching, five different forms of each scale were constructed.

9. Minutes of the third conference of the Elementary School Intelligence Board, 17 and 18 October 1919, pp. 63–70, LTP.

10. Ibid., p. 68.

11. Robert M. Yerkes and Helen M. Anderson, "The Importance of Social Status as Indicated by the Results of the Point Scale Method of Measuring Mental Capacity," *Journal of Educational Psychology* 6(1915):137–50. Other investigators were also pointing to the importance of social-class differences in intelligence. See James W. Bridges and Lillian E. Coler, "The Relation of Intelligence to Social Status," *Psychological Review* 24(1917):1–31; S. L. Pressey and J. B. Thomas, "A Study of Country Children in (1) a Good and (2) a Poor Farming District by Means of a Group Scale of Intelligence," *Journal of Applied Psychology* 3(1919):283–86; and Luella W. Pressey, "The Influence of Inadequate Schooling and Poor Environment upon the Results with Tests of Intelligence," *Journal of Applied Psychology* 4(1920):91–96. The latter two reports pointed to the role of environmental factors in accounting for social-class differences.

12. Minutes, p. 68.

13. "Report of the Committee on Intelligence Tests," p. 1.

14. Mention was also made about sex differences in a supplement to the test manual. Girls scored higher than boys at every age. The sex difference was equivalent to six months of mental age. However, their difference was deemed to be too inconsequential to justify separate sex norms (*National Intelligence Tests, Supplement No. 3 to Manual of Directions*, Yonkers, N.Y.: World Book Company, 1924, pp. 13–14). Samelson points out that, unlike race differences, no conclusions were drawn about innate group differences in the case of sex. See Franz Samelson, "Putting Psychology on the Map," in *Psychology in Social Context*, ed. Allan R. Buss (New York: Irvington, 1979), pp. 103–68.

15. "Report of the Committee on Intelligence Tests," p. 25.

16. Ibid., p. 24.

17. Roger T. Lennon, "Foreword," in *Intelligence Perspectives 1965: The Terman-Otis Memorial Lectures*, eds. Orville G. Brim, Jr., Richard S. Crutchfield, and Wayne H. Holtzman (New York: Harcourt, Brace and World, 1966), pp. vii–x.

18. "Report of the Committee on Intelligence Tests," p. 30. The remaining four forms of each scale were published in 1921.

19. LMT and Edith D. Whitmire, "Age and Grade Norms for the National Intelligence Tests, Scales A and B, *Journal of Educational Research* 3(1921):124–32; and *National Intelligence Tests, Supplement No. 3*, 1924, p. 6.

20. Whipple, "The National Intelligence Tests," p. 16.

21. Frank N. Freeman, *Mental Tests: Their History, Principles, and Applications* (Boston: Houghton Mifflin, 1926), pp. 165–66.

22. Caspar W. Hodgson to LMT, 13 January 1920; and Ernest Hesse to LMT, 28 June 1920, LTP.

23. These norms were available in October 1922, after an initial set based on a sample of thirty thousand. *Terman Group Test of Mental Ability, Manual of Directions* (Yonkers, N.Y.: World Book Company, 1926).

24. LMT to Hodgson, 15 October 1923, LTP.

25. Truman L. Kelley to LMT, 11 September 1920, LTP.

26. "Dr. L. M. Terman at the University of Stanford," p. 4, MSP (typed).

27. Two levels of the test were constructed: the primary level for grades two and three and the advanced level for grades four through eight.

28. See Murray Levine, "The Academic Achievement Test: Its Historical Context and Social Functions," *American Psychologist* 31(1976):228–38 for a discussion of the history of educational testing.

29. Truman L. Kelley, Giles M. Ruch, and LMT, *Stanford Achievement Test, Manuals of Directions for Primary Examination and Advanced Examination* (Yonkers, N.Y.: World Book Company, 1923.)

30. A. E. Wiggam, Interview with LMT, 14 and 15 December 1925, LTP.

31. LMT, *The Intelligence of School Children* (Boston: Houghton Mifflin, 1919).

32. Ibid., pp. 291–313.

33. LMT, "The Use of Intelligence Tests," p. 20.

34. Virgil E. Dickson, "The Relation of Mental Testing to School Administration" (Ph.D. dissertation, Stanford University, 1919); and LMT, "The Use of Intelligence Tests."

35. LMT, "The Use of Intelligence Tests"; and LMT to Flexner, 7 January 1919, LTP.

36. LMT, "The Use of Intelligence Tests," p. 31.

37. See Paul D. Chapman, "Schools as Sorters: Lewis M. Terman and the Intelligence Testing Movement, 1890–1930" (Ph.D. dissertation, Stanford University), Ann Arbor, Mich.: University Microfilms, 1980, No. 80-11615, pp. 120–29, 136–41.

38. Kimball Young, *Mental Differences in Certain Immigrant Groups* (Eugene, Ore.: University of Oregon Press, 1922).

39. Ibid., p. 94.

40. Ibid. The average IQ for the American children was 100; for the Latin children, 83.

41. These data were summarized in Carl C. Brigham, *A Study of American Intelligence* (Princeton, N.J.: Princeton University Press, 1923).

42. Young, during his graduate-student career, presents an interesting case of opposing influences. He had first been trained in sociology and social psychology by W. I. Thomas at the University of Chicago. This convinced him that intellectual performance was largely determined by social learning (Young to Seagoe, 16 February 1968, MSP). When he arrived at Stanford for his doctoral work in the fall of 1919, he took Terman's seminar on mental measurement and engaged in an "intellectual free-for-all" with his new mentor. Based on his dissertation, Young was obviously won over to Terman's point of view. However, by 1923, when he was a faculty member at the University of Oregon, he began to return to the position of Thomas and the "Chicago" school regarding the importance of cultural influences. See Chapter 5 for mention of Young's criticisms of the testing movement. Young's leaning to Thomas can be detected in Kimball Young, "The History of Mental Testing," *Pedagogical Seminary* 31(1923):1–48.

43. Young, *Mental Differences*, pp. 69, 97.

44. Chapman, "Schools as Sorters," pp. 133–36.

45. Ibid., pp. 120–29, 136–41.

46. "The Work of the Commission on the Revision of Elementary Education," attached to letter of Margaret S. McNaught to LMT, 3 May 1919, LTP (typed).

47. See Richard Hofstadter, *Anti-intellectualism in American Life* (New York: Knopf, 1962), pp. 323–58.

48. "The Work of the Commission," p. 4.

49. McNaught to LMT, 3 May 1919, LTP.

50. Margaret S. McNaught, "Introduction," in Lewis M. Terman, Virgil E. Dickson, D. N. Sutherland, Raymond Franzen, C. R. Tupper, and Grace Fernald, *Intelligence Tests and School Reorganization* (Yonkers, N.Y.: World Book Company, 1922), p. viii.

51. LMT et al., *School Reorganization*.

52. LMT, "The Problem," in LMT et al., *School Reorganization*, pp. 1–31, quote p. 3.

53. Ibid., p. 20.

54. Ibid., p. 21.

55. Ibid.

56. LMT, "Editor's Introduction," in Virgil E. Dickson, *Mental Tests and the Classroom Teacher* (Yonkers, N.Y.: World Book Company, 1923), pp. xiv–xv.

57. LMT, "The Conservation of Talent," *School and Society* 19(1924):359–64.

58. See David B. Tyack, *The One Best System: A History of American Urban Education* (Cambridge, Mass.: Harvard University Press, 1974), pp. 198–216; and Chapman, "Schools as Sorters," pp. 156–89.

59. LMT, "Were We Born That Way?" *World's Work* 44(1922):655–60, quote pp. 657–59.

60. LMT, "The Problem," p. 28.

61. LMT, "Editor's Introduction," in Dickson, p. xv.

62. For an analysis of the meritocracy model and its inadequate empirical support, see Samuel Bowles and Herbert Gintis, *Schooling in Capitalist America: Educational Reform and the Contradictions of Economic Life* (New York: Basic Books, 1976), pp. 102–24. The term "meritocracy" was introduced by the British sociologist Michael Young in his satirical book, *The Rise of the Meritocracy* (Baltimore: Penguin Books, 1958). However, the concept of a social hierarchy based on ability was implicit in the work of Galton and the mental-testing movement.

63. LMT to Yerkes, 10 June 1921, LTP, regarding the availability of Robert M. Yerkes, ed., *Psychological Examining in the United States Army*, vol. 15, *Memoirs of the National Academy of Sciences* (Washington, D.C.: Government Printing Office, 1921).

64. Cornelia James Cannon, "American Misgivings," *Atlantic Monthly* 129(1922):145–57.

65. James Reed, "Robert M. Yerkes and the Mental Testing Movement," in *Psychological Testing and American Society, 1890–1930*, ed. Michael M. Sokal (New Brunswick, N.J.: Rutgers University Press, 1987), pp. 75–94.

66. Cannon, "American Misgivings," pp. 151, 154–56.

67. See Franz Samelson, "On the Science and Politics of the IQ," *Social Research* 42(1975):467–88.

68. Cited in Nicholas Pastore, "The Army Intelligence Tests and Walter Lippmann," *Journal of the History of the Behavioral Sciences* 14(1978):316–27, quote p. 321.

69. George B. Cutten, "The Reconstruction of Democracy," *School and Society* 16(1922):477–79, quote p. 478.

70. Yerkes, *Psychological Examining*, pp. 785–91.

71. Ibid., p. 785. This was also consistent with Terman's report of an average mental age of 13.4 found for 653 white enlisted men who were tested with the Stanford-Binet. See LMT, "Mental Growth and the I.Q.," *Journal of Educational Psychology* 22(1921):325–41, 401–7.

72. Yerkes, *Psychological Examining*, p. 785.

73. Ibid., Table 333, p. 790. There was some ambiguity as to whether the "moron" classification was a mental age of less than thirteen or less than twelve. However, the percentages cited reflect the mental age of thirteen as the dividing point. See Pastore, "The Army Intelligence Tests," p. 318.

74. Walter Lipmann, "The Mental Age of Americans," *New Republic* 32(1922):213–15; "The Mystery of the 'A' Men," ibid.: 246–48; "The Reliability of Intelligence Tests," ibid.: 275–77; "The Abuse of the Tests," ibid.: 297–98; "Tests of Hereditary Intelligence," ibid.: 328–30; "A Future for the Tests," *New Republic* 33(1922):9–10; and "A Defense of Education," *Century Magazine* 106(1923):95–103.

75. Lippmann, "The Mental Age of Americans," p. 215.

76. Lippmann, "The Abuse of the Tests," p. 298.

77. Terman had categorized the data into three age levels: five to eight years, nine to eleven years, and twelve to fifteen years. See LMT, Grace Lyman, George Ordahl, Louise Ellison Ordahl, Neva Galbreath, and Wilford Talbert, *The Stanford Revision and Extension of the Binet-Simon Scale for Measuring Intelligence* (Baltimore: Warwick and York, 1917), p. 97.

78. Lippmann, "Tests of Hereditary Intelligence," p. 329.

79. Paul R. Farnsworth to Seagoe, 9 August 1972, MSP. Farnsworth, in referring to Terman's reaction, commented that according to those who were close to him at the time, "he literally trembled with rage."

80. LMT, "The Great Conspiracy on the Impulse Imperious of Intelligence Testers, Psychoanalyzed and Exposed by Mr. Lippmann," *New Republic* 33(1922):116–20. See also Walter Lippmann, "The Great Confusion: A reply to Mr. Terman," *New Republic* 33(1922):145–46.

81. LMT, "Mental Growth and the I.Q.," *Journal of Educational Psychology* 22(1921):325–41, 401–07. Another psychologist, Frank N. Freeman, addressed Lippmann's criticism about mental age by pointing out that the fact that the draftees had been out of school for five to ten years worked against them. Therefore, he questioned the advisability of making comparisons between adults and schoolchildren on the same test. See Frank N. Freeman, "The Mental Age of Adults," *Journal of Educational Research* 6(1922):441–44.

82. James McKeen Cattell to LMT, 3 January 1922 [sic], LTP. The year typed on the letter is an error as the articles appeared in late 1922. The correct year is 1923.

83. E. G. Conklin to LMT, 6 February 1923, LTP.

84. Yerkes, 2 January 1923, LTP. In fact, Yerkes felt compelled to write to Lippmann, who was a former student of his (see Samelson, "Putting Psychology on the Map," p. 133). Boring also appeared to have some concerns about the Terman-Lippmann debate and attempted his own resolution in the *New Republic* (see Edwin G. Boring, "Intelligence as the Tests Test It," *New Republic* 35(1923):35–37).

85. Howard C. Warren to LMT, 5 February 1923, LTP.

86. LMT to Jessie Chase Fenton, 12 March 1923, LTP.

87. William C. Bagley, "Educational Determinism; or Democracy and the I.Q.," *School and Society* 15(1922):373–84; LMT, "The Psychological Determinist; or Democracy and the I.Q.," *Journal of Educational Research* 6(1922):57–62; and William C. Bagley, "Professor Terman's Determinism: A Rejoinder," *Journal of Educational Research* 6(1922):371–85. Bagley's articles were reprinted, in large part, with a series of related papers in William C. Bagley, *Determinism in Education* (Baltimore: Warwick and York, 1925).

88. Bagley, *Determinism in Education*, p. 32.

89. LMT, "The Psychological Determinist," pp. 60–62.

90. This was Terman's definition of intelligence. See LMT, "Intelligence and Its Measurement," *Journal of Educational Psychology* 12(1921):127–33.

91. John Dewey, "Individuality Equality and Superiority," *New Republic* 33(1922):51–63, quote pp. 61–62.

92. See John C. Almack, James F. Bursch, and James C. DeVoss, "Democracy, Determinism and the I.Q.," *School and Society* 18 (1923): 292–95; Truman L. Kelley, "Again: Educational Determinism," *Journal of Educational Research* 8(1923):10–19; and Guy M. Whipple, "The Intelligence Testing Program and Its Objectors—Conscientious and Otherwise," *School and Society* 17(1923):561–68, 596–604.

93. To achieve their egalitarian social goals, Bagley and Dewey had very different models of education. Bagley argued for a traditional, structured academic curriculum and was highly critical of Dewey's individualized, nonconventional progressive education with its emphasis on social values. For a discussion of Bagley's role as a critic of progressive education, see I. L. Kandel, *William Chandler Bagley: Stalwart Educator* (New York: Bureau of Publications, Teachers College, 1961).

94. For an analysis of the variety of interpretations about Darwinian thought, see Donald C. Bellomy, " 'Social Darwinism' Revisited," *Perspectives in American History*, New Series I (1984): 1–129.

95. See Hamilton Cravens, *The Triumph of Evolution: American Scientists and the Hereditary-Environment Controversy, 1900–1941* (Philadelphia: University of Pennsylvania Press, 1978) for an analysis of the intellectual shift that occurred in the 1920s.

96. In completing this section on the testing debate, mention should be made of the fact that there were several related controversies during the early 1920s that were accentuated with the published results of the army testing. There was a brief exchange between Terman and Beardsley Ruml over the conceptual basis of intelligence, with Ruml criticizing the lack of a theoretical rationale. See Beardsley Ruml, "Intelligence and Its Measurement," *Journal of Educational Psychology* 12(1921):143–44; and Truman L. Kelley and LMT, "Dr. Ruml's Criticism of Mental Test Methods," *Journal of Psychology* 18(1921):459–65. There were also two other testing debates that Terman was less directly involved with. These were the association of mental deficiency with antisocial behavior and the ethnic-racial differences in tested intelligence as related to immigration policy. See Cravens, *The Triumph of Evolution*, pp. 224–51 for an overview of these two controversies. In the early twenties, Terman did shift his position on the association of mental deficiency with antisocial behavior. This is discussed in a later section of this chapter (see "Other Ventures in Applied Psychology").

97. LMT to F. S. Hoyt, 13 November 1921, LTP.

98. LMT, *Medical Inspection, Hygiene Teaching, Physical Training, and Special Schools for Defectives in Portland, Oregon: Report of the Survey of the Public School System of Portland* (Yonkers, N.Y.: World Book Company, 1914).

99. Lennon, "Foreword," pp. viii–ix; and LMT to Hoyt, 13 November 1921, LTP.

100. For discussion of the background of World Book and Terman's association see Henry L. Minton, "Lewis M. Terman and the 'World' of Test Publishing," paper presented at the annual meeting of the American Psychological Association, Los Angeles, August 1985.

101. Hodgson to LMT, 2 August 1921, LTP.

102. Memorandum, LMT to William C. Ferguson, 20 April 1923, LTP.

103. Ibid.

104. LMT to Hoyt, 13 November 1921, LTP.

105. Hodgson to LMT, 1 December 1922; and Arthur S. Otis to LMT, 4 January 1923, LTP.

106. Hodgson to LMT, 18 January 1923, LTP.

107. LMT to Hodgson, 26 January 1923, LTP.

108. Freeman, *Mental Tests*, pp. 187–90; and Chapman, "Schools as Sorters," pp. 165–72.

109. When Harcourt, Brace and World acquired the Psychological Corporation in 1970, the firm was renamed Harcourt Brace Jovanovich.

110. LMT et al., *Genetic Studies of Genius*, vol. 1: *Mental and Physical Traits of a Thousand Gifted Children* (Stanford, Calif.: Stanford University Press, 1925), p. 3.

111. LMT, "The Mental Hygiene of Exceptional Children," *Pedagogical Seminary* 22(1915):529–37.

112. LMT, *The Intelligence of School Children*, pp. 165–267.

113. LMT et al., *Genetic Studies*, vol. 1, p. 4.

114. Cubberley to Wilbur, 19 May 1919; and Wilbur to Cubberley, 7 June 1919, ECP.

115. LMT et al., *Genetic Studies*, vol. 1, p. 4.

116. LMT, "The Intelligence Quotient of Francis Galton in Childhood," *American Journal of Psychology* 28(1917):209–15.

117. Galton's early display of intellectual prowess did not prepare him particularly well for academic success. Once he left the tutelage of his family, his academic record was rather mediocre. See Raymond E. Fancher, "Biographical Origins of Francis Galton's Psychology," *Isis* 74(1983):227–33.

118. LMT, "An Experiment in Infant Education," *Journal of Applied Psychology* 2(1918):219–28.

119. LMT and Jessie C. Fenton, "Preliminary Report on a Gifted Juvenile Author," *Journal of Applied Psychology* 5(1921):163–78.

120. Fenton to Seagoe, 8 June 1967, MSP.

121. LMT, "Biographical Note on Henry Cowell," *American Journal of Psychology* 37(1925):233–34.

122. Keith Sward to Seagoe, 2 April 1967, MSP.

123. LMT et al., *Genetic Studies*, vol. 1, pp. 5–17.

124. For histories of child development and longitudinal studies, see John E. Anderson, "Child Development: An Historical Perspective," *Child Development* 27(1956):181–96; and Robert R. Sears, "Your Ancients Revisited: A History of Child Development," in *Review of Child Development Research*, vol. 5, ed. E. Mavis Hetherington (Chicago: University of Chicago Press, 1975), pp. 1–73.

125. Ruch's work in developing the achievement test was related to the development of the Stanford Achievement Test, coauthored with Kelley and Terman.

126. In following-up the gifted sample since 1970, Robert Sears and his research collaborators discovered some errors in the original scoring of the Stanford-Binet tests. As a result, a few of the subjects had IQs a little below the 135 cutoff point for the group. See LMT, Robert R. Sears, Lee J. Cronbach, and Pauline S. Sears, *Terman Life Cycle Study of Children of High Ability, 1922–1982* (Ann Arbor, Mich.: Inter-University Consortium for Political and Social Research, 1983), p. 1.

127. LMT et al., *Genetic Studies*, vol. 1, pp. 19–37.

128. Grades one and two were initially canvassed using only the Stanford-Binet. However, to make the work of the field assistants manageable, grades one and two were eliminated from the survey in November 1921 (ibid., p. 8).

129. Florence L. Goodenough to LMT, 22 January 1922, LTP.

130. LMT to Goodenough, 27 January 1922, LTP.

131. There were actually several control groups used, although they were each drawn primarily from the population of California schoolchildren. For the Stanford-Binet and the Stanford Achievement Test, the control groups were the standardization samples used in developing the tests. For those instruments specially constructed for the gifted study, the control groups were drawn largely from the same schools that contributed to the gifted sample. See LMT et al., *Genetic Studies*, vol. 1, pp. 45, 177, 291, 393, 445, 461.

132. LMT and Melita H. Oden, *Genetic Studies of Genius*, vol. 4: *The Gifted Child Grows Up; Twenty-five Years' Follow-up of a Superior Group* (Stanford, Calif.: Stanford University Press, 1947), p. 7. These figures were corrected from those reported in earlier volumes.

133. Terman acknowledged this possibility but felt that it was not a factor since the vast majority of nominations were made by women teachers. He also pointed out that the sex ratio of those qualifying was higher than the sex ratio of the original nominations. These points, notwithstanding, do not address the possible bias in favor of boys in both the nomination and testing situations. For Terman's discussion, see LMT et al, *Genetic Studies*, vol. 1, pp. 50–51.

134. LMT et al., *Genetic Studies*, vol. 1, p. 12. The data collection during the second year of the study was supported by an additional Commonwealth grant.

135. The summary results are taken from the updated description in LMT and Oden, *Genetic Studies*, vol. 4, pp. 11–57.

136. No estimates were made about Chinese and Japanese children. This was due to the fact that, for the most part, these children attended segregated schools; and these schools were not canvassed.

137. Ibid., p. 57.

138. LMT et al., *Genetic Studies*, vol. 1, pp. 639–40.

139. Catharine M. Cox, *Genetic Studies of Genius*, vol. 2: *The Early Mental Traits of Three Hundred Geniuses* (Stanford, Calif.: Stanford University Press, 1926).

140. LMT, "Editor's Preface," in Cox, *Genetic Studies of Genius*, vol. 2, p. vi.

141. Ibid., pp. viii–ix.

142. For discussions about the problems with Cox's study see Gould, *The Mismeasure of Man*, pp. 183–88; and Jeffrey M. Blum, *Pseudoscience and Mental Ability: The Origins and Fallacies of the I.Q. Controversy* (New York: Monthly Review Press, 1978), pp. 73–75.

143. Yoakum and Yerkes, *Army Mental Tests*, pp. 188–203.

144. See Samuel Haber, *Efficiency and Uplift: Scientific Management in the Progressive Era, 1890–1920* (Chicago: University of Chicago Press, 1964); and Robert H. Wiebe, *The Search for Order: 1877–1920* (New York: Hill and Wang, 1967).

145. Sometime after the war the name was changed to the Bureau of Management Research (Bureau of Management Research folder, LTP).

146. Ibid., lecture outlines.

147. See Michael M. Sokal, "The Origins of the Psychological Corporation," *Journal of the History of the Behavioral Sciences* 17(1981):54–67.

148. Cattell to LMT, 3 September 1919, LTP.

149. Cattell to Wilbur, 22 November 1919, LTP. Terman thanked Cattell for his endorsement (LMT to Cattell, 24 December 1919, LTP).

150. Minutes of the first meeting of the Board of Directors, Psychological Corporation, 2 June 1921, LTP.

151. LMT to Cattell, 14 June 1921, LTP.

152. LMT to Cattell, 21 February 1923, LTP.

153. Minutes of the meeting of the California Branch of the Psychological Corporation, 10 February 1923, LTP, quoted in Sokal, "The Origins of the Psychological Corporation," p. 60.

154. Sokal, "The Origins of the Psychological Corporation."

155. LMT, "Fred Nelles Practical Idealist," *Journal of Delinquency* 11(1927):212–14.

156. LMT, "Editorial," *Journal of Delinquency* 12(1928):193–95.

157. J. Harold Williams and LMT, *Whittier State School Biennial Report: Psychological Survey of the Whittier State School. Preliminary and Final Reports* (Whittier, Calif.: Whittier State School, 1914); and LMT and J. Harold Williams, *Relation of Delinquency and Criminality to Mental Deficiency* (Whittier, Calif.: Whittier State School, 1915).

158. LMT, "Research on the Diagnosis of Pre-Delinquent Tendencies," *Journal of Delinquency* 9(1925):124–30, quote p. 124.

159. Vernon M. Cady, "The Estimation of Juvenile Incorrigibility," *Journal of Delinquency, Monograph No. 2* (1923); and A. S. Raubenheimer, "An Experimental Study of Some Behavior Traits of the Potentially Delinquent Boy" (Ph.D. dissertation, Stanford University, 1923).

160. LMT, "Research on the Diagnosis of Pre-Delinquent Tendencies"; and LMT, "Forword," in Cady, "The Estimation of Juvenile Incorrigibility," pp. 3–4.

161. See Cravens, *The Triumph of Evolution*, pp. 241–51.

162. Franklin S. Fearing, "Some Extra-Intellectual Factors in Delinquency," *Journal of Delinquency* 8(1923):145–54.

163. LMT, "Intelligence Tests in Colleges and Universities," *School and Society* 13(1921):481–94.

164. LMT, "Adventures in Stupidity: A Partial Analysis of the Intellectual Inferiority of a College Student," *Scientific Monthly* 14(1922):23–38.

165. LMT and Karl M. Cowdery, "Stanford's Program of University Personnel Research," *Journal of Personnel Research* 4(1925):263–67.

166. Terman's interest in furthering measurement in higher education was also expressed in his capacity as editor for World Book's Measurement and Adjustment Series. He encouraged Ben D. Wood, who was involved in educational research at Columbia University to publish a monograph. See Ben D. Wood, *Measurement in Higher Education* (Yonkers, N.Y.: World Book Company, 1923).

167. Report of the Committee on Qualifications for Psychological Examiners and Other Psychological Experts, December 1919, LTP.

168. Proposed Constitution and By-Laws of the American Association of Clinical

Psychologists (as revised after the meeting of 28 December 1918), LTP. The AACP became the section of Clinical Psychology within APA in 1920.

169. In 1921 Terman also served on an APA committee, chaired by Boring, dealing with general membership requirements. Minimum qualifications recommended included a Ph.D. and "acceptable published research." Report of the APA Committee on Requirements for Membership, 1 September 1921, LTP.

170. LMT, "The Status of Applied Psychology in the United States," *Journal of Applied Psychology* 5(1921):1–4.

171. E. G. Boring, "Statistics of the American Psychological Association in 1920," *Psychological Bulletin* 17(1920):271–78.

172. See John M. O'Donnell, "The Crisis of Experimentalism in the 1920s: E. G. Boring and the Uses of History," *American Psychologist* 34(1979):289–95.

173. LMT, "The Status of Applied Psychology," p. 4.

174. LMT, "The Mental Test as a Psychological Method," *Psychological Review* 31(1924):93–117.

175. Ibid., p. 97.

176. Ibid., p. 98.

177. Ibid., p. 100.

178. Ibid., p. 112.

179. Ibid., p. 114.

180. Ibid., p. 117.

181. See Lee J. Cronbach, "The Two Disciplines of Scientific Psychology," *American Psychologist* 12(1957):671–84.

182. Yerkes to LMT, 18 December 1923, LTP.

183. Yerkes to LMT, 6 December 1923, LTP.

184. L. L. Thurstone to LMT, 20 December 1923, LTP.

185. LMT to Gesell, 1 December 1919, AGP.

186. LMT to Gesell, 19 January 1920, AGP.

187. LMT to Yerkes, 11 May 1920, LTP.

8. *Midcareer (1923–1932)*

1. LMT, "The Stanford Department of Psychology (1922–1942)," Faculty File, Stanford University Archives, Stanford, Calif., July 1945, quote p. 1 (typed).

2. See LMT, "Frank Angell: 1857–1939," *American Journal of Psychology* 53(1940):138–41.

3. For a full-length biography of Martin, see Miriam Allen deFord, *Psychologist Unretired: The Life Pattern of Lillien J. Martin* (Stanford, Calif.: Stanford University Press, 1948). See also Gwendolyn Stevens and Sheldon Gardner, *The Women of Psychology*, vol. 1: *Pioneers and Innovators* (Cambridge, Mass.: Schenkman, 1982), pp. 89–96.

4. Frederick C. Dommeyer, "Psychical Research at Stanford University," *Journal of Parapsychology* 39(1975):173–205.

5. See Dommeyer, "Psychical Research at Stanford University" for a discussion of the controversy surrounding T. W. Stanford's intentions regarding this gift.

6. Cubberley to Wilbur, 23 September 1920, RWP.

7. Frank Angell to Wilbur, 21 April 1920, RWP.

8. J. E. Coover to Wilbur, 31 August 1920, RWP.

9. LMT to Wilbur, 15 January 1921, RWP.

10. Angell to Wilbur, 28 February 1921, RWP.

11. LMT to Wilbur, 15 January 1921, RWP.

12. Cubberley to Wilbur, 14 February 1922 and 5 March 1922, RWP.

13. Cubberley to Wilbur, 14 February 1922, RWP.

14. Cubberley to Wilbur, 5 March 1922, RWP.

15. E. G. Boring, "Edward Garrigues Boring," in *A History of Psychology in Autobiography*, eds. E. G. Boring, Herbert J. Langfeld, Heinz Werner, and Robert M. Yerkes, vol. 4 (New York: Russell and Russell, 1952), pp. 27–52.

16. E. G. Boring, "Lewis Madison Terman: 1877–1956," *Biographical Memoirs of the National Academy of Sciences* 33(1959):414–40.

17. LMT to Wilbur, 16 January 1921, RWP.

18. Ibid., memorandum on E. G. Boring attached.

19. Ibid.

20. Cubberley to Wilbur, 5 march 1922, RWP.

21. E. G. Boring to Wilbur, 13 March 1922, RWP.

22. LMT to Wilbur, 23 March 1922, RWP.

23. See John M. O'Donnell, "The Crisis of Experimentation in the 1920s: E. G. Boring and the Uses of History," *American Psychologist* 34(1979):289–95. O'Donnell points out that Boring's concern about the growing dominance of applied psychology was a central motive in the writing of his *History of Experimental Psychology* published in 1929.

24. LMT, "The Status of Applied Psychology in the United States," *Journal of Applied Psychology* 5(1921):1–4.

25. Boring to Wilbur, 30 March 1922, RWP.

26. Telegram from Boring to Wilbur, 29 March 1922, RWP.

27. Telegram from Wilbur to Boring, 3 April 1922, RWP.

28. Boring, "Edward Garrigues Boring."

29. Boring to Wilbur, 4 April 1922, RWP.

30. Walter R. Miles, "Walter R. Miles," in *A History of Psychology in Autobiography*, eds. E. G. Boring and Gardner Lindzey, vol. 5 (New York: Appleton-Century-Crofts, 1967), pp. 221–52.

31. Cubberley to Wilbur, 5 March 1922, RWP.

32. Miles, "Walter R. Miles," pp. 234–35.

33. Wilbur to Walter R. Miles, 5 April 1922, RWP.

34. LMT to Yerkes, 19 January 1985, LTP.

35. Cubberley to Wilbur, 14 February 1922, RWP.

36. LMT to Yerkes, 19 January 1955, LTP.

37. M. E. Haggerty to LMT, 29 April 1922.

38. Memorandum from LMT to Wilbur, 9 May 1922, RWP.

39. Wilbur to LMT, 27 May 1922, RWP.

40. LMT, "The Stanford Department of Psychology," p. 1.

41. LMT to Gesell, 1 December 1919, AGP.

42. LMT to Yerkes, 11 May 1920, RYP.

43. Wilbur to Angell, 27 May 1922, RWP.

44. LMT, "Frank Angell," p. 141.

45. *Stanford University: Announcement of Courses:* 1922/23, p. 189.

46. Interview with Hilgard, 1 March 1984.

47. Dommeyer, "Psychical Research at Stanford University," p. 186.

48. LMT, "The Stanford Department of Psychology," pp. 2–5.

49. *Stanford University: Announcement of Courses:* 1932–1933, p. 278.

50. LMT to Boring, 3 August 1927, LTP.

51. Boring to LMT, 17 January 1927, LTP. Boring had a troubled personal relationship with Köhler at this time. The two did not get along very well when Köhler was being considered for a Harvard faculty appointment. See Michael M. Sokal, "The Gestalt Psychologists in Behaviorist America," *American Historical Review* 89 (1984):1240–63.

52. Boring to LMT, 6 October 1931; Boring to LMT, 7 April 1933; and LMT to Boring, 11 April 1933, LTP.

53. LMT to Boring, 11 April 1933, LTP.

54. LMT to Boring, 13 August 1931, E. G. Boring Papers, Harvard University Archives, Cambridge, Mass. Quoted in Sokal, "The Gestalt Psychologists in Behaviorist America," p. 1249.

55. Boring to LMT, 6 October 1931, LTP.

56. LMT to Alvin Johnson, 12 June 1933, LTP. Johnson was head of the "University in Exile" at the New School for Social Research, an organization concerned with placing refugee academics.

57. Samuel C. Kohs to Seagoe, [1967], MSP.

58. LMT to Abraham A. Roback, 27 November 1950, LTP. "Jewish" was removed as a correct response in the 1960 revision of the Stanford-Binet.

59. LMT to Beardsley Ruml, 4 February 1926, LTP.

60. LMT to J. A. Sellards (with attached prospectus), 7 February 1927; and LMT to R. E. Swain (with attached prospectus), 5 January 1932, LTP.

61. LMT and Walter R. Miles, "A Program of Psychological Research on the Later Period of Maturity," memorandum, 12 April 1928, LTP.

62. Miles, "Walter R. Miles," p. 240.

63. Memorandum on the Stanford Citizenship Course, 26 September 1923, LTP.

64. The most representative exposition of Terman's views on intelligence and democracy was presented in LMT, "Were We Born That Way?" *World's Work* 44(1922):655–60.

65. "Dr. L. M. Terman at the University of Stanford," MSP (typed).

66. LMT to Hodgson, 11 May 1926, LTP.

67. Hodgson to LMT, 3 May 1926 and 20 May 1926, LTP.

68. See J. Pearce Mitchell, *Stanford University 1916–1941* (Stanford, Calif.: Stanford University Press, 1958), pp. 47–56.

69. Barbara S. Burks, Dortha W. Jensen, and LMT, *Genetic Studies of Genius* vol. 3, *The Promise of Youth: Follow-up Studies of a Thousand Gifted Children* (Stanford, Calif.: Stanford University Press, 1930).

70. Yerkes to LMT, 9 April 1924; and Max Rosenberg to LMT, 16 May 1924, LTP. Over the years until Rosenberg's death in 1931, the two men struck up a friendship. Terman, in a letter to Rosenberg's sister, praised his "humanitarian spirit" and was grateful for his kindness (LMT to Emilie Oppenheimer, 19 May 1931, LTP).

71. Burks, Jensen, and LMT, *Genetic Studies*, vol. 3, p. 22.

72. Ibid., p. 475.

73. Ibid., pp. 153–61.

74. The final version of the M-F test is contained in LMT and Catharine Cox Miles,

Sex and Personality: Studies in Masculinity and Femininity (New York: McGraw-Hill, 1936), pp. 482–530.

75. Burks, Jensen, and LMT, *Genetic Studies*, vol. 3, p. 161.

76. Ibid., pp. 328–31.

77. Ibid., pp. 471–72.

78. Leta S. Hollingworth to LMT, 3 January 1921, LTP.

79. Burks, Jensen, & LMT, *Genetic Studies*, vol. 3, pp. 467–69. This section appeared in the last chapter, which was written by Terman.

80. Ibid., p. 468.

81. Ibid., p. 482.

82. LMT and Margaret Lima, *Children's Reading: A Guide for Parents and Teachers* (New York: Appleton, 1926).

83. Barbara S. Burks, "I.Q. Farming," [1924], Child Prodigies box, Gilbreth folder, LTP (typed).

84. Terman kept a folder on "Child Prodigies" among his papers. This folder is part of the collection of his papers at Stanford.

85. Lillian M. Gilbreth to Barbara S. Burks, 8 October 1923, LTP.

86. For a biography of Lillian M. Gilbreth, see Edna Yost, "Gilbreth, Lillian Moller," in *American Women of Science* (Philadelphia: Stokes: 1943).

87. Burks, "I.Q. Farming," p. 9.

88. Ibid., pp. 1–2. It should be noted that the restrictive immigration act was passed by the United States Congress in 1924.

89. LMT to Ruml, 11 April 1923, LTP.

90. "Heredity of Gifted Children, Search for Funds 1923–24" folder, LTP.

91. LMT to Rosenberg, 18 February 1925, LTP.

92. An influential report of this study appeared in Barbara S. Burks, "The Relative Influence of Nature and Nurture Upon Mental Development: A Comparative Study of Foster Parent-Foster Child Resemblance and True Parent-True Child Resemblance," *Yearbook of the National Society for the Study of Education* 27, part 1 (1928):219–316.

93. Frank N. Freeman, Karl J. Holzinger, and Blythe C. Mitchell, "The Influence of Environment on the Intelligence, School Achievement, and Conduct of Foster Children," *Yearbook of the National Society for the Study of Education* 27, part 1 (1928):103–217.

94. LMT, "Were We Born That Way?" p. 650.

95. LMT to W. F. Book, 12 April 1929, LTP.

96. Minutes of the Executive Meeting of the Division of Anthropology and Psychology of the National Research Council, 27 December 1919, LTP.

97. Walter V. Bingham, memorandum, National Research Council, Division of Anthropology and Psychology, [1920], LTP.

98. Ibid., p. 3.

99. LMT to Secretary, Japanese Association of America, 21 February 1920, LTP.

100. "Dr. L. M. Terman at the University of Stanford."

101. LMT, "Were We Born That Way?" p. 660; and Marvin L. Darsie, "The Mental Capacity of American-Born Japanese Children," *Comparative Psychology Monograph* 3(1926): Number 15.

102. Terman did point out to Bingham that Kimball Young's doctoral study of racial groups in San Jose fitted in with Bingham's proposal. LMT to Bingham, 5 February 1920, LTP.

103. On eugenics see Mark M. Haller, *Eugenics: Hereditarian Attitudes in American*

Thought (New Brunswick: Rutgers University Press, 1963); and Daniel J. Kevles, *In the Name of Eugenics: Genetics and the Uses of Human Heredity* (New York: Knopf, 1985).

104. LMT, "Were We Born That Way?" pp. 658–59; and "Intellegent Classes Are Decreasing: Dr. Terman Questions Future, Sees Menace to World Civilization," *Palo Alto Times*, 1923 (month and date not available on clipping in Terman papers).

105. "Intelligent Classes Are Decreasing."

106. LMT to Irving M. Fisher, 5 July 1922, LTP.

107. Fisher to LMT, 19 November 1923, with attached copy of Report of the Committee on Selective Immigration of the Eugenics Committee of the United States of America, LTP.

108. For a discussion of the role of the mental-testing movement on restrictive immigration, see Franz Samelson, "Putting Psychology on the Map: Ideology and Intelligence Testing," in *Psychology in Social Context*, ed. Allan R. Buss (New York: Irvington, 1979), pp. 103–68.

109. Leon F. Whitney to LMT, 23 September 1925, LTP.

110. LMT to Whitney, 24 June 1930, LTP.

111. Guy Irving Burch to LMT, 8 October 1930, LTP.

112. LMT to Burch, 25 June 1935, LTP.

113. Terman was also a member of the Eugenics Section of the Commonwealth Club of California. In 1935 he resigned for financial reasons but indicated he thoroughly believed in the work of the club. LMT to Secretary, Commonwealth Club, 2 July 1935, LTP.

114. LMT to Whitney, 1 September 1927, LTP.

115. Minutes, meeting of the Commonwealth Club of California, San Francisco, 7 January 1926, LTP.

116. LMT, "Comments on the Norwegian Program for Race Hygiene," July 1930, LTP (typed).

117. "The Human Betterment Foundation," *Eugenics* 2, Number 3 (1929):17–21.

118. E. S. Gosney to LMT, 4 March 1927, LTP.

119. "The Human Betterment Foundation," p. 19; and Paul Popenoe, "The Institute of Family Relations," *Journal of Juvenile Research* 15(1931):92–100.

120. LMT to Gosney, 9 March 1927, LTP.

121. Haller, *Eugenics*, p. 138.

122. *Human Sterilization Today* (Pasadena, Calif.: Human Betterment Foundation, [1936]), p. 8, LTP.

123. *Collected Papers on Eugenics Sterilization in California* (Pasadena, Calif.: Human Betterment Foundation, 1930); and E. S. Gosney and Paul Popenoe, *Sterilization for Human Betterment* (New York: Macmillan, 1930).

124. Paul Popenoe, "Annual Report of the Secretary of the Human Betterment Foundation for the Year Ending February 13th, 1934," LTP (mimeographed).

125. LMT, *The Measurement of Intelligence* (Boston: Houghton Mifflin, 1916), pp. 6–7; and LMT, "Feeble-Minded Children in the Public Schools of California," *School and Society* 5(1912):161–65.

126. LMT to Paul Popenoe, 8 February 1934, LTP.

127. Gosney to LMT, 16 March 1938, LTP. For background on the institute, see "The Institute of Family Relations."

128. LMT to Gosney, 9 April 1938, LTP.

129. Ibid.

130. LMT, "The Possibilities and Limitations of Training," *Journal of Educational Research* 10(1924):355–43.

131. Ibid., p. 340.

132. Ibid., p. 343. That this was Terman's suggestion to the society is indicated in Guy M. Whipple, "Editor's Preface," *Yearbook of the National Society for the Study of Education* 27, part I (1928):viii–ix.

133. Mauritz Johnson, ed., *The Seventy-Ninth Yearbook of the National Society for the Study of Education* (Chicago: University of Chicago Press, 1980), part 1, p. 330.

134. LMT, "Introduction," *Yearbook of the National Society for the Study of Education* 27, part 1 (1928):1–7, quote p. 3.

135. Ibid., p. 4.

136. Burks, "The Relative Influence of Nature and Nurture."

137. Freeman, Holzinger, and Mitchell, "The Influence of Environment."

138. LMT to Guy M. Whipple, 11 November 1927, LTP.

139. Rather unfairly, Terman also invited Barbara Burks to contribute a written discussion to the yearbook on her study and the Freeman study. See Barbara S. Burks, "Comments on the Chicago and Stanford Studies of Foster Children," *Yearbook of the National Society for the Study of Education* 27, part 1 (1928):317–21. In her comments Burks was more critical of the Chicago study than her own Stanford study.

140. LMT to Whipple, 3 December 1927, LTP.

141. William C. Bagley to LMT, 17 December 1927, LTP.

142. LMT to Bagley, 5 January 1928, LTP.

143. Bagley to LMT, 9 January 1928, LTP.

144. LMT, "The Influence of Nature and Nurture upon Intelligence Scores: An Evaluation of the Evidence in Part I of the 1928 Yearbook of the National Society for the Study of Education," *Journal of Educational Psychology* 19(1928):362–69.

145. Ibid., p. 369.

146. LMT to Bagley, 18 January 1928, LTP.

147. Frank N. Freeman, "An Evaluation of the Evidence in Part I of the Yearbook and Its Bearing on the Interpretation of Intelligence Tests," *Journal of Educational Psychology* 19(1928):374–80, quote p. 378.

148. Guy M. Whipple, "Editorial Impression of the Contribution to Knowledge of the Twenty-Seventh Yearbook," *Journal of Educational Psychology* 19(1928):389–96.

149. William C. Bagley, "The Significance of Unambiguous Evidence Regarding Environmental Influences," *Educational Administration and Supervision* 14(1928):441–50.

150. Arthur I. Gates, "Observed Facts and Theoretical Concepts," *Journal of Educational Psychology* 19(1928):381–88.

151. See Frank N. Feeman, "Charles Hubbard Judd," *Psychological Review* 54(1947):59–65.

152. Charles H. Judd, "Intelligence as Method of Adaptation," *Journal of Educational Psychology* 19(1928):397–404, quote p. 397.

153. Bird T. Baldwin and Lorle I. Stecher, *The Psychology of the Preschool Child* (New York: Appleton, 1924).

154. Bird T. Baldwin, "Heredity and Environment—Or Capacity and Training?" *Journal of Educational Psychology* 19(1928):405–09, quote p. 408.

155. Correspondence between Terman and Yerkes, 1920–1922, LTP.

156. LMT to Yerkes, 10 June 1921, LTP.

157. Yerkes to LMT, 10 August 1922, LTP.

158. LMT to Yerkes, 13 May 1921, LTP.

159. Yerkes to LMT, 24 December 1924, LTP.

160. Yerkes to LMT, 9 April 1924, LTP.

161. LMT to Yerkes, 16 October 1925 and 6 May 1927, LTP.

162. Boring, "Lewis Madison Terman," p. 414.

163. Boring to LMT, 3 December 1925, LTP.

164. Boring to LMT, 14 April 1930, LTP.

165. Boring to LMT, 17 January 1927, LTP.

166. LMT to Boring, 26 January 1927, LTP.

167. Edwin G. Boring, *Psychologist at Large: An Autobiography and Selected Essays* (New York: Basic Books, 1961), p. 56.

168. Boring to LMT, 3 June 1930, LTP.

169. Boring to LMT, 17 January, 1927; and LMT to Boring, 3 August 1927, LTP.

170. Boring to LMT, 30 June 1930, LTP.

171. LMT to Boring, 11 April 1933, LTP.

172. LMT, "Review of *The Mental Growth of the Child*, by Arnold Gesell," *Science* 51(1925):445–46.

173. LMT to Gesell, 4 September 1925, AGP.

174. LMT to Goodenough, 22 May 1925, LTP.

175. LMT to Catharine M. Cox, 2 March 1927 and 19 April 1927, LTP.

176. Letter to the author from Anne Roe, 12 April 1983.

177. Correspondence between Terman and J. H. Russell, 1925–1956, LTP.

178. Murchison to LMT, 20 August 1928, LTP.

179. Murchison to LMT, 14 September 1928, LTP.

180. LMT to Murchison, 8 May 1930, LTP; and LMT, "Trails to Psychology," in *A History of Psychology in Autobiography*, vol. 2, ed. Carl Murchison (Worcester, Mass.: Clark University Press, 1932).

181. Ibid., p. 328.

182. FET, "Special Comments," [1974], pp. 11–12, MSP.

183. LMT to William H. Burnham, 2 May 1924, LTP.

184. LMT to Burnham, 16 December 1924, LTP.

185. LMT to Burnham, 25 November 1931, LTP.

186. "Confidential" letter, undated, circulated by C. H. Thurber; acknowledged by LMT to Thurber, 26 May 1924, LTP.

187. Douglas Fryer to LMT, 6 January 1933, LTP.

188. FET, "Special Comments," pp. 12–13.

189. Diary of Anna Minton Terman, 1923–1927, in the possession of her granddaughter, Doris Tucker.

190. Sward to Seagoe, 2 April 1967, MSP.

191. LMT to Kelley, 4 November 1929, LTP.

192. LMT, "I Was Lucky," 1953, p. 13, LTP (typed).

193. Diaries of Anna Minton Terman, 1923–1927 and 1928–1931, in the possession of Doris Tucker.

194. Interview with Hilgard, 1 March 1984.

195. Diaries of Anna Minton Terman, 1923–1927 and 1928–1931.

196. LMT, "I Was Lucky," pp. 10–13.

197. LMT to Harris J. Ryan, 22 November 1927; and Frank P. Deering to LMT, 26 January 1938, LTP.

198. FET, "Special Comments," pp. 33–34.

199. LMT to Gesell, 14 December 1924, AGP.

200. "In a Shadow," unpublished manuscript (case study) of Helen Terman Mosher by her daughter, Doris Tucker, 1970, in the possession of Tucker.

201. Interview with Tucker, 18 and 19 August 1985.

202. Interview with Fred W. Terman (son of Fred E. Terman), 16 December 1983.

203. Interview with Tucker, 18 and 19 August 1985.

204. Roger G. Barker to Seagoe, 19 September 1967, MSP.

205. LMT to Gesell, 30 July 1925, AGP.

206. LMT to Boring, 10 July 1931, LTP; and interview with Fred W. Terman, 16 December 1983.

207. Diaries of Anna Minton Terman, 1923–1927 and 1928–1931; and FET, "Special Comments," pp. 12–14b.

208. Tucker, "In a Shadow"; and FET, "Special Comments," pp. 14a–14b.

209. Diary of Anna Minton Terman, 1923–1927.

210. Letter to the author from E. Lowell Kelly, 9 January 1984.

211. Interview with Hilgard, 1 March 1984.

212. Anna Minton Terman, "My Trip Abroad" (diary of her trip to Copenhagen, June–September 1932), in the possession of Doris Tucker.

213. Diaries of Anna Minton Terman, 1923–1927 and 1928–1931.

214. May V. Seagoe, *Terman and the Gifted* (Los Altos, Calif.: William Kaufmann, 1975), p. 131.

215. Interview with Hilgard, 1 March 1984.

216. Harry F. Harlow to Seagoe, 17 July 1967, MSP.

217. Interview with Tucker, 18 and 19 August 1985.

218. Diary of Anna Minton Terman, 1923–1927.

219. Ibid.; and Diary, 1928–1931.

220. Interview with Tucker, 18 and 19 August 1985.

221. Helen Terman Mosher to Seagoe, [1967], MSP.

222. Ibid.

223. Seagoe, *Terman and the Gifted*, p. 131.

224. Interviews with Tucker, 18 and 19 August 1985; and Fred W. Terman, 16 December 1985.

225. Interview with Tucker, 18 and 19 August 1985.

226. Entry of 23 March 1928, Diary of Anna Minton Terman, 1928–1931.

227. Helen Terman Mosher to Seagoe, [1967], MSP.

228. LMT, "Trails to Psychology," p. 309.

229. LMT et al., *Psychological Factors in Marital Happiness* (New York: McGraw-Hill, 1938), p. 376.

9. New Directions (1932–1942)

1. LMT to Cox, 19 April 1927, LTP.

2. LMT and Catharine Cox Miles, *Sex and Personality: Studies in Masculinity and Femininity* (New York: McGraw-Hill, 1936).

3. Havelock Ellis, *Man and Woman: A Study of Human Secondary Sexual Characters* (London: Walter Scott, 1894).

4. See Helen Thompson Wooley, "A Review on the Recent Literature on the Psychology of Sex," *Psychological Bulletin* 7(1910):335–42. Also see Rosalind Rosenberg, *Beyond Separate Spheres: Intellectual Origins of Modern Feminism* (New Haven, Conn.: Yale University Press, 1982); and J. G. Morawski, "The Measurement of Masculinity and Femininity: Engendering Categorical Realities," *Journal of Personality* 53(1985): 196–223 for historical overviews of the psychology of sex differences and masculinity-femininity.

5. Joseph Jastrow, *The Psychology of Conviction* (Boston: Houghton Mifflin, 1918).

6. LMT and Miles, *Sex and Personality*, pp. 1–10.

7. Ibid., pp. 61–63, 120–21.

8. Ibid., pp. 164–66.

9. Ibid., p. 179.

10. LMT to Cox, 19 April 1927, LTP.

11. Curtis G. Benjamin to LMT, 15 February 1937; and LMT to Benjamin, 20 February 1937, LTP.

12. E. B. Reuter, "Sex and Personality," *American Journal of Sociology* 42(1937):753–54; and David Wechsler, "Sex and Personality," *American Journal of Psychology* 49(1937):328–29.

13. One contribution was the fact that the Terman-Miles M-F test served as the model for the development of subsequent measures of masculinity-femininity. See Miriam Lewin, "Psychology Measures Femininity and Masculinity, 2: From '13 Gay Men' to the Instrumental-Expressive Distinction," in *In the Shadow of the Past: Psychology Portrays the Sexes*, ed. Miriam Lewin (New York: Columbia University Press, 1984), pp. 179–204.

14. LMT and Miles, *Sex and Personality*, pp. 451–70.

15. Ibid., pp. 451–52.

16. For an evaluation of the Terman-Miles M-F test, see Miriam Lewin, "Rather Worse Than Folly? Psychology Measures Femininity and Masculinity, 1," in *In the Shadow of the Past*, ed. Lewin, pp. 155–78. For a general consideration of the measurement of masculinity-femininity, see Morawski, "The Measurement of Masculinity and Femininity."

17. LMT and Miles, *Sex and Personality*, p. 70.

18. See Vern L. Bullough, *Sexual Variance in Society and History* (New York: Wiley, 1976), pp. 635–49.

19. Letter to the author from Kelly, 9 January 1984.

20. See LMT and Miles, *Sex and Personality*, pp. 239–58 for a report on the study with homosexuals.

21. Ibid., p. 240

22. Ibid., p. 257.

23. Ibid.

24. Ibid., p. 248.

25. Ibid.

26. Ibid., p. 260.

27. Ibid., pp. 257–58.

28. Ibid., p. 243.

29. Havelock Ellis, *Psychology of Sex: A Manual for Students* (New York: Long and Smith, 1933).

30. LMT and Miles, *Sex and Personality*, pp. 256–57.

31. Ibid.

32. Ibid., pp. 321–41. Maud Merrill gathered these data and coauthored the chapter on the results with Terman. In order to obtain a sample of female homosexuals Terman had initially contacted several women colleagues, including Leta S. Hollingworth (LMT to Hollingworth, 2 April 1929, LTP) and Kay Banham Bridges (LMT to Bridges, 11 April 1929, LTP). He hoped they might know of "cases," but these contacts did not produce any leads.

33. Ibid., pp. 577–79.

34. Ibid., pp. 259–83.

35. Terman and Kelly referred to this as a "moderate correlation." Ibid., p. 282.

36. Ibid.

37. Ibid., p. 283.

38. For a discussion of the male homosexual subculture around 1920, see George Chauncey, Jr., "Christian Brotherhood or Sexual Perversion? Homosexual Identities and the Construction of Sexual Boundaries in the World War One Era," *Journal of Social History* 19(1985):189–211.

39. LMT, "Trials to Psychology," in *A History of Psychology in Autobiography*, vol. 2, ed. Carl Murchison (Worcester, Mass.: Clark University Press, 1932), p. 330.

40. For a recent biography and analysis of Havelock Ellis's works, see Phyllis Grosskurth, *Havelock Ellis: A Biography* (New York: Knopf, 1980).

41. LMT and Miles, *Sex and Personality*, p. 468.

42. Ibid., p. 452.

43. Ibid., p. viii.

44. Personal correspondence, Container 15, Files 1 and 32, LTP.

45. LMT to Yerkes, 8 September 1952, LTP.

46. Robert L. Dickinson to LMT, 28 January 1935, LTP.

47. George W. Henry, *Sex Variants: A Study of Homosexual Patterns*, vol. 1 (New York: Hoeber, 1941), pp. vii–viii.

48. Another instance of this was Terman's recommendation to Lowell Kelly that his name as coauthor for the sections on homosexuality in *Sex and Personality* be limited to footnotes. This is because Terman believed it would not be desirable for Kelly's career to have his name closely linked to such a taboo topic as homosexuality. Kelly refers to this in a letter written to the author, 9 January 1984.

49. Letter to the author from George Chauncey, Jr., 27 May 1987.

50. George W. Henry, *Sex Variants: A Study of Homosexual Patterns*, vols. 1 and 2 (New York: Hoeber, 1941).

51. For a more extensive discussion of the Henry study and the Committee for the Study of Sex Variants, see Henry L. Minton, "Femininity in Men and Masculinity in Women: American Psychiatry and Psychology Portray Homosexuality in the 1930s," *Journal of Homosexuality* 13(1)(1986):1–21.

52. LMT to Russell G. Leiter, 13 November 1952, LTP.

53. LMT, "Kinsey's 'Sexual Behavior in the Human Male': Some Comments and Criticisms," *Psychological Bulletin* 45(1948):443–59.

54. Letter to the author from Kelly, 9 January 1984.

55. The three books on marriage were Katherine Bement Davis, *Factors in the Sex Life of Twenty-Two Hundred Women* (New York: Harper and Brothers, 1929); G. V. Hamilton, *A Research in Marriage* (New York: Albert and Charles Boni, 1929); and Robert L. Dickinson and Lura Beam, *A Thousand Marriages* (Baltimore: Williams and Wilkins, 1931).

56. These series of events recalled by Kelly are also reflected in the Terman-Kelly correspondence of 1931–33, LTP.

57. Kelly to LMT, 12 November 1933; and LMT to Kelly, 22 November 1933, LTP.

58. Paul Popenoe, "The Institute of Family Relations," *Journal of Juvenile Research* 15(1931):92–100.

59. LMT et al., *Psychological Factors in Marital Happiness* (New York: McGraw-Hill, 1938).

60. Ibid., pp. 366–78.

61. Robert G. Bernreuter, "The Evaluation of a Proposed New Method for Constructing Personality Trait Tests of Foster Parent-Child Resemblance and True Parent-Child Resemblance" (Ph.D. dissertation, Stanford University, 1931).

62. LMT et al., *Psychological Factors in Marital Happiness*, pp. 145–66.

63. Ibid., p. 146.

64. Ibid., p. 368.

65. Ibid., pp. 366–78.

66. Ibid., p. 375.

67. In 1940 Terman used his marital questionnaire (slightly revised) as part of his follow-up study of the gifted. In 1951 he reported data on orgasm adequacy for about six hundred wives of this group. The pattern of results was similar to the 1938 study. However, he and his collaborators were now more noncommittal as to whether inadequacy was biological or psychological. See LMT, Nancy Bayley, Helen Marshall, Olga W. McNemar, Melita H. Oden, and Ellen B. Sullivan, "Correlates of Orgasm Adequacy in a Group of 556 Wives," *Journal of Psychology* 32(1951):115–72. As another part of the gifted follow-up, Terman reported that his revised marital questionnaire successfully predicted those couples who divorced. See LMT and Paul Wallin, "The Validity of Marriage Prediction and Marital Adjustment Tests," *American Sociological Review* 14(1949):497–504.

68. See Leonard S. Cottrell, "Review of *Psychological Factors in Marital Happiness*," *American Journal of Sociology* 44(1939):570–74; Rudolf Pintner, "Review of *Psychological Factors in Marital Happiness*," *American Journal of Psychology* 52(1939):656; and Robert R. Sears, "Review of *Psychological Factors in Marital Happiness*," *Character and Personality* 7(1938–1939):349–50.

69. Havelock Ellis to LMT, 11 November 1938; Dickinson to LMT, 2 December 1938; G. V. Hamilton to LMT, 10 January 1939; and LMT to Hamilton, 13 January 1939, LTP.

70. LMT to Benjamin, 13 January 1939, LTP. Terman made similar comments in a letter to Kelly, 8 December 1938, LTP.

71. Harry L. Hollingworth, "Review of *Psychological Factors in Marital Happiness*," *Psychological Bulletin* 36(1939):191–97, quote p. 191.

72. See Cottrell, "Review of *Psychological Factors*"; and Sears "Review of *Psychological Factors*."

73. Cottrell and Sears in their reviews also pointed to such limitations of the question-

naire data. Furthermore, Cottrell criticized the atomistic nature of the personality questionnaire. In fact, the Bernreuter Personality Inventory has not proven to be a well constructed or valid measure. See Donald J. Veldman, "Review of the *Bernreuter Personality Inventory*," in *Personality Tests and Reviews*, ed. Oscar K. Buros (Highland Park, N.J.: Gryphon Press, 1970), pp. 1150–52.

74. LMT, "The Effect of Happiness or Unhappiness on Self-Report Regarding Attitudes, Reaction Patterns, and Facts of Personal History," *Psychological Bulletin* 36(1939):197–292.

75. Kelly to LMT, 2 December 1938, LTP.

76. LMT to Kelly, 8 December 1938, LTP.

77. LMT and Winifred B. Johnson, "Methodology and Results of Recent Studies in Marital Adjustment," *American Sociological Review* 4(1939):307–24. Kelly reported on the follow-up of his longitudinal study in his 1954 American Psychological Association presidential address (letter to the author from Kelly, 9 January 1984).

78. LMT and Maud A. Merrill, "Report of Progress of Research by Lewis M. Terman and Maud A. Merrill under Social Science Research Grants," October 1931, LTP (mimeographed).

79. For an evaluation of the 1916 Stanford-Binet, see Anne Anastasi, *Psychological Testing* (New York: Macmillan, 1954), pp. 176–78; and Jerome M. Sattler, *Assessment of Children's Intelligence* (Philadelphia: Saunders, 1974), pp. 100–101.

80. LMT and Merrill, "Report of Progress," 1931.

81. LMT and Maud A. Merrill, *Revised Stanford-Binet Scale* (Boston: Houghton Mifflin, 1937); and LMT and Maud A. Merrill, *Measuring Intelligence: A Guide to the Administration of the New Revised Stanford-Binet Tests of Intelligence* (Boston: Houghton Mifflin, 1937).

82. LMT and Maud A. Merrill, "Report of Progress of Research by Lewis M. Terman and Maud A. Merrill under Social Science Research Grants," March 1938, LTP (mimeographed).

83. LMT to Joseph L. Pollock, 7 July 1949, LTP. Terman's rationale was that choosing A and B would lead to confusing A with the 1916 edition of the test.

84. For discussion of these changes, see LMT and Merrill, *Measuring Intelligence*, pp. 3–51; and LMT, "The Revision Procedures," in Quinn McNemar, *The Revision of the Stanford-Binet Scale: An Analysis of the Standardization Data* (Boston: Houghton Mifflin, 1942), pp. 1–14.

85. Anastasi, *Psychological Testing*, p. 182.

86. LMT and Merrill, *Measuring Intelligence*, p. 48.

87. LMT, *The Measurement of Intelligence* (Boston: Houghton Mifflin, 1916), p. 72.

88. Although Terman had moderated his views, his 1916 book, *The Measurement of Intelligence*, remained in print until 1952 (C. A. Ulrich to LMT, 19 May 1952, LTP).

89. William E. Spaulding to LMT, 23 March 1937; Dorothy Molodetsky to LMT, 24 March 1937; and Mary H. Bressler to LMT, 25 March 1937, LTP. For a discussion of the Psychologists' League, see Lorenz J. Finison, "Unemployment, Politics, and the History of Organized Psychology," *American Psychologist* 31(1976):747–55.

90. LMT to Molodetsky, 1 April 1937, LTP.

91. Spaulding to LMT, 9 April 1937; and LMT to Spaulding, 19 April 1937, LTP.

92. Maud A. Merrill to George Davol, 18 April 1945, LTP.

93. See Anastasi, *Psychological Testing*, pp. 193–203; and Sattler, *Children's Intelligence*, pp. 101–04.

94. David Wechsler, *The Measurement of Adult Intelligence* (Baltimore: Williams and Wilkins, 1939).

95. LMT to G. M. Fenollosa, 6 April 1953; and Fenollosa to LMT, 31 March 1955, LTP.

96. LMT and Maud A. Merrill, *Stanford-Binet Intelligence Scale*, 3d ed. (Boston: Houghton Mifflin, 1960).

97. Robert L. Thorndike, Elizabeth P. Hagan, and Jerome M. Sattler, *Stanford-Binet Intelligence Scale*, 4th ed. (Chicago: Riverside, 1985). One reviewer points out that this latest revision is more similar in structure and content to the Wechsler scales than it is to its predecessors. See Philip E. Vernon, "The Demise of the Stanford-Binet Scale," *Canadian Psychology* 28(1987):251–58.

98. LMT and Quinn McNemar, *Terman-McNemar Test of Mental Ability* (Yonkers, N.Y.: World Book Company, 1941).

99. *Manual of Directions, Terman-McNemar Test of Mental Ability* (Yonkers, N.Y.: World Book Company, 1941).

100. Anastasi, *Psychological Testing*, p. 216.

101. See Oscar K. Buros, ed., *Tests in Print II* (Highland Park, N.J.: Gryphon Press, 1974).

102. Terman was only actively involved in the 1929 and 1940 revisions. Truman L. Kelley, along with Richard Madden and Eric F. Gardner, carried out the 1953 revision (Roger T. Lennon to LMT, 30 January 1951, LTP).

103. The royalty difficulties also affected returns from Terman's other publications with World Book. These included the Terman Group Test and some edited books.

104. LMT to Hodgson, 16 December 1930; and LMT to Hodgson, 20 October 1931, LTP.

105. Hodgson to LMT, 9 April 1931; LMT to Kelley, 31 January 1934; and Kelley to LMT, 2 March 1934, LTP.

106. Hodgson to Hoover, 15 June 1935; and Wilbur to Hodgson, 22 June 1935, RWP.

107. Kelley to LMT and G. M. Ruch, 4 July 1933; and LMT to Kelley, 12 July 1933, LTP.

108. Wilbur to Daphne Hodgson, 18 February 1938, RWP.

109. LMT to O. S. Reimold, 22 November 1933; and Reimold to LMT, 10 April 1935, LTP.

110. LMT to Ferguson, 18 July 1947, LTP.

111. Ibid.

112. Quinn McNemar, "Quinn McNemar," in *A History of Psychology in Autobiography*, vol. 7, ed. Gardner Lindzey (San Francisco: Freeman, 1980), pp. 305–33.

113. LMT to Ferguson, 18 July 1947, LTP.

114. Kelley to LMT, 2 March 1944, LTP.

115. LMT to Ferguson, 18 July 1947, LTP.

116. LMT to Kelley, 18 September 1922, LTP.

117. LMT to Kelley, 20 July 1933, LTP.

118. LMT to Ruch, 20 December 1938, LTP.

119. Correspondence between LMT and Ruch, 15 February 1938 to 24 September 1940, LTP.

120. Ruch to LMT, 17 September 1940; and Ferguson to LMT, 14 January 1941, LTP.

121. LMT to Ferguson, 10 December 1943. Terman received word from Ruch's younger brother, Floyd, who had also been a psychology graduate student at Stanford.

122. Ibid.

123. Frances W. Burks to LMT, 16 June 1943, LTP.

124. Although Terman did not participate in the next revision of the Stanford Achievement Test (1953), he prevailed on the World Book Company to limit Kelley's participation. He was concerned that if Kelley had primary control, the test would lose its practical value (LMT to Ferguson, 18 July 1947, LTP).

125. George D. Stoddard, *The Pursuit of Education: An Autobiography* (New York: Vantage Press, 1981), p. 54.

126. Ibid.

127. Bird T. Baldwin, "Heredity and Environment—Or Capacity and Training?" *Journal of Educational Psychology* 19(1928):405–09.

128. Wellman had received her Ph.D. under Baldwin, and at the time of his death they were engaged to marry (interview with Marie Skodak Crissey, 15 January 1982). Also see Beth L. Wellman, "Contributions of Bird Thomas Baldwin to Child Development," *Journal of Juvenile Research* 14(1930):1–7.

129. Beth L. Wellman, "Iowa Studies on the Effects of Schooling," in *The Thirty-Ninth Yearbook of the National Society for the Study of Education*, part 2 (Bloomington, Ill.: Public School Publishing, 1940), pp. 377–99. For a review of the Iowa studies and the 1940 IQ debate, see Henry L. Minton, "The Iowa Child Welfare Research Station and the 1940 Debate on Intelligence: Carrying on the Legacy of a Concerned Mother," *Journal of the History of the Behavioral Sciences* 20(1984):160–76.

130. Harold M. Skeels, "Some Iowa Studies of the Mental Growth of Children in Relation to Differentials of the Environment: A Summary," in *The Thirty-Ninth Yearbook*, part 2, pp. 281–308; and Marie Skodak, *Children in Foster Homes: A Study of Mental Development*, University of Iowa Studies in Child Welfare, vol. 16, no. 1 (Iowa City: University of Iowa Press, 1939).

131. Skeels, "Some Iowa Studies on the Mental Growth of Children," pp. 296–300.

132. Interviews with Ronald Lippitt, 14 January 1982; Marie Skodak Crissey, 15 January 1982; and Orlo L. Crissey, 15 January 1982.

133. George D. Stoddard, "Intellectual Development of the Child: An Answer to the Critics of the Iowa Studies," *School and Society* 51(1940):529–636; and George D. Stoddard, *The Meaning of Intelligence* (New York: Macmillan, 1943), pp. 123–46, 414.

134. Stoddard, *The Pursuit of Education*, p. 54.

135. LMT to Gosney, 13 January 1939, LTP.

136. LMT, "Personal Reactions of the Yearbook Committee," in *The Thirty-Ninth Yearbook*, part 1, pp. 460–67, quote p. 461.

137. Florence L. Goodenough, "New Evidence on Environmental Influences on Intelligence," in *The Thirty-Ninth Yearbook*, part 1, pp. 307–65; and Florence L. Goodenough, "Personal Reactions of the Yearbook Committee," ibid., pp. 449–451.

138. George D. Stoddard, "Personal Reactions of the Yearbook Committee," in *The Thirty-Ninth Yearbook*, part 1, pp. 456–59; and Beth L. Wellman, "Personal Reactions of the Yearbook Committee," ibid., pp. 468–71.

139. Stoddard, *The Meaning of Intelligence*, p. 116.

140. Goodenough to LMT, 18 October 1938, FGP.

141. Goodenough to Hollingworth, 5 April 1939, FGP.

142. Ibid.

143. Goodenough to LMT, 8 April 1939, FGP.

144. McNemar, in *A History of Psychology in Autobiography*, p. 320.

145. Quinn McNemar, "A Critical Examination of the University of Iowa Studies of Environmental Influence Upon the IQ," *Psychological Bulletin* 37(1940):63–92; and Beth L. Wellman, Harold M. Skeels, and Marie Skodak, "Review of McNemar's Critical Examination of Iowa Studies," *Psychological Bulletin* 37(1940):63–92.

146. Wellman, Skeels, and Skodak, "Review of McNemar," p. 93.

147. McNemar, in *A History of Psychology in Autobiography*, p. 320.

148. Ibid.

149. George D. Stoddard to LMT, 4 March 1939, LTP.

150. Paul R. Hanna to LMT, 3 April 1939, LTP.

151. Stoddard, *The Pursuit of Education*, p. 59. On the program Terman was listed as the speaker. Stoddard's name was not included ("Outline of Program, Conference on Educational Frontiers, July 7–9, 1939," LTP) (mimeographed).

152. Stoddard, *The Pursuit of Education*, p. 59.

153. Interview with Sears, 16 March 1984.

154. Edgar Z. Friedenberg, personal communication, 5 July 1985.

155. Wiggam to LMT, 29 June 1939; and LMT to Wiggam, 10 July 1939, LTP.

156. Barbara S. Burks to LMT, 13 November 1939, LTP.

157. Burks to LMT, 29 May 1940, LTP.

158. Ben D. Wood to LMT, 26 July 1939, LTP.

159. LMT to Wood, 29 July 1929, LTP.

160. LMT to Goodenough, 3 October 1939, LTP.

161. Goodenough to LMT, 31 October 1939, FGP.

162. H. H. Remmers to LMT, 27 July 1939, LTP.

163. Kelly to LMT, 18 January 1940, LTP.

164. Goodenough to LMT, 8 November 1939, FGP.

165. Benjamin R. Simpson, "The Wandering IQ: Is it Time for it to Settle Down?" *Journal of Psychology* 7(1939):351–67.

166. LMT to Benjamin R. Simpson, 16 March 1939, LTP.

167. Simpson to LMT, 9 March 1940, LTP.

168. LMT to Simpson, 12 March 1940, LTP. Terman was more muted in his criticism of Stoddard in his communications with G. M. Ruch. Ruch supported Terman, but Stoddard had been Ruch's favorite graduate student. Ruch's solution to his dual allegiance was to place the blame with Wellman (Ruch to LMT, 17 June 1939; and LMT to Ruch, 7 March 1940, LTP).

169. Stoddard, "Intellectual Development of the Child."

170. LMT to Goodenough, 1 May 1940, FGP.

171. Ferguson to LMT, 26 April 1940, LTP.

172. LMT to Ferguson, 1 May 1940, LTP.

173. LMT to Ferguson, 17 October 1949, LTP.

174. Hazel M. Cushing to Goodenough, 7 November 1941; and Goodenough to Cushing, 13 November 1941, FGP. In this exchange reference was made to the Spokane, Washington, school superintendent, Orville C. Pratt, debunking the use of IQ tests because of various reports of the variability of scores over time.

175. LMT to Ferguson, 7 October 1940, LTP.

176. Stoddard eventually went on to become the president of the University of Illinois. See Stoddard, *The Pursuit of Education*.

177. LMT to Goodenough, 25 October 1941; and Goodenough to LMT, 31 October 1941, FGP.

178. Interviews with Lippitt, 14 January 1982; and Skodak-Crissey, 15 January 1982.

179. LMT to Yerkes, 8 January 1951, LTP.

180. Interview with Sears, 16 March 1984.

181. Farnsworth to Seagoe, 9 August 1972, MSP.

182. George D. Stoddard and Beth L. Wellman, "Environment and the IQ," in *The Thirty-Ninth Yearbook*, part 1, pp. 405–42, quote p. 431.

183. For a more extensive discussion of these problems see Minton, "The Iowa Child Welfare Research Station"; and Langdon E. Longstreth, "Revisiting Skeels' Final Study: A Critique," *Developmental Psychology* 17(1981):620–25.

184. For a review of the more recent studies, see Henry L. Minton and Frank W. Schneider, *Differential Psychology* (Monterey, Calif.: Brooks/Cole, 1980), pp. 120–29, 433–40.

185. FET, "Hoover Poll of Stanford Faculty," memorandum, 22 February 1980, FTP. Wilbur was the secretary of the interior under Hoover's federal administration.

186. May V. Seagoe, *Terman and the Gifted* (Los Altos, Calif.: William Kaufmann, 1975), pp. 151–63. Seagoe provides extensive detail about the Hoover-Stanford affair based on documents provided to her by Fred Terman. These documents are deposited in the Hoover Institution at Stanford (FET, "Hoover Poll of Stanford Faculty").

187. "Our Nation's Foreign Policy," circular, 21 August 1941, LTP (mimeographed).

188. LMT, "Leadership in the Present Emergency," unpublished manuscript with the notation, "for release on Mon., Aug. 18," LTP (typed). Although the year is not indicated, it is clear from the contents that it was 1941. This paper does not appear to have been published in any newspaper as there are no clippings in the Terman papers.

189. Seagoe, *Terman and the Gifted*, p. 153.

190. Hoover to Edwin A. Cottrell, 22 September 1941, LTP.

191. "Herbert Hoover's Questionnaire," *San Francisco Chronicle*, 27 September 1941.

192. LMT to Stanford colleagues, 24 September 1941, LTP.

193. "Hoover's Poll of Faculty Shows 60% of Professors Oppose Dynamic Defense," *The Stanford Daily*, 2 October 1941.

194. LMT, "Hoover Poll Misleading; Terman Says," *Palo Alto Times*, 3 October 1941.

195. Seagoe, *Terman and the Gifted*, pp. 156–57.

196. Ibid.; and FET to Seagoe, 20 March 1974, MSP.

197. Seagoe, *Terman and the Gifted*, pp. 158–62. Unlike the Hoover poll, it was decided to restrict the sample to full-time faculty.

198. LMT to Wilbur, 15 October 1941, quoted in Seagoe, *Terman and the Gifted*, p. 149.

199. Hoover to LMT, 30 October 1941, LTP. Hoover knew Terman personally. They lived only a short distance from one another on the Stanford campus. The Termans attended the victory celebration in Hoover's home when he won the presidential election in 1928 (Diary of Anna Minton Terman, 1928–1931).

200. Seagoe, *Terman and the Gifted*, pp. 162–63. Terman wrote a conciliatory note in reply to Hoover, stating that it was inevitable that friends should differ, but that such differences should not lead to termination of friendship (referred to in Seagoe, *Terman and the Gifted*, p. 162).

201. Maud A. Merrill to Goodenough, 9 December 1941, FGP.

202. Ibid.; and LMT to Roger G. Barker, 4 February 1942, LTP.

203. Quinn McNemar and Maud A. Merrill, eds., *Studies in Personality* (New York: McGraw-Hill, 1942), p. vii.

204. Robert S. Woodworth, "Introduction," in *Studies in Personality*, pp. 3–11.

205. Ibid., p. 3.

206. Ibid., p. 11.

207. LMT to "Incredibly Devoted Friends," 19 January 1942, quoted in Seagoe, *Terman and the Gifted*, p. 169.

208. See Seagoe, *Terman and the Gifted*, pp. 205–10 for a list of the Ph.D. and M.A. research sponsored by Terman. Before 1923 all of the students he directed were in education. From 1923 on the majority were in psychology. The only education student he directed after 1930 was Seagoe, who completed her dissertation in 1934.

209. McNemar, in *A History of Psychology in Autobiography*, p. 319.

210. Letter to the author from Barker, 16 April 1983.

211. Barker to Seagoe, 19 September 1967, MSP.

212. McNemar, in *A History of Psychology in Autobiography*, pp. 318–19; and letters to the author from Barker, 16 April 1983, and Kelly, 9 January 1984.

213. McNemar, in *A History of Psychology in Autobiography*, pp. 318–19.

214. Ibid., p. 319.

215. Ibid.

216. Interview with Hilgard, 1 March 1984.

217. Roger G. Barker, "Settings of a Professional Lifetime," *American Psychologist* 37(1979):2137–57. In this article, the author provides a detailed description of the setting and atmosphere of the evening seminars. The seminars have also been described by Kelly (letter to the author from Kelly, 9 January 1984) and by Hilgard (interview, 1 March 1984).

218. Barker, "Settings of a Professional Lifetime," p. 2141.

219. Letter to the author from Neal E. Miller, 11 April 1983.

220. Miles A. Tinker to Seagoe, 18 January 1968, MSP; and letters to the author from Barker, 16 April 1983, and Kelly, 9 January 1984.

221. Harlow to Seagoe, 5 July 1967, MSP.

222. Harlow to LMT, 22 November 1954, LTP.

223. Letter to the author from Barker, 16 April 1983.

224. Interview with Hilgard, 1 March 1984.

225. Robert R. Sears, "Robert R. Sears," in *A History of Psychology in Autobiography*, vol. 7, ed. Gardner Lindzey (San Francisco: Freeman, 1980), pp. 395–433.

226. Interview with Sears, 16 March 1984. Sears had first met Terman when he was tested at the age of six. His father, Jesse Sears, was a colleague and friend of Terman.

227. "Terman 'Retires' but Goes on Working: 'Prodigies' are his Hobby," *Palo Alto Times*, 4 June 1942; and "Lewis Madison Terman," *Stanford Alumni Review* 43(1941–1942):22–23.

10. Retirement from Teaching (1942–1956)

1. LMT, "The Stanford Department of Psychology (1922–1942)," Faculty File, Stanford University Archives, Stanford, Calif., July 1945, quote pp. 11–12.

2. Ibid.

3. Interview with Hilgard, 1 March 1984.

4. LMT "The Stanford Department of Psychology (1922–1942)."

5. According to Fred E. Terman, the department had also been rated in 1925 as seventh among psychology departments in the country (FET, "Special Comments," [1974] p. 36, MSP).

6. Ibid.

7. See "Final Report of Graduate Education," *The Chronicle of Higher Education*, 19 January 1983.

8. LMT to Wilbur, 30 May 1944, LTP. Wilbur retired as Stanford president in 1942.

9. LMT, "The Stanford Department of Psychology (1922–1942)," p. 4.

10. LMT to Wilbur, 30 April 1942, LTP.

11. LMT to Boring, 13 October 1937, LTP.

12. LMT to Barker, 1 January 1945, LTP.

13. Nathan Van Patten (director of the Stanford Libraries) to LMT, 11 May 1940; and LMT to A. F. Kuhlman (Joint University Libraries), 4 September 1940, LTP.

14. Kuhlman to LMT, 9 October 1956, LTP.

15. LMT, "Ten Vows of the Stanford Emeriti Graduates of 1942," 1942, LTP (mimeographed).

16. Ibid.

17. LMT, "I Was Lucky," 1953, pp. 13–14, LTP (typed).

18. LMT to Charles H. Warren, 28 July 1935, LTP.

19. These lectures were the prestigious Silliman Lectures. Terman's scheduled topic was "Studies in Human Intelligence." LMT to Warren, 28 July 1935 and 30 November 1936, LTP.

20. Anna Minton Terman to Sibyl Walcutt Terman, 9 January 1943 and 25 January 1943, FTP; May V. Seagoe, *Terman and the Gifted*, (Los Altos, Calif.: William Kaufmann, 1975), p. 170; and interview with Fred W. Terman, 16 December 1983.

21. "Frederick Emmons Terman: Life and Career," guide for the Frederick E. Terman Papers, FTP.

22. Anna Minton Terman to Sibyl Walcutt Terman, 9 January 1943 and 25 January 1943, FTP.

23. LMT to Robert Gordon Sproul, 29 April 1943 and 18 May 1943, LTP.

24. Anna Minton Terman to Sibyl Walcutt Terman, 28 July 1943, FTP.

25. LMT to Sibyl Walcutt Terman, 17 September 1943, FTP.

26. LMT to FET, 15 September 1943, FTP.

27. Anna Minton Terman to Sibyl Walcutt Terman, 18 March 1944, FTP.

28. Anna Minton Terman to Sibyl Walcutt Terman, 29 May 1944, FTP.

29. Anna Minton Terman to Sibyl Walcutt Terman, 18 November 1944, 8 May 1945, and 27 August 1945, FTP.

30. LMT to Gesell, 19 December 1945 and 19 August 1946, LTP.

31. LMT to Elizabeth M. Bonbright, 8 October 1946, LTP.

32. LMT to Bonbright, 23 June 1947, LTP.

33. LMT to Miles, 29 June 1949, LTP.

34. LMT and Melita H. Oden, *Genetic Studies of Genius*, vol. 4: *The Gifted Child Grows Up; Twenty-five Years' Follow-up of a Superior Group* (Stanford, Calif.: Stanford University Press, 1947).

35. Ibid., pp. 66–77.

36. A summary of these results is provided in LMT and Melita H. Oden, *Genetic*

Studies of Genius, vol. 5: *The Gifted Group at Midlife: Thirty-five Years' Follow-up of the Superior Child* (Stanford, Calif.: Stanford University Press, 1959), pp. 21–22.

37. LMT and Oden, *Genetic Studies*, vol. 4, p. 349. This investigation was limited to men because it was felt that the achievement of women was difficult to estimate and often the outcome of extraneous circumstances.

38. Ibid., pp. 349–52.

39. Ibid., p. 352.

40. LMT and Oden, *Genetic Studies*, vol. 5.

41. Ibid., pp. xi–xiii, 23–27. The field workers in the 1940–52 follow-up were Nancy Bayley, Helen Marshall, Melita H. Oden, Alice Leahy Shea, and Ellen Sullivan. Helen Marshall had the distinction of being part of each field follow-up, beginning with the first in 1921. Her presence provided personal continuity for the field study procedures.

42. By 1955, 104 of the original group of 1,528 subjects had died.

43. LMT and Oden, *Genetic Studies*, vol. 5, pp. 143–52. See also LMT, "Scientists and Nonscientists in a Group of 800 Gifted Men," *Psychological Monographs* 68(1954): No. 7 (Whole No. 378).

44. Also rounding out the overall pattern were the data obtained from spouses and children. The spouses had high educational achievement and were generally of high intellectual caliber. The IQ testing of the offspring also revealed superior intellectual functioning. These children had an average IQ of 133. See LMT and Oden, *Genetic Studies*, vol. 5, pp. 136–42.

45. See Merle R. Sumpton, Dorothy Norris, and LMT, "Special Education for the Gifted Child," in *The Forty-Ninth Yearbook of the National Society for the Study of Education*, part 2 (Chicago: University of Chicago Press, 1950), pp. 259–80; and LMT and Melita H. Oden, "Major Issues in the Education of Gifted Children," *Journal of Teacher Education* 5(1954):230–32.

46. LMT, "The Discovery and Encouragement of Exceptional Talent," *American Psychologist* 9(1954):221–30.

47. The head of the selection committee was Yerkes. Terman wrote Yerkes that he was glad he had accepted the invitation. His talk was better received than he had hoped. He reported that he got the "biggest ovation" of his life. The hall seated twenty-five hundred and a thousand had to be turned away (LMT to Yerkes, 1 April 1954, LTP).

48. Harvey C. Lehman, *Age and Achievement* (Princeton, N.J.: Princeton University Press, 1953).

49. LMT to Harvey C. Lehman, 10 August 1945, LTP.

50. LMT to L. P. Eisenhart, 25 February 1952, LTP. Terman pointed to Lehman's poor literary style and lack of interpretation.

51. Eisenhart to LMT, 12 February 1952, LTP.

52. LMT to Boring, 6 March 1952, LTP.

53. LMT to Boring, 28 April 1953, LTP.

54. "Foreign Students' Dreams Come True under Novel New Scholarship Project," *Santa Barbara News-Press*, 25 July 1948.

55. LMT to Bonbright, 25 January 1955, LTP.

56. LMT to Bonbright, 17 June 1946, LTP.

57. LMT to Wilbur, 16 October 1946, LTP.

58. Jeanette S. Nelson to Alvin P. Eurich, 31 March 1948, LTP.

59. Eurich to Nelson, 6 April 1948, LTP.

60. "Foreign Students' Dreams Come True."

61. LMT correspondence with Bonbright and Winifred Johnson, 1946–1955, LTP.

62. LMT to R. E. Wallace Sterling, 9 March 1953, LTP.

63. LMT to Bonbright, 25 January 1955, LTP.

64. A. E. Wiggam, *Exploring Your Mind with the Psychologists* (New York: Blue Ribbon Books, 1928), pp. 213–72.

65. LMT to Wilbur, 6 November 1941, LTP.

66. LMT to DeWitt Wallace, 19 February 1948, LTP.

67. LMT, Typescript of radio address for the "Quiz Kids Program," 7 December 1947, LTP.

68. LMT to John Llewellen, 16 December 1947, LTP.

69. LMT to Eliza Merrill Hickok, 27 March 1947, LTP.

70. LMT, Typescript of "Quiz Kids Program."

71. FET, "Special Comments," p. 16.

72. These files, which are confidential, are part of the Terman papers and are located in Stanford University's psychology department.

73. LMT, "Trails to Psychology," in *A History of Psychology in Autobiography*, vol. 2, ed. Carl Murchison (Worcester, Mass.: Clark University Press, 1932), pp. 298–305.

74. Interview with Lee J. Cronbach, 29 March 1984.

75. LMT, Robert R. Sears, Lee J. Cronbach, and Pauline S. Sears, *Terman Life Cycle Study of Children of High Ability, 1922–1982* (Ann Arbor, Mich.: Inter-University Consortium for Political and Social Research, 1983), p. 1.

76. Interview with Sears, 16 March 1984.

77. "Disposal of Assets of Lewis M. and Anna B. Terman," attached to letter from Avery J. Howe to LMT, 29 October 1948. LTP.

78. FET, "Special Comments," p. 16.

79. Robert T. Sears, "Foreword," in LMT and Oden, *Genetic Studies*, vol. 5, pp. vii–ix.

80. Helen Marshall and Melita H. Oden, "The Status of the Mature Gifted Individual as a Basis for Evaluation of the Aging Process," *The Gerontologist* 2(1962):201–06; and Melita H. Oden, "The Fulfillment of Promises: 40-Year Follow-up of the Terman Gifted Group," *Genetic Psychology Monographs* 77(1968):3–93.

81. Sears to Willie L. Lowe, Jr., 22 November 1968, LTP.

82. LMT et al., *Terman Life Cycle Study, 1922–1982*, p. 1.

83. Interview with Sears, 16 March 1984. For a recent report see Robert R. Sears, "Sources of Life Satisfactions of the Terman Gifted Men," *American Psychologist* 32(1977):119–28. See also LMT et al., *Terman Life Cycle Study, 1922–1982*.

84. The latest reported figures are for the 1977 follow-up. The total sample numbered 917 with a few more men than women. The average age was seventy-one. See Robert R. Sears, "The Terman Gifted Children Study," paper presented at the annual meeting of the American Psychological Association, Los Angeles, August 1981.

85. Terman and Oden, *Genetic Studies*, vol. 4, pp. 1–2. Also by this time organizations, such as the American Association for Gifted Children and the National Association for Gifted Children, played active roles in promoting the interests of the gifted. Terman was honorary vice-president of the former and a member of the board of the latter.

86. Robert R. Sears (interviewed, 16 March 1984) and Lee J. Cronbach (interviewed, 29 March 1984) have each indicated how being a subject in the study benefited their

own educational and career development. There are also many instances of this kind in the file folders of the gifted subjects.

87. "Prodigious Failure," *Time*, 31 July 1944, pp. 60, 62.

88. Ibid., p. 62.

89. LMT, *The Measurement of Intelligence* (Boston: Houghton Mifflin, 1916), p. 12.

90. LMT, "Were We Born That Way?" *World's Work* 44(1922):655–60, quote p. 657.

91. Another limitation of Terman's study was the failure to follow-up the control groups. For the gifted children in the study, the fact that they were so identified had an impact on their future development. Additionally, Robert Sears points out that it would have been helpful to have included treatment variations with a comparable gifted group. Cohorts from later periods of time would also have added to the usefulness of the study. See Robert R. Sears "Your Ancients Revisited: A History of Child Development," in *Review of Child Development Research*, vol. 5, ed. Mavis Hetherington (Chicago: University of Chicago Press, 1975), pp. 1–73.

92. See LMT and Leona E. Tyler, "Psychological Sex Differences," in *Manual of Child Psychology*, ed. Leonard Carmichael, 2d ed (New York: Wiley, 1954), pp. 1064–1114; and LMT and Paul Wallen, "The Validity of Marriage Prediction and Marital Adjustment Tests," *American Sociological Review* 14(1949):497–504.

93. LMT, "Kinsey's 'Sexual Behavior in the Human Male': Some Comments and Criticisms," *Psychological Bulletin* 45(1948):443–59.

94. Alfred C. Kinsey, Wardell B. Pomeroy, and Clyde E. Martin, *Sexual Behavior in the Human Male* (Philadelphia: Saunders, 1948).

95. Morris L. Ernst and David Loth, *American Sexual Behavior and the Kinsey Report* (New York: Greystone Press, 1948), quote p. 11.

96. LMT et al., *Psychological Factors in Marital Happiness* (New York: McGraw-Hill, 1938).

97. LMT and Catharine Cox Miles, *Sex and Personality: Studies in Masculinity and Femininity* (New York: McGraw-Hill, 1936).

98. Wardell B. Pomeroy, *Dr. Kinsey and the Institute for Sex Research* (New York: Harper and Row, 1972), p. 91. Pomeroy's book is based upon his close professional relationship with Kinsey as well as on the Kinsey papers in the Archives of the Institute for Sex Research, Indiana University, Bloomington, Indiana.

99. LMT, "Kinsey's 'Sexual Behavior in the Human Male'," p. 443.

100. Ibid., pp. 458–59.

101. Ibid., p. 459.

102. Ibid., p. 458.

103. LMT to Alfred C. Kinsey, 2 October 1946, LTP.

104. Pomeroy, *Dr. Kinsey*, p. 247.

105. Ibid., p. 290.

106. Ibid., pp. 293–94.

107. As Pomeroy points out, Yerkes was a close friend of Terman and could hardly be expected to give Kinsey unqualified support.

108. Kinsey to LMT, 29 November 1948, LTP. In his reply (LMT to Kinsey, 10 December 1948, LTP), Terman recommended several mathematical statisticians, including Frederick Mosteller. As events unfolded, Mosteller served on a committee of the American Statistical Association that was given the task of evaluating the 1948 Kinsey Report on statistical grounds. This assessment was generally a positive one. See William G. Cochran, Frederick Mosteller, and John W. Tukey, *Statistical Problems of the Kinsey*

Report on Sexual Behavior in the Human Male (Washington, D.C.: American Statistical Association, 1954).

109. LMT to Yerkes, 21 December 1948, LTP.

110. Pomeroy, *Dr. Kinsey*, pp. 291–94.

111. See Kinsey et al., *Sexual Behavior*, p. 31. Kinsey was critical of Terman's use of questionnaires rather than direct interviewing, as well as his failure to analyze the effects of different educational levels. These criticisms raised questions about the reliability of Terman's data and the generalizability of his conclusions.

112. LMT to Yerkes, 8 September 1952, LTP.

113. Ibid.

114. See Loren Baritz, *The Servants of Power: A History of the Use of Social Science in American Industry* (Middletown, Conn.: Wesleyan University Press, 1960).

115. See Pomeroy, *Dr. Kinsey*; and Cornelia V. Christenson, *Kinsey: A Biography* (Bloomington, Ind.: Indiana University Press, 1971).

116. See Ludwig von Bertalanffy, *Problems of Life: An Evaluation of Modern Biological Thought* (New York: Harper, 1952); and Wayne W. Reese and Willis Overton, "Models of Development and Theories of Development," in *Life-Span Developmental Psychology: Research and Theory*, eds. L. R. Goulet and Paul B. Baltes (New York: Academic Press, 1970), pp. 115–45.

117. Alfred C. Kinsey, "Criteria for a Hormonal Explanation of the Homosexual," *Journal of Clinical Endocrinology* 1(1941):424–28. In the volume on male sexual behavior, Kinsey dismissed both psychological and biological causal explanations (Kinsey et al., *Sexual Behavior*, pp. 615, 658–59).

118. For a discussion and explication of Kinsey's views on sex, see Paul Robinson, *The Modernization of Sex* (New York: Harper and Row, 1976), pp. 42–119.

119. Kinsey et al., *Sexual Behavior*, p. 661. Kinsey's analysis of sexual preference as a problem of choice is one of the passages that Terman chose as an example of Kinsey's passing moral judgment (Terman, "Kinsey's 'Sexual Behavior in the Human Male'," p. 457).

120. Robinson, *The Modernization of Sex*, p. 50.

121. Kinsey et al., *Sexual Behavior*, p. 16.

122. Robinson, *The Modernization of Sex*, p. 51.

123. Kinsey concluded from his data that thirty-seven percent of the adult male population had at least some homosexual experience (Kinsey et al., *Sexual Behavior*, p. 663).

124. See Terman, "Kinsey's 'Sexual Behavior in the Human Male'," pp. 446–50; Kinsey et al., *Sexual Behavior*, pp. 82–119; and Pomeroy, *Dr. Kinsey*, pp. 291–92.

125. Cochran et al., *Statistical Problems of the Kinsey Report*, p. 2.

11. *Reflections (1942–1956)*

1. LMT, "My Faith," 1948, p. 6, LTP (typewritten).

2. LMT, "Trails to Psychology," in *A History of Psychology in Autobiography*, vol. 2, ed. Carl Murchison (Worcester, Mass.: Clark University Press, 1932), p. 330.

3. G. B. Lal to LMT, 29 August 1947, LTP.

4. LMT to Yerkes, 20 June 1949, LTP.

5. Ibid.

6. LMT, "My Faith," p. 2.

7. Ibid.

8. See LMT, "Were We Born that Way?" *World's Work* 44(1922):655–60; and LMT, "Education and the Democratic Ideal," *Educational Forum* 7 (1943): Supplement number 3, pp. 5–8, 10.

9. "Terman 'Retires' but Goes on Working," *Palo Alto Times*, 4 June 1942.

10. LMT, "Editor's Introduction," in Virgil E. Dickson, *Mental Tests and the Classroom Teacher* (Yonkers, N.Y.: World Book Company, 1923), pp. xiv–xv, quote p. xv.

11. "Terman 'Retires' but Goes on Working."

12. LMT to Boring, 16 February 1945, LTP.

13. Ibid.

14. LMT, "Some of the Things I Think About," 1942, LTP (handwritten).

15. LMT, "The Discovery and Encouragement of Exceptional Talent," *American Psychologist* 9(1954):221–30.

16. LMT to Nicholas Pastore, 4 March 1948, LTP.

17. Pastore to LMT, 26 February 1948, LTP.

18. Pastore's dissertation was published in 1949. See Nicholas Pastore, *The Nature-Nurture Controversy* (New York: King's Crown Press, 1949). In this final version the one change was placing Terman within the liberal group.

19. Pastore to LMT, 26 February 1948; and LMT to Pastore, 4 March 1948, LTP.

20. LMT to Pastore, 4 March 1948, LTP.

21. See Pastore, *The Nature-Nurture Controversy*, pp. 85–95.

22. Anne Anastasi, "Review of *Nature-Nurture Controversy*," *Science* 111(1950):45–46.

23. Pastore, *The Nature-Nurture Controversy*, p. 15.

24. Pastore also referred to the "radical" as someone who believed in the necessity of thorough change in social, political, and economic institutions. He appeared to view radicalism as a more extreme form of liberalism, and his basic hypothesis was that environmentalism was associated with either liberalism or radicalism.

25. See Arthur A. Ekrich, Jr., *Progressivism in America: A Study of the Era from Theodore Roosevelt to Woodrow Wilson* (New York: Franklin Watts, 1974); and Robert H. Wiebe, *The Search for Order: 1877–1920* (New York: Hill and Wang, 1967).

26. This analysis is drawn from Henry L. Minton, "Lewis M. Terman and Mental Testing: In Search of the Democratic Ideal," in *Psychological Testing and American Society, 1890–1930,* ed. Michael M. Sokal (New Brunswick, N.J.: Rutgers University Press, 1987), pp. 95–112. For another discussion of the relationship between Terman's liberal orientation and his work, see Russell Marks, "Lewis M. Terman: Individual Differences and the Construction of Social Reality," *Educational Theory* 24(1974):336–55.

27. See Donald C. Bellomy, " 'Social Darwinism' Revisited" *Perspectives in American History,* New Series I (1984)1–129.

28. See Donald K. Pickens, *Eugenics and the Progressives* (Nashville: Vanderbilt University Press, 1968); and Kenneth M. Ludmerer, *Genetics and American Society: A Historical Approach* (Baltimore: Johns Hopkins Press, 1972), pp. 7–43.

29. See Hamilton Cravens, *The Triumph of Evolution: American Scientists and the Heredity-Environment Controversy, 1900–1941* (Philadelphia: University of Pennsylvania Press, 1978) for an analysis of the intellectual shift that occurred in the 1920s. Also see Franz Samelson, "From 'Race Psychology' to 'Studies in Prejudice': Some Observations on the Thematic Reversal in Social Psychology," *Journal of the History of the Behavioral Science* 14(1978):265–78.

30. For discussions of these repudiations, see Cravens, *The Triumph of Evolution;* and Stephen Jay Gould, *The Mismeasure of Man* (New York: Norton, 1981).

31. LMT, "Some of the Things I Think About"; and LMT, "A Lesson in Window Dressing," 1941, LTP (typewritten). In the first unpublished paper Terman wrote an analysis of the totalitarian threat to democracy. In the second paper, which may have been circulated to his Stanford colleagues, Terman wrote about the dangers of sponsoring political action groups without knowing all of the policies they advocated. He described his own experience of allowing his name to appear as a sponsor for a civil liberties group. When he learned that the group was radical in its policies, he withdrew his support.

32. Gordon W. Allport to LMT, 6 January 1942; and LMT to Allport, 14 January 1942, LTP.

33. LMT to Yerkes, 12 September 1947, LTP.

34. LMT to Yerkes, 21 October 1947, LTP.

35. LMT to Boring, 21 July 1950, LTP.

36. Ibid.

37. Ibid.

38. LMT to Edward C. Tolman, 23 October 1952, LTP.

39. LMT to Tolman, 28 October 1952, LTP.

40. LMT to Yerkes, 15 July 1952, LTP.

41. LMT to Boring, 31 July 1952, LTP.

42. LMT to Yerkes, 17 December 1952, LTP.

43. LMT to Yerkes, 27 February 1953, LTP.

44. LMT to Frederick E. Jackson, 28 February 1956, LTP.

45. LMT to Mrs. Guy M. Whipple, 12 September 1941, LTP.

46. LMT, "Review of *Leta S. Hollingworth: A Biography*, by H. L. Hollingworth," *Journal of Applied Psychology* 28(1944):357–59.

47. LMT to Roe, 30 June 1943, LTP.

48. LMT, "Barbara Stoddard Burks (1902–1943)," *Psychological Review* 51(1944):136–41. Seventy-five entries were listed at the end of the article, under "Publications of Barbara S. Burks."

49. LMT to Yerkes, 13 August 1944, LTP.

50. Correspondence between LMT and Yerkes, 1945–1955, LTP.

51. LMT to Yerkes, 19 April 1949, LTP.

52. LMT to Yerkes, 13 November 1951, LTP.

53. Yerkes to LMT, 3 December 1951, LTP.

54. LMT to Yerkes, 26 May 1952, LTP.

55. LMT to Ada Yerkes, 22 April 1954, LTP.

56. LMT to Ada Yerkes, 11 August 1955, LTP.

57. Ada Yerkes telegram to LMT, 4 February 1956, LTP.

58. LMT telegram to Ada Yerkes, 4 February 1956, LTP.

59. Neither Boring nor Terman thought much of John Dewey's contribution to psychology. Boring to LMT, 3 June 1952; and LMT to Boring, 18 June 1952, LTP.

60. LMT to Boring, 28 April 1953, LTP.

61. LMT to Boring, 13 January 1955, LTP.

62. LMT to Yerkes, 7 August 1950, LTP.

63. LMT to Boring, 16 May 1950, LTP.

64. LMT, "Trails to Psychology," pp. 318–19.

65. LMT, "Review of *Human Nature and the Social Order*, by E. L. Thorndike," *Science* 94(1941):236–37.

66. Edward L. Thorndike to LMT, 2 June 1943, LTP.

67. Thorndike to LMT, 2 October 1946, LTP.

68. LMT to Robert L. Thorndike, 11 August 1949, LTP.

69. Godfrey H. Thomson to LMT, 29 October 1941, LTP.

70. Correspondence between LMT and Thomson, 1947–1955, LTP.

71. Thomson to LMT, 13 July 1952, LTP.

72. LMT to Jennie Thomson, 18 August 1955, LTP.

73. Goodenough to LMT, 20 February 1947, LTP.

74. LMT to Goodenough, 22 April 1947, LTP.

75. Goodenough to LMT, 27 June 1949, LTP.

76. Florence L. Goodenough, *Mental Testing: Its History, Principles, and Applications* (New York: Rinehart, 1949).

77. LMT to Yerkes, 18 May 1948, LTP.

78. Ibid.

79. Esther Morris to FET, 8 May 1976, FTP.

80. Lucille Miller to FET, 14 March 1976; and Blanche Cockrun to FET, 31 March 1976, FTP.

81. Morris to FET, 8 May 1976, FTP.

82. Hazel Gross to FET, 25 February 1976, FTP; and diary of Anna Minton Terman, 1923–1927.

83. John Terman to LMT, 18 August 1954; and LMT to John Terman [1954], FTP.

84. LMT to P. C. Emmons, 7 May 1956, LTP.

85. "Frederick Emmons Terman: Life and Career," Guide for the Frederick E. Terman Papers, FTP.

86. LMT to FET, 30 June 1942, FTP.

87. Correspondence by LMT to FET, 1942–1945, FTP.

88. LMT to FET, 18 September 1942, FTP.

89. LMT to FET, 12 November 1945, FTP.

90. FET, "Special Comments," [1974], p. 35, MSP.

91. FET to Morris, 30 December 1977, FTP.

92. Annabelle Spencer to FET, 21 June 1976, FTP.

93. Barbara S. Burks, Dortha W. Jensen, and LMT, *Genetic Studies of Genius*. vol. 3 *The Promise of Youth: Follow-up Studies of a Thousand Gifted Children* (Stanford, Calif.: Stanford University Press, 1930), pp. 338–39.

94. Ibid., p. 339.

95. Interviews with Fred W. Terman, 16 December 1983; and Terence Terman, 7 April 1984.

96. "Frederick Emmons Terman: Life and Career."

97. Wallace Sterling to LMT, 9 October 1950; and LMT to Sterling; 13 October 1950, LTP.

98. "Frederick Emmons Terman, Stanford Engineer, Dies at 82," *New York Times*, 22 December 1982.

99. Anna Minton Terman to Fred and Sibyl Terman, 28 July 1943, FTP; and Doris Tucker, "In a Shadow," unpublished manuscript, 1970.

100. Tucker, "In a Shadow."

101. FET, "Supplementary Notes," 1974, MSP.

102. Interview with Tucker, 18 and 19 August 1985.

103. Interviews with Fred W. Terman, Terence Terman, and Doris Tucker. Fred W. and Terence were Fred's two oldest sons and Doris was Helen's oldest daughter. Doris also reported some of her sister Anne's memories. Lewis, the youngest son of Fred, had relatively little contact with his grandparents.

104. "A Man Who Measures Minds," *San Francisco Chronicle*, 11 April 1937.

105. Cockrun to FET, 31 March 1976, FTP.

106. Interviews with Fred W. Terman and Terence Terman.

107. Interview with Tucker.

108. Ibid., personal communication.

109. Interviews with Fred W. Terman, Terence Terman, and Tucker.

110. Interview with Tucker.

111. LMT to Boring, 28 May 1954, LTP; and LMT to John Terman [1954], reply to John Terman's letter of 18 August 1954, FTP.

112. LMT to Yerkes, 19 September 1955, LTP.

113. LMT to Jessie Roth, 6 January 1956, FTP; and LMT to Yerkes, 8 December 1955, LTP.

114. William T. Shea to LMT, 13 July 1953, LTP.

115. LMT to Shea, 17 December 1953 and 11 October 1955, LTP.

116. LMT, "I Was Lucky," 1953, p. 14 LTP (typed).

117. LMT to Coy, 4 April 1956, LTP; and "Mrs. Terman Passes Away at Age of 79," *Palo Alto Times*, 27 March 1956.

118. LMT, "Trails to Psychology," p. 309.

119. "Mrs. Terman Passes Away at Age of 79."

120. Interview with Tucker.

121. LMT to Jennie Thomson, 17 April 1956, LTP.

122. Goodenough to LMT, 2 May 1956, LTP.

123. Ibid., note attached by Melita H. Oden

124. LMT to Goodenough, 15 May 1956, LTP.

125. LMT to Boring, 12 April 1956; and LMT to Ada Yerkes, 19 April 1956, LTP.

126. LMT to Ada Yerkes, 28 May 1956, LTP.

127. LMT to Ada Yerkes, 12 July 1956, LTP.

128. LMT to Jennie Thomson, 8 November 1956, LTP.

129. Oden to Jennie Thomson, 7 January 1957, LTP.

130. "Dr. Lewis M. Terman, Renowned Stanford Psychologist Passes," *Palo Alto Times*, 22 December 1956.

131. Oden to Jennie Thomson, 7 January 1957, LTP.

132. Robert R. Sears, Paul R. Farnsworth, Quinn McNemar, and Paul Wallin, "Memorial Resolution, Lewis Madison Terman, 1877–1956," Faculty File, Stanford University Archives (mimeographed).

133. May V. Seagoe, *Terman and the Gifted* (Los Altos, Calif.: William Kaufmann, 1975), p. 182. Private services were held in Palo Alto ("Dr. Lewis M. Terman, Renowned Stanford Psychologist Passes").

134. Melita H. Oden, "The Gifted Child at Mid-Life," paper presented at the Conference on the Gifted Child, Stanford University, 13 April 1957.

Epilogue

1. Kohs to Seagoe, [1967], MSP.

2. "Jewish" was included as one of the correct responses for the word "shrewd" on the vocabulary test of the Stanford-Binet. Terman alluded to the clannishness of Jews in a comment to Gesell. In 1916, during a visit to New York's Coney Island, he declared: "I had never thought there were so many Jews in the world! All the Ghetto was there." LMT to Gesell, 17 July 1916, AGP.

3. Barker to Seagoe, 19 September 1967; and Sward to Seagoe, 2 April 1967, MSP.

4. Albert Walton to Seagoe, 10 June 1967; and Young to Seagoe, 16 February 1968, MSP.

5. Interview with Tucker, 18 and 19 August 1985.

6. E. G. Boring, "Lewis Madison Terman: 1877–1956," *Biographical Memoirs of the National Academy of Sciences* 33(1959):414–40.

7. LMT to Wilbur, 16 October 1946, LTP.

8. See Michel Foucault, *Madness and Civilization* (London: Tavistock, 1967); and Michel Foucault, *History of Sexuality, Vol. 1* (New York: Vintage, 1980). For an analysis of the mental-testing movement from Foucault's perspective, see Nikolas Rose, "The Psychological Complex: Mental Measurement and Social Administration," *Ideology and Consciousness* 5(1979):5–68.

9. See Edmund V. Sullivan, *A Critical Psychology: Interpretation of the Personal World* (New York: Plenum, 1984); Kenneth J. Gergen, "The Social Constructionist Movement in Modern Psychology," *American Psychologist* 40(1985):266–75; and Henry L. Minton, "Emancipatory Social Psychology as a Paradigm for the Study of Minority Groups," in *Dialectics and Ideology in Psychology*, ed. Knud S. Larsen (Norwood, N.J.: Ablex, 1986), pp. 257–77.

Bibliographic Note

The major resource for the preparation of this book has been the Lewis M. Terman Papers, located at the Stanford University Archives. This collection includes a complete exchange of correspondence from about 1920 until 1956, the time of Terman's death. Unpublished manuscripts, memoranda, newspaper clippings, and research data are also included. In addition, other collections at the Stanford University Archives provided relevant material. Ellwood P. Cubberley and Ray Lyman Wilbur were Stanford administrators who worked closely with Terman, and their papers bearing on Terman were useful. Terman's son, Frederick E. Terman, was an engineering dean and subsequently a provost at Stanford. His papers contain some items that his father passed on to him, most notably information about family genealogy. The collection also includes correspondence between Fred Terman and his parents, as well as with his father's family.

Information about Terman's childhood is sparse. His 1932 autobiographical chapter in Carl Murchison's edited series is the only published account. The Frederick E. Terman Papers contain some oral history that was passed on about family life while Terman was growing up. However, there is very little of this, and such data are always subject to the bias of selective memory. No contemporary records of Terman's childhood exist, such as diaries kept by him or his parents and siblings, school records, or family correspondence. We must, therefore, rely almost exclusively on Terman's own memories of his childhood as set down in his autobiography. As in the case of oral history, such memories are subject to selectivity and distortion. Recognizing these limitations, Terman's recollections do provide a fairly detailed account of his formative years.

Records about Terman's student years at Indiana University are available at the Indiana University Archives. Terman's correspondence with G. Stanley Hall is available in the G. Stanley Hall Papers at Clark University. Terman's professional correspondence before World War I was rather limited, but material is available from the collections of three of his major correspondents during this period. His exchanges are included in the Robert M. Yerkes Papers at Yale University, the Arnold Gesell Papers at the Library of Congress, and the H. H. Goddard Papers at the Archives of the History of American Psychology at the University of Akron. In addition to the Terman correspondence from 1920 on, which is contained in the Stanford University Archives, his exchanges with Boring are in the E. G. Boring Papers at the Harvard University Archives. His exchanges with Goodenough are in the Florence L. Goodenough Papers at the University of Minnesota Archives.

Another source of archival data is included in the May V. Seagoe Papers at the Archives of the History of American Psychology at the University of Akron. Seagoe, a former student, wrote a biography of Terman that was published in 1975 (*Terman and the Gifted*, published by William Kaufmann). Her book focused on Terman's personal life and his career achievements but tended to neglect the broader social and historical context of his work. Nevertheless, Seagoe generously provided the opportunity for future scholars to make use of the valuable material she collected for her book. She had received letters from a number of individuals who knew Terman. Many of these colleagues and former students are now deceased. Her papers also contain an extensive set of notes and comments on her manuscript by Terman's son Fred. Fred and his sister Helen (both are now deceased) also provided written information about their parents.

There are a number of individuals who have offered personal impressions of Terman. The following all answered, through correspondence, my request for this information: Roger G. Barker, Jean Carson Challman, Dale B. Harris, C. Mansel Keene, E. Lowell Kelly, Neal E. Miller, and Anne Roe. Several others afforded me the opportunity to conduct interviews with them. These include Nancy Bayley, Lee J. Cronbach, Ernest R. Hilgard, Robert R. Sears, and Ruth Tinsley Storey. In addition, Ronald Lippitt, Marie Skodak Crissey, and Orlo L. Crissey granted me interviews on a related research project, which dealt with the 1940 debate on intelligence between George D. Stoddard and Terman. Family impressions and recollections were obtained from interviews with three of Terman's grandchildren: Fred W. Terman, Terry Terman, and Doris Tucker. Doris Tucker also permitted me to choose several of the photographs reproduced in this book and to make use of her grandmother's surviving diaries.

Bibliography of Published Works by Lewis M. Terman

1904 "A Preliminary Study in the Psychology and Pedagogy of Leadership."
Pedagogical Seminary 11:413–51.

1905 "A Study in Precocity and Prematuration." *American Journal of Psychology* 16:145–83.

1906 "Genius and Stupidity: A Study of Some of the Intellectual Processes
of Seven 'Bright' and Seven 'Stupid' Boys." *Pedagogical Seminary*
13:307–73.

1907 "Scholarship and the Professional Training of Teachers." *Educator-Journal* 7:375–77, 447–50.

1908 "Child Study: Its Reasons and Promise." *University of California Chronicle* 11:145–58.

"Factors of Safety." *New England Magazine* 39:508–12.

"The Point of View, Confessions of a Pedagogue." *Scribner's Magazine*
43:505–08.

1909 "Commercialism: The Educator's Bugbear." *School Review* 17:193–95.

"Education Against Nature." *Harper's Weekly* 53:17.

"Pathology of School Discipline." *New England Magazine* 41:479–84.

"Waste on Phonic Drills." *Educator-Journal* 9:433–36.

1911 "The Binet-Simon Scale for Measuring Intelligence: Impressions Gained
by the Application Upon Four Hundred Non-Selected Children."
Psychological Clinic 5:199–206.

"Medical Inspection of Schools in California." *Psychological Clinic* 5:57–
62.

"Paradoxes of Personality, or Muckraking in the Psychology of Character." *New England Magazine* 44:371–74.

"Relation of the Manual Arts to Health." *Popular Science Monthly* 78:602–
09.

"A School Where Girls are Taught Home-Making." *Craftsman* 20:63–68.

"Some Paradoxes of Personality." *Out West* 1:201–04.

1912   "Does Your Child Stutter?" *Harper's Weekly* 56:12.

"Evils of School Life." *Harper's Weekly* 56:24.

"A New Apostle of Childhood." *Educator-Journal* 12:585–88.

"Professional Training for Child Hygiene." *Popular Science Monthly* 80:289–97.

Review of "Normal Child and Primary Education," by Arnold Gesell. *Journal of Educational Psychology* 3:526–27.

"School Clinics, Dental and Medical." *Psychological Clinic* 5:271–78.

"Survey of Mentally Defective Children in the Schools of San Luis Obispo, California." *Psychological Clinic* 6:131–39.

(With H. G. Childs.) "A Tentative Revision and Extension of the Binet-Simon Measuring Scale of Intelligence." *Journal of Educational Psychology* 3:61–74, 133–43, 198–208, 277–89.

1913   (With David Starr Jordan.) "The Contribution of School Hygiene to Human Conservation." *Dietetic and Hygienic Gazette* 29:489–90.

"Juvenile Suicide." *Harper's Weekly* 58:13–14.

"Psychological Principles Underlying the Binet-Simon Scale and Some Practical Considerations for Its Correct Use." *Journal of Pyscho-Asthenics* 18:93–104.

"A Report of the Buffalo Conference on the Binet-Simon Tests of Intelligence." *Pedagogical Seminary* 20:549–54.

Review of "School Hygiene," by Fletcher B. Dresslar. *Science* 38:625–26.

(With A. Hocking.) "The Sleep of School Children: Its Distribution According to Age, and Its Relation to Physical and Mental Efficiency." *Journal of Educational Psychology* 4:138–47, 199–208.

"The Sleep of the Feeble-minded." *Training School Bulletin* 9:150–53.

"Social Hygiene: The Real Conservation Problem." *North American Review* 198:404–12.

"Suggestions for Revising, Extending, and Supplementing the Binet Intelligence Tests." *Journal of Psycho-Asthenics* 18:20–33.

The Teacher's Health: A Study in the Hygiene of an Occupation. Boston: Houghton Mifflin.

"Tragedies of Childhood." *Forum* 49:41–47.

(With D. S. Jordan.) "World Congress for Child Welfare." *San Francisco Call*, Sunday Magazine (August).

1914   "Concerning Psycho-Clinical Expertness." *Training School Bulletin* 11:9.

(With Ellwood P. Cubberley.) "Educational Work a Stanford University in Behalf of Backward and Feeble-minded Children." *Sierra Education News* 10:501.

"The Effects of School Life Upon the Nutritive Processes, Health, and the Composition of the Blood." *Popular Science Monthly* 84:257–64.

(With E. B. Hoag.) *Health Work in the Schools.* Boston: Houghton Mifflin.

The Hygiene of the School Child. Boston: Houghton Mifflin.

Medical Inspection, Hygiene Teaching, Physical Training and Special Schools for Defectives in Portland, Oregon. Report of the Survey of the Public School System of Portland. Yonkers, N.Y.: World Book Company.

"Precocious Children." *Forum* 52:893–98.

"Recent Literature on Juvenile Suicides." *Journal of Abnormal Psychology* 9:61–66.

"Review of Meumann on Tests of Endowment." *Journal of Psycho-Asthenics* 19:75–94, 123–34, 187–99.

Review of "Problems of Educational Readjustment," by David S. Snedden. *Stanford Alumnus* 15:174–76.

Review of "School Health Administration," by Louis W. Rapeer. *Science* 39:725–26.

"The Significance of Intelligence Tests for Mental Hygiene." *Journal of Psycho-Asthenics* 18:119–27.

"The Sleep of School Children." *Child* 4:804–10.

"Teeth and Civilization." *Forum* 51: 418–24.

(With E. P. Cubberley.) "To Help Backward School Children." *Stanford Alumus* (April).

"A Vocabulary Test." *Youth's Companion* 88:672.

(With J. Harold Williams.) *Whittier State School Biennial Report: Psychological Survey of the Whittier State School.* Preliminary and Final Reports. Whittier, Calif.: Whittier State School.

1915 (With others.) "Buildings and Health." In *Report of the Survey of the Public School System of Salt Lake City, Utah.* Salt Lake City: Part 3, pp. 221–98.

"Earache, a Danger Signal." *Youth's Companion* 89:10.

"Impressions of the Eighth Annual Congress of the American School Hygiene Association." *Child* 6:77–79.

"Measuring Intelligence." *California Outlook* 18:4–5.

"The Mental Hygiene of Exceptional Children." *Pedagogical Seminary* 22:529–37.

"Protecting the Teeth." *Mother's Magazine* 10:110.

(With J. H. Williams.) *Relation of Delinquency and Criminality to Mental Deficiency.* Whittier, Calif.: Whittier State School.

Research in Mental Deviation Among Children: A Statement of the Aims and Purposes of the Buckel Foundation. Stanford, Calif.: Stanford University Press.

Review of "Osceola: An Educational Utopia," by Ellwood P. Cubberley. *Stanford Alumnus* 16:180–82.

(With H. E. Knollin.) "Some Problems Relating to the Detection of Borderline Cases of Mental Deficiency." *Journal of Psycho-Asthenics* 20:3–15.

(With others) "The Stanford Revision of the Binet-Simon Scale and Some Results from the Application to 1,000 Non-Selected Children." *Journal of Educational Psychology* 6:551–62.

1916 "The American School Hygiene Association." *Social Service Review* 4:23.

"Assaying Intelligence." *Stanford Illustrated Review* 2:174–75.

"The Binet Scale and the Diagnosis of Feeblemindedness." *Journal of Criminal Law and Criminology* 7:530–43.

"The Building Situation and Medical Inspection." In *Denver School Survey*, part 5. Denver.

"The Measurement of Intelligence." In *Young People's Encyclopedia*. Chicago: Hudson Bellows.

The Measurement of Intelligence. Boston: Houghton Mifflin.

(With others.) "Mentality Tests: A Symposium." *Journal of Educational Psychology* 7:348–60.

Review of "Being Well Born," by M. F. Guyer. *Sierra Education News* 12:170.

Review of "The Criminal Imbecile," by Henry H. Goodard. *Journal of Delinquency* 1:56–57.

Review of "Man: An Adaptive Mechanism," by George W. Crile. *Journal of Delinquency* 1:158–60.

Review of "Mendelism and the Problem of Mental Defect," by Karl Pearson. *Journal of Delinquency* 1:102–04.

Review of "Self Reliance," by Dorothy Canfield Fisher. *Sierra Education News* 12:554.

"Review of the Vineland Translation of Articles by Binet and Simon." *Journal of Delinquency* 1:256–72.

"Some Comments on Dr. Haines' Comparison of the Binet-Simon and Yerkes-Bridges Intelligence Scales." *Journal of Delinquency* 1:115–17.

The Stanford Revision of the Binet-Simon Tests. Boston: Houghton Mifflin.

1917 "Feeble-minded Children in the Public Schools of California." *School and Society* 5:161–65.

"The Intelligence Quotient of Francis Galton in Childhood." *American Journal of Psychology* 28:209–15.

"The Mental Powers of Children and the Stanford Revision and Extension of the Binet-Simon Intelligence Scale." *Child* 7:287–90.

(With others.) "The Stanford Revision and Extension of the Binet-Simon Scale for Measuring Intelligence." *Educational Psychology Monographs*, no. 18.

"A Trial of Mental and Pedagogical Tests in a Civil Service Examination of Policemen and Firemen." *Journal of Applied Psychology* 1:17–29.

1918 (With Virgil Dickson and Lowry Howard.) "Backward and Feeble-minded Children in the Public Schools of 'X' County, California." In *Surveys in Mental Deviation in Prisons, Public Schools, and Orphanages in California.* Sacramento: California State Board of Charities and Corrections, pp. 19–45.

"Errors in Scoring Binet Tests." *Psychological Clinic* 12:33–39.

"An Experiment in Infant Education." *Journal of Applied Psychology* 2:219–28.

"Expert Testimony in the Case of Alberto Flores." *Journal of Delinquency* 3:145–64.

(With D. Wagner.) "Intelligence Quotients of 68 Children in a California Orphanage." *Journal of Delinquency* 3:115–21.

(With H. E. Knollin.) "A Partial Psychological Survey of the Prison Population of San Quentin, California, Based on Mental Tests of 155 Consecutive Entrants." In *Surveys in Mental Deviation in Prisons, Public Schools, and Orphanages in California.* Sacramento: California State Board of Charities and Corrections, pp. 6–19.

(With Irene Cuneo.) "Stanford-Binet Tests of 112 Kindergarten Children and 77 Repeated Tests." *Pedagogical Seminary* 25:414–28.

"Tests of General Intelligence." *Psychological Bulletin* 15:160–67.

(With M. B. Chamberlain.) "Twenty-three Serial Tests of Intelligence and Their Intercorrelations." *Journal of Applied Psychology* 2:341–54.

"The Use of Intelligence Tests in the Army." *Psychological Bulletin* 15:177–87.

"The Vocabulary Test as a Measure of Intelligence." *Journal of Educational Psychology* 9:452–66.

1919 "Dental Clinics." In *Bulletin No. 60.* Washington, D.C.: Children's Bureau, U.S. Department of Labor, pp. 234–37.

The Intelligence of School Children. Boston: Houghton Mifflin.

"Some Data on the Binet Test of Naming Words." *Journal of Educational Psychology* 10:29–35.

1920 (With others.) *National Intelligence Tests, with Manual of Directions.* Yonkers, N.Y.: World Book Company.

(With Jessie M. Chase.) "The Psychology, Biology and Pedagogy of Genius." *Psychological Bulletin* 17:397–409.

"Scholarship and Success." *Stanford Cardinal* 29:265–66.

Terman Group Test of Mental Ability. Yonkers, N.Y.: World Book Company.

"The Use of Intelligence Tests in the Grading of School Children." *Journal of Educational Research* 1:20–32.

1921   (With Edith D. Whitmire.) "Age and Grade Norms for the National Intelligence Tests, Scales A and B." *Journal of Educational Research* 3:124–32.

(With Truman L. Kelley.) "Dr. Ruml's Criticism of Mental Test Methods." *Journal of Philosophy* 18:459–65.

(With others) "Intelligence and Its Measurement: A Symposium." *Journal of Educational Psychology* 12:127–33.

"Intelligence Tests in Colleges and Universities." *School and Society* 13:481–94.

"Mental Growth and the I.Q." *Journal of Educational Psychology* 12:325–41, 401–07.

"Methods of Examining: History, Development and Preliminary Results." In *Psychological Examining in the United States Army. Memoirs of the National Academy of Sciences*, edited by Robert M. Yerkes, vol. 15, part 2, pp. 299–546. Washington, D.C.: Government Printing Office.

(With Jessie Chase Fenton.) "Preliminary Report on a Gifted Juvenile Author." *Journal of Applied Psychology* 5:163–78.

"The Status of Applied Psychology in the United States." *Journal of Applied Psychology* 5:1–4.

(With J. C. Fenton and Giles M. Ruch.) *Suggestions for Children's Reading*. Stanford, Calif.: Stanford University Press.

Suggestions for the Education and Training of Gifted Children. Stanford, Calif.: Stanford University Press.

"$20,000 Grant by Commonwealth Fund of New York for Work with Gifted Children." *School and Society* 13:694–95.

1922   "Adventures in Stupidity: A Partial Analysis of the Intellectual Inferiority of a College Student." *Scientific Monthly* 14:23–38.

"The Great Conspiracy, or the Impulse Imperious of Intelligence Testers, Psychoanalyzed and Exposed by Mr. Lippmann." *New Republic* 33:116–20.

(With others.) *Intelligence Tests and School Reorganization*. Yonkers, N.Y.: World Book Company.

"Mental Measurement Work Told." *Stanford Illustrated Review* 23:44, 457, 464.

"A New Approach to the Study of Genius." *Psychological Review* 29:310–18.

"The Problem." In *Intelligence Tests and School Reorganization*, pp. 1–31. Yonkers, N.Y.: World Book Company.

"The Psychological Determinist, or Democracy and the I.Q." *Journal of Educational Research* 6:57–62.

Review of "Intelligence of High School Seniors," by William F. Book. *Indiana University Alumni Quarterly* 9:443–44.

"Were We Born That Way?" *World's Work* 44:655–60.

1923 Editor's Introduction of Virgil E. Dickson, *Mental Tests and the Classroom Teacher*. Yonkers, N.Y.: World Book Company.

Editor's Introduction to Ben D. Wood, *Measurement in Higher Education*. Yonkers, N.Y.: World Book Company.

Forward to Vernon M. Cady, *The Estimation of Juvenile Incorrigibility*. Whittier, Calif.: California Bureau of Juvenile Research.

(With others.) *Report of Subcommittee of Leland Stanford Junior University Committee on Scholarship and Student Ability*. Stanford, Calif.: Stanford University Press.

(With others.) *School Organization and Administration*. Yonkers, N.Y.: World Book Company.

(With T. L. Kelley and G. M. Ruch.) *Stanford Achievement Test*. Yonkers, N.Y.: World Book Company.

1924 "American Psychological Association." *Science* 59:546–48.

"Conservation of Talent." *School and Society* 19:359–64.

Editor's Introduction to Louise Stedman, *Education of Gifted Children*. Yonkers, N.Y.: World Book Company.

(With J. C. DeVoss.) "The Educational Achievements of Gifted Children." In *Yearbook of the National Society for the Study of Education*, vol. 23, part 1, pp. 169–84.

Introduction to Maurice A. Bigelow, *Adolescence*. New York: Funk and Wagnalls.

"Mental Measurements." *Washington Education Journal* 3:133–36, 151.

"The Mental Test as a Psychological Method." *Psychological Review* 31:93–117.

"The Physical and Mental Traits of Gifted Children." In *Yearbook of the National Society for the Study of Education*, vol. 23, part 1, pp. 155–67.

"The Possibilities and Limitations of Training." *Journal of Educational Research* 10:335–43.

"Tests and Measurements of Gifted Children." *Washington Education Journal* 3:172–73, 189–190.

1925 "Bright Children Upset Notions About Genius." *New York Times*, 19 July, section 8, p. 14.

Editor's Introduction to Arthur S. Otis, *Statistical Method in Educational Measurement*. Yonkers, N.Y.: World Book Company.

Editor's Introduction to Joseph Peterson, *Early Conceptions and Tests of Intelligence*. Yonkers, N.Y.: World Book Company.

(With others.) *Genetic Studies of Genius*. Vol. 1, *Mental and Physical Traits of a Thousand Gifted Children*. Stanford, Calif.: Stanford University Press.

"Research on the Diagnosis of Pre-delinquent Tendencies." *Journal of Delinquency* 9:124–30.

Review of "The Mental Growth of the Child," by Arnold Gesell. *Science* 61:445–46.

(With Karl M. Cowdery.) "Stanford Program of University Personnel Research." *Journal of Personnel Research* 4:263–67.

1926 "Biographical Note on Henry Cowell." *American Journal of Psychology* 37:233–34.

(With Margaret Lima.) "Children's Reading." *National Education Association Journal* 15:169–70.

(With Margaret Lima.) *Children's Reading: A Guide for Parents and Teachers.* New York: Appleton (2nd ed., 1931).

Editor's Introduction to Norman Fenton, *Self-Direction and Adjustment.* Yonkers, N.Y.: World Book Company.

Editor's Introduction to Florence L. Goodenough, *Measurement of Intelligence by Drawings.* Yonkers, N.Y.: World Book Company.

Catharine Cox, assisted by Lewis M. Terman and others. *Genetic Studies of Genius.* Vol. 2, *The Early Mental Traits of 300 Geniuses.* Stanford, Calif.: Stanford University Press.

"Independent Study Plan at Stanford University." *School and Society* 24:96–98.

"The 1927 Yearbook of the National Society for the Study of Education, on the Possibilities and Limitations of Training." *School and Society* 23:404–06.

"The Possibilities and Limitations of Training." *Journal of Educational Research* 13:371–73.

Review of "Elementary Psychology," by Arthur I. Gates. *Journal of Educational Psychology* 17:214–16.

1927 Editor's Introduction to Truman L. Kelley, *Interpretation of Educational Measurements.* Yonkers, N.Y.: World Book Company.

Editor's Introduction to Giles M. Ruch and George D. Stoddard, *Tests and Measurements in High School Instruction.* Yonkers, N.Y.: World Book Company.

Editor's Introduction to Frederic L. Wells, *Mental Tests in Clinical Practice.* Yonkers, N.Y.: World Book Company.

"Fred Nelles, Practical Idealist." *Journal of Delinquency* 11:212–14.

Review of "Behaviorism," by John B. Watson, *American Journal of Psychology* 38:135–38.

Review of "Gifted Children: Their Nature and Nurture," by Leta S. Hollingworth, *Journal of Educational Research* 15:63–64.

1928 "Editorial." *Journal of Delinquency* 12:193–95.

Editor's Introduction to Clark L. Hull, *Aptitude Testing.* Yonkers, N.Y.: World Book Company.

"Growth Through Professional Reading." *National Education Association Journal* 17:137–38.

"The Influence of Nature and Nurture upon Intelligence Scores: An Evaluation of the Evidence in Part I of the 1928 Yearbook of the National Society for the Study of Education." *Journal of Educational Psychology* 19:362–73.

"Introduction to: Nature and Nurture. I. Their Influence Upon Intelligence." In *Yearbook of the National Society for the Study of Education*, vol. 27, part 1, pp. 1–7.

"Testing for the Crime Germ." *Sunset* 60:24–25, 54–56.

"Ultimate Influence of Standard Tests." *Journal of Educational Research* 17:57–59.

1929 "Ability and Personality Tests." *Independent Education* 3:5–6.

(With J. C. Almack.) *The Hygiene of the School Child*. Revised and enlarged. Boston: Houghton Mifflin.

(With T. L. Kelley, G. M. Ruch, et al.) *New Stanford Achievement Test*. Yonkers, N.Y.: World Book Company. (Revised 1940, 1953.)

(With Catharine Cox Miles.) "Sex Difference in the Association of Ideas." *American Journal of Psychology* 41:165–206.

1930 Editor's Introduction to Gertrude H. Hildreth, *Psychological Service for School Problems*. Yonkers, N.Y.: World Book Company.

Editor's Introduction to I. N. Madsen, *Educational Measurement in the Elementary Grades*. Yonkers, N.Y.: World Book Company.

(With Barbara S. Burks and Dortha W. Jensen.) *Genetic Studies of Genius*. Vol. 3, *The Promise of Youth: Follow-up Studies of a Thousand Gifted Children*. Stanford, Calif.: Stanford University Press.

"Talent and Genius in Children." In *The New Generation*, edited by V. F. Calverton and S. D. Schmalhausen, pp. 405–24. New York: Macaulay.

1931 "Editorial." *Child Study* 9:1.

Editor's Introduction to Rachel Stutsman, *Mental Measurement of Preschool Children*. Yonkers, N.Y.: World Book Company.

"Educational Psychology." In *Biology in Human Affairs*, edited by E. M. East, pp. 94–122. New York: McGraw-Hill.

"The Gifted Child." In *Handbook of Child Psychology*, edited by Carl A. Murchison, pp. 568–84. Worcester, Mass.: Clark University Press.

Introduction to Douglas Fryer, *The Measurement of Interests in Relation to Human Adjustment*. New York: Holt.

"Psychology and the Law." *Los Angeles Bar Association Bulletin* 6:142–53.

1932 Editor's Introduction to Jack W. Dunlap and Albert K. Kutz, *Handbook of Statistical Monographs, Tables, and Formulas*. Yonkers, N.Y.: World Book Company.

Editor's Introduction to Carleton Washburne, *Adjusting the School to the Child*. Yonkers, N.Y.: World Book Company.

"Intelligence Tests." In *White House Conference on Child Health and Protec-*

tion, Growth and Development of the Child, Part 4, Appraisal of the Child, pp. 26–60. New York: Century.

"Mentally Superior Children." In *White House Conference on Child Health and Protection*, Growth and Development of the Child, Part 4, Appraisal of the Child, pp. 61–75. New York: Century.

(With Maud A. Merrill.) "Preliminary Notes on a Revision of the Stanford-Binet Scale." *Psychological Bulletin* 28:589.

"Trails to Psychology." In *A History of Psychology in Autobiography*. Vol. 2, edited by Carl A. Murchison pp. 279–332. Worcester, Mass.: Clark University Press.

1933   (With B. S. Burks.) "The Gifted Child." In *Handbook of Child Psychology*. 2d ed., edited by Carl A. Murchison, pp. 773–801. Worcester, Mass.: Clark University Press.

Introduction to M. E. Bennett, *College and Life*. New York: McGraw-Hill.

1934   "The Measurement of Personality." *Science* 80:605–08.

"Objective of Social Control and Motivation in a Planned Society." In *Proceedings of the 4th Annual Social Science Research Conference of the Pacific Coast*, pp. 48–51.

"The Present Status of Personality Measurement." *Psychological Bulletin* 31:584.

1935   (With M. A. Merrill.) "Analysis of Intelligence Test Scores." In *Practical Applications of the Punched Card Method in Colleges and Universities*, edited by G. W. Baehne, pp. 230–34. New York: Columbia University Press.

Introduction to Norman Fenton, *The Delinquent Boy and the Correctional School*. Claremont, Calif.: Claremont Colleges Guidance Center.

(With Winifred B. Johnson.) "Personality Characteristics of Happily Married, Unhappily Married, and Divorced Persons." *Character and Personality* 3:290–311.

(With Paul Buttenweiser.) "Personality Factors in Marital Compatibility." *Journal of Social Psychology* 6:143–71, 267–89.

"Psychology." In *University Training and Vocational Outlets*, edited by C. G. Wrenn, pp. 61–64. Stanford, Calif.: Stanford University Press.

(With Roger G. Barker.) Review of "A Dynamic Theory of Personality," by Kurt Lewin. *Character and Personality* 4:91–92.

1936   (With E. Lowell Kelly and C. C. Miles.) "Ability to Influence One's Score on a Typical Paper-and-Pencil Test of Personality." *Character and Personality* 4:206–15.

(With C. C. Miles.) *Attitude-Interest Analysis Test*. New York: McGraw-Hill.

(With C. C. Miles.) *Sex and Personality: Studies in Masculinity and Femininity*. New York: McGraw-Hill.

(With Quinn McNemar.) "Sex Differences in Variational Tendency." *Genetic Psychology Monographs* 18: no. 1.

1937 (With M. A. Merrill.) *Measuring Intelligence.* Boston: Houghton Mifflin.

(With M. A. Merrill.) *Revised Stanford-Binet Scale.* Boston: Houghton Mifflin. (3d revision, 1960.)

1938 (With C. C. Miles.) *Manual of Information and Directions for Use of Attitude-Interest Analysis Test.* New York: McGraw-Hill.

(With others.) *Psychological Factors in Marital Happiness.* New York: McGraw-Hill.

1939 "Educational Suggestions from Follow-up Studies of Intellectually Gifted Children." *Journal of Educational Sociology* 13:82–89.

"The Effect of Happiness or Unhappiness on Self-Report Regarding Attitudes, Reaction Patterns, and Facts of Personal History." *Psychological Bulletin* 36:197–202.

"The Gifted Student and His Academic Environment." *School and Society* 49:65–73.

(With W. B. Johnson.) "Methodology and Results of Recent Studies in Marital Adjustment." *American Sociological Review* 4:307–24.

Review of "Plan for Marriage," by J. K. Folsom, ed. *American Journal of Sociology* 45:136–37.

Review of "The Student and His Knowledge," by William S. Learned and Ben D. Wood. *Journal of Higher Education* 10:111–13.

1940 "Frank Angell: 1857–1939." *American Journal of Psychology* 53:138–41.

"Intelligence in a Changing Universe." *School and Society* 51:465–70.

"Personal Reactions of the Yearbook Committee, National Society for the Study of Education." In *Yearbook of the National Society for the Study of Education*, vol. 39, part 1, pp. 460–67.

"Psychological Approaches to the Biography of Genius." *Science* 92:293–301.

(With Melita H. Oden.) "The Significance of Deviates. II. Status of the California Gifted Group at the End of Sixteen Years. III. Correlates of Adult Achievement in the California Gifted Group." In *Yearbook of the National Society for the Study of Education*, vol. 39, part 1, pp. 67–89.

(With W. B. Johnson.) "Some Highlights in the Literature of Psychological Sex Differences Published Since 1920." *Journal of Psychology* 9:327–36.

1941 Introduction to Lowry S. Howard, *The Road Ahead.* Yonkers, N.Y.: World Book Company.

Review of "Human Nature and the Social Order," by E. L. Thorndike. *Science* 94:236–38.

Review of "Sex in Development," by Carney Landis et al. *American Journal of Psychology* 54:453–55.

"Should the Historian Study Psychology?" *Pacific Historical Review* 10:2, 209–16.

(With Q. McNemar.) *Terman-McNemar Test of Mental Ability*. Yonkers, N.Y.: World Book Company.

1942   Editor's Introduction to Leta S. Hollingworth, *Children Above 180 I.Q.* Yonkers, N.Y.: World Book Company.

"The Revision Procedures." In *The Revision of the Stanford-Binet Scale*, Quinn McNemar, pp. 1–14. Boston: Houghton Mifflin.

"The Vocational Successes of Intellectually Gifted Individuals." *Occupations* 20:493–98.

1943   "Education and the Democratic Ideal." *Educational Forum* 7:supplement, 5–8

Forward to Grace M. Fernald, *Remedial Techniques in Basic School Subjects*. New York: McGraw-Hill.

1944   "Barbara Stoddard Burks (1902–1943)." *Psychological Review* 51:136–41.

Review of "Leta S. Hollingworth: A Biography," by H. L. Hollingworth. *Journal of Applied Psychology* 28:357–59.

1946   Editor's Introduction to Raymond B. Cattell, *The Description and Measurement of Personality*. Yonkers, N.Y.: World Book Company.

(With W. B. Johnson, George Kuznets, and Olga W. McNemar.) "Psychological Sex Differences." In *Manual of Child Psychology*, edited by Leonard Carmichael, pp. 954–1000. New York: Wiley.

Review of "How a Baby Grows: A Study in Pictures," by Arnold Gesell. *Science* 103:60.

The Stanford Study of Gifted Children: Condensed Summary 1921–1946. Stanford, Calif.: Stanford University Press.

1947   "Factors in the Adult Achievement of Gifted Men." In *Miscellanea Psychologica Albert Michotte*, pp. 371–81. Louvain, Belgium: Institut Superieur de Philosophie.

(With M. H. Oden.) *Genetic Studies of Genius*. Vol. 4, *The Gifted Child Grows Up; Twenty-five Years' Follow-up of a Superior Group*. Stanford, Calif.: Stanford University Press.

"Marital Adjustment and Its Prediction." In *Successful Marriage*, edited by M. Fishbein and E. W. Burgess, pp. 113–26. New York: Doubleday. (Rev. ed., 1955.)

"Psychological Approaches to the Biography of Genius." *Occasional Papers on Eugenics*, no. 4. London: The Eugenics Society and Hamish Hamilton Medical Books.

Review of "The Psychology of Human Differences," by Leona Tyler. *Journal of Applied Psychology* 32:216–17.

Review of "22 Cells in Nuremberg," by Douglas M. Kelley. *Psychological Bulletin* 44:483–84.

1948 "Kinsey's 'Sexual Behavior in the Human Male': Some Comments and Criticisms." *Psychological Bulletin* 45:443–59.

1949 "A Critique of the Evaluations of the Study of Bernadine G. Schmidt entitled: 'Changes in Personal, Social, and Intellectual Behavior of Children Originally Classified as Feeble-minded.' " *Journal of Exceptional Children* 15:228–30.

Review of "Psychologist Unretired: The Life Pattern of Lillien J. Martin," by Miriam Allen deFord. *California Medicine* 70:141–42.

1949 (With Paul Wallin.) "The Validity of Marriage Prediction and Marital Adjustment Tests." *American Sociological Review* 14:497–504.

1950 "Predicting Marriage Failure from Test Scores." *Marriage and Family Living* 12:51–54.

(With M. R. Sumption and Dorothy Norris.) "Special Education for the Gifted Child." In *Yearbook of the National Society for the Study of Education*, vol. 49, pp. 259–80.

1951 (With Nancy Bayley, Helen Marshall, O. W. McNemar, and M. H. Oden.) "Correlates of Orgasm Adequacy in a Group of 556 Wives." *Journal of Psychology* 32:115–72.

Review of "The New You and Heredity," by Amram Scheinfeld. *Psychological Bulletin* 48:457–58.

(With M. H. Oden.) "The Stanford Studies of the Gifted." In *The Gifted Child*, edited by Paul Witty, pp. 20–46. Boston: D.C. Heath.

1952 Review of "Predicting Adjustment in Marriage," by Harvey J. Locke. *Sociology and Social Research* 36:339–42.

1953 Foreword to Harvey C. Lehman, *Age and Achievement*. Princeton, N.J.: Princeton University Press.

(With M. A. Merrill.) "1937 Stanford-Binet Scales." In *Contributions Toward Medical Psychology*, edited by A. Weider, pp. 510–21. New York: Ronald Press.

Review of "A History of Psychology in Autobiography," vol. IV, edited by E. G. Boring, H. S. Langfeld, H. Werner, and R. M. Yerkes. *Psychological Bulletin* 50:477–81.

Review of "Mental Prodigies," by F. Barlow. *Journal of Applied Psychology* 37:325–26.

1954 "The Discovery and Encouragement of Exceptional Talent." *American Psychologist* 9:221–30.

(With M. H. Oden.) "Major Issues in the Education of Gifted Children." *Journal of Teacher Education* 5:230–32.

(With Leona Tyler.) "Psychological Sex Differences." In *Manual of Child Psychology*. Revised edition edited by Leonard Carmichael, pp. 1064–1114. New York: Wiley.

"Scientists and Nonscientists in a Group of 800 Gifted Men." *Psychological Monographs* 68: no. 7 (whole no. 378).

1955   "Are Scientists Different?" *Scientific American* 192:25–29.
       Foreword to Beatrice Lantz, *Easel Age Scale*. Los Angeles: California
       Test Bureau.
       "Louis Leon Thurstone (1877–1955)." *Yearbook of the American Philosoph-
       ical Society*, pp. 504–8.
1956   *Concept Mastery Test*. New York: Psychological Corporation.
       Review of "Selection and Guidance of Gifted Students for National
       Survival," edited by Arthur E. Traxler. *Contemporary Psychology* 1:359.
1958   "What Education for the Gifted Should Accomplish." In *Yearbook of the
       National Society for the Study of Education*, vol. 57, part 2, pp. 15–19.
1959   (With M. H. Oden.) *Genetic Studies of Genius*. Vol. 5, *The Gifted Group at
       Mid-life: Thirty-five Years' Follow-up of the Superior Child*. Stanford,
       Calif.: Stanford University Press.

Index